THE X-CULTURE HANDBOOK OF COLLABORATION AND PROBLEM SOLVING IN GLOBAL VIRTUAL TEAMS

THE X-CULTURE HANDBOOK OF COLLABORATION AND PROBLEM SOLVING IN GLOBAL VIRTUAL TEAMS

EDITED BY

Vas Taras

PUBLISHED BY UNC GREENSBORO UNIVERSITY LIBRARIES

Suggested citation: Taras, Vas. *The X-Culture Handbook of Collaboration and Problem Solving in Global Virtual Teams*. Greensboro: UNC Greensboro University Libraries, 2022.

doi: https://doi.org/10.5149/ 9781469669809_Taras

Project Editor: Theo Papageorge

The nature of global virtual collaboration is constantly changing. New online collaboration tools become available seemingly every day, creating new challenges and requiring new best practices. We encourage readers to build upon and develop our content. We would appreciate if you shared your work so that we could use it to further develop this book and to keep up with the developments in the field. Please email Vas Taras at v_taras@uncg.edu.

ISBN 978-1-4696-6979-3 (paperback: alk. paper)
ISBN 978-1-4696-6980-9 (open access ebook)

Published by the UNC Greensboro University Libraries
Distributed by the University of North Carolina Press
www.uncpress.org

CONTENTS

ACKNOWLEDGMENTS

This handbook on global virtual collaboration is a product of global virtual collaboration. Thirty-two co-authors from twenty-three countries produced this book, collaborating virtually, across time zones and cultural differences, and relying on online communication tools. We thank the X-Culture global community for bringing us together, and we thank the many IT companies, from Google and Zoom to Microsoft and Dropbox, for providing the tools for virtual communication.

CHAPTER 1

A Brief History of Global Virtual Teams

SUSAN GODAR, WILLIAM PATERSON UNIVERSITY

STEFAAN VAN RYSSEN, GHENT UNIVERSITY

Today, when a team project is assigned in a class, many students immediately set up virtual team channels. They swap email addresses and mobile phone numbers, establish cloud-based sharing accounts to gather information and review others' input, and use scheduling software to set meeting times for both F2F and online chats. This is true for projects ranging from ones done completely within a single classroom to those spanning multiple continents. The easy availability of technology has opened a multitude of opportunities to enhance student learning, particularly in the arena of international business.

This has not always been so. In the following sections, we will interweave the history of GVTs with the history of the technology that facilitated those teams. During the period from 1990–2019, we saw teams transform from being a training device for students to being real-time consultants to the business.

Early Student Collaborations – Through 1999

Pre-Internet

Professors have long worked to connect their students with those in other countries. In the days before the internet, those connections were primarily "pen pal" types of arrangements. Someone returning from her own international teaching experience, participating in a Fulbright grant or other exchange programs, would have her class write letters to students from her exchange school. Alternatively, a professor would meet someone from another country at a conference and have his students write to his new colleagues. Due to the time it takes for mail to cross borders, these professors did not usually have a specific academic objective beyond informal learning about another country through the eyes of a contemporary.

Businesses were, of course, focused on the accomplishment of a project, and relying on international teams to develop products for multiple markets in their home countries and abroad. For example, as Augusta S.p.A., an Italian helicopter manufacturer (now a part of Leonardo), worked with Bell Helicopter in Texas or with Westland in the U.K. to refine products, they relied on face-to-face (F2F) meetings interspersed with telexes, faxes, and phone conversations. While businesses were seeking ways to reduce the time and cost of trans-border product development, the technology was not yet available.

Using the Internet for Knowledge Exchange

In 1992, the first articles started to appear in business magazines about the concept of "virtual" teams (Hall, 1992). Teams with members located in far-flung locales could meet via the Internet and talk in real-time without being F2F or making expensive telephone calls. With technology like Lotus Notes and 1-2-3, team members could look at the same information at the same time and work through problems together. There was, however, a great deal of hand-wringing and fretting about whether this technological solution to project work would or could ever match the richness of F2F meetings.

On the academic side, there was a growing awareness of the importance of "international experience" for students who would be entering this new workplace. This need for experience was, of course, more salient in the USA than in Europe. Travel within Europe became easy after the passage of the Schengen agreement in 1985, which made it possible to cross borders without visas or special documents. It was, however, important for the students to have more than a tourist experience, as they needed to learn to work with people from other countries.

However, setting up a mechanism for that to happen was difficult. It was very costly to send US students abroad, or European students to the US or Asia. Although the growth of the World Wide Web was highly touted as a way for people in different countries to communicate, a significant problem faced by academics trying to connect students was a lack of technological expertise. Web pages needed to be hand-coded in HTML, and the use of most technology was expensive, both in terms of money and in time devoted to set-up.

To introduce students to the concept of working with others in a non-F2F configuration, several models were used in academe. The easiest to implement utilized two schools within the same country. In this way, students could participate in virtual teams. However, this did not facilitate the achievement of cross-national learning objectives.

A small number of universities had a simpler solution than others. Those universities with international satellite campuses taught the same course on two or more campuses and connected their students for a project using teleconferencing. When they utilized the equipment well, this was very effective. INSEAD offered the same business course to their campuses in Singapore and France and soon found that students were not learning anything about the other country – a major course objective. The solution was easily found when they opened the link between the two classrooms for periods before and after each class for informal communications. This gave the students the same opportunity that students have in a F2F class: they could chat with one another as the classroom filled or emptied (Fayard, 2006).

Most complex were those projects that ran in multiple schools spread across multiple countries. According to their article, Stefaan Van Ryssen of Hogeschool Gent, in Ghent, Belgium, sent an email to Sue Godar, then at St. Mary's College of Maryland on December 26, 1996, asking if she would be interested in having her class work with his on a transnational project that they named Marctica. They recruited another school to join them: The University of Texas – Brownsville. (Van Ryssen & Godar, 2000)

During the project, self-selected small student groups from the three colleges primarily communicated through email. The plan was that students had to find matching partners using a website where they wrote short biographies in the hopes of putting together well-matched teams. Once formed, the intercontinental teams would move on to searching for a product for analysis. Finally, each team would write a paper comparing the marketing of the product in the USA versus Belgium and their experiences in managing communications within their virtual team. These team papers would be graded by each team member's respective teacher.

There were numerous problems with the implementation of this plan. The first was that each school had slightly different break times during the spring term, and every team took any school break as a reason to stop working. Some students were comfortable with email programs, while for others, it was a brand-new experience. An extra hurdle for the Belgian students was the language barrier. Coming from the northern, Dutch-speaking majority in Belgium, English was their third language. This was perhaps the biggest issue to resolve in the introductory phase of the project. For example, picking a product to focus on involved a good deal of negotiations and lots of frustration when negotiating styles clashed or when language was misunderstood – valuable learning experiences.

The three professors involved more-or-less monitored the progress of the teams as they worked at the task at hand. Some teams had internal weekly contact, while others hardly communicated at all. They found that GVTs had some of the same problems that F2F teams had, especially with students dedicating different amounts of effort to the project. As usual, this caused more frustration for more ambitious or grade-conscious group members.

Over the next four years, the professors involved changed universities or dropped out due to the complexity of the project. Others were recruited, and in the final iteration of the project, held during the 2001 spring term, teams from Belgium, the US, France, and Argentina participated.

As GVT projects in general grew, so did the logistical challenges. If managing a project with two colleges in one country using the same language is a challenge, imagine what happens when the team consists of groups from four colleges where four different languages are spoken. There may be a very different number of students in each class, and participants are in different time zones and have different cultural backgrounds. The number of possible problems grows exponentially.

For example, a trio consisting of colleges from France (Lille), the UK (Edinburgh) and Belgium (Ghent) tried to solve one of these problems, i.e., mismatched class size, by having groups of different sizes, but that led to orphaned students who could not find a team and problems blamed on too-large or too-small group sizes. In the end, the professors forced students into teams, explaining that one can't always have one's way in business. In the end, some teams broke up, and final papers written by groups of two or even a single student were submitted. The experience was never repeated.

While faculty participants were solving some of the communication problems with this type of project, the technology was changing to enhance the process. This created both opportunities and challenges as more and more schools participated in GVT projects.

Rapid expansion – 2000–2010

Technology Availability

By the early 2000s, technologies that could be used to support GVTs were rapidly being introduced. As a sample, the following messaging systems were readily available:

Table 1.1 From Ferris & Minielli, 2004

Asynchronous Messaging	Synchronous Messaging
E-Mail	Instantaneous interactive messaging (IMs)
Audio & Video E-mail with webcams	Chat systems
Electronic Bulletin Boards	
Discussion lists	
Weblogs	
SMS	

These tools and proprietary groupware packages like WebCT fostered the fast growth of these teams, as both faculty and students did not have to engage in additional learning to prepare for projects.

Word of mouth

The expansion of GVTs was fostered by spreading the word about them through articles in journals and presentations at conferences. For example, in 2001, Hogeschool Ghent received an EU grant to hold a conference on how to create and manage such teams.[1] The improvement in technology also made GVT participation easier. With the growth in online courses, the Web was moving from mere entertainment to a strong tool for education.

New use for old technology

Part of the utility of the Web in these projects was the ability to utilize some of the Electronic Meeting Systems software initially developed in the 1950s. With the Web, this type of software could easily be deployed for use by multinational teams. Some of the software programs were simple Group Support Systems (GSS). The purpose of a GSS is to facilitate communication within a team. According to Shirani (2006), a GSS allows three things to happen:

- Parallel communication. People can be entering comments at the same time as others are commenting. They do not need to "wait their turn," but instead can comment while they still remember what they wanted to say without intervening distractions.
- Anonymous comments. Without names attached to ideas, others can focus on what was said and not on who said it. This may also lead to a more open discussion with more input from participants who may be shy or uncertain.
- Transcribing all dialog. The whole of the meeting can be read later to answer questions that might arise.

A more complex system was a GDSS, a Group Decision Support System. Within these systems, participants can vote on decisions, and the decisions can be ranked (Roszkiewicz, 2007). In both GSS and GDSS, the ability to provide a transcription of the meeting offered a great opportunity for researchers. They could read the transcript to study how the material was shared, how conflicts were resolved, and how the teams worked as project problems arose. Paul, Samarah, Seetharaman & Mykytyn (2004) estimated that 90% of the research using these techniques to study and improve the functioning of GVTs was done using student samples. This meant that some of the GVTs existed only to gather data and involved little student social interaction. In others, the data was a side benefit of the teamwork that the students performed.

For example, in a collaboration between students at the University of Southern Illinois at Carbondale and the Indian Institute of Management, Calcutta, the researchers attempted to show that, while conflict management in a GVT was influenced by cultural differences, the style of conflict management could be mediated by using a GDSS. In the experiment, students were working on price setting for graduate versus undergraduate courses. Relative to Hofstede's Individualism trait, half of the student teams were homogenous while the others were heterogeneous. Using a web-based GDSS, students could anonymously comment and vote on various proposals. The use of this tool served to reduce the differences

---

1   It was at this conference that Van Ryssen, Godar, and Jean-Marc Lehu (participating faculty from the Sorbonne in France) met for the first time.

in the way heterogeneous and homogeneous teams handled conflict (Paul, Samarah, Seetharaman & Mykytyn, 2004). This type of research was beneficial to both businesses and academia as each expanded its use of GVTs.

New technology and old problems

When Skype was introduced in 2003, it became possible for members of GVTs to communicate in real-time and see one another at very little cost. No technology beyond a laptop and Skype software were required. While this made it possible to have "virtual F2F" meetings, it also made everyone more aware of the problems that differences in language proficiency cause in team processes. European business and marketing professors generally understand the need for professionals to be at least bilingual and, specifically in Belgium, to master three languages. This concern is not as strong in most Anglophone universities. Most UK and USA students do not bother to learn or are not encouraged to learn a second language. This often causes an imbalance in workloads when more proficient students do more work and is something non-English speaking professors need to consider.

In a project between colleges in Buenos Aires and Ghent, the language issue was even further illustrated. About half of the Belgian students in Ghent were taking Spanish as a fourth language. Furthermore, the class welcomed a number of international students from the Erasmus Exchange program of the European Commission. At any time, students were talking in ten or more languages, including Finnish, German, Italian, Greek, and various dialects of Spanish. For the project, however, the lingua franca had to remain English, the second language to practically all. The Argentine and Belgian professors were very much aware of the danger that Spanish-speaking students in Belgium would stick together, creating an imbalance in groups. The professors had to force mixed groups with, for example, Czech, Dutch, Finnish and Spanish students. One of the supervising faculty, Stefaan Van Ryssen, set a strict policy that all discussions in class be exclusively in English, leaving the students to speak whatever they liked outside.

As technology improved and became a normal part of "smart classrooms," it became much easier to launch a course project that included participants from multiple nations. The marginal cost to both faculty and students was very low. There were some situations, however, in which that was not the case. In an attempted GVT involving Ghent and a university in China, the faculty soon found that there was a substantial difference in access to technology. The Chinese students were severely hampered in terms of limited availability of computer time, forcing some students to do their work at 4 a.m. This project was curtailed for the benefit of all.

2010 & Beyond

X Culture

In 2010, the largest GVT project to date was launched by Dr. Vas Taras at the University of North Carolina – Greensboro. In the very first semester of X-Culture, approximately 400 students from 7 universities around the globe participated. According to their current LinkedIn profile:

> X-Culture is a large-scale international experiential learning project that involves over 3,500 MBA and business students from 100 universities from 40 countries on six continents every semester. The students are placed in global virtual teams of about seven, with each student coming from a different country. Working with people from around the globe and dealing with cultural differences, time-

zone dispersion, and global communication challenges, the teams complete a consulting project for a multi-national company.

X-Culture is experimenting with various crowd-sourced problem solving and hopes to develop a process that would allow crowds of amateurs to outperform experts. Our ultimate goal is to do to the business consulting industry what Wikipedia did to the Encyclopedia Britannica. (http://www .linkedin.com/company/x-culture, downloaded April 20, 2019)

As X-Culture has grown, businesses have recognized the benefit that this massive group of GVTs can bring. Businesses are now submitting projects to be studied by these student teams, and they are covering some of the infrastructure costs of this academic enterprise.

Core competence

In 2016, almost twenty years after Van Ryssen contacted Godar, the Yale School of Management added a new core course to their MBA curriculum: Global Virtual Teams (Yale, 2016). They recognize that learning to operate successfully in an environment with GVTs is a "must" for their students. Thus, the week before classes start, they put students through training on the use of the systems, international cultural differences, and GVT etiquette. Later in the semester, the Yale students are teamed with students from other countries to solve a real-world consulting project, with some of the research paid for by sponsoring corporations.

From a training exercise to consulting

What is notable about both X-Culture and the Yale course is that students are using current projects submitted by corporations. While GVTs were first introduced to give students experience in working with multinational team members because it was a need identified by businesses, now businesses are finding the teams to be of benefit in making a recommendation on actual problems. The teams have moved beyond a training device or a setting for research on how to improve processes, to being true consultants to business.

The Future

As noted in the introduction to this chapter, students now automatically make projects "virtual." The technology keeps improving, making it easier and less expensive to go virtual. Utilizing the tools that this generation of college students use in their personal relationships, e.g., Snapchat, Facebook Groups, Dropbox, Doodle, etc., will be a universal expectation of new college graduates entering the workplace. Functioning well on a GVT will be a required skill.

We also anticipate that projects will gamify, which would allow students to change sides and swap groups. As companies look for more innovative solutions to their problems, this could be a true advantage in a crowd-sourced world. The answers to those problems may well lie outside the product or industry boundaries we now use. With gamification, we anticipate that the name of GVT may change to GVS, Global Virtual Squads, ready to be deployed anywhere, anytime.

References

Fayard, A. (2006). One School/Two Campuses: A Socio-Technical Approach for Building the Distributed Classroom, in Teaching and Learning with Virtual Teams, Hershey: Information Science Publishing, ed. Ferris, S.P. & Godar, S.H. 194–220.

Ferris, S.P. & Minielli, M.C. (2004). Technology and Virtual Teams, in Virtual and Collaborative Teams: Process, Technologies and Practice, Hershey: Idea Group Publishing, ed. Godar, S.H. & Ferris, S.P., 193–212.

Hall, R. W. (1992). Catching up with the times. Business Horizons, 35(4), 6–14.

Paul, S., Samarah, I. M., Seetharaman, P., & Mykytyn Jr., P. P. (2004). An Empirical Investigation of Collaborative Conflict Management Style in Group Support System-Based Global Virtual Teams. Journal of Management Information Systems, 21(3), 185–222.

Roszkiewicz, R. (2007). GDSS: The Future of Online Meetings and True Digital Collaboration? Seybold Report: Analyzing Publishing Technologies, 7(1), 13–17.

Shirani, A. I. (2006). Sampling and pooling of decision-relevant information: Comparing the efficiency of face-to-face and GSS supported groups. Information & Management, 43(4), 521–529.

Van Ryssen, S. & Godar, S.H. (2000). Going International without Going International: Multinational Virtual Teams. Journal of International Management, 6(1), 49–60.

Yale (2016), Inside the Global Virtual Teams Course, https://som.yale.edu/news/2016/07/inside-the-global-virtual-teams-course

CHAPTER 2

Foundations of Global Virtual Teams

LEI WENG SI, MACAO INSTITUTE FOR TOURISM STUDIES

The Beginning of GVTs

The simple definition of a GVT is a distributed team located in different places, which could be within a city or different regions of the world, that works together and aims to achieve a common goal or objective. In fact, virtual teams may have existed not only for the last decade but may trace back to the early 1980s. In the 1980s, when telecommunication started to grow rapidly, telephones became available for offices and homes, and J.C. Penny started to hire home-based call center agents. Some work could be done at home, which enabled workers to stay home and got work done at the same time. Throughout the twentieth century, the development of telecommunication technology has not just modernized the way we communicate but also created a type of new working mode—telework. Facsimile machines, cellular phones, and PCs were all important communication tools before the Internet era, facilitating work being carried out from different locations. Facsimile machines were a necessity for offices in the old days. Documents were transmitted within seconds from different parts of the world to an office. Cellular phones enable a high level of workers' mobility, while PCs serve many functions in an office and at home. All of these laid the foundation of virtual team operation. Current internet technology has empowered the possibility of telework and the creation of virtual teams. Internet and World Wide Web have revolutionized our ways of life as well as ways of work. Working from different parts of the world had never been possible without WiFi, smartphones, and cloud computing nowadays. Global Virtual Teams became the latest development in the world of work and corporate circles of the 21st century.

GVTs' Emergence

The internet penetration rate and fierce competition among multinational companies are believed to be the main driving forces behind the emergence of GVTs. In particular, physical boundaries are being minimalized by internet technology. Multinational companies are able to fully internalize their operations by establishing GVTs to race around the clock in a competitive global business environment. Developed countries such as the U.S. and Europe, are believed to have taken the lead in establishing GVTs in the early days. As revealed from the statistics by the International Telecommunication Union (ITU, 2019) in Figure 1, Europe and America have the highest internet penetration rate since 2009. The CIS (The Commonwealth of Independent States) countries have been quickly catching up since 2015. Other continents, such as Africa, the Arab States and the Asia Pacific have been showing similar trends in internet penetration. With the increasing level of internet penetration in different continents and countries, GVTs become more feasible to form than in the old days when the internet was not so popular across the world. Internet penetration is probably the first and foremost criteria to establish workable and effective GVTs, and one can imagine that GVTs would not function well with a poor internet connection which hampers communication among the GVT's members.

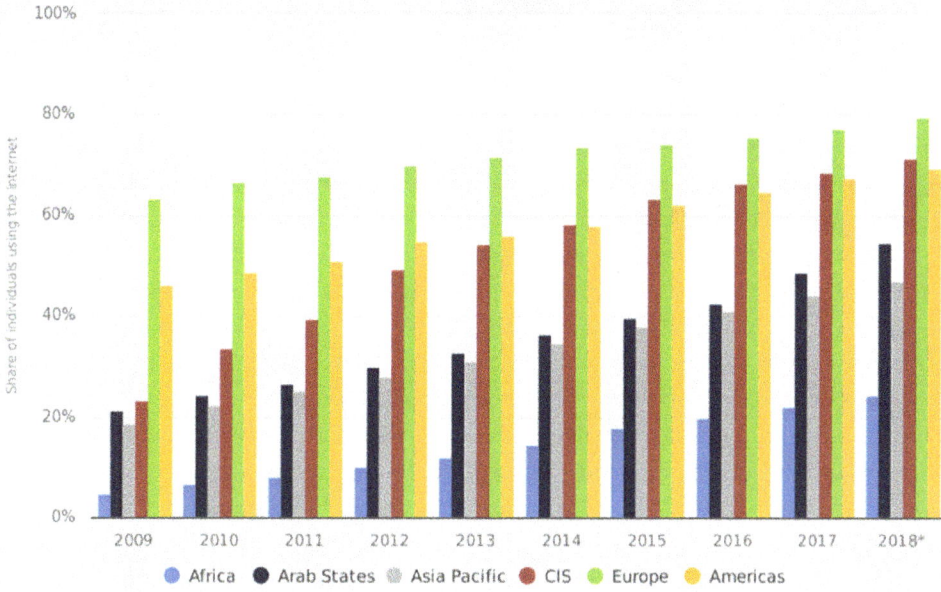

Fig 2.1 Global Internet Penetration Rate from 2009 to 2018, by Region
Source: Statista (ITU, 2019)

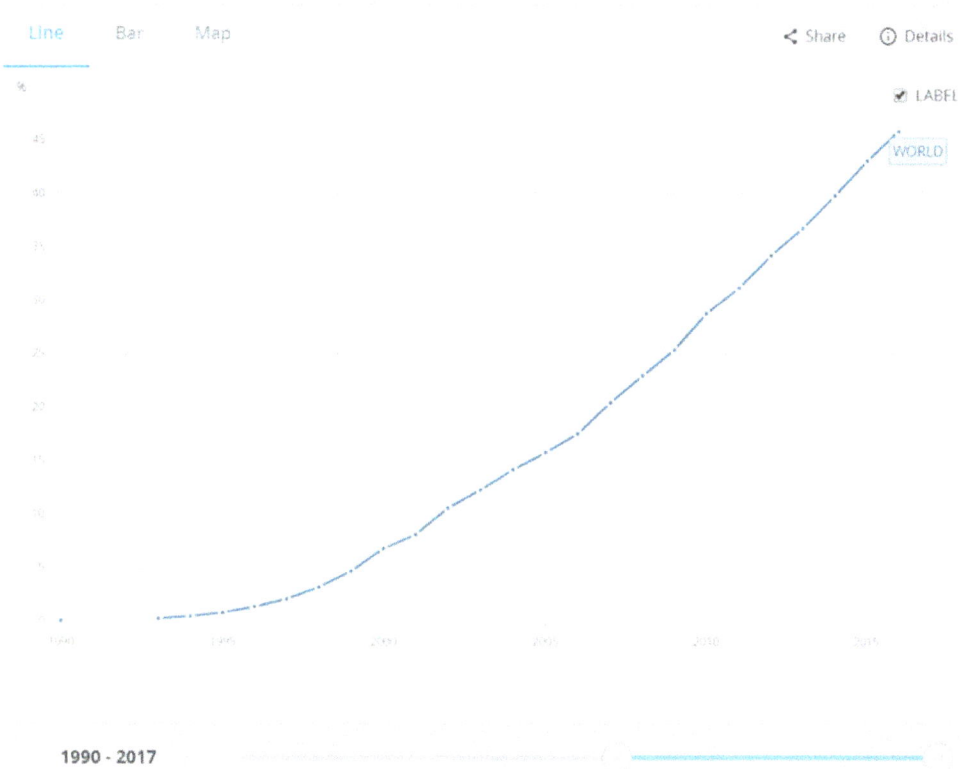

Fig 2.2 Individuals using the Internet (% of population)
Source: The World Bank (TheWorldBank, 2019)

When scrutinizing the statistics of Individual Internet Usage by TheWorldBank (2019), as shown in Figure 2, one can see the rapid upsurge of individual internet usage during the second decade of the new millennium. The two statistics illustrate a possible timeline of the emergence of GVTs: it started after the millennium and has grown rapidly ever since. Despite the rapid internet penetration, mobile usage and mobile network developments also contribute to the effectiveness of GVTs operation around the globe. From the GSM mobile network of before to the recent testing of the 5G mobile network, the download speed on mobile devices is expected to take a great leap forward. Mobile devices with good internet connections enable not only instant messaging, but smooth video conferencing (e.g., FaceTime) and possible future speedy downloading of massive data. These are all important catalysts to speed up the popularity of GVTs and its efficiency. With a mobile device and a stable mobile network, a team member of a GVT could simply work anywhere he/she prefers and perform more or less the same as another member stations in the head office of a multinational corporation.

Furthermore, according to the World Development Report 2016: Digital Dividends by Minges (2016), there exists a positive relationship between internet broadband penetration and economic growth. For example, it is estimated that for every 10 percentage point increase in broadband penetration, there was a 2.14% increase in GDP in China. In Germany, for each 10% increase in broadband penetration growth, GDP growth increases by 0.255. Thus, the internet penetration rate is no doubt one of the biggest driving force behind GVTs' operation as well as economic development and growth.

Companies Pioneered GVTs—Mini Cases of Multinational Corporations

IBM

IBM is one of the pioneering multinational corporations that established GVTs, dating back as early as 2006. An initiative named the IBM 2006 InnovationJam gathered over 150,000 employees, family members, business partners, and IBM clients from 104 countries to identify new business foci. On the technology side, IBM also built virtual spaces to examine its usage patterns for training, collaboration, immersive events, remote mentoring, business rehearsals, new employee orientation, joint software development, and many other business areas. Table 1 explains the detailed usage of virtual space at IBM (Cherbakov, Brunner, Smart, & Lu, 2009) and its benefits.

Table 2.1 IBM Usage of Virtual Spaces and Benefits

Business Activity	Capabilities	Benefits
Events e.g., IBM Academy of Technology Conference	• VoIP • Cater to different sizes of meetings, from small team meetings to large formal conferences	• Reduced travel time and cost • Eliminate meeting expenses • Engaging a broader audience.
Mentoring and Knowledge Exchange e.g., Metaverse managers speed mentoring	• Integration with enterprise directory • Private (location proximity-based) chat • Social spaces and games to build stronger connections	• Remote interaction with SMEs • Cross-cultural networking • Exchange of knowledge

Business Activity	Capabilities	Benefits
New employee orientation e.g., Fresh Blue program in China and India	• Content co-creation as a teaming activity • Exploration of career opportunities	• Establish quick connections with new and experienced IBMers • An engaging way to teach company history and culture • Practice English and presentation skills
Rehearsals	• Simulation of complex business activities • Execution, recording, and playback of business scenarios.	• Efficient on-the-job learning in a safe social environment. • Remote interaction with SME. • Team building
Software Development e.g., Bluegrass – Rational Jazz Team Concert IDE Plug-in	• Artifact representation • 3D modeling • Visualize software team activities	• Enable globally distributed teams • Visibility into presence and work of the team • Modeling without advanced skills
System Management e.g., Energy-efficient data center	• Simulation of systems usage and loads (such as CPU, memory). • Visual representation of servers, racks, networking, power and cooling equipment • Alerts rendering through integration with systems management software (such as IBM Tivoli)	• Remote monitoring problem determination and resolution • Remote systems management • Modeling and simulations of space, power and cooling planning • Simulation of disaster recovery scenarios.
White-board brainstorming	• Brainstorming across different virtual spaces and channels, including Metaverse, OpenSim, Sametime, Web. • REST-Style API for additional third-party development. • Sametime plug-in	• Boost productivity by generating, categorizing, and capturing ideas • Generate solutions without limitations of physical spaces and time • media channels in real time (Web 2D/ and 3D) • Data Mining with persisted ideas.

Different forms of GVTs are established by using the technologies available at IBM in order to carry out varies types of business activities virtually. More importantly, the types of technology employed to support IBM GVTs activities include Active Worlds, Forterra OLIVE™, OpenSim, Second Life, Torque, and Unity3D. For example, Active Worlds (AW) is regularly used regularly to hold events and collaboration activities, such as learning and development activities for employees.

Coca Cola

Aside from tech companies like IBM that have the ability to employ and develop different kinds of technology to enable GVTs and carry out all sorts of virtual activities, non-tech companies like Coca-Cola have also joined the trend of establishing GVTs to cope with the fast-paced global world. With the aim of improving operational efficiency and reducing costs, Coca-Cola Latin America has started to form a virtual team to support and implement certain management functions of Coca-Cola in Latin America

(Anonymous). 2008 was the first time that Coca-Cola made investments with the goal of developing its leaders' capability to work in a virtual environment. Appointed leaders were trained to experience and validate their leadership practices in a virtual environment, and leaders underwent a two-month intensive program consisting of:

- A series of six online web seminars held over a two-week period:
  - Setting the scene; introduction to participants, facilitators, the program, the tools and technologies
  - Effective participation in virtual teams
  - A framework for effective virtual teams
  - Team spirit and motivation
  - Personal skills, coaching, and action learning
  - Hands-on with Wikis, social networks, and survey tools
- Participation in a social network team room
- One to one telephone coaching
- Collaboration tools, including social networks, survey tools, and wikis
- Assessments, audits, and analysis
- Action learning sets.

In addition, a follow-up to the action learning project was carried out six weeks after the intensive training. Business benefits were found, namely, that team leaders could free themselves up to work more strategically, and teams become mature, faster, and more self-sufficient.

Google

One of the technology giants, Google, employs nearly 100,000 workers located in more than 50 countries, 150 cities, and across five continents. GVTs are a common form of organizational structure at Google. Colleagues work with colleagues who they have never met in person but only over the internet. Employees at Google very commonly work across different time zones, cultures, and languages. In view of this, Google's People Innovation Lab (PiLab) spent two years studying more than 5,000 employees in order to understand how to keep things in place when employees are spread out all over the world. One of the statements by Veronica Gilrane, manager of Google's People Innovation Lab, was encouraging: "We were happy to find no difference in the effectiveness, performance ratings, or promotions for individuals and teams whose work requires collaboration with colleagues around the world versus Googlers who spend most of their day to day working with colleagues in the same office. Well-being standards were uniform across the board as well. Googlers or teams who work virtually find ways to prioritize a steady work-life balance by prioritizing important rituals like a healthy night's sleep and exercise just as non-distributed team members do" (Ludema, 2019).

The research results are concluded with six important recommendations in operating GVTs. They are:

1. **Get to know your people**: Personal conversation is always a good icebreaker before getting to the meeting agenda. Google recommends a small causal chat before each online meeting to set up the rapport and learn about colleagues' preferences on the meeting schedule, regarding a particular day of a week and a convenient time of a day, for example.

2. **Set clear boundaries**: The researchers of the project recommend setting clear norms that are then stated explicitly in order not to leave any chance for confusion. Ways of communication, e.g., expected response time, meetings attendance and schedule, e.g., vacation and private hours, are to be set and communicated clearly.

3. **Forge connections**: Connecting the team and colleagues together is crucial, no matter how far away colleagues are from each other. It is recommended to connect colleagues on a personal level by using one-on-one meetings to exchange experiences. It is important to bring the whole team together in one location for special occasions, e.g., celebrating a work achievement, to build up in-person interaction. Anyone who cannot make it to the occasion should still be connected virtually and make the person feel engaged and part of the occasion.

4. **Putting it together**: The research team reports that "we found managers leading by example and making an extra effort to get to know distributed team members can be extra impactful, and a little rapport goes a long way." Managers or team leaders are advised to spend the time and resources needed to take care of their team members, especially in the virtual workplace.

5. **Create a supportive environment**: Technologies to support virtual work, video conferencing, and cloud computing, for example, should be made available at all times.

6. **Trusting your teammates**: Team leaders and managers should always trust their team members and should not micromanage their remote team members. Instead, work goals and priorities should be clear at all times. The research result also suggests creating a rhythm of the team's work, with a regular communication schedule in place.

GVTs are very common in many different industries, as illustrated by the cases of IBM, Coca-Cola, and Google. GVTs certainly offer advantages and disadvantages to corporations. Managers or team leaders nowadays are expected to be equipped with the skills to manage GVTs. They will be asked to manage a GVT at some point in their business operation, making it inevitable that they need to understand their characteristics and operations. The three corporations discussed above have a long history of using GVTs. Having the technology to support the operation of GVTs, as described in the case of IBM, and the necessary training and advice available to GVT managers and team leaders are the critical success factors in running GVTs, as shown by Coca Cola and Google. In addition to what multinational corporations are working on to enhance the benefits earned from GVTs, graduate schools also see the need to introduce courses on GVT management. Post-graduate courses of GVTs management developed by world elite universities, for example, at Yale University and the University of Southern California, are available. GVTs were introduced by Yale School of Management as a course at the post-graduate level in 2016.

GVTs Tomorrow

According to the statistics of the 2017 State of Telecommuting in the U.S. by Global Workplace Analytics, the trend of the U.S. workforce working remotely will increase up to fifty percent by 2020. A similar increase is expected in the U.K., Australia, and other OECD countries. In the U.S., there are currently around 3.7 million employees who work from home. These people are mainly telecommuters, have a college education, and earn a salary of at approximately $58,000 a year (ULTATEL, 2018). In a study conducted by Virgin Media, it states that 58% of UK workers think the traditional office will not exist by 2020 (Media, 2011). 56% believe they will work from home or from a remote hub, rather than commuting to work, and 83% feel that technology has enabled them to become more productive in the last ten years. A recent study by IBISWorld shows that "by 2050, it is estimated that one in five Australians will telework." Furthermore, a survey done by the Society for Human Resource Management with 397 randomly selected human resources profession from the Society for Human Resource Management shows that multinational corporations are twice more likely (66%) to operate virtual teams than those U.S.-based only operations (28%). In addition, government agencies are the least likely to use virtual teams (9%) (Minton-Eversole, 2012).

GVTs are very much rooted in the offering of telework or flexible working by corporations. Many human resource reports and statistics, as shown above, illustrate well that teleworking or flexible working is already widely implemented and will continue rising as an important trend in the near future. Challenges in operating GVTs will emerge and remain as an obstacle to reaping the potential benefits to be offered. Thus, corporations will have to come up with strategies to tackle the potential challenges. In a white paper produced by O2, they suggest three important ingredients to manage flexible working. They are 1. Hardware; 2. Connectivity and 3. Applications. Hardware refers to smartphones and tablets, connectivity refers to businesses offering connectivity to employees via home broadband for logging on to work email and other company systems over the internet, and applications refer to free or low-cost video-calling, such as FaceTime and Skype, which can help colleagues to work together. Alongside these three main ingredients, Google and Evernote have recently produced a document called the Virtual Team Driver's License (Scheunemann & Bühlmann, 2018). It serves as a survival guide to operating virtual teams and identifies three fundamental problems in operating them as: 1. Data overload, 2. Communication overload, and 3. Cognitive overload.

A typical scenario of a person engaging in a GVT is:

7 AM. Smartphone alarm. 15 minutes of email—some urgent because it's from around the world, and those teams are headed home shortly. Business before and during breakfast. Facebook, messaging, and multiple chat channels during the commute. Upon arrival at the office, you're already behind because you never caught up with yesterday's work. Meetings all day, virtual and otherwise. And just when you're finishing up for the day, another office in another time zone just got started. This may feel like a bad day at work, but it's really a bad way to work.

The document provides helpful suggestions to operate GVT. They are:

1. **Hiring the right staff, who are:**
   - Self-management skills (good time management, good energy management)
   - Above-average self-motivation
   - Very strong oral and written communication skills
   - Naturally proactive
   - High level of integrity
   - Ability to thrive under a low-touch, highly flexible management style
   - Being okay without a regular, social workplace environment
   - Affinity for different forms of communication technology.

2. **Getting to know the team:**
   - It is suggested to have a face-to-face onboarding that achieves the below:
       i. Understanding the team mission to establish a clear, common direction.
      ii. Faster and stronger relationship-building with the rest of the team, as well as others in the office.
     iii. Understanding (or helping to create) defined rules of collaboration.
      iv. Taking time to get to know each other on a personal level to further strengthen tea bonds
       v. Shared interests and better understanding.
   - Learn the difference – Virtual team members, especially managers, should learn the differences of different team members, e.g., employment laws, holiday policies, cultural considerations, and share with local team members.
   - Mission-critical clarity – Effective role clarity must include goals and milestones for each team member. It is best to practice the 3Ws: Who does What by When.

3. **How remote teams stay on track:**
   - Using the right channel for the right reason
   - Using commute time smartly
   - Addressing the potential language barrier
   - Run productive meetings.

4. Trust is the key:

Teams	Groups
Shared leadership roles	Strong leader
Individual and mutual accountability	Individual accountability is dominant
Open-ended discussion and active problems solving	Focus on efficiency in meetings

   - Hold a "getting-to-know-each-other" session as soon as possible
   - A leader should always lead by example and keep agreements.
   - Hold honest sharing sessions of success and failures
   - Leadership from the bottom up.

As we can see from the survival guide produced by Google and Evernote, the future of GVTs face fewer technological challenges but more people challenges, such as assuring that the right type of people is utilized in a GVT, the working mode of GVTs, and trust and leadership within GVT operation. These are more pressing issues to be concerned with regarding the GVTs of tomorrow. In addition, recent studies discovered that GVTs might cause feelings of isolation from team members. Furthermore, according to a survey done by the European Union in 2015 (Eurofound, 2017), the stress level of highly mobile workers is higher than others who telework. Operating virtual teams will surely remain a challenge to many corporations in the near future. In view of the benefits and potential challenges offered by GVTs, balance will probably be the key for corporations to steer towards in the near future as they operate GVTs. For example, they will need to gauge the level of engagement a GVT member should have, how often the GVTs should get together in person in order to achieve team building, and how teams can establish trust.

Percentage of workers reporting they feel stress at work

Always or most of the time, by work location

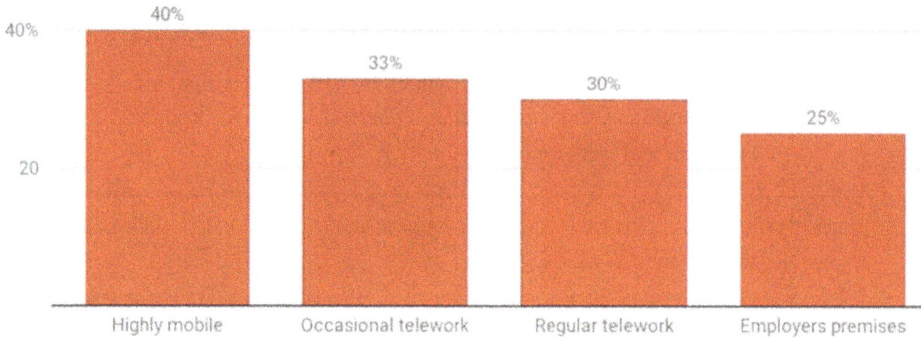

Source: European Working Conditions Survey 2015

Fig 2.3 Worker Percentage Graph

Criterion and Characteristics of GVTs

The popularity of the internet and modern technology has changed many aspects of organizations, particularly regarding team structure and formation. In the old days, teams were usually formed within a single office location. Team members normally had daily face-to-face contact and worked together to accomplish a company's mission or goals. Meetings usually took place in a boardroom with all team members physically present. Today, the emergence of GVTs is almost inevitable for companies having overseas operations, and even small and medium enterprises may hire talents overseas to assist in their daily operations or projects. GVTs are normally formed to achieve a common goal or complete an assigned project, with team members distributed in different locations. Electronic communication is the main mode of communication. This includes emails, video conferencing, mobile messaging, and the usage of cloud storage for document sharing and access. It is very often that team members may not meet each other in person before starting to work on a project, and team members only communicate via electronic communication and working toward a common goal.

There are three common characteristics of GVTs, which are: 1) members share the same working goal and mission; 2) members are located in different locations; and 3) members communicate via various forms of electronic communication. Additionally, there are another four characteristics, which are that 1) members live in different time zones; 2) members have not met each other in person before or after the project/task is complete; 3) members come from different cultural backgrounds; and 4) members speak different native languages but use one common working language, for example, English. Based on the characteristics of GVTs, a comparison is formed to see the major difference between traditional teams and GVTs.

Table 2.2 Illustrates the major difference between a traditional team and GVTs.

Traditional Team	GVTs
Working in the same location	Working in different geographic locations
Face-to-face contact	Non-face-to-face contact via different means of digital communication
Live in the same cultural environment	From different cultural backgrounds
Formal meeting before work starts	Meeting over screens before work starts
Similar work routine/schedule due to being in the same time zone	Different work routines/schedules due to being in different time zones
A similar level of technology at work	Different levels of technology at work

The types of GVTs could be categorized into five types. They are: parallel teams, project development teams, functional teams, service teams, and offshore ISD teams.

Parallel Teams exist alongside a company and are normally responsible for research and development, design, and innovation.

Project Development Teams normally consist of members from different functional teams. They form and work together to achieve a project goal.

Function Teams normally consist of members with the same specialties or expertise and perform together in achieving a common goal or function.

Service Teams are similar to function teams. They mainly provide services to supplement the company's operation and production.

Offshore ISD Teams are independent service providers to which a company can outsource parts of work to. They normally work together with an onshore team.

A company may have different GVTs operating 24x7 around the globe to increase the companies' productivity and service levels to customers. IBM employs more than 350,000 people from different countries, which each possess their own unique cultural background. According to IBM, the benefits in running GVTs are not limited to increasing efficiency and productivity but also include great staff satisfaction, cutting costs, and saving on space (IBM, 2017). Having flexible work schedules and working remotely offers greater job satisfaction to employees of GVTs. GVTs also enable IBM to reduce office operation costs, as GVT members are free to work from home most of the time. GVT team members use many different forms of digital communication, email and instant messaging for example, to handle daily tasks. IBM believes that allowing people to work at the hours when they are naturally most productive can boost performance and morale, and adopts a Results Oriented Work Environment (ROWE). Members of GVTs at IBM have a large range of flexibility with their work, with variables ranging from location to schedule all placed under the employees' control. In addition, IBM uses collaborative software to help GVT members to build trust and enhance communication between team members.

Challenges of GVTs

There are many benefits offered by establishing GVTs, as shown in the examples illustrated by IBM earlier; however, challenges in implementing and operating GVTs also exist. Based on the differences identified in Table 2 (The Major Difference Between Traditional Teams and GVTs), challenges become more prominent for GVTs composed of members coming from around the globe. Below are a few large challenges when operating GVTs.

- Time zone difference
- A lack of face-to-face communication
- The language barrier that exists when members are from different countries and the working language is not a member's native tongue
- Cultural differences
- Different work practices rooted in cultural differences
- Limited social opportunities.

Time Zone Difference

A typical challenge faced by GVTs is to find a common meeting time online. This is a challenge that team members living in different time zones will have to cope with. For example, a team member living in Asia may need to stay up late into the evening in order to teleconference with a team member living in the U.S. or vice versa.

Lacking face-to-face communication

In a traditional working environment, team members see each other every day during office hours, making it easy for conversation between the members of a workplace to happen. Teammates can have lunch together and socialize during break time. Quite often, minor work issues are informally discussed, and small collaborations are easily had via face-to-face chats, making it easy to reach agreements on how to proceed. However, this kind of convenience and opportunity is missing from GVTs. Oftentimes, members of GVTs are working alone and have minimal interaction with colleagues.

Limited Opportunities to Social

Due to the lack of face-to-face communication, opportunities to socialize with colleagues or members are practically nonexistent. Developing social relationships becomes a challenge for GVTs. Without seeing a colleague or co-worker face-to-face, there exist limited opportunities to connect on a personal level.

Cultural Difference

It is fairly common that GVT members come from many different nationalities. Fostering and embracing an inclusive virtual working environment is essential to run GVTs. Due to the potential cultural differences, there are many more challenges that arise around issues such as language and work practices that do not exist with traditional teams.

Language Barrier

Having a set working language is common in GVTs. Nevertheless, due to the nature of GVTs, members' cultural backgrounds can be very diverse. Even when using English as a working language, misunderstandings and misinterpretations of written messages or texts can happen, which has the potential of hindering work effectiveness and efficiency. This scenario is especially prominent when English is not any member's native tongue.

Different work practices rooted in cultural difference

Work practices can vary from one culture to another. With the diversity that exists in GVTs, these differences may have an impact on their operation. For example, punctuality and respecting deadlines may be practiced very differently by people coming from different cultures. Due to these potential shortcomings, a clear understanding of work practices must be aligned at the time of the GVT's establishment.

To mitigate potential issues, ways to improve GVT communications become critical to the success of any GVT. GVT communication is mostly text-based, as members read, write, and send reports via electronic mediums, e.g., e-mail. This type of cooperation, based mostly on text exchanges, can become risky due to the missing connectedness and cues that can only be established through face-to-face communication. Thus, having regular video chats with the GVT's members will be critical to cultivating its connection. Teammate connection is a fundamental building block of trust, team spirit, and team identity in all teams' formation and operation. GVTs are no exception, and careful and thoughtful planning is necessary to facilitate connection among the members.

Definition of Global Virtual Teams

The definition of GVTs has evolved over time. The simple definition defines a GVT as a distributed team located in different places, where people in different regions of the world work together and aim to achieve a common goal or objective. According to the Financial Times Lexicon, which provides a glossary of words and phrases selected by Financial Times editors, GVTs embrace the concept that team members can engage in and deliver projects with limited or no direct physical interaction with other members, allowing multinational enterprises to draw on the widest talent pool available among their global employee base. Teams typically never meet face-to-face and conduct all project work using VOIP (Voice Over Internet Protocol) technology and other virtual meeting applications, such as SharePoint (Global Virtual Teams, 2019). "Virtual team" is used to define a broad range of activities and various forms of technology-supported working styles (Anderson, McEwan, Bal, & Carletta, 2007). Another definition suggests that virtual teams are distributed work teams whose members are geographically dispersed and coordinate their work predominantly with electronic information and communication technologies, such as via e-mail, video-conferencing, and telephone (Hertel, Geister, & Konradt, 2005).

The level of internationality in a GVT can have significant geographic variation. For example, a GVT can be comprised of team members in different locations within the same region, such as within North America, Asia, or Western Europe. However, a GVT can also consist of team members located over a few continents and operating under different time zones, such as in Asia, Northern Europe, and South America. For example, suppose a multinational information technology company seeking to develop a product is allocated the relevant internationally located staff to accomplish the task as a Global Virtual Team. The senior project manager is located in the head office of the firm in Silicon Valley, the project manager is located in the Asia regional office in Beijing, China, and the project leader is located in Bangalore, India, along with another ten staff working from home at different Indian states.

GVTs emerged in approximately the mid-1990s, when many multinational companies, such as Goodyear, Texas Instruments, and General Electric, had begun exporting the team idea to their overseas' branches located in Asia, Europe, and Latin America and integrating human resources internationally.

At the same time, communication technology took a great leap forward when the internet became available not only in universities but enterprises and households. Started in the year 2000 and developing over the following decade, virtual teams have been formed in many different multinational enterprises in order to take advantage of time zone differences and increase productivity levels.

References

Anderson, A. H., McEwan, R., Bal, J., & Carletta, J. (2007). Virtual team meetings: An analysis of communication and context. Computers in Human Behavior, 23(5), 2558–2580.

Anonymous. Coca-Cola Latin America - a virtual programme to develop
organisational capability and capacity for Managing Virtual Teams. Retrieved from
https://towardsmaturity.org/elements/uploads/Coca_Cola_LA_Managing_Virtual_Teams.pdf

Cherbakov, L., Brunner, R., Smart, R., & Lu, C. (2009). History of virtual worlds environment in IBM. Retrieved from https://www.ibm.com/developerworks/library/ws-virtualspaces/index.html

Eurofound. (2017). Sixth European Working Condition Survey - Overview report (2017 update). Retrieved from Luxembourg: https://www.eurofound.europa.eu/sites/default/files/ef_publication/field_ef_document/ef1634en.pdf

Global Virtual Teams. (2019). Lexion. Retrieved from http://lexicon.ft.com/Term?term=global-virtual-teams

Hertel, G., Geister, S., & Konradt, U. (2005). Managing virtual teams: A review of current empirical research. Human resource management review, 15(1), 69–95.

IBM. (2017, Nov 24, 2017). The Key Benefits of Having a Virtual Team. Retrieved from https://developer.ibm.com/answers/questions/414966/the-key-benefits-of-having-a-virtual-team/

ITU. (2019). Global Internet Penetration Rate from 2009 to 2018, by Region. Retrieved from https://www.statista.com/statistics/265149/internet-penetration-rate-by-region/

Ludema, J. J., Amber. (2019). What Google Has Learned About Remote Work: Six Tips. Retrieved from https://www.forbes.com/sites/amberjohnson-jimludema/2019/05/09/what-google-has-learned-about-remote-work-six-tips/#790dbd7146d1

Media, V. B. (2011). Measuring the benefits of agility at work report. Retrieved from Virgin Business Media: https://www.virginmediabusiness.co.uk/

Minges, M. (2016). Exploring the Relationship Between Broadband and Economic Growth. World Developement Report Digital Dividends. Retrieved from http://pubdocs.worldbank.org/en/391452529895999/WDR16-BP-Exploring-the-Relationship-between-Broadband-and-Economic-Growth-Minges.pdf

Minton-Eversole, T. (2012). Virtual Teams Used Most by Global Organizations, Survey Says. Retrieved from https://www.shrm.org/resourcesandtools/hr-topics/organizational-and-employee-development/pages/virtualteamsusedmostbyglobalorganizations,surveysays.aspx

Scheunemann, Y., & Bühlmann, D. B. (2018). The virtual teams driver's license. Retrieved from https://www.thinkwithgoogle.com/_qs/.../mktdesign-757-virtual-team-whitepaper.pdf

TheWorldBank. (2019). Individuals using the Internet (% of population). Retrieved from https://data.worldbank.org/indicator/IT.NET.USER.ZS?end=2017&start=1990&view=chart

ULTATEL. (2018). Fifty Percent of U.S. Workforce Will be Remote by 2020; ULTATEL's Cloud-Based Technology Paves the Way. Retrieved from https://markets.businessinsider.com/news/stocks/fifty-percent-of-u-s-workforce-will-be-remote-by-2020-ultatel-s-cloud-based-technology-paves-the-way-1015773617

Theories of Virtual Teams, International Teams, and Global Virtual Collaboration

SERDAR KARABATI, ISTANBUL BILGI UNIVERSITY

Cooperation and working together have been an important part of human history. Complex tasks and projects, such as mass hunting or building a pyramid, were only possible thanks to collaboration, though sometimes forcedly, among a group of individuals. Collaboration requires that everyone involved has a mutual understanding of the expectations, rights, and obligations of the group members. We must also note that collaboration is only possible when members engage their energies in informing, sharing, and helping in a manner specific to the activity at hand.

Our modern institutions thrive thanks to collaboration. Linguist and developmental psychologist Michael Tomasello uses the example of shopping for food at a supermarket, a relatively simple activity, to explain the extent of collaboration surrounding us. A supermarket is full of products, each with a specific label, detailed information about ingredients if it is a packaged good and a price tag. Entering the store gives the customers the right to purchase items for the posted price but also subjects them to the obligation of not stealing or destroying items. Customers expect the products to be healthy and free of toxins or other such issues, trusting the producers and relying on the obligation of the retailer and the government to control these producers. The transactions are completed with the use of paper money or a credit card, both of which are exchange mediums in the complex institutional structure under which financial activities take place. People also follow behavioral norms, such as not removing items from another customer's cart and standing in line.

Today, teams are viewed as central building blocks in a wide variety of applied contexts and industries like the military, spaceflight, healthcare, and sports (Driskell, Salas, and Driskell, 2018). Increased global competition and the pressure for fast innovation are the two main reasons for the transformation to team-based work models. In addition, increased labor mobility and the rise of multinational enterprise have led to organizations and work groups whose members come from a wide range of ethnic, national, and cultural backgrounds (Hays-Thomas, 2004). Therefore, management scholars strive to understand work teams from a variety of lenses, including a cross-cultural perspective.

The scientific interest by management scholars in work groups and teams started with the famous Hawthorne studies, conducted at an electric factory of the same name during the 1920s and the 1930s. The interest in work teams started to peak in the 1980s, as organizations across the globe have started to shift from rigid bureaucratic structures towards more organic designs (Jimenez, Boehe, Taras, and Caprar, 2017). Mechanistic organizations are highly formal, centralized, and highly structured, with an emphasis on divisionalization. They are the descendants of Weber's bureaucracies. Unlike mechanistic organizations, organic organization thrives on the power of relationships, flexible procedures, and a network-like communication. Organic organizations can react quickly and easily to changes in the environment, which is why they are said to be the most adaptive form of organization

What is a team?

A team is "a collection of individuals who are interdependent in their tasks, who share responsibility for outcomes, who see themselves and are seen by others as an intact social entity, embedded in one or more larger social systems and who manage their relationships across organizational boundaries" (Tirmizi, 2008). The terms "team" and "group" are sometimes used interchangeably; however, we differentiate these two along several dimensions. As summarized in the below table, teams are characterized by a stronger emphasis on commonality, a goal that requires shared leadership and mutual accountability.

Building Interpersonal Trust	Building Task-based Trust
✓ Sharing meals	✓ Keeping team commitments to deadlines
✓ Socializing after business hours	✓ Constantly delivering high-quality work
✓ Sharing personal information and hobbies	✓ Reliable, helpful, cooperative behavior
✓ Exchanging pictures	
✓ Non-job-related communication	

Accountability: An obligation or willingness to accept responsibility or to account for one's actions.

As defined by Pearce and Conger, shared leadership is an interactive influence process among individuals in groups for which the objective is to lead one another to the achievement of group or organizational goals.

There are various forms of teams. Firstly, teams are classified according to their level of formality. A project team established and officially recognized by management, for example, is a highly formal team. Teams can also be permanent or temporary. The senior management team of an organization or an ethics committee at a university are relatively permanent, structured around fixed, formal roles. A task force, on the other hand, is highly formal but temporary. In naval operations, for example, a task force can be assembled using ships from different divisions and squadrons without requiring a permanent fleet reorganization. Task forces can be easily dissolved following the completion of the operational task. Teams also differ according to the level of similarity and interdependence between the tasks of team members. For example, in synchronized artistic swimming, swimmers rely on a similar set of skills for success in their routines. On the other hand, during surgery, the surgeon, surgeon's assistant, anesthesia provider, circulating nurse, and other team members such as the surgical technologist focus on different tasks as they operate on the patient.

What the team does:

Do things – make a product or market a service;
Run things – devise an organization's mission statement and strategy;
Recommend things – offer alternative solutions to problems.

Project teams

According to one estimate, 65 percent of all work done in modern organizations is project-based. Teamwork in organizational settings demands intelligent management of several processes, namely transition processes, action processes, and interpersonal processes (Marks, Mathieu, and Zaccaro, 2001). Mission analysis, goal specification, and strategy formulation are dimensions of transition phase processes. Action phase processes involve the monitoring of progress toward goals, team control and backup, and coordination of activities. Specific to interpersonal processes are the issues of conflict management, motivation and confidence building, and management of emotions.

Project teams face numerous challenges in different phases of these three processes. However, many companies are solely concerned with controlling the action phase processes, by implementing rigid guides to dictate behavior and by using statistical methods and techniques such as total quality management to monitor outcomes. Despite these kinds of strict approaches, the rate of project failure does not seem to be decreasing. A survey of IT and software projects, for example, revealed that only 39% of all projects were delivered on time, on budget, complete with required features and functions (Standish Group, 2012). A bulk of 43% was late, over budget, and/or with less than the required features and functions, and 18% were either canceled prior to completion or delivered but never used. That is because most of the tools and techniques account largely for the rational, technical components of project management, but they overlook the interpersonal and emotional components (Gallup, 2012).

High-performing organizations successfully complete 89 percent of their projects, while low performers complete only 36 percent successfully. This difference in success results in high-performing organizations wasting nearly 12 times less than low performers (PMI, 2014).

Effectiveness of teams

Effectiveness and success of teams depend on several factors, some of which have to do with the characteristics and strengths of the organization or the company. Some of the major organizational factors that affect teams' success are overall training of organizational members, the performance management system used, and having or not having a company culture that promotes teamwork. X-Culture promotes the idea that teamwork is valuable and that students should develop their collaboration skills, thus creating a climate suitable for achieving effectiveness. However, although most participants in X-Culture are likely to have similar educational backgrounds, we should not assume that every student possesses the necessary experience to work in a team, and more specifically, in a virtual setting. Team effectiveness may also depend on the similarity of weights allocated to X-Culture assessment by different professors. This is why there is a requirement for professors in X-Culture that at least 20 percent of the course grade should be tied to the quality of the project their students are involved in.

The effectiveness of a team also depends on its composition and the characteristics of its members. Team size, for example, is a critical factor foremost because it changes the duration of communication. We can see that it takes more than four times longer in a 10-member team for the members to talk to each other on a one-on-one basis (44 dyads) than for a 5-member team (10 dyads). Team size also affects decisions about the way available resources will be managed and shared. The general rule is that it is highly difficult to sustain a good performance in teams with more than 15 people (Jones and Bearley, 2001). Of course, this is not to say that a smaller team will always be more successful. Studies on communication in teams suggest that the quality of the exchange is more important to team performance than the volume of information shared. We may also say that communication is somewhat more critical in decision-making teams (facts) for performance than in creative teams (ideas).

In addition to size, allocation of roles and diversity are two other factors that considerably determine a work team's success. However, findings on these two aspects of teams are not conclusive. Some studies reveal that the experience and skill of those in core roles in a team are more critical than the skill set of members in other roles. Others suggest that members should be selected to ensure that various roles are filled because teams have different needs. This question is interrelated with the diversity of teams (in terms of gender, ethnicity, age, education, etc.), which, again, is an issue that requires careful attention.

Meredith Belbin, an English researcher and management consultant promoted the idea that the effectiveness of a team relies on the correct distribution of roles. The scientific evidence for Belbin's team roles model is not very strong, but it continues to be popular among practitioners because of its insight into team dynamics. According to the Belbin model, a team needs to have the properties of a "balanced team" with the presence of nine diverse roles, which can be categorized into action-oriented roles, people-oriented roles, and thinking roles (Smith, Jennings, and Castro, 2006). Action-oriented roles mainly have to do with task demands, broadly defined. A shaper, for example, is the driving force of a group and ensures that the team does not lose momentum or dwindle to inactivity. The implementer, on the other hand, is practical, reliable, efficient, and turns ideas into actions. Upon first thought, you may conclude that a team will be highly successful when it has more people who possess the qualities of the Shaper and the Implementer. However, as much as a project requires action, it also needs to be monitored for the quality of the results. This is exactly where the Completer role comes in. The Completer not only polishes the work for errors but also assures the accuracy of the project by meticulously checking for corrections.

People-oriented roles are especially critical in coordination and conflict resolution. The Coordinator clarifies the goals for others and fulfills the responsibility of treating all contributors in the team on their merits and without prejudice. The Resource Investigator, on the other hand, is outgoing and enthusiastic and has the capacity for developing contacts for the exploration of opportunities outside the company. The Teamworker is cooperative, perceptive, and diplomatic and responds to revive team spirit during moments of friction or crisis.

The third group, which consists of thinking roles, concerns expertise and analysis. The Monitor Evaluator is the analyzer of problems. This role requires a level of judgment ability that is crucial when the success or failure of a task relies on a few critical decisions. The Specialist contributes to a narrow topic by only dwelling on technicalities and providing in-depth expertise. They are especially needed in cases where services or products are based on rare skills and knowledge. A Plant, on the other hand, is the person in the team who generates proposals and solves complex problems in a novel way with his/her imaginative capabilities.

Members of high-performing teams tend to have better interpersonal skills and possess more expertise in their subject area.

Another major factor that plays an important role in team effectiveness and success is personality. Personality, of course, is a very complex issue that deserves its own discussion, but, overall, teams composed of members with high levels of conscientiousness tend to function and perform better. On the other hand, negative traits such as lower emotional stability is a risk factor for team success. In fact, lower emotional stability is an exclusion factor in selecting members, especially for teams that will work in isolated, extreme environments such as a research station in Antarctica, a remote excavation site, or a space mission. This is because emotionally unstable; irritable people are considered high-cost interaction partners who are less likely to be approached for friendship and advice. Conscientious individuals, on the other hand, are more likely to be approached for work-related advice and information and to bridge the flow of information between team members.

Persons with high scores on Conscientiousness organize their time and their physical surroundings, work in a disciplined way toward their goals, strive for accuracy and perfection in their tasks, and try to make decisions carefully. Conversely, persons with low scores on this personality dimension tend to be unconcerned with orderly surroundings or schedules, avoid difficult tasks or challenging goals, are satisfied with work that contains some errors, and make decisions on impulse or with little reflection (visit www.hexaco.org for more details).

The complexity of team projects

Teams are never perfect and are full of complexities, and thus may show various task or performance-related problems. However, even when there is no technical reason to justify a collaborative effort, teams may be preferred over individual work because of the fact that teams can increase employees' participation, motivation, and the overall satisfaction they take from their jobs. Let's briefly take a look at the challenges we face in team projects.

The complexity of a team project can be described over several dimensions. The first dimension is the number of distant locations. The team can be in a single room, in different rooms, or in multiple locations. In global projects, the team members are located at least in two different countries. When all participants are in geographical locations close to each other, face-to-face meetings can be easily organized to solve any problem. As the distances increase, however, the team must rely more on virtual tools for communication. Another factor is the time zones. If the team members are based in the same location or in different locations in the same time zone, communication and coordination are relatively easy. It becomes highly difficult to organize meetings in common work hours, however, when the project team is composed of members residing in completely different time zones.

An important factor that adds to the complexity of teamwork is the number of different organizations. If project team members are working for a single department in one company, coordination is relatively easy. However, it becomes more difficult to manage the team when members are from multiple departments. The complexity level is even greater when members are representing multiple companies. The innovative outer structure of the Bird's Nest Stadium constructed for the 2008 Olympic Games in Beijing, for example, required the collaboration of architects, designers, and engineers from Herzog & De Meuron Architekten, Arup Sport, and the China Architecture Design and Research Group.

If team members are from different countries, potential cultural differences become the source of both positive outcomes and challenges. We usually expect that diversity originating from traditions of different nations and regions will reduce groupthink and improve collective creativity. In addition, motivation and satisfaction often increase as many people enjoy working in cross-cultural environments because of the rich exchanges and novel experience gained. Nevertheless, this diversity can sometimes be the source of conflicts and misunderstandings. Building trust among team members and overcoming feelings of isolation and detachment due to cultural differences becomes a challenge.

Groupthink is a psychological term used to describe the mode of thinking that persons engage in when concurrence seeking becomes so dominant in a cohesive group that it tends to override realistic

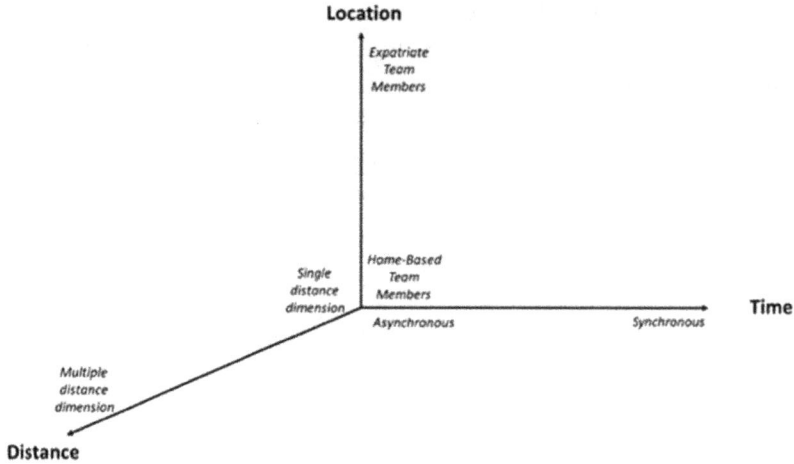

Fig 3.1 Location-Distance Graph
From Jimenez et al. (2017)

appraisal of alternative courses of action. This kind of problem may arise simply because group members value harmony and coherence above rational thinking. At meetings, all members are amiable and seek complete concurrence, which is likely to be recognized erroneously as consensus. The term was first introduced in an article by psychologist Irving Janis, who had conducted an extensive study of group decision-making under conditions of stress.

Remedies for groupthink

- If you are in a leadership position, avoid stating your preferences or your decision on the issue at the beginning of meetings.
- Have one member play devil's advocate or the role of critical evaluator at the group's meetings to challenge the majority position.
- Hold a "second-chance" meeting (after reaching a preliminary consensus about what seems to be the best decision) to allow every member to rethink the entire issue.

Although in most situations, the global business language is English, the manner in which people communicate is still largely dependent on their native language or their level of proficiency in English. Most speakers of English as a second language will be limited by their knowledge of specific expressions, vocabulary and often by their ability to make analogies or understand jokes. On the other hand, native English speakers face difficulties because they sometimes need to limit their vocabulary and expressions and must confirm that their ideas are well understood by others.

Least complex	Extremely complex
Members are in the same country in locations in the same time zone, they all speak the same native language, and they belong to similar (sub)cultures.	Members reside in countries in different time zones, they all speak a different native language, and they belong to dissimilar cultures.

International (cross-cultural) teams

International teams are championed largely because we expect that cultural diversity will provide the necessary skills and views needed in the global work arena. However, findings regarding the effectiveness of international teams are mixed. A study on football teams in five big European leagues, for example, has revealed that the higher the level of cultural differences in a team, the less successful it is (Maderer, Holtbrügge, and Schuster, 2014). On the other hand, an analysis of the box office performance of German movies in international markets has revealed that movies produced by a diverse central production team (i.e., the producer, the director, leading actors, and the cinematographer) had higher export performance, in addition to their domestic success (Meiseberg and Ehrmann, 2013). Some have suggested that international teams are better when the task or the activities involve exploration rather than performance towards specific goals. From this perspective, international teams are expected to be good at strategy formulation and the production of creative ideas but weaker in the actual implementation of products or services.

The major challenge in culturally heterogeneous teams is that cultural biases may distort communication and trust. Every individual is exposed to specific norms within their culture, and their socialization may shape the way they react to certain issues and problems. Paradoxically, it may be more difficult to recognize the impact of culture on one's own values, attitudes, and behavior than it is to recognize it in others. This potential drawback is a precursor to errors in judgment because it may fuel the perception that "everyone is wrong." Thus, cultural diversity can be extremely challenging, as members of a group will struggle to understand the sources of problems, manage conflict, and keep the team socially integrated.

Various concepts and dimensions are used to classify cultures around the world. Here, we focus on three of them, namely, high-versus low-context, power distance, and uncertainty avoidance. Edward T. Hall proposed the concept of high-versus low-context as a way of understanding different cultural orientations. In his view, a high-context culture is one in which people are deeply involved with each other in intimate relationships. In a high-context culture, individuals keep their inner feelings under strong self-control, and information is mostly shared indirectly through simple messages with deep meaning. A low-context culture is one in which people are highly individualized, and there is relatively little involvement with others, especially in business-related relationships. As a consequence, social hierarchy and relationships impose less on individuals' decisions, and communication between people is relatively direct, explicit, and non-personal. In low-context cultures, the mass of the information comes from the explicit code, that is, from the words, sentences, and grammar. Therefore, what is important is what is said, rather than how it is said or the environment within which it is said.

Geert Hofstede, a Dutch researcher, and consultant introduced the concepts of power distance and uncertainty avoidance in the early 1980s. Power distance is the extent to which less powerful members accept unequal distribution of power or inequality. In high power distance cultures, subordinates tend to look to their superiors for direction and expect them to tell them what to do. In low power-distance cultures, the relationship between subordinates and superiors is consultative in nature. Uncertainty avoidance, on the other hand, is the extent to which the members of a culture feel threatened by ambiguous and unknown situations. Differences in power distance orientation and uncertainty avoidance among members may affect the manner a team works. If a member of a team is from a high power distance culture, s/he may be more sensitive about status differences among the team and may restrict or deprioritize her/his contact with members whom s/he perceives to have lower status, especially when s/he perceives herself/himself to hold a higher status. To avoid the stress that comes from ambiguity, individuals from high uncertainty avoidance cultures may be inclined to ask many questions even about trivial issues or ask the same questions to different people in the team. This type of behavior may create the perception that the person is apprehensive or non-trusting. Trust is an important factor in teamwork because individuals with high (vs. low) trust in other people are more likely to behave cooperatively in the face of uncertainty and conflicting interests. Unlike traits and personality, which are largely hereditary, differences in trust among individuals stem from cultural factors rather than being determined by genetic markers (Van Lange, 2015).

Culture, according to Geertz, a leading cultural anthropologist, is "a system of inherited conceptions expressed in symbolic forms by means of which men communicate, perpetuate, and develop their knowledge about and attitudes toward life." Hofstede has defined culture as "the collective programming of the mind that distinguishes the members of one group or category of people from others."

All of this brings us to the importance of intercultural competence. Despite irritations with others' behaviors that may not conform to their expectations, members in teams may control themselves to avoid conflicts. However, we can say that if a team stops seeing cultural differences as important, it may run the risk of performing poorly. A damaging pattern may emerge when members ignore their differences by saying, for example, "We are all engineers, so we understand each other, it doesn't matter that we are from Finland or Belgium." Teams must understand that effective communication and the ability to change perspectives are highly critical in intercultural settings.

Intercultural competence is the ability to communicate effectively and appropriately in intercultural situations, to shift frames of reference appropriately, and adapt behavior to cultural context. It largely rests on two qualities:
Respect: recognizing the diversity of others as social equals and examining one's own cultural assumptions to validate other perspectives, values, and behaviors.
Openness: the recognition and acceptance of multiple ways of interpreting situations and withholding premature judgment towards others.

Virtual teams

Since the birth of the internet, developments in communication technologies have accelerated the use of alternative work arrangements across firms and industries around the globe. There are several methods to utilize online communication technologies to complete work-related tasks. When an employee uses online communication technologies to work on their tasks partially or completely outside the actual workplace, it is called telework. When a group of teleworkers work for and report to the same manager, it becomes a virtual group. A virtual team is different from a virtual group because group members in the latter interact with each other to accomplish specific goals collaboratively. You may also see large entities of distributed work, such as open-source software projects or scientific collaborations, which are typically initiated by an individual or a group of researchers. These kinds of collaborations do not necessitate a formal organizational structure and they are called virtual communities.

Virtual teams are work arrangements where team members from geographically dispersed places work interdependently to achieve common goals, using electronic media, online collaboration tools, and project management software.

Globalized organizations widely adopt virtual teams as a primary way to structure work in areas such as information technology, software development, consulting, product development, and treatment of patients (Gilson et al., 2015; Mesmer-Magnus et al., 2011). Virtual teams are becoming common practice because the reductions in office requirements, duplication costs, travel expenses, and logistical expenditures lead to savings for the firm (Robbins and Judge, 2007). In addition to cost-related benefits, virtual teams help organizations become more flexible against growing competition, provide greater access to talent or technical experts, and allow proximity to customers across the globe (Binder, 2007). Virtual teams also decrease the environmental impact of work organizations by lessening the use of cars and vehicles, helping reduce carbon emissions.

The main benefits of virtual teams for individuals are higher flexibility, control, and empowerment. These characteristics may lead to various positive outcomes. Due to the fact that there are fewer cues indicating the status and position of members in high-virtuality environments, minority and low-status members may have more influence than in traditional teams. In addition, the flexibility of virtual teams gives people with low mobility (due to handicaps or responsibilities) a better chance of integration into the work life. We may also say that virtual teams have more potential than typical work arrangements to create jobs in less developed regions, despite difficulties in internet connectedness. Thus, virtual teams have a potential to increase social equalization.

A recent survey by RW3 CultureWizard with more than 1300 participants across the globe shows that corporate teams are becoming increasingly virtual, and 41% never meet in person. Corporate teams are also becoming increasingly global. In the same survey, 48% of the respondents mentioned that more than half of the teams included members from other countries. This is up from a 33% in 2012. What is more striking is that 85% of respondents say that virtual teamwork is extremely or somewhat critical to their job and business success.

Main reasons for companies to adopt virtual teamwork:

- Savings in travel expenses and logistical expenditures
- Increased flexibility against global competition
- Greater access to talent and technical experts
- Proximity to customers across the globe.

This is not to say that global virtual teams are perfect or free from problems. The major drawback in virtual settings is the lack of face-to-face interaction, which may be critical in understanding the full context of how people communicate, as well as for managing conflict and establishing trust. This is why face-to-face teams sometimes lead to better performance outcomes by allowing greater efficiency in the use of resources, better knowledge sharing, and faster decision-making (Purvanova, 2014). However, most professionals still believe that the advantages of virtual teams outweigh the challenges for the reasons outlined above. Younger generations, and especially millennials, tend to have high levels of familiarity with computer- or smartphone-mediated technologies, and therefore, unlike earlier generations, they do not perceive the use of technology as a major challenge (Gilson et al., 2015). For that reason, reliance on virtuality in different life domains is likely to further increase, making all of the above issues even more critical.

Major challenges in global virtual teamwork:

- Members showing no participation
- Slow pace of decision-making
- Conflicts in role expectations by team members
- Follow-through of team members.

A note on virtuality

The line between virtual and non-virtual teams is not always clear. Even when all the members are in the same office, teams use technological tools like e-mail and instant messaging. Instead of using an either-or categorization, it is best to consider virtuality just another aspect of teamwork like diversity or number and types of roles (Hertel, Geister, and Konradt, 2005). What defines the virtuality of a team is not the use of virtual tools per se, but the informational value and synchronicity of the exchanges between the members (Kirkman and Mathieu, 2005). For example, when the members of an architectural team employ technologies that convey rich information, such as a 3D animation, their exchanges are less virtual than when they use technologies that provide less valuable information. The second aspect we need to consider is synchronicity (simultaneousness), which refers to exchanges that occur in real-time. The opposite of it is asynchronous exchanges, which involve a time lag. Asynchronous exchanges may degrade communication quality and weaken team coordination, but they also allow members to take time to consider both the message and their response. When teams use tools that mimic face-to-face interactions (e.g., videoconferencing), the exchange should be described as comparatively much less virtual due both to media richness and simultaneousness.

Synchronicity

Synchronous exchanges occur in real-time, whereas asynchronous exchanges involve a time lag.

Brief insights and recommendations

X-Culture asks each team to write a charter at the beginning of the project. A team charter is a good way to start a collective effort and set the norms, so teams should take this task seriously. A team charter is important because it is also likely to increase cohesiveness, which predicts members' motivation to stay/stay active in the group.

In X-Culture, teams are formed by randomly selecting members from a large list of participants. Therefore, there is no guarantee that every team will have all the right characteristics or the optimal level of "conscientiousness." Some teams will have more students who are organized and dutiful, while others will have less of these types of students. It is helpful for X-Culture professors to remind students about their responsibilities in regard to other team members. Personalities do not change in a short time, but it is possible to seed the norms that will help teams perform better, despite their differences.

A "sufficient" "healthy dose" of generalized trust is adaptive, especially for many social interactions that take place with others one does not know well. However, people from certain cultures are less prone to trust others. Also, remember that it is more difficult to establish trust in diverse teams. Therefore, teams should start by focusing on similarities and commonalities first, rather than differences.

Team trust is important both in face-to-face and virtual teams. However, it is more critical for performance in virtual teams (see Breuer, Hüffmeier, and Hertel, 2016).

We know from research on attribution, impression formation, attitudes, and stereotyping that "bad is stronger than good." We as humans tend to pay more attention to negative stimuli than to the positive. Therefore, remember that negative perceptions, errors, or negative developments in teamwork will have a greater impact on teamwork and the quality of your project.

Even small differences in expression matter. Refer to differences as an asset (positive) rather than difficulty (negative).

Trust does not mean that team members should not monitor each other's performance. Remember, however, that monitoring is beneficial to the team only when it is inherent to the task and when it is perceived to support team members to perform their tasks, keep on track, and achieve common goals.

To facilitate shared leadership, team members must view their tasks and responsibilities as interdependent and their performance as a collective outcome. It is important to note that shared leadership may have a more constrained meaning and a limited effect if most members are from high power distance and collectivistic cultures. In those cases, shared leadership can be complemented with the leadership of a designated team leader. These are not necessarily contradictory processes.

X-Culture teams are relatively diverse. Members usually come from four or five different countries and, although they are likely to have similar educational backgrounds, they tend to differ in their values. Always keep in mind that the customs and traditions of different nations and regions may help the team reduce groupthink and improve collective creativity. Try to utilize diversity to the benefit of the team and the project.

A certain amount of conflict is necessary for team success and performance. However, students should be warned against the perils of task conflict turning into a relationship conflict. Task conflict is an awareness of differences in viewpoints and opinions about a group task, which, of course, comes with animated discussions and personal excitement. If this excitement turns into personal issues such as dislike among group members and feelings such as annoyance, the team is at risk of dissolving.

Studies with space mission personnel showed that humor might be a key factor in team compatibility, conflict resolution, and coping. However, the perceived meaning and usefulness of humor are not independent of culture and the social power relationship between the participants. Therefore, students should be careful with political jokes and the like until they get to know each other well.

Do not use humor directed at another participant. Generic or self-deprecating humor is more likely to work than humor directed at someone else. Observe the team members' reactions following a joke made in the group.

Communication is somewhat more critical in decision-making teams for performance than in creative teams. And task-related communication and knowledge sharing are highly critical in virtual teams. Teams in X-Culture should use online chats and discussion boards to facilitate communication.

Teams should try to decrease virtuality from time to time, by using tools like videoconferencing that mimic face-to-face interactions, in order to build trust, increase information sharing, and simultaneousness.

Also, try to make the best of asynchronous exchanges. Try to develop a norm that pushes members to return to asynchronous exchanges with preparation and useful information that contributes to the task in question. Use the different working times to the team's advantage by creating a 'follow-the sun' implementation, reducing the duration of sequential tasks.

CHAPTER 4

How Working in Teams is Different from Working Alone

WILLIAM H.A. JOHNSON, THE PENNSYLVANIA STATE UNIVERSITY ERIE—THE BEHREND
COLLEGE, SAM AND IRENE BLACK SCHOOL OF BUSINESS

What is a team, and why are they important?

A team is a group of people charged with interacting to accomplish a stated goal. It is essentially a way to structure a project, which is defined as an effort to achieve a goal and that has a beginning, middle, and end. In essence, a team is a group of people engaged in a project.

Teams put a man on the moon. It was a team that created the famous Macintosh computer, then the first iPad, and eventually the iPhone at Apple. For many students, it is with a team that they must work to get a major semester-long project done—whether they like it or not. Indeed, teams are everywhere in corporate and organizational life; the team is inescapable. As a way to get things done, how are teams different from cases where someone works alone? That is, what is the difference between working alone and working in a team on a project? And how can you make sure that your teams are more effective?

This chapter discusses these differences and provides examples of when, where, and how working in teams can be of benefit so that you can achieve superior results. To start, research suggests that teams are most necessary for doing complex work that involves the input of many people to achieve a final successful goal of significance. The teams from cases of historic technological advancements referenced above required a lot of different knowledge sets, as well as creative ideas to be shared and coalesced into achievable technical outcomes. One person alone could not have invented and created the iPhone—in fact, in these cases, there were actually teams of teams involved!

So, to begin, when we think about utilizing a team to achieve our goals, we need to be clear about the complexity of the problem(s) we are trying to solve. Simple problems can often be solved by an individual and their individual knowledge of the areas needed to create a solution. Writing a paper or story can be achieved by one person if they have adequate background knowledge for it. Large but uncomplex problems can be solved by homogenous teams, which are teams of individuals with similar background knowledge and demographics. Here, the idea is to break down the work and make it more efficient and productive for each individual in the team to work on their set. In such cases, it is not creativity that is needed, but rather more time in the day, as one person can only do so much work. The mapping of the human genome is an example of one such large but somewhat homogenous team effort.

However, in many cases, we are interested in teams that create something new, e.g., a new product or simply a new idea. Unfortunately, in many classroom examples, the homogenous team approach is what students use. One student does one section of a report, other works on a second section, and so on. However, the main objective of most classroom team projects is not simply the efficient production of a report but rather the creation of new and interesting ideas, which require more of a heterogeneous approach (i.e., more diversity). Such pasted-together reports show their low value, as students merely walk through the process, and the final product is something any one of the students on the team could have produced themselves if given enough time. A truly effective team produces a report that neither of the individuals on the team could have done themselves because the final product is a synergy of the ideas and efforts of each of the team members. It is as if the team had become one, though still of many.

To do this, teams need members who have certain similarities and also certain differences. For example, using the same language, including any technical jargon that is used, provides consistency of communication. Having shared goals for what the project should achieve and agreement on the processes and procedures involved is needed. It also helps to have knowledge sets that differ so that each team member brings his or her own value to the team. For example, global virtual teams charged with solving complex problems such as the market entry strategy for an organization may involve issues of marketing, finance, production, and other functional areas. In such cases, the value of creating a heterogeneous team with members that have different knowledge sets to add to the team output is readily apparent. The old expression, "two heads are better than one," applies here specifically because of the need for creativity and synergy.

Let us examine the difference between working alone and working in a team. Working alone means being solely responsible for the work and the outcome of the project. Again, in this situation, you are on your own. Of course, working alone does not mean any interacting or working with others (if you want to do a good job). However, it does mean that the final outcome is the responsibility of you alone. For example, students working on a project for which they want to achieve a great grade (and also actually learn something new) will potentially consult their librarian, experts in the area of study, companies that might be doing business in the field, etc. Depending on the help of others plays a part in all valuable projects, but working alone means doing all the tasks of the project alone, which includes initiating and implementing the contacts with others that are required for full information to complete the project. As such, working in a team—even a homogenous one meant to break up the work tasks—can be helpful in saving time and energy on a large and worthy project.

So, we can see that there are pros and cons to working in a team versus working alone. Working in a team means being responsible for the group effort and sharing in both the workload and the outcome of the project. It means understanding that the shared goals of the team are "owned" by everyone in the team. The team must act as one "unit." The old adage from the story of the Three Musketeers, "All for one and one for all," comes to mind as the mantra of a great team.

It means that responsibility is shared, and ultimately you may be required to step up and deliver even when you may feel that you are doing most of the work. This can be one of the pressing issues that people in a team must confront. You may ask yourself, "Couldn't I have done this work myself and not have to worry about the rest of the team?" This may be true. However, quite often, the time spent working in a team is not more than when one works alone and even can be shorter and less intense. Being part of something greater than oneself can bring pride and meaning to one's work. It is true that the time saved from working as a group and sharing the load can be offset by the time needed for coordination, which is not necessary when you are working alone.

However, this notion that you are doing most of the work may or may not be true because perception is so important in teamwork. Sometimes, people perceive that they are doing all the work but are not; other times, it is the other way around. This also means that communication is essential to a successful team process and its outcome. This is one reason that self-review (in addition to peer review) is an essential part of evaluating teamwork. You need to ask yourself: am I really getting involved with making my team the best that it can be?

Being positive and setting team goals (particularly at the beginning of a project) is paramount to success. Being closed-minded and negative can be a self-fulfilling prophecy when starting a project with others. This is due to the fact that if you believe that working together is a waste of time, then, of course, it will (seem to) be! Too often, poorly performing teams are that way because of initial negative perceptions put forth by pessimistic teammates. However, research suggests that teams are generally more effective than solo work when, as mentioned, a project is large and complex and requires creativity. So, why not start out with a positive, go-getting attitude? My experience as an instructor of courses that use team-based projects is that such teams are always more effective and get better outcomes, including grades, than solo-run projects or teams with negative attitudes.

Still not convinced? It is true that some people ultimately prefer one way to work over the other (team vs. solo), and this is usually based on their previous experience with project work. Preferences for the various types of work situations can also vary due to demographics and cultural perspectives. For example, research suggests that individuals from the newest generation to enter post-secondary education, Gen-Z, prefer to do work as an individual rather than in teams (and that this is the opposite of Millennials, who apparently prefer teams)! Again, though, these are mostly preferences based on personal bias. There are pros and cons of both ways of working on a project, which we briefly explore in this chapter. That is, both approaches can have positive results, but many projects will require teamwork and can be superior to what can be achieved alone.

In the end, teams are an essential and valuable way of doing projects, whether your personal preferences are for teamwork or solo work. In job settings and other situations, such as in the military and at school, you will be forced to work in teams—and for a good reason, as we have seen and will continue to explore. Teamwork can be fruitful and a prime mechanism for achieving high-value outcomes for many projects.

Advantages of Working Alone

Of course, though it may seem selfish, the primary advantage of working alone is that all benefits accrue to you alone. You do all the work, and you get all the glory (or go down in flames with a failed project!) This is like a company that decides to create its own standalone business when entering a new country rather than to partner with an existing local company. All the profits will be theirs from the new venture. (Of course, we'll see the disadvantage of such a stance soon.)

As we saw earlier, working alone may not mean being alone when a project requires the collection of outside information to be completed. Depending on the requirements for outside information, the time and effort involved in communication with others may be less. Less communication effort is needed when the only communication is with a limited number of stakeholders/references that you might rely on for the project, rather than fellow project members.

A true advantage of working alone, however, is to be able to book and do most tasks around your own time schedule. The time for working is dependent only on your own schedule unless you must accommodate the schedule of another stakeholder or reference person when speaking with them.

If you have the time and energy, working alone can provide for tremendous learning, but as with most things, this is dependent on the tasks required to complete the goal(s) successfully. That is, when working alone, you get to learn everything yourself and do not have to worry about second-hand news or information from team colleagues. It is quite easy to imagine, however, how quickly these advantages can turn into disadvantages, which we will now examine.

Disadvantages of Working Alone

It should go without saying that working alone means all the work for a project is done by you alone. For some people who are shy or do not like social interaction, this can seem like the best mode to work. But, as we have seen, most worthwhile projects require social interaction with others like references anyway. As such, in fact, a disadvantage for shy people working alone is that they may have to cold call on a lot of stakeholders/references to do a good job. In such cases, it may be more comfortable for such individuals to work closely with team members they trust who may be more comfortable with the tasks of contacting and interacting with these stakeholders/references.

Doing all the work yourself also means the time required for a project should allow enough for each element of the project. You cannot delegate work without paying for it, like one might do to get consulting work done. Note that even in this situation, you add extra time coordinating with the paid consultant—an example of a stakeholder/reference that takes time to work with.

I mentioned earlier that working alone can lead to a lot of self-learning. However, this can also lead to an insular view of the project, one where you may not see what is needed because of your personal blind spots about your own strengths and weaknesses and other things that might be needed for a successful project. This is the 'two heads are better than one' aspect. Any reflection or advice on how well you are doing will depend on whether you ask stakeholders/references directly yourself.

Another related major disadvantage is that you own all the mistakes, and the learning curve for doing a great job can be high. Thus, the creativity of working alone can be wanting. This does not mean that creativity is not possible when working alone. I have argued in the past, using knowledge management theory, that words alone can often lead to unexpected creativity because one is not constrained by previous knowledge sets. For example, if your project was to learn how to play the piano on your own, then you would have to spend a lot of time experimenting with fingering, chords, melody, etc. In doing so, you may create new uncharted musical expressions, but you are also just as likely to never get anything that sounds quite right. If you take lessons with a teacher, you will learn the proper techniques but may never actually be creative (that is, allow yourself to just go with the flow of the music and play unconstrained); they call it "vamping" in music, and this is considered a no-no in the classical piano world. Having a teacher can be envisioned as being like working in a team, in that it is likely to be more productive when another person is involved. However, a true team consists of equal players (that is, equal in stature as when a team is said to be egalitarian), and when people of similar aptitudes come together in a team, they may indeed be more creative as a group. Here, you might imagine musicians who already know the basics of music coming together to form a band and, in doing so, creating new and undiscovered songs together. As such, the probability of being creative is highest when you are part of an interacting, coordinated team—just like a good band.

So, now let's look more at the advantages of working in a team.

Advantages of Working in a Team

Many of the advantages of working in teams contrast with the disadvantages of working alone. From your own personal point of view regarding time and energy, teams allow you to share in the workload needed to complete a successful and valuable project rather than doing it all yourself.

As mentioned already, the interaction and honest, constructive feedback within the team setting can often create better, more creative, and higher-quality outcomes. A student of mine once got kicked out of his team for lack of effort. His reward was to double his effort because he was then on his own. At the end of the project, I could easily examine the two resulting reports (the one from his old team and his own) to compare. Sure enough, the solo project was less creative and less well done than the team project. One could argue that this was due to the student's poor work habits. In this case, the student was actually not bad academically and was intelligent and studious. His problem had to do with some scheduling issues that should have been dealt with upfront and more quickly. His final report was not bad, but it could have been better, and he could have done less actual work in the long run if he had shared it with his teammates. Isn't it obvious that it would have been much better for him if he had worked more diligently with his team in the first place?

So, the major advantage of teams is that they allow for more creative outcomes and the sharing of the workload.

Disadvantages of Working in a Team

The major disadvantage of working in a team has to do with the coordination issues (often using up time) and, in many cases, the inevitable clash of personalities. There are well-studied findings on the development process for any team (see the chapter in this volume on the life cycle of a typical team: e.g., forming, storming, norming, performing). The time individuals save from the delegation of various tasks may be taken up by the time needed to stay focused and communicate with the rest of the team. These time coordination issues often mean that working in a team can take more in terms of start-up time, and thus, long-term projects are more amenable to teamwork. Indeed, most school team projects are semester-long. Many business team projects (like the R&D projects discussed at the beginning of this chapter) take up many quarters, if not years.

Regardless of the relationship with other team members, the project must be completed, which means that sometimes having bad luck with a bad team leads to as much work as when working alone. Freeloading and disagreements among team members do happen. Thus, there is always a risk to working in teams, which hopefully ends up being worth it, as in the old adage, "nothing ventured, nothing gained." That is, we know teams produce more creative and better outcomes for highly complex projects. The key is to understand these potential issues and immediately deal with them upfront.

The methods mentioned next should help mitigate or eliminate these risks.

Overall Analysis: The Trade-offs of Team and Solo Work

Overall, you can see that the often-noted perception that teams take up more time and energy than working alone is actually false. If the project is worthwhile and expected to lead to a successful outcome, it will take up a lot of time regardless. The extra time needed for the coordination of team members will often be offset by the extra time needed to devote to doing each task on one's own in a solo effort.

Now that we know something about how working in team differs from working alone, the last couple of sections in the chapter discuss the things that you and your team can do to make your team projects more effective and less stressful with higher quality outcomes.

How to Be a Team that Excels

In concluding this chapter, I discuss a technique that has been found to be useful in creating highly effective teams, focusing primarily on producing an operative team contract as the basis for conducting work within the team.

Methods That Help Maximize Team Performance—The Team Contract

The first realization that should be clear to maximizing success for any team is that communication is essential to team performance. There is just no getting around the fact that the difference between poor-performing teams and high-performing teams is almost always due to communication issues (and this includes personality mismatches).

One of the most important things a team can do is to negotiate and create a team contract at the beginning of the project. Creating a team contract at the beginning of the project will help with communication and the process of managing the team as a group. A team contract is a written device that specifies the mutual understandings of the team players about what the project is and how it will be managed. It is like the rules of the game in any team sport. Though it would definitely help, you might not always like everyone on your team; however, if you all understand the rules of the game and you agree about what you want to finally achieve then successful teamwork (even with people you would not otherwise work with) is possible.

The first part of the team contract should be to specify what the end goal of the project will be. Otherwise, how will we know when we are finished? Here, the team should be clear about the endgame, though not necessarily definitive. In other words, our final goal may be, for example, the production of a report, yet, of course, at the beginning, we do not know what the content of the report will be. However, we may, for instance, know that we are charged with doing a report on marketing a new product. That will help frame how we might then conduct the teamwork.

The second major part of the contract should spell out how the team will interact. For example, what days and times will we meet? If a team leader is not delegated already, the election of someone to that position is useful, making it that there is one person who is the 'go to' person for the team as well as for outsiders wishing to communicate with the team. It also helps to have a discussion in the first meeting as to who has what prior expertise and interests in order to determine who will be responsible for specific sections and knowledge brought to the project.

The contract should set out all of these elements. Unlike a legal contract, the team contract is really the constitution of the team containing all the aspects and procedures to be used during the project. Instead of taking members to court if there is an issue (like it might happen with a business contract breech), the team contract helps to shed light on what to do if there is a problem. As such, a third major section of the contract should specify what happens when a major issue arises for which the team must do something. For example, how will decisions be made? Will the team demand consensus on an issue (that is, all members must agree to the action or decision for it to happen) or will the team go by majority rule vote (that is, where all members vote on the issue and a 50% plus 1 agreement wins)? In such cases, any procedure or method is possible as long as the team agrees to it upfront at the beginning when the team contract is being formed.

Part of this contract section on procedural issues may also include what to do about potential free-loading. Again, the team must agree upfront to the procedural rules to be used, but once written and agreed to, the rules will be enforced. For example, the team might agree that with a two-thirds or higher vote among members, a teammate accused of being a freeloader will be expelled from the team. This may seem harsh, but the negative effects of freeloading behavior can be even more pervasive if nothing is agreed to upfront about what to do about it, should it arise.

As such, the expectations of all team members are set within the team contract and the process used to create it. Anything the team feels is needed to make sure the project is run smoothly could be included, as long as everyone agrees or is made to agree, as in cases where your boss says so. For example, you may have teams that specify the distribution of outcomes based on each individual teammate's inputs. In academic projects, this means that the grades may be re-distributed based on the work efforts and inputs of different teammates (if agreed to upfront and with the teacher, of course)! In such cases, some people might feel that the team leader should get a little more credit due to his or her extra effort, etc. In most cases, it is also helpful to have a final editor of the completed report so that any work that was disjointed and done as separate pieces of work does not look that way for the finished product. That is, the final report should look holistic as if written by one person, though it is the product of the team (i.e., many people).

As the team contract is essentially the constitution of the team project, as the constitutions of most free nations, it must be signed by all team members and then held as the law (of what to do) throughout the course of the project.

The chapter's appendix includes a template of such a team contract that you can use and modify for your own needs in the teamwork that you are doing now.

Methods That May Be Used in Mitigating Potential Negative Issues That Arise Over Time

The creation of a team contract mentioned earlier can help when the team suffers some setback. Students in the courses I have taught over the years have sometimes had to refer to the document to determine how to treat a team member who is not contributing.

Also, the use of peer review grading (or peer review without grades that acts as a feedback communication device) is another method to encourage all team members to stay focused on the team goal and to act as a unit. Recall that working on a team means sharing both the workload and the outcome of the project. Peer review and evaluation, combined with peer grading, means that if one does not share in the 'workload' of the team, then one cannot also share in the 'outcome' of the team. In the X-Culture program, that outcome would be points or a grade for a course.

Finally, the ultimate use of an arbitrator may be necessary for cases when the team contract cannot be used alone- such as a belligerent teammate or a team shirker who just won't get better. Here, your teacher, manager, officer or another superior who is often responsible for forming you into a team can act as a facilitator or arbitrator and hopefully get the team back on track.

Ultimately, however, it is the responsibility of the team to perform. A good attitude is of the utmost importance and a willingness to work as a team, for the team, is essential. To paraphrase the great inventor, Thomas Edison: "Aspiration is 1% inspiration and 99% perspiration!"

Good luck with your work in teams and also remember that you get out what you put in again, to quote another wise man, the great Paul McCartney of the Beatles: "In the end, the love you take is equal to the love you make …" (quote from the song 'The End' from the album Abbey Road).

Appendices

Example of Guidelines for Writing Team Contract in an Academic Setting[1]

RATIONALE

According to concepts from Organizational Behavior, there are five stages of team development: forming, storming, norming, performing, and adjourning. During the forming stage, teams tend to communicate in polite indirect ways rather than more directly. The storming stage, characterized by conflict, can often be productive, but may consume excessive amounts of time and energy. In this stage, it is important to listen well to differing expectations. Next, during the norming stage, teams formulate roles and standards, increasing trust and communication. This norming stage is characterized by agreement on procedures, reduction in role ambiguity, and increased "we-ness" or unity. These developments generally are precursors to the performing stage, during which teams achieve their goals, are highly task-oriented, and focus on performance and production. When the task has been completed, the team adjourns.

To accelerate a team's development, a team contract is generated to establish procedures and roles in order to move the team more quickly into the performing stage. This process of generating a team contract can actually help jump-start a group's collaborative efforts by immediately focusing the team members on a definite task. The group members must communicate and negotiate in order to identify the quality of work they all wish to achieve and the level of group participation and individual accountability they all feel comfortable with.

Successful team performance depends on individual personal accountability. In a team environment, individuals are usually effectively motivated to maximize their own rewards and minimize their own costs. However, conflicts can arise when individualistic motives or behaviors disrupt team-oriented goals. For example, conflict can stem from an unequal division of resources. When team members believe they are receiving too little for what they are giving, they sometimes reduce their effort and turn in work of lower quality. Such "free-riding" occurs most frequently when individual contributions are combined into a single product or performance, and individual effort is perceived as unequal. At this point, some individual team members may take on extra responsibilities while other team members may reduce their own efforts or withdraw from the team completely. These behaviors may engender anger, frustration, or isolation—resulting in a dysfunctional team and poor quality of work. However, with a well-formulated team contract, such obstacles can usually be avoided.

---

1 I adapted this from a template used at the University of Texas at Austin. Apparently, the template has been reproduced a number of times in different courses in different universities such that it is impossible to determine the author of the original first draft. I have used this template in my courses for many years and it is very useful as a guide for how to create a team contract.

Team Contract Assignment

Your team contract template is divided into three major sections:

1. Establishing team procedures
2. Identifying expectations
3. Specifying the consequences for failing to follow these procedures and fulfill these expectations.

As the basic purpose of this team contract is to accelerate your team's development, to increase individual accountability for team tasks, and to reduce the possibility for team conflict, make your contract as specific as possible: (a) specify each task as detailed as possible, (b) specify each step in a procedure or process as detailed as possible, (c) specify the exact person(s) responsible for each specific task, and (d) specify the exact time and exact place for completion or submission of each task. The more specifically you describe your team expectations, roles, and procedures, the greater chance you have for a successful team experience.

Use the Team Contract template to discuss and finalize your team roles, procedures, and standards. Complete, sign, and submit a copy of your finalized contract to Instructor.

Once your team contract has been developed, your team is ready to begin work on collaborative assignments. However, you may soon find that your team is not working as well as you had hoped. This is normal but needs to be attended to immediately. Perhaps your team is simply not following the established contract procedures or roles as strictly as you should be, or perhaps you need to change some of the procedures or roles as outlined in your contract. Call a team meeting immediately to discuss and resolve the challenges your team is facing; do not delay. Seek guidance from your instructor to resolve any conflicts so that you will have the most positive team experience possible.

TEAM CONTRACT

Team Name: _____

Team Members:

Team Procedures

1. Day, time, and place for regular team meetings:

2. Preferred method of communication (e.g., e-mail, cell phone, wired phone, Blackboard Discussion Board, face-to-face, in a certain class) in order to inform each other of team meetings, announcement, updates, reminders, problems:

3. Decision-making policy (by consensus? by majority vote?):

4. Method for setting and following meeting agendas (Who will set each agenda? When? How will team members be notified/reminded? Who will be responsible for the team following the agenda during a team meeting? What will be done to keep the team on track during a meeting?):

5. Method of record keeping (Who will be responsible for recording & disseminating minutes? How & when will the minutes be disseminated? Where will all agendas & minutes be kept?):

```
Team Expectations
```

Work Quality

1. Project standards (What is a realistic level of quality for team presentations, collaborative writing, individual research, preparation of drafts, peer reviews, etc.?):

2. Strategies to fulfill these standards:

Team Participation

1. Strategies to ensure cooperation and equal distribution of tasks:

2. Strategies for encouraging/including ideas from all team members (team maintenance):

3. Strategies for keeping on task (task maintenance):

4. Preferences for leadership (informal, formal, individual, shared):

Personal Accountability

1. Expected individual attendance, punctuality, and participation at all team meetings:

2. Expected level of responsibility for fulfilling team assignments, timelines, and deadlines:

3. Expected level of communication with other team members:

4. Expected level of commitment to team decisions and tasks.

```
Consequences for Failing to Follow Procedures and Fulfill Expectations
```

1. Describe, as a group, you would handle infractions of any of the obligations of this team contract:

2. Describe what your team will do if the infractions continue:

a) I participated in formulating the standards, roles, and procedures as stated in this contract.

b) I understand that I am obligated to abide by these terms and conditions.

c) I understand that if I do not abide by these terms and conditions, I will suffer the consequences as stated in this contract.

Signed:

1) _____Date:_____

2) _____Date:_____

3) _____Date:_____

4) _____Date:_____

5) _____Date:_____

Fig 4.1 Team Contract PDF

CHAPTER 5

Communication in GVTs

ANA MARIA SOARES, UNIVERSITY OF MINHO

The following key points will be addressed in this chapter:

1. Effective communication is the key to successful collaboration in Global Virtual Teams (GVTs).
2. There are several reasons for communication failure in cross-cultural contexts.
3. Communication is a process for sharing meaning and information that involves different components.
4. Communication has informational and relational functions. The importance of these functions may vary cross-culturally.
5. Examples of how culture (cultural values; verbal vs. non-verbal communication and style/ conventions and practices), language and situational-related challenges impact communication.
6. To improve the quality of communication, it is important to plan how the group will communicate and define guidelines for communication

1. Introduction

Communication is an important requirement for successful collaboration. It has been estimated that communication takes up more than 75% of project managers' time. However, communication in Global Virtual Teams (GVTs) faces a number of unique challenges due to the cultural, language, and situational specificities of this form of collaboration compared to face-to-face teams.

GVT team members are from different cultures, different geographic regions, different time zones, and may speak different languages. Communication in these circumstances has been the object of several pieces of research. For example, Shachaf (2009) studied the effects of cultural diversity and Information and communications technology (ICT) on team effectiveness. The findings of this research suggested that cultural diversity positively impacts decision-making but has a negative impact on the accuracy of communication. In practice, this means that culturally diverse teams may reach better decisions but also suffer from miscommunication issues, including slower speech, difficulties with translation, and less accurate communications.

Thus, differences in cultural expectations may distort communication and impair mutual understanding. This can be because communication is not face-to-face and/or because there are cultural differences in non-verbal and context communication. Barna (1985) pointed out six reasons for the failure of intercultural communication:

1. False assumptions of similarity,
2. Language,
3. Nonverbal misunderstanding,
4. The presence of misconceptions and stereotypes,

5. The tendency to evaluate,

6. High anxiety.

All these situations can lead to communication breakdowns and hinder a GVT's effectiveness. Therefore, ensuring effective and timely communications requires certain adaptations, learning processes, and adequate expectations. Members of GVTs need to define and implement adequate collaboration procedures, including how to communicate (communication guidelines), which encompass when and through which channels feedback should be given, as well as the timeline for answering.

In this chapter, we address the importance and requirements of communication in GVTs. We start by defining the concept, components, and functions of communication. Then we present the challenges to communication in GVTs, which we list under three main groups: challenges due to culture-related, language-related, and situational-related differences. Several recommendations to deal with these challenges are listed. To conclude, communications guidelines to avoid miscommunication in GVTs are suggested.

2. Communication: concept, component, and functions

Communication is the process of sharing meaning and information. This implies that communication only happens when both parties share content and understanding. This process can have differing degrees of intentionality. To better understand how communication works, we can break it down to its elements.

2.1 Communication process

We all communicate and often do not think a lot about the process unless something goes wrong, making us realize we were not successful in expressing our ideas. To understand the requirements for effective communication in GVTs, it is important to know the elements of a communication process. Several models have been proposed to capture the elements needed for effective communication. Figure 1 below displays these elements and their interrelation based on the seminal work of Schramm (1971).

Sender/source – Individual with an idea he/she wishes to transmit and who initiates the communication.

Message – Content being communicated.

Channel – Medium of transmission; refers to the means through which the message is sent to its intended audience.

Receiver – The recipient of the message.

Encoding – The process of translating information into symbols representing the content being communicated.

Decoding – Interpreting the meaning of the received symbols; it is the process through which the receiver understands the communication.

Noise – Anything that interferes with communication and affects its effectiveness.

Feedback – Response from the recipient.

Bearing in mind these components of communication and how they are interrelated allows us to identify some general requirements for effective communication, which ensures that the intended meaning is properly received and understood, leading to the fruitful exchange of ideas, debate and group

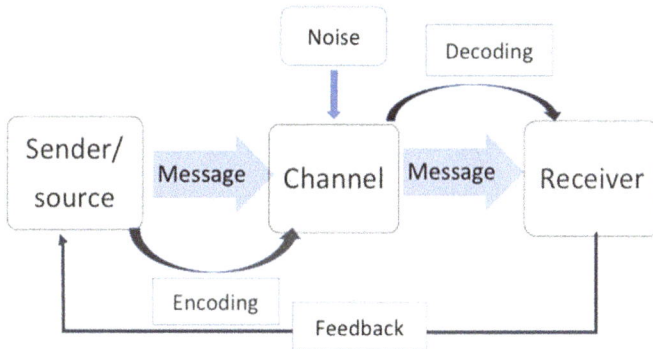

Fig 5.1 Components and process of communication
Source: Adapted from Schramm (1971)

collaboration. Take the encoding process: the meaning and understanding of symbols into which ideas are encoded may vary. In verbal communication, words are used to encode one's thoughts.

In a GVT setting, the language of communication may be a commonly-spoken language, often English. However, the English level of non-English native speakers may vary significantly, and if not all team members are equally familiar with the meaning of some words, specific expressions, etc., the message may not be properly understood. One recommendation for improving communication effectiveness when not all team members are native speakers is to avoid using slang, idioms, and regional expressions. Also, it is advised to pay attention to unexpected reactions to your words; these may signal some difficulty in decoding, i.e., interpreting and understanding the content.

Gestures and other forms of nonverbal communication also carry meaning. However, all team members may not understand the meaning of these nonverbal symbols in the same way. Check if your team members are following your ideas and do not be afraid to ask for clarifications, for example, by asking: "Do you understand what I mean?" and/or "What do you mean?"

The model also shows the importance of the channel or medium. This needs to be an adequate medium for both sender and receiver and needs to be mutually agreed in the first meetings of the group in which guidelines for collaboration should be established.

Noise refers to form on disruption in the communication process and can take many forms, such as other stimuli that draw attention away from the message and/or disrupt the communication process. Thus, possible sources of interference must be dealt with, including issues such as the quality of the internet connection, the screen size (laptop vs. mobile phone), etc.

Recommendations:
Avoid using slang, idioms, and regional expressions.
Pay attention to unexpected reactions to your words
Be concise.
Focus on listening.
Make an effort not to be misled by stereotypes.
Do not assume you understand what is being said and double-check you understood/were understood whenever needed.

Limit sources of disruption in the communication (quality of internet connection; screen size of a medium), etc.

2.2 Functions of communication

Communication may serve many functions. Two central functions of communication are informational and relational. The informational function refers to conveying information to others, while the relational function refers to developing and maintain relationships.

As will be further developed below, team members from different cultures may attach differing importance to these communication functions. Specifically, people from independent cultures may "place more emphasis on outcome-oriented aspects of the communication, such as clarity and effectiveness" while people from interdependent cultures "tend to place more emphasis on other-oriented aspects of the communication, such as avoiding hurting the hearer's feelings and minimizing imposition" (Miyamoto and Schwarz, 2006, p. 541). People from interdependent cultures may feel the need to show that they are attentive to the conversation by providing constant feedback (e.g., uh, uh; yeah…) and adjust the level of politeness to the status of the receiver.

Recommendations:
Do not assume that small talk is a waste of time.
Bear in mind that communication serves both to convey information and to maintain the relationship.

3. Challenges to communication in GVTs

There are several challenges to communication in GVTs. We will group them under three main groups: culture-related, language-related, and situational-related challenges.

3.1 Culture-related differences challenges

We have addressed culture, why culture is important and standardized approaches to culture elsewhere in this book. So, by now, you are familiarized with the sphere of culture, cultural differences, and their implications. In this section, we will focus on how these dimensions impact communication.

3.1.1 Cultural dimensions

Recognizing the cultural values of where team members come from helps understand behaviors and the correct interpretation of attitudes and increases productive behavior.

Hofstede's cultural dimensions (Hofstede, 1984) are used to show some of the communicational consequences of each dimension:

Power distance (PD):

as discussed, this dimension refers to power and status within societies. Some of the ways PD may impact communication pertain to the dynamics of group collaboration and expressing opinions and disagreement. In high power distance countries, individual characteristics such as age, social and professional status influence how a person communicates with others and expects others to communicate with him/her. Thus, high and low PD team members may have different attitudes and behavior concerning expressing disagreement, making oneself heard, and participating in the decision-making processes.

Since status is important for high PD cultures, the use of a formal register and honorary titles may be adopted, while in low PD cultures, informal language is accepted.

PD and communication

Team members from high PD:

- Value the use of signs/titles of status and hierarchy
- May use more formal language and titles
- May have difficulty in addressing older colleagues by the first name
- May find it difficult to express disagreement.
- May expect to be told what to do

Team members from low PD:

- Use informal language
- Expect to be seen as equal
- Express disagreement, expect to be heard, and participate in decision-making.

Individualism-collectivism:

Since this dimension has implications for how individuals relate to groups, there may be implications relevant for communication, particularly in regards to assigning tasks among group members.

In what concerns the functions of communication, it has been argued that team members of individualist cultures place more emphasis on the informational function of communication, while members of collectivist cultures place more emphasis on the relational function (Miyamoto and Schwarz, 2006) as relationships are very important to people from collectivistic cultures.

In general, team members from individualist cultures may enjoy more flexibility in executing tasks that they have been assigned and prefer challenging and competitive environments.

Since in-group harmony is valued by collectivistic cultures, team members from these cultures may express themselves in more moderate ways and prefer indirect modes of communication (Smith, 2011).

Individualism-collectivism and communication:

Team members from individualistic cultures:

- See communication as a way to convey information
- Enjoy working independently.

Team members from collectivistic cultures:

- Value communication as a means to build and maintain relationships
- May communicate their ideas more moderately to preserve group harmony.

Masculinity-Femininity (M-F):

This dimension refers to dominant values in cultures. Masculine cultures emphasize individual achievement and competition, while feminine cultures emphasize social nurturing and quality of life.

Team members from feminine cultures are more prone to sharing personal stories, are more focused on seeking consensus and concerned with balancing the contributions of the different members, and listen more carefully. In contrast, team members from masculine countries tend to be more assertive and aggressive, interrupt more, and may come across as attempting to dominate the conversation.

Masculinity-femininity and communication

Teams members from feminine cultures:

- Focus on building connections by sharing experiences and asking questions
- Focus on seeking consensus
- May nod their head to show that they are listening.

Teams members from masculine cultures

- May be more prone to tell information rather than ask questions
- May be more assertive.
- Only nod their head if they agree.

Uncertainty avoidance (UA):

Uncertainty avoidance refers to the extent to which people feel uncomfortable with less structured, ambiguous situations. In high UA cultures, there are typically many laws and regulations to avoid vagueness and prevent ambiguity. Hence, individuals from high avoidance cultures may prefer more structured environments, instructions, and tasks. They may be likely to prefer more planning, guidance, control, and feedback in task assignments and have a lower tolerance for ambiguity. Decisions are also more likely to be based on consensus.

Members from low UA cultures may be more relaxed about ambiguous/less structured situations and may prefer more flexibility in how they complete their tasks.

Uncertainty avoidance and communication

Team members from high UC cultures:

- May prefer structured tasks.

Team members from low UA cultures

- May be more relaxed with ambiguous situations and tasks
- May be more willing to take risks.

Recommendations

- Encourage all team members to express their views and participate in decision-making.
- Do not assume that no objections to your ideas are a synonym of agreement.

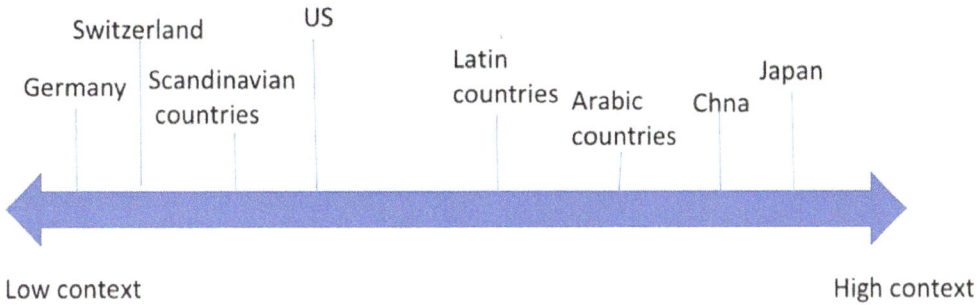

Fig 5.2 Some examples of low context and high context cultures

Source: Own elaboration

- Discuss collaboration rules and task allocation between members.
- Address collaboration expectations and address group collaboration rules.

3.1.2 Verbal vs. nonverbal communication:

Nonverbal communication encompasses elements such as body language, posture, situational cues, and tone of voice, all of which carry meaning. The importance of verbal versus nonverbal communication may vary widely. A relevant framework to understand this difference is Hall's low context and high context classification (Hall, 1976) (Figure 2). Hall is an anthropologist who studied communication within cultures in the '70s. He proposed that cultures can be classified based on the importance of explicit vs. implicit communication.

In **High context cultures,** communication is implicit and indirect, while in **Low context cultures**, communication is explicit and direct.

Thus, in high context cultures, not all information is explicit and transmitted through verbal communication. If you are not familiar with the contextual cues, you may miss part of the meaning being communicated. Low context cultures, on the contrary, rely primarily on verbal language to convey the intended meaning. People from these cultures may be perceived as too direct or too blunt by people from high context cultures.

Hence, communication between team members from high and low context cultures may be affected. Some of the challenges low context culture members may encounter when working with high context are:

- Information may be lost because low context members cannot read the context.
- High context culture members avoid saying "no" and tend not to be straightforward.

On the opposite side, some of the challenges high context culture members may encounter when working with low context team members are:

- They may feel uncomfortable with the direct, blunt communication style.
- Being direct may be seen as being impolite by low-context team members.

Misunderstandings derived from differences in non-verbal behavior can be harder to detect than language inaccuracies. Nonverbal communication includes the voice, i.e., pitch, tone, facial expressions, the body, distance between speakers, gestures, among others (Gallois and Callan, 1997). The usage of nonverbal communication may vary significantly among cultures and may lead to misinterpretations. Because nonverbal communication expresses emotions and mood while words convey information, misunderstandings based on nonverbal behavior may be unconscious and more difficult to detect.

Examples:

- Smiling in Japan may reflect nervousness and social discomfort.
- The Japanese may feel that Americans are emotional because they speak loudly; Americans may think the Japanese are reserved because they speak softly.

In some countries, people are more prone to using large gestures, talking with their hands, or speaking louder. This does not mean that they are aggressive or angry.

A specific case is the meaning of emblematic gestures in different cultures. One study about similarities and differences in gestures across cultures (Matsumoto and Huang, 2013) identified three groups of situations: (1) Different gestures with the same verbal meaning: "come," "emotional closeness," "God bless you," "hello," and "I don't agree," for example; (2) The same forms with different meanings: the "ring," for instance, can mean "A-OK," "money," or other messages and bringing both hands together in the front and bowing may mean "thank you", "hello" or "goodbye"; bringing both hands to the sides of one's head and pointing the index finger may mean "the devil", "angry" in others, and "horny" among others; (3) unique gestures, in which an emblem for a message exists in one culture but not another, such as the message for "apology," for instance, which occurs only in South Asia; the message for "hunger" occurs only in East Asia; and the message for "day after tomorrow" occurs only in the Middle East.

Recommendations

When communicating with members from different cultures, is mindful of different communication styles:

- People from high context cultures may not appreciate attempts to get right to the point, but this does not mean they are averting the topic;
- People from low context cultures may not appreciate talking around the subject.

3.1.3 Differences in style, conventions, and practices

Another level of communication refers to the style we adopt when addressing others. The style of communication concerns the register, i.e., type of language (Gallois and Callan, 1997): when addressing, for example, a judge in court, we will use a different communication style than the one we use when talking to close friends. Cultures differ in their rules regarding appropriate styles for each context. In general, English has a narrower range of formal styles than other languages, such as Chinese and Japanese. Since this may be very difficult to manage for foreign speakers, it may lead to being perceived as either too formal or too casual.

Some situations in which this may be more noticeable are when expressing disagreement, giving bad news, giving orders, etc. In general, assertive communication may be mistakenly interpreted as aggression in some cultures.

The dynamics of talking and establishing a dialogue can also vary cross-culturally. In some cultures, people are very talkative, while in others, it is considered very rude to interrupt when someone is talking and can lead to a blockage of communication. This can happen, for example, in a dialogue between people from South American and Scandinavian countries.

3.2 Language-related challenges

For a long time, it was believed that words were mere labels for objects and that the only differences between languages were the sounds used to designate such objects. However, many experts now believe that language affects how we see and interpret the world. This is something that linguists and other academics have studied for some time and is still an object of controversy. In general, studies found that some languages lack designations for some concepts because those concepts do not exist in their culture. Thus, languages act as "a filter, enhancer, or framer of perception and thought." This means that there exist clear relationships between language and thought patterns.

In practice, what this means is that people can only perceive concepts for which their language as a word. In other words, languages affect the way you think and the way you act.

For example, studies show that Greeks tend to interrupt others because their language puts important information at the beginning of the sentence, while Germans do not interrupt because they put the most important information at the end of the sentence.

Studies also show that bilinguals answer survey questions differently depending on the language.

- In English: more task-oriented, less family-oriented
- In Spanish/Arabic: more relationship-oriented.

3.2.1 Communicating in a foreign language

Verbal communication is hampered by the fact that some or all members may be expressing their ideas in a non-native language. When communicating with foreign-language speakers, different levels of language competence may cause frustration and failures in communication. When the command of the chosen work language of team members is poor, it may be necessary to repeat information and check that information is being correctly understood. Strong accents may also hinder understanding. This may lead to delays, misunderstandings, and lower levels of accuracy.

Some of the frequent mistakes found when using a foreign language are the following:

- Use of simple language
- Not engaging
- Tendency to over-explain.

3.2.2 Same words, different meanings?

Speaking the same language is not a guarantee that misunderstanding will never occur. The differences in meaning, expressions, and slang between the languages spoken in different countries may lead to funny or embarrassing situations or, in the worst-case scenario, to a lack of communication or even trouble. Examples include British English and American English or Portuguese and Brazilian

Portuguese, among many others. There are plenty of online resources where you can get further information about the differences between British and American English, for example https://pt.scribd.com/doc/16522472/List-of-Words-Having-Different-Meanings-in-British-and-American-English and https://en.oxforddictionaries.com/usage/british-and-american-terms Some of the most emblematic examples of different meanings are:

	British English	American English
Jumper	Sweater	Someone about to jump
Trainer	Sports shoes	Someone who trains people or animals
Pants	Underwear	Trousers
Biscuit	Cookie	A kind of bread/scone

3.3 Situational-related challenges

Situational-related changes refer to the fact that GVTs are virtual teams, based in different geographical locations with different time zones who have to communicate using technological communication tools.

3.3.1 Virtual teams

The fact that GVT members are working in different geographical locations may be a challenge to communication. Studies suggest, however, that distance is not necessarily a constraint to effective communication. An aspect that seems to be more relevant is the quality of communication. In fact, one study showed that the depth and focus of communication were more important than frequent, superficial conversations. Thus, to the extent that GVTs manage to have frequent, positive, and continuous communication, geographical dispersion should matter less. Nevertheless, the distance narrows the options for communication modes, which allows frequent face-to-face communication. Contrary to collocated teams, which may socialize during coffee and lunch breaks, for example, and thus bond, improve the quality of relationships, and develop trust, GVTs lack these opportunities to develop group cohesiveness. This may hinder the development of trust between group members (Small and Jogeva, 2017), which can be an issue, as trust is fundamental for effective group collaboration.

The choice of virtual tools for communication needs to bear in mind that positive communication requires more than just task-oriented communication. "Increased reliance on electronic communication can lead to misunderstandings, which can erode team communication and productivity, and inhibit the type of social interaction within a team that leads to innovation and success" (Daim et al., 2012, 203). Hence, the chosen virtual tools must allow not only for informal communication and for more than just verbal or written communication. As mentioned, we communicate to a great extent through nonverbal communication such as body language and facial expressions. These nonverbal cues carry a richness of information and meaning that may be important for positive communication, relationship building and establishing and developing trust. Face-to-face communication tools need to be used, in addition to other collaborative tools. Remote communication lacks this dimension of communication.

Different locations also mean different time zones. This may restrict the timing for communications to overlapping working hours and may favor asynchronous communication tools, such as email, rather than synchronous communication tools. However, it is important to also find adequate meeting times and synchronous communication, which are important for richer interaction.

3.3.2 Communication tools

Although Information and Communication Technology (ICT) provides multiple effective options for voice and image communication, technical problems may happen, or members may feel less comfortable with remote communication. Consequently, the lack of physical proximity may exacerbate misunderstandings, erode interpersonal relationships, hinder the natural flow of communication, lead to miscommunication, and hamper the development of trust among members.

Communication tools have advantages and limitations. Thus, the GVT should discuss which communication tools are more adequate and preferred by its members in order to choose between face-to-face vs. audio/text communication tools, as well as synchronous vs. asynchronous communication tools. Important nonverbal communication is missing in some communication tools, which lowers the accuracy of communication being transmitted and causes anxiety (Daim et al., 2012). A study showed that videoconferencing was useful for mitigating problems and allowing people to see each other's body language. However, often connection problems such as poor internet connections lead people to prefer using audio-conferencing. In this study, email was the most used communication tool; however, it was mentioned that emails were often badly written, which could cause misinterpretations. It was also used after meetings in order to put in written form the main content from virtual meetings.

Recommendations:

- Use different communication tools
- Use videoconferencing whenever possible. If there is a poor connection, use your camera during at least the first part of the meeting to greet everyone and bond. Then, if necessary, it can be turned off for better quality.

3 - Defining communications guidelines

In order to improve the quality of communication, it is important to plan how the group will communicate and define guidelines regarding communication tools, timing, providing feedback, etc. to avoid communication breakdowns.

For voice communication, Smith (2001, cited in Daim et al., 2012) recommends the following guidelines: (a) establish a timeline for the response; (b) define what to do if the receiver cannot provide all of the information requested, or not quickly enough; (c) define how and when senders may be contacted; (d) create a protocol for what to do if the sender thinks a message could be misunderstood; and (e) plan what to do if a receiver does not understand a message.

In written communications, the requested actions should appear in the final paragraph.

Recommendations:
Be clear regarding the response that is expected to the message.
In lengthy messages, provide a summary of the main ideas.

References

Daim, T. U., Ha, A., Reutiman, S., Hughes, B., Pathak, U., Bynum, W. and Bhatla, A. (2012). Exploring the communication breakdown in global virtual teams. International Journal of Project Management. Elsevier Ltd, 30(2), pp. 199–212. doi: 10.1016/j.ijproman.2011.06.004.

Gallois, C., & Callan, V. J. (1997). Communication and culture: A guide for practice. John Wiley & Sons Inc.

Hall, Edward T. (1976). Beyond Culture. Garden City, NY: Anchor Press.

Hofstede, G. (1984). Culture's consequences: International differences in work-related values (Vol. 5). sage.

Matsumoto, D., & Hwang, H. C. (2013). Cultural similarities and differences in emblematic gestures. Journal of Nonverbal Behavior, 37(1), 1–27.

Miyamoto, Y., & Schwarz, N. (2006). When conveying a message may hurt the relationship: Cultural differences in the difficulty of using an answering machine. Journal of Experimental Social Psychology, 42(4), 540–547.

Schramm, W.A. (1971). The nature of communication between humans, in Schramm, W.A. and Roberts, D.F. (Eds), The Process and Effects of Mass Communication, University of Illinois Press, Urbana, IL.

Smal, A., & Jõgeva, E. (2017). Communication challenges in managing global virtual teams: the experience of project managers (Master's thesis). University of Gothenburg

Smith, P. B. (2011). Communication styles as dimensions of national culture. Journal of Cross-cultural psychology, 42(2), 216–233.

CHAPTER 6

Free-Riders in GVTs

VAS TARAS, THE UNIVERSITY OF NORTH CAROLINA AT GREENSBORO, X-CULTURE, INC.

The Problem

As organizations shift from hierarchical and rigid bureaucratic structures to more organic orga-nizational designs, work teams become more prevalent. In recent years, this trend has been signified by a ubiquity of Global Virtual Teams (GVTs). Various studies suggest that between 50 and 70 percent of all white-collar workers in OECD countries at least occasionally work on proj-ects that require some form of virtual collaboration. Of those, 20 to 35 percent involve collaborations across national borders, and the number of such interactions is increasing (c.f., Duarte & Snyder, 2011; Kurtzberg, 2014).

The reliance on virtual communication has fundamentally changed how team members gather, share, exchange information, make decisions, and monitor progress. Virtual teams offer a number of advan-tages, including flexibility with respect to geography and timing. One problem with virtual teams is that the physical and psychological distance of its members exacerbates the fundamental team problem of free-riding (Pillis & Furumo, 2007).

The term 'Free Riding' was first introduced in the economics literature (Olson, 1965) and later extended to the management literature (Jones, 1984). A form of social loafing, free-riding refers to "a tendency for individuals to fail to participate in collectively profitable activities in the absence of coer-cion or individual incentives" (Stigler, 1974, p. 359).

Decades of research in social psychology, organizational psychology, and communication have shown that the social context creates a powerful set of forces that influence group members' cognitions and behaviors, in particular with respect to preventing deviant behaviors and social loafing (Burnstein & Vinokur, 1973; Hackman, 1987; Maass & Clark, 1984). Virtual groups represent a substantially different social context than face-to-face groups (Hackman, 2002). In traditional collocated teams, social obli-gation and reciprocity among team members arises from closer acquaintanceship, shared experiences, common interests, and integration in one another's personal networks, including those external to the team. The separation in time, space, and geography of the members of virtual teams greatly weakens common social forces, thereby removing social pressures that minimize free-riding (Falk & Fischbacher, 2006). Moreover, cultural differences, which are an inherent feature of GVTs, further dissociate team members from their team and inhibit social and team identities, which further exacerbates the free-rider problem.

We propose that the damaging effects of free-riding on virtual team performance is non-linear and multi- dimensional. That is, the performance loss is neither limited nor proportional to the loss of labor due to free-riding and instead is much greater (Figure 1). The most obvious performance cost due to free-riding is forfeiture of labor. However, a team's performance is further damaged by the increased coordination and internal maintenance cost necessitated by free-riding. Once free-riding occurs, the workflow gets broken and deadlines can be missed, creating process loss by requiring intensified process management efforts to resolve coordination problems and develop a new plan.

Further, probably the most devastating effect of free-riding is that it damages team morale, thereby triggering what we call the "rotten apple" vicious cycle. Free-riding induces feelings of injustice, which undermines team morale and effort, leading to more free-riding. Soon enough, conflicts occur, a blame game starts, and team performance collapses. One "rotten apple" spoils the entire barrel.

With the growing ubiquity of GVTs and the acuteness of the free-riding problem under this form of work design, a study that could explain the mechanisms by which free-riding damages team performance and experimentally test the effectiveness of commonly available strategies for minimizing free-riding would make a major contribution to HRM literature and practices.

Unfortunately, studying free-riding in GVTs is extremely difficult and even prohibitive in most cases because of the difficulties associated with obtaining continuous and reliable access to a sizable team-level sample of corporate GVTs performing comparable tasks. Furthermore, lab-based studies do not lend themselves well to replicating the cultural, geographic, and temporal contextual issues that must be captured for a full understanding of GVT effectiveness.

We are in a unique position to overcome the above challenges. Our quasi-experimental study on the mechanisms of free-riding and strategies for dealing with the problem will be based on our priority access to X-Culture (www.X-Culture.org), a large-scale international business collaboration project that involves about 1,000 GVTs annually (500 twice a year) comprised of 3,000 MBA and business students and working professionals from all six continents (Taras et al., 2012; Taras et al., 2013). Working in GVTs where each member is from a different country, the project participants rely on virtual communication and face the challenge of collaborating across time zones and cultures, a real business challenge, real rewards, and possible real losses. Furthermore, we will have a unique opportunity to study free-riding in GVTs longitudinally, manipulate various factors, including team composition and treatment, and have sizable samples in each of the variety of treatment conditions. The proposed study can offer a major leap forward in terms of the research design possibilities, richness, and validity of the findings from earlier research on GVTs.

Theoretical Basis

The goal of the proposed study is twofold. First, we will explore the mechanisms by which free-riding affects group dynamics and performance. Second, we will examine the comparative effectiveness of various commonly available strategies for preventing and dealing with free-riding in GVTs.

Free-Riding Mechanisms

As discussed earlier, we hypothesize that the effect of free-riding is comprised of multiple components, which makes its effect non-linear and much greater than what the expected performance loss from reduced labor loss only would be. As illustrated in Figure 1, we propose that the performance losses due to free-riding stem from (1) labor force loss, (2) coordination loss, and (3) morale loss. While the effect of the reduced labor force is linear and directly proportional to the percent of the team member's time lost due to free-riding, the combined effect of all three components leads to a disproportionally rapid performance loss in response even to a minor occurrence of free-riding. For example, a loss of input from a single member due to free-riding in a team of ten will lead to a performance loss greater than 10 percent.

Figure 1. Performance Loss due to Free-Riding

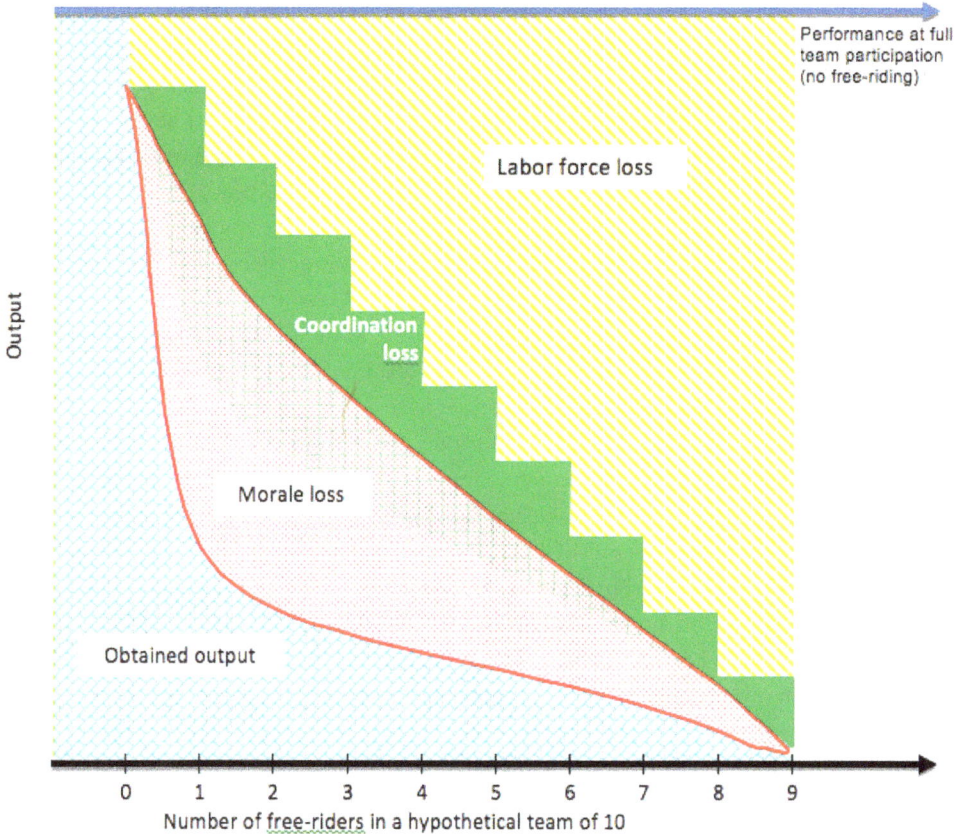

Fig 6.1 Performance Loss due to Free-Riding.

The proposed study will also assess the exact magnitude of the performance loss due to free-riding in response to the different number and percent losses in the labor force and will attempt to model the exact shape of the performance loss function. Figure 2 illustrates the key components of our hypothesized mechanism by which free-riding damages team dynamics and performance.

Different factors contribute to the probability of free-riding at different stages of team life. Accordingly, different forms of intervention are possible and suitable at these different times.

Intervention Opportunity 1

The first intervention opportunity to minimize the chances of free-riding presents itself when the team is being formed. At this stage, it is still possible to manipulate key team characteristics to remove the factors contributing to free-riding. Several factors are hypothesized to play a role at the team forming stage:

Team size: Larger teams are more likely to experience free-riding. As the group size increases, it becomes easier to "hide" social loafing. Furthermore, a diffusion of responsibility hinders the motivation to contribute (Darley & Latane, 1968). When people work alone, the responsibility is then concentrated in one person and any shirking will be immediately linked to the person. In groups, the responsibility is shared. As the team size increases, each person assumes less responsibility, which makes identifying the shirking more difficult. A lack of contribution can go unnoticed, which limits motivation and effort.

Team diversity: The similarity-attraction theory postulates that people tend to associate with those who are similar and therefore familiar to them either in terms of such easily observable attributes as race, ethnic, origin or social status, or in terms of more subtle attributes such as attitudes and beliefs (Williams & O'Reilly, 1998). Therefore, homogeneity facilitates, and diversity hurts group integration and cohesion (Watson & Kumar, 1992). As diversity increases, the members of the team have less in common, have less trust, feel less connected, and the sense of social reciprocity and obligation that prevents free-riding vanishes (Jarvenpaa & Leidner, 1999; Katsikeas, Skarmeas, & Bello, 2009). Furthermore, the social queues and communicating patterns are more likely to differ across cultures, making misunderstandings likely. The genuine effort made to contribute, along with a desire to connect, may go unnoticed due to misinterpretation of the signals because of cultural or demographic differences (Barna, 1985; Maznevski, 1994; Shaw & Barrett-Power, 1998; Wlotko & Federmeier, 2012). The challenges will only be aggravated by the virtual nature of collaboration, where low-context low-media-richness communication channels further limit opportunities for effective social exchange (Hambley, O'Neill, & Kline, 2007a, 2007b). In other words, two separate smaller teams will have a greater output than that of one larger team equal in size to the sum of the two teams.

The difficulty of entry: Prior research has shown that difficulty of entry makes membership in the team more valuable, which in turn leads to greater team commitment, cohesion, and effort (Burgess & Turner, 2000). In teams where membership depends on the ability to pass rigorous selection tests and survive challenging initiations, team members not only perceive their membership on the team as more exclusive and valuable but will feel stronger social and affective ties to their team members, as they feel they have more in common and are more committed. This, in turn, reduces the perceived diversity of the group and, ultimately, free-riding.

If confirmed, the hypothesis suggests that free-riding can be minimized by administering team member selection tests and publicizing the test difficulty and the low acceptance rate.

Acquaintanceship: Group members that are closely acquainted with one another are more interpersonally attracted, feel more social obligation and reciprocity, tend to contribute a greater effort toward a common goal, display more citizenship behavior, and shirk less. One of the reasons free-riding is more common in virtual teams is because in the virtual context, interactions tend to be less personal and more task-focused. Low media-richness of the communication media (e.g., email) and limited opportunities for interactions outside of work often result in members of virtual teams not being acquainted with each another on a personal level. The cultural differences that often are an inherited feature of GVTs only make it more difficult to learn about other team members, as their unfamiliar background context provides fewer queues and associations.

Intervention Opportunity 2

After free-riding occurs, we hypothesize that it is possible to stop this behavior by understanding how free-riding causes the "rotten apple" vicious cycle and removing the factors that perpetuate the cycle. As illustrated in Diagram 2, the key factor that induces further free-riding behavior is the perception of injustice. If free-riding occurs, the free-rider is seen as someone who gets the same benefits while contributing less. As it is not fair that the free-rider's contribution-reward ratio is better than that of the other

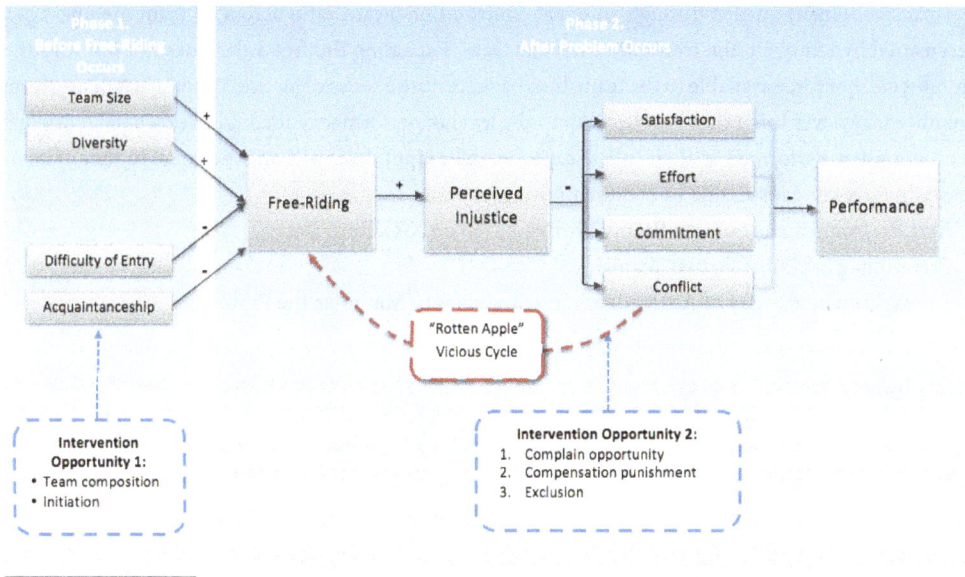

Fig 6.2   Free-Riding in Global Virtual Teams: Nature and Prevention Model

team members, the rest of the team tries to restore justice. Usually, two basic options are available. First, the personal outcomes (rewards or punishments) can be adjusted to reflect the different levels of contribution. In this case, the free-rider's lower performance would be associated with lower personal gains. Unfortunately, adjusting the rewards/punishments is not always within the power of the team members.

Second, if rewards cannot be adjusted, the only other way to equalize the contribution-reward ratio across the team members is to lower one's own performance (Adams, 1965). Lowering one's performance not only ensures that one's contribution-reward ratio will be closer to that of the free-rider, but each team member has an incentive to follow the free-rider behavior as soon as possible. The sooner one stops contributing, the better one's final contribution-reward ratio will be. The team member who stops contributing last will end up with the lowest reward-performance ratio. Accordingly, we hypothesize that intervention strategies that restore perceived justice in a team will be effective in stopping free-riding behavior after it occurs. Several interventions are available:

Opportunity to complain: The simplest strategy could be allowing the team members to formally complain about the free-rider. While this approach does not remove the problem per se, it ensures that the management knows of the injustice in the team and gives the team members hope that justice will be restored. This may be a less effective strategy than the more radical ones described below, but it is likely to at least temporarily break the "rotten apple" cycle.

Reduced compensation: Formal reduction of the compensation of the free-rider will likely be more effective than the strategy detailed above, as it not only gives hope that justice will be restored but also provides a specific readily observable adjustment: free-riders get less. The free-rider can be punished by reducing his/her pay (in corporate teams) or grade (in academic teams). This would be especially effective if compensation hinged on peer evaluations. This way, the team can be sure that punishment through a reduction of the compensation resides with the team members and, thus, is inevitable.

Exclusion: Finally, justice through an equal contribution-award ratio across all team members can be ensured by removing the free-rider from the team. Excluding the free-rider does not improve the amount of labor force available to the team, but it does restore a sense of justice. While a loss of one team member may never bring the team back up to the level of performance it could have when all original team members performed to their fullest capacity, the output drop will only be equal to that of labor loss, while avoiding losses due to coordination and morale.

Extracts from Papers on Free-Riding Written Based on X-Culture Data

Free-Riding in Global Virtual Teams:

An Experimental Study of Antecedents and Strategies to Minimize the Problem

Abstract

Free-riding is a major problem in workgroups, particularly in global virtual teams (GVTs). This study explores the mechanisms by which free-riding affects group dynamics and performance in GVTs, and experimentally tests several commonly available strategies to alleviate the problem. The study was conducted using 2,163 GVTs composed of 15,453 people from over 40 countries who worked on real business challenges presented by international companies. The results confirmed that the damage caused by free-riding is disproportionately higher than the loss in manpower, and that many strategies implemented before the team started working on the project and/or after the problem of free-riding occurred can be remarkably effective in preventing and mitigating the problem. Presented here are the initial results of the study.

Main Findings

In the proposed study, we examined a large sample of global virtual teams doing comparable and consequential work over an extended period. Although the results of the study yet again showed how damaging free-riding is, the results of our experiments are very encouraging: free-riding can be effectively dealt with. Indeed, free-riding appears to not only reduce the manpower available to the team but also leads to process losses and the undermining of team morale, thereby further damaging team performance. However, several interventions appear to significantly reduce the problem.

At the onset of the project, creating teams that are smaller, more homogeneous and less dispersed can reduce the free-riding rate by about 25%. If team member diversity is desired and cannot be compromised, prompting team members to get to know each other on a personal level is likely to help in preventing free-riding. Investing just a few minutes in meeting team members in the first days of the project can significantly reduce free-riding down the road.

When free-riding occurs, doing nothing is the worst option. Up to 17% of team members (or more than one per team in teams of 4 to 10 people in size) are likely to free-ride in these conditions. Letting team members complain but doing nothing about it is not likely to solve the problem, although just the possibility of a complaint will bring a noticeable improvement. Regular peer evaluations will help further, especially if the results are shared with the team members.

In conclusion, the most effective strategy was the complete removal of the free-riders. Even though only a very small number of project participants were removed (less than 2% or just one per 50 teams), the threat of exclusion did wonders, with free-riding dropping by about 50%.

Free-Riding Prevention Strategies	N	# of Free-riders	% of Free-riders
1. Nothing	847	1.09	16.97
2. Complain, no action	343	1.03	15.22
3. Complain, peer-evaluations not shared	382	1.00	14.17
4. Complain, peer-evaluations shared	82	0.94	13.19
5. Exclude if repeated complaints received	509	0.56	9.00
Grand Total	2,163	0.99	14.82

The Other Side of the Barricades: Interviewing the Free-Riders, Not Their Managers and Co-Workers, On the Reasons Of and Ways to Deal With Free-Riding in GVTs

Abstract

Based on a unique sample of 86 documented "free-riders" from 750 teams that completed a long-term international business consulting project, this study attempts to understand the reasons for and ways to deal with low performance in the GVT context by looking at the problem through the eyes of the guilty party, as opposed to the accounts of their active team members or project managers. Hundreds of pages of qualitative interview data are coded and analyzed. The findings are discussed with respect to HR managerial implications and future research directions.

Main findings and implications

Positive responses despite negative experience. Despite their unsatisfactory performance, most free-riders remain positive about the project and their team. So, problems of this nature do not necessarily mean the team member is a loss for the organization. They appear to remain committed to the organization and their co-workers and, given another chance, will likely do better.

Don't expect an admission of guilt. Even when faced with well-documented evidence of their unsatisfactory performance, most free-riders will not admit guilt. Many will agree that their performance was poor, but the clear majority will attribute the problem to external causes. This is alarming, as it means most free-riders do not recognize that they themselves can control their performance in GVTs.

The first days of teamwork are critically important, as free-riding tends to take root in the forming and storming stages. The issue is almost always due to problems related to these initial contacts and interactions. If the team survives these initial stages, free-riding is much less likely to occur later. Moreover, about a quarter of to-be free riders could be detected (and excluded) even before the project commences. Leadership and training are very important at the team member selection stages, as well as at the beginning of the project.

Communication is the key. If we were to provide the best recommendation for dealing with the problem, it would be better inter-member communication. Most free-riders are not lazy, irresponsible people. Under different circumstances, most would have turned out to be productive members of the teams. However, due to a lack of communication, they fail to get involved or later fail to resolve a conflict or figure out what and how should be done. Better communication can preclude or resolve most of the problems surrounding free-riding.

Withholding Effort in Teams: A Meta-Analytic Synthesis of Empirical Evidence on Social Loafing, Free Riding, and Free-Loading in Teams

Abstract

By means of a meta-analysis of 101 publications (112 independent samples, 458 data points) on social loafing, free-loading, and free-riding, we investigated the predictors and consequences of withholding effort in teams (WET). Our database includes samples from a variety of populations, including students, lower-level employees, and managers. We meta-analytically tested the predictive power of 36 different factors on WET that represented team member characteristics, team dynamics, work design, and the effects of WET on 6 team outcomes representing possible team performance and psychological results. The findings are remarkably consistent: a number of factors reliably predict WET, and the occurrence of WET dramatically damages team performance and dynamics. The results clearly indicate that WET has a negative effect on team performance and team member well-being, but proper team member selection, team dynamics management, and work design can substantially alleviate the problem. Underexplored but promising areas in the extant literature are identified and directions for future research are provided.

Main Findings

The best predictors of free-riding are listed below.

Less free-riding if:

- Team members score high on consciousness (a personality trait) (r= -0.42)
- Membership in the team is prestigious (r= -0.55)
- Regular feedback (r= -0.41)
- Individual effort is tracked (r= -.38)

More free-riding if

- Team members think others shirk (r=0.40)
- Bullying in teams (r =0.46)
- Team morale low (r=0.52)
- Trust is low (r=0.42)
- Perceived injustice (r= 0.55)

Consequences of free-riding

- Team performance down (r= -0.37)
- Burnout (r= 0.46)
- Team cohesion down (r= -0.62)
- Motivation down (r= -0.35)

CHAPTER 7

Culture, Cross-Cultural Differences and Cross-Cultural Conflicts

SWATI DHIR, INTERNATIONAL MANAGEMENT INSTITUTE, NEW DELHI, INDIA

MAMATA MOHAPATRA, INTERNATIONAL MANAGEMENT INSTITUTE, NEW DELHI, INDIA

1. Introduction

Confirming the basic need for belongingness, we tend to want to be accepted and be recognized as a valuable part of a group. The drive to belong manifests in personal spaces, with family, friends, sports groups, club and travel groups, in professional spaces like being in a team, and in academic areas such as with a lab group, for example. Notably, people only come together as a group when they share a common goal or interest: a common workplace, common areas of interest, a common place of origin, common language, or common behavior. People communicate, cooperate, and interact with a group member to maintain group cohesiveness and harmony within diversity. Coming from different backgrounds and upbringings, every individual is different, and therefore everyone posits a different opinion, which influences the discussion and decision-making process. When people from different cultural backgrounds come together and form a group, it usually faces conflicts because of its variance in opinions. The opinion variation is the function of one's upbringing, orientation towards life, and, most importantly, his/her experiences in life. In such a case, it is necessary for the management to create a healthy environment of appreciating the differences and accepting the ideas that are in the best interest of the group and organization. Organizations need to create a culture by encouraging interactions among employees, where each other's differences are appreciated and utilized to reduce conflict and get the best possible solution to a problem.

The dynamic management system of an organization contributes to the growth of diverse cultural perspectives. Accepting diversity requires open-minded people who accept individual differences with positivity. Unfortunately, due to limited exposure to the world of diverse cultural artifacts, we tend to become rigid, fixed within limited mental boundaries, and closed to different opinions. It would certainly be difficult for a single individual to experience and understand the embedded beliefs and assumptions of all cultures. However, when the organization provides us with the opportunity to explore the world of diversity by sharing each other's views, perspectives, beliefs, and assumptions, it becomes easy to understand and appreciate those differences. Since the business world is moving towards globalization, the organization tries to understand the customer preferences to set their business up, as the customer perspective is considered important to develop strategies and plan business. It has been seen that organizations that ignore these aspects fail in the long term if they have not been able to customize their businesses as per the cultural requirements of the given place. There might be conflicts because of cultural priorities. However, the moment we accept the fact that the differences exist, we start making attempts to understand and behave accordingly. Therefore, the key to success while managing cross-cultural issues is accepting and appreciating the differences by understanding its genesis and core philosophy without any implicit biases.

This chapter explains the concept of culture, its influence in different business contexts and highlights the interdependence of global culture in the business context. An attempt will be made to delineate cross-cultural differences and ways of handling cross-cultural conflicts in the most appropriate manner to minimize productivity losses.

2. Culture and management

Organizational culture is an intangible phenomenon in any organization. It is very difficult to see the tangent aspects of culture, and organizational culture is deeply embedded in any organization, which at times is visible by the behavior of a group of employees together. The founder's philosophy, beliefs, assumptions, and values are reflected in the artifacts of various organizational policies. Organizational culture can be influenced by founder and top management beliefs in terms of innovative culture, bureaucratic culture, non-hierarchical culture, and a participative culture. A successful company needs a good alignment between an individual's orientation and the company's values and beliefs.

Gone are the days when only a handful of companies and conglomerates were associated with terms like "global" and "multinational." The modern business must now operate in an ecosystem where competition is not bound by geographical boundaries. For a business to sustain and thrive, it is important that it transcends national boundaries. The aggregate amount of global e-commerce was \$27.7 trillion in 2016, and the size of business-to-business (B2B) e-commerce was six times larger than business-to-consumer (B2C) e-commerce (World Trade Statistical Review, 2018). Companies like Honda, Tata, and McDonald's operate in more than a hundred countries to achieve their goals, and even a small incense enterprise in India must source the bamboo sticks from Vietnam or China. International business is not a new concept; trade across national boundaries has been in existence for centuries. However, the current times' cultural considerations are imperative with the advent of wireless technology, which is continuously shrinking the world and turning it into a global village.

Cross-cultural management underlines the importance of taking into consideration the differences in cultures and preferences of employees and clients, which is constituent of people from different parts of the world. It helps the comparison of organizational behavior across different countries and cultures and leads towards a better understanding of the interactions between all the culturally diverse stakeholders of a certain business.

2.1 Understanding cross-cultural differences

In order to understand cultural differences, it is very important to understand individual behavior. Patterns of the behavior of employees from Italy, the USA, and India will vary because of the difference in their perceptions and attitudes, which in itself could be a manifestation of their varied cultural influences. For example, in the USA, direct instructions and commands are preferred over indirect ones, but if one was to go to the eastern part of the world and find themself in Japan, they would witness an abundance of indirect communication, where a lot of emphases is placed upon the development of interpersonal relationships, the impact of body language, and other forms of non-verbal communication. Cross-cultural differences can potentially vary significantly, and in management, they can exist in the form of language, etiquette, hierarchy, behavior, tolerance level, rules, material objects, and the like. Managers adept at working with a team of people from different countries are in high demand, as they help the business modify and adapt its tactics so that it can effectively compete on a level playing field.

2.2 Appreciating and accepting the differences

Cross-cultural differences can only become a hindrance in getting desired results if there is rigidity in the workplace. Working in cross-cultural teams calls for flexibility and respect. Learning from generalizations may help, but many times it also leads to distorted ideas about cultures. Hence, although these generalities may be helpful, they should not be relied upon completely; the idea is to observe and learn about the differences in order to overcome them. The interaction must be carried out responsibly and with sensitivity. McDonald's, which is known for its hamburgers around the world, opened its first-ever vegetarian-only outlets in India after being in the business for over 70 years in over 100 countries, recognizing and taking into account the religious sentiments of its customers.

2.3 Issues due to cross-cultural differences

In the workplace, the difference in religious beliefs, ethnicity, language, and other cultural differences may potentially lead to a cultural clash. Additionally, the differences in working practices and communication styles between departments, with clients, with other companies, and between senior management and other people in the workforce can further lead to distress and potentially derail the organization's goals and objectives. While studies suggest that diversity is positively linked with creativity, there are also instances where cultural differences and their lack of recognition have resulted in delayed execution and, in some cases, the total failure of projects.

3. Studies on culture in management

In the last few decades, studies on the cultural impact of organizational management and economics have been getting unprecedented attention. With the predominant influence of globalization in every aspect of human life, the cultural perspective has expanded drastically. In this regard, researchers are now exploring and addressing the multidimensional, multicultural, and cross-cultural influence on the workplace. Rousseau (1990) has proposed a multicultural ring model. These rings are "organized from readily accessible (outer layers) to difficult to access (inner layers)," which covers all key elements, namely, artifacts, pattern behavior, norms, values, and beliefs of culture (Rousseau, 1990, p. 158). Further, understanding and managing organizational culture is important as it serves as the fundamental issue in organizational change (Pettigrew et al., 2003). Globalization, with its multicultural implications, has become an indispensable factor in strategic management (Amaram, 2007). Since the industrial revolution, cultural diversity has bloomed as immigrants started sharing a significant part of the population and labor force (Copeland, 1988). Today, in the 21st century, while workforce demographic diversity has been continually expanding, these changes offer both opportunities and challenges. The diverse nature of the workforce and the amalgamation of cultural artifacts and knowledge institutions attract researchers to conduct in-depth studies in the related areas with intriguing results.

1. Positivist view: The possibility of exploring the culture through values and exact observations. Positivist assumptions believe that the culture of any organization is a function of logical deductions and uses an instrumental perspective of understanding the people's orientation and adapting to the top management's philosophy with the necessary rationale.
2. Interpretive view: People use meanings in systems to organize their actions and Emic positioning in strong contrast to the etic constructs (cultural dimensions). It contrasts with the

positivist view in such a way that it believes more in the subjective understanding of the individual's behavior by interpreting in the given context. It refers to the very close reading, deep understanding, and decoding of the subjective experiences of the given context. In the context of cross-cultural aspects, the interpretive views might be more closely related to reality. No matter how much one has gathered the objective information about the given culture, the real understanding comes with appropriate interpretation.

3. Critical view: Postmodern, critical, and postcolonial perspectives focus on the influence of societal and structural elements in work. Critical views of culture believe that the real aspects of any concept lie very deep in its core and need to be decoded by removing multiple layers. A critical view of culture argues that one can observe the objective aspects by going through the formal approach, or one can observe structure and patterns at some level, but these objective measures and subjective observations might be biased and might not be truly neutral. Therefore, to understand the real core of any culture, one needs to understand the cultural genesis by multiple lenses.

4. Cross-cultural conflicts

A conflict can occur between any two parties—it could be between nations, organizations, individuals, or ethnic groups. When this conflict occurs between groups or individuals of different social, ethnic, or national backgrounds who belong to separate cultures, it is called cross-cultural conflict. Social inheritance and shared way of life of members of a social group mold an individual's perception. Cross-cultural conflicts actually cross over the fringes of these perceptions and can potentially make way for miscommunication and misinterpretation among people and organizations belonging to different cultures. This cultural difference can potentially aggravate the conflict irrespective of the reason for the conflict. It is very important to understand and sensitize employees towards cultural differences to diminish the probability of cross-cultural conflicts, as they can be detrimental to an organization's performance.

4.1 Kinds of conflicts

In organizational behavior, the conflicts can be organized under four types: Interpersonal Conflict, Intrapersonal Conflict, Intragroup Conflict, and Intergroup Conflict. Cross-cultural conflicts are plausible in the latter three. A difference in perception and personalities between two individuals may lead to interpersonal conflict. However, the organization relies more on teams to get the job done. Team conflicts are categorized as Relationship Conflict and Task Conflict.

4.2 Reasons for conflict

Conflict generally arises when two or more individuals differ or disagree on a particular topic. In a culturally diverse workplace, people differ on demographic origin, ethnicity, religion, caste, class, gender, language, social and educational background, beliefs, financial status, and so on (Bhadury, Mighty, & Damar, 2000). These distinctive qualities, resulting from cultural diversity collectively or individually, influence one's sense of identity. Therefore, if every individual does not get the appreciation and recognition that they are entitled to as a member of the group, frustration, and conflict because of the ignorance of diversity occurs.

4.3 Conflicts in GVTs due to mode of communication

The ever-improving technology and ongoing globalization have made many organizations form Global Virtual Teams (GVTs). Conflict in GVT is often aggravated by communication delays, time zone differences, and lack of face-to-face contact due to space-time dispersion. Five types of communication problems are found to contribute to misunderstanding in virtual teams: failure to communicate contextual information; failure to communicate information evenly; differences in the salience of information to individuals; differences in speed of access to information, and interpretation of the meaning of silence (Chatman & Barsade,1995). The causes of these problems cited were the geographic dispersion of team members, the information load, and the slow rate and feedback lag of communication media (Desanctis & Monge, 1999).

4.4 Differences between regular conflict & cross-cultural conflict

In a regular conflict, there is a serious disagreement between two parties about something. A regular conflict often deals with the interests of either party. However, a cross-cultural conflict may arise out of the difference in perception about methods of communication, the concept of time and punctuality, or something as trivial as eye contact, which may or may not have to do anything with the interests of either party. Cross-cultural conflict often manifests out of ignorance of the foreign culture, customs, and values.

4.5 Do conflicts in cross-cultural teams differ from conflicts in traditional teams?

Conflict in teams can be classified as relationship conflict and task conflict (Pinkley, 1990). Relationship conflict involves personal issues such as mutual dislike, personality clashes, and annoyance among team members. Differences in point of view and opinions in the context of team tasks are known as task conflict, which is usually devoid of the intense negative emotions commonly associated with relationship conflict (Jehn & Mannix, 2001). Task conflict deals with issues of duty and resource delegation, such as who should do what and how much responsibility each person should get. There is no conclusive study on which type of conflict is more evident in traditional or cross-cultural teams. But, cultural (including national and linguistic) diversity has been found to induce conflict in global virtual teams much more than in traditional teams (Kankanhalli et al, 2006).

Generally, the global virtual team comprises people from diverse cultures and backgrounds. These people in the team have rarely met or interacted with each other. The cultural differences can cause conflict among such virtual team members. These people from different cultures differ with respect to their values, communication style, personality, and working style. For example, for people from collectivistic cultures, the value, goals, and needs of the group are more important than that of the individual, whereas in individualistic cultures, the needs, aspirations, and value of the individual are given more priority. In another instance, people from masculine cultures are oriented more towards heroism, assertiveness, achievement, and material rewards, whereas people from feminine cultures are more oriented towards cooperation, caring, modesty, and quality of life. Another reason for that could include the perception of the national culture of the countries involved. Having a common template to scan the culture of any country might not discount the hard reality of individual differences. Also, cultural differences have a large effect on global virtual teams, due to the lack of in-person interaction, and it can be more difficult to resolve conflicts in this more distant situation.

Another important dimension of conflicts in cross-cultural teams is dispersion. This is defined as the degree to which the members of a team are working across national boundaries. The virtual team may be formed due to the specific nature of the work, and it can be dissolved when the purpose is fulfilled. This causes the relationship between the members to be temporary. Thus, group cohesiveness among the global virtual team members is also low as compared to face-to-face teams. Also, a lack of informal relationships and face-to-face interactions adds in lowering the cohesiveness among groups, thus promoting conflict.

5. Misalignment of organizational culture and national culture

In an organization, organizational culture is not the only determinant that impacts work behavior. A general assumption is that employees from the same organization will exhibit similar behavior, even when their nationalities are different. This assumption is based on a belief that organizational culture fades or wipes the impact of national culture on employees from the same organizations. In such a case, the differences will only be taken into account when a project involves foreign clients. This fact is quite contradictory, as the work behavior does contain the influences of national culture. Employees and managers bring their cultural and ethnic backgrounds to the workplace, as studies show that more than half of the dissimilarities observed in the behavior and attitude of employees can be explained by their national culture. For businesses to run efficiently, it is very important that these operating differences are recognized and used to the business' advantage, rather than ignoring them, attempting to brush them under the rug, and letting them cause problems.

Cultural differences seem more prevalent among the executives of multinational organizations, which have more diversity in terms of nationality compared to organizations with most employees of the same nationality (Adler & Gunderson, 2008). The fact is that one cannot assume that executives working within the same organization should behave in the same way, given that every organization has its own unique cultural values. However, national culture cannot erase or diminish organizational culture. Hence, to reduce the likelihood of cross-cultural conflicts, one needs to accept the hard wiring of national culture much before an individual actually reaches their employment opportunities. Though organizations try to incorporate more global processes, systems, and policies to provide a more acceptable and familiar environment to their expatriates, the reality is that the national cultural values of individuals are not easily detached.

5.1 Understanding different work behaviors across cultures

Work behaviors across cultures are usually very different from one another. Depending upon the nature of the behavior under consideration, the influence of culture varies. National cultures have been observed to show a dominant effect on behavior, which puts more stress on moral values and consists of a robust social component. While professional culture looks to have a dominant effect on behavior, this shows more of an allegiance to task components and puts stress on competence values or practices. Work behaviors in Indian organizations show more signs of having the influence of national culture, while in North American organizations, professional culture is more on display.

5.2 Culture shock

Culture shock can be explained as the feeling of disorientation that one experiences when someone is removed from his or her familiar setting and culture to a foreign place with a noticeably different culture. While a feeling of fascination with one's new surroundings is common, adjusting to a foreign culture can cause practical issues in the workplace. For example, an American will find nothing wrong in choosing a watch as a perfect business gift, but if he chooses to gift this to his Chinese partners, it would not be received well as the watch, to them, represents death. It is very important for the individuals working in cross-cultural teams to absorb these shocks in the early stages of their respective tenures and learn the differences very quickly.

5.3 Stereotypes prevalent in the organizational context

According to the Oxford English Dictionary, a stereotype is "a widely held but fixed and oversimplified image or the idea of a particular type of person or thing." This meaning holds true in a business context, where a certain image, which may or may not be a true representation of reality, gets propagated. For example, although many steps are being taken by organizations to eliminate biases and stereotypes, it is a difficult task, and not many are successful. Even a country like the USA, where employees are from all around the world, is still not untouched by stereotypes. Some common stereotypes that are present are that British employees are uptight, Asians are hardworking, Americans are innovative, etc.

5.4 Managing a culturally diverse workforce

The flow of technological advancement and its impact on the workforce makes it imperative for management to seek suitable approaches for effectively managing culturally diverse personnel in the workplace. Managing diversity is crucial, as it represents unique characteristics that make individual differences. Cultural diversity further affects one's self-concept or identity and, consequently, one's perspective about others. So, managing a culturally diverse workforce requires a unique managerial style (Seymen, 2006). Diversity, on the one hand, has beneficial effects like enhancing the public image, better job satisfaction, and morale, as well as increased innovation and creativity by providing alternate solutions to a problem. On the other hand, diversity creates conflicts and tension, which increases accidental cost, training cost, turnover, and reduced productivity and performance. A multicultural and cross-cultural workforce in an organization and therefore requires training to facilitate integration and coherence to create a homogeneous workgroup. People of such a group are more likely to accept different views and opinions, and are open to change and diversity. This ultimately helps in reducing conflict and leads to a perceptible increase in job performance and productivity

5.5 Global organizations becoming more similar

There is a popular belief that with every passing year, with revolutionary technologies entering the businesses atmosphere, organizations are becoming more and more similar. This belief is equally correct and incorrect. When the emphasis is put on macro-level issues such as organizational structure, technology, and processes adopted and used, the organizations exhibit a lot of similarities. However, when the focus is shifted towards micro-level issues, especially dealing with employee behavior, organizations appear unique compared to one another. Strategies and organizational structures in India, Japan, and Switzerland may appear similar, but the employees working in them who are Indian, Japanese, and Swiss still continue to exhibit their own distinct cultural behavior.

6. Communicating across cultures

Cross-cultural communication is the process of sending and receiving messages between people belonging to different cultural backgrounds, which can lead to different interpretations of verbal as well as other forms of communication. The method of communication may be spoken words, written texts, or other forms of communicating, such as behavioral signs like gestures or facial expressions. In order to communicate across cultures, one-on-one conversations, meetings, telephone calls, documents, or emails, everything is available to use. In order to have successful communication, what is important is that the message delivered is understood and perceived the same way that it was intended to be.

6.1 Communication styles

How people communicate in different cultures can be explained by the concepts of high-context and low-context. The basic difference between them is determined by the extent to which the meaning of the communication is conveyed by using actual words used or implied by the context. If unspoken information is being transferred subtly or indirectly, this type of communication is classified as high-context. In places like Japan, Mexico, and the Middle East, emphasis is put on long-term relationships. In terms of communication, a lot is conveyed nonverbally in the form of gestures and facial expressions, and these places can be classified as high-context cultures. In low-context cultures, information exchange is predominantly preferred in the form of direct written or spoken words, and rarely is there a scope of implied meaning. In low-context cultures such as Germany and the USA, people provide the meaning explicitly in the message itself.

6.2 Non-verbal communication in different cultures of the world

Non-verbal communication comprises more than half of our communication. People exchange information in ways beyond words, and non-verbal cues add force to verbal messages by complementing or contradicting them. They can also substitute a verbal message entirely. For instance, a "yes" can be communicated simply by nodding one's head. The form of nonverbal communication, however, varies on the basis of the country and its culture, and similar non-verbal communications can have different meanings in different cultures. Therefore, it is especially essential for employers and employees to have some basic understanding of nonverbal cues in a foreign culture they may be working in. A high-context culture relies heavily on nonverbal elements of communication. On the contrary, a low-context culture will mostly utilize direct communication through words. Even though they are different, each culture type will have its own merits and thus should not be compared to another.

6.3 Cross-cultural misperception

If a boat is shown to a Sri Lankan and a German and asked about its use, it is very likely that one will get different answers. If a series of cards of cricket equipment and ice hockey is shown to Indians and Canadians, it is very likely that Indians will see and remember them all as cricket equipment, and Canadians will see and remember them as ice hockey equipment. It is the varied personal and cultural experiences of these people that make them perceive these things the way they do. This phenomenon of seeing the same things in different ways, is due to growing up in different cultural contexts. An understanding of forms of nonverbal communication is effective in an international profession. Eye contact is perceived as equality in North and Latin America, while Asian cultures avoid eye contact to demonstrate respect. Looking into an adult's eyes will be perceived as defiance in Ghana.

6.4 Cross-cultural misinterpretation

Assigning meaning to observations gives way to interpretation. The same observations can be associated with different meanings by people belonging to different cultures and countries. The difference between the observation and its assigned meaning in a certain context can lead to misinterpretation. A wink of an eye can be interpreted as rude by the Chinese, while the same gesture is very likely to be seen as a romantic or sexual invite by Latin Americans. Nigerians wink to hint at their children to leave the room. An "OK" sign conveys acceptability in the US but means "money" in Japan. French, Argentinian and Portuguese will interpret the symbol to signify zero or nil, and some Eastern European countries consider it to be the sign equivalent of a swear word.

6.5 Cross-cultural misevaluation

The universal expressions of anger, sadness, fear, disgust, surprise, and happiness can also be different in terms of the extent of their expression across cultures. Thus, when people from different cultures communicate, they can misevaluate each other and offend each other unintentionally. An American will react more aggressively to an accidental touch than a Japanese person. Latin Americans also prefer less personal space, and Indians won't mind sharing their own space with others.

7. Leveraging cultural diversity

There are many studies that support the assertion that one of the attributes of organizations that leads to higher profits is organizational diversity and the inclusion of employees who come from diverse cultures. Innovation and creativity are often linked to the diversity of experience and opinion that comes together when people from diverse cultural backgrounds exchange ideas with each other. Workforce diversity is considered a key driver of innovation and creativity of thought. This kind of creativity is not only necessary in order to create a long-term competitive advantage, but is also something that firms often struggle to achieve. It has been argued and established through studies that cultural diversity can become a true source of competitive advantage for organizations, as evidenced by increased profit, market share, and sales.

7.1 Managing conflicts

Conflicts are a natural element of organizational processes. Most conflicts in organizations are a matter of disagreement and thus should not be viewed as negative. If managed properly, conflicts can give rise to certain benefits. Conflicts can be appropriately handled to ensure good social relations between employees. A healthy approach to conflict management must include open communication and creative alternatives that ensure respect and mutual respect for both parties.

The reasons for conflicts change with each stage of team development. There is less conflict during the initial stages, since team members are trying to understand each other. During the stage when a team assigns roles for its members, the conflict is regarding their status and the team's operating rules. Task-oriented stages result in conflicts related to possible ways of performing tasks. The conflict level lowers at the final stages, since the focus is on implementing the already made decisions.

Conflict management, not resolution, is more appropriate as not all conflicts can be resolved. Identifying the source of conflict as healthy or unhealthy makes it easy to work on. Legitimate reasons can include the difference in expectations, objectives, and actions. Unhealthy sources are not related to tasks and spring for power, rewards, and goal competitiveness between individuals and groups. Personal grudges can also drive conflicts.

7.2 Approaches to handling conflict: Reactive vs. proactive approaches

A reactive approach involves reacting only after the problem has arisen. It lacks preplanning and might reflect an ignorant attitude of team leaders. This approach avoids the participation of employees to keep conflict at bay and reflects poor communication. The benefits of this approach are that it reflects good fire-fighting problem-solving skills of managers, but the conflict can get out of hand and grow into an insurmountable issue by the time it is identified. Moreover, a proactive approach prevents conflicts so that they don't arise and thus involves planning and preparing for conflicts. It will require developing approaches to identifying conflicts in their nascent stages and create space for the expression of disagreement so that problems don't go unaddressed. The most successful way in a proactive approach is creating an environment for safe communication. The issues with this approach are that it needs time and effort on the part of managers and leaders, and every conflict cannot be successfully averted in advance.

7.2.2 Confronting vs. avoidance approach

Aggressively approaching conflict with the hope of winning over the other party is a confronting approach. The side effect of this approach is that it prioritizes winning over making a balanced decision. The confrontation approach is high on assertiveness and low on cooperativeness. The avoidance approach is an attempt to ignore the problem and denying that there is an issue; team members just hope that the issue goes away by itself and not confront it. The avoidance approach is low on assertiveness as well as cooperativeness.

7.3 Optimization of conflicts

Conflicts are not always bad. An optimum level of conflict is required to get a different perspective on the same issue. Most of the time, we get so involved in our approach that it becomes difficult to appreciate or experiment with a new thought. Hence, it is very important to have better outcomes. Also, our environmental conditioning helps us to think differently. An individual's thought process is very much influenced by the beliefs, assumptions, and values a person carries from his/her family and society. X-culture provides a platform to students where there is a great diversity between their backgrounds, putting them in the position to try these various approaches.

7.4 Cultural invisibility

Cultural invisibility occurs when managers and organizations fail or refuse to see culture as a detriment to the day-to-day operations of an organization. The amplified version of this is known as cultural blindness, where the managers completely blind themselves to gender, race, and ethnicity. North American cultural norms often encourage such behavior. This approach causes problems by confusing the recognition of cultural differences with the judging of people by their differences, which are two very different things.

7.5 Cultural synergy

Through the management of cultural diversity in an organization, managers align its strategies, structure, and practices with the patterns of the cultural diversity of the employees and clients. Such an approach recognizes both the differences and the similarities between different cultures, which leads to the composition of a global organization that transcends the distinct cultures of its stakeholders. It is based on the principle that no one culture's way is inherently superior.

8. Discussion and conclusion

Cultures are characterized by different behaviors, communication styles, and norms; that is why it becomes very important to recognize these differences and have an awareness about them. Discouraging stereotyping is one of the ways to avoid conflicts. Stereotypes with negative connotations can lead to distorted expectations about behavior and misinterpretations, which can be expensive for an organization. To avoid cross-cultural misunderstandings, one should avoid using the lens of one's own culture to see others' behaviors, values, and beliefs. In order to eradicate this possibility of a biased view, it is important that resources are invested in learning about different cultures from a neutral point of view. This entails researching the customs and behaviors of different cultures and developing an appreciation for why people follow these unique customs and display such behaviors. It is clear that countries have unique cultures, but cultures vary among teams and organizations too. One should take the time to study the context and person, including the various cultures to which they belong – this can include the national culture, vocational culture, and a company's corporate culture. It is the responsibility of the organization and employees to promote the appreciation of cultural differences. Also, understanding the cultural context of other persons or organizations can be filled with opportunities to capitalize on different values, beliefs, priorities, and preferences. For global virtual teams, many channels such as online chat, email, intranet, and group chat could be used for conflict resolution, along with normal techniques such as negotiation, mediation, and facilitation, to name a few.

Maintaining a diverse workforce is harder than recruiting culturally diverse people. Identification and understanding of diversity are essential for making an appropriate strategy to sustain a culturally diverse work culture, where people appreciate and accept each other's different points of view and work coherently for the betterment of the organization. Additionally, a successful company that retains a culturally diverse workforce is likely to serve as a role model for others in the multicultural global market. In such an organization, all employees feel connected and worthy of the company, which not only grows the employee's self-esteem but also increases the commitment and loyalty of employees towards their organization.

References

Adler, N. J., & Gundersen, A. (2007). International dimensions of organizational behavior. Cengage Learning.

Amaram, D. I. (2007). Cultural diversity: Implications for workplace management. Journal of Diversity Management, 2(4), 1-6.

Bhadury, J., Mighty, E. J., & Damar, H. (2000). Maximizing workforce diversity in project teams: A network flow approach. Omega, 28(2), 143-153.

Chatman, J. A., & Barsade, S. G. (1995). Personality, organizational culture, and cooperation: Evidence from a business simulation. Administrative Science Quarterly, 40(3), 423-443.

Copeland, L. (1988). Making the Most OF Cultural Differences at the Workplace. Personnel, 66(6), 52-60.

Desanctis, G., & Monge, P. (1999). Introduction to the special issue: Communication processes for virtual organizations. Organization Science, 10(6), 693-703.

Jehn, K. A., & Mannix, E. A. (2001). The dynamic nature of conflict: A longitudinal study of intragroup conflict and group performance. Academy of Management Journal, 44(2), 238-251.

Kankanhalli, A., Tan, B. C., & Wei, K. K. (2006). Conflict and performance in global virtual teams. Journal of management information systems, 23(3), 237-274.

Pettigrew, A.M.(ed.), Whittington, R., Melin, L., Sanchez-Runde, C., Van den Bosch, F.A.J., Ruignok, W. and Numagami, T. (2003). Innovative forms of Organising, London: Sage Publications.

Pinkley, R. L. (1990). Dimensions of conflict frame: Disputant interpretations of conflict. Journal of applied psychology, 75(2), 117-126.

Rousseau, D.M. (1990). Assessing Organisational Culture: The Case for Multiple Methods. In Schneider, B. (Ed.), Organisational Climate and Culture, Oxford: JosseyBass.

Seymen, O. A. (2006). The cultural diversity phenomenon in organisations and different approaches for effective cultural diversity management: a literary review. Cross Cultural Management: An International Journal, 13(4), 296-315.

World Trade Statistical Review. (2018). Retrieved from https://www.wto.org/english/res_e/statis_e/wts2018_e/wts2018_e.pdf

CHAPTER 8

Focusing on Culture in X-Culture

Cross-Cultural Differences and Conflicts in Global Virtual Teams

DARIA PANINA, MAYS BUSINESS SCHOOL, TEXAS A&M UNIVERSITY

Introduction

Teams are common in all types of organizations. With the rise in globalization, culturally diverse teams are becoming increasingly common as well. Recent studies report that between 50% and 70% of all white-collar workers in OECD countries at least occasionally work on virtual collaboration projects (Jimenez et al., 2017). According to the 2018 Trends in High-Performing Global Virtual Teams (GVT) survey, 89% of corporate employees serve on at least one GVT. Of the 1,620 respondents from 90 countries, almost everyone reported being on a virtual team, and 88% of them stated that participation in GVTs was critical to their productivity (RW3 CultureWizard, 2018). Companies who use GVTs do it to improve productivity, minimize travel costs, and support the global nature of the projects, according to the survey by SHRM (Minton-Eversole, 2012). Although the use of GVTs by global businesses and organizations is commonplace, there are reports that at least half of such global virtual projects fail to meet their objectives due to the inability of team members to manage the complexities of the team processes (Jimenez et al., 2017). The biggest challenges identified by the participants of GVTs were interactions with team members who do not participate, timeliness and responsiveness in team interactions, and differing expectations for how to manage and how to be managed. Most of the problems that are cited in the surveys are caused by cultural misunderstandings and can be avoided.

Business schools are helping students to be prepared for the culturally diverse working environment. It is the priority of business schools to offer students opportunities to develop cross-cultural skills and competencies and learn to function in diverse teams. One possible teaching method that helps grow an appreciation for culture in teams is utilizing group-based experiential learning projects. Research shows that such projects represent an effective approach to teaching IB and cross-cultural competencies, as well as virtual collaboration skills (Gonzales-Perez et al., 2014).

Group experiential learning activities such as the X-Culture project are designed to give business students the opportunity to experience cross-cultural group processes and the nuances of virtual collaboration. Overall, students who participate in X-Culture have two assumptions. The first assumption is that all X-Culture participants are students who are taking similar classes, listen to similar music, wear similar clothes, and thus culture does not really matter. The second assumption is that millennials are born with communication technology, and it cannot possibly present any problems for them.

To their surprise, most of the students who participate in X-Culture run into problems while interacting with their teammates or completing the project virtually and have to find solutions to the wide variety of cultural and technological issues they face. This chapter summarizes the most commonly mentioned cultural challenges of GVT management and offers ways to overcome them, as identified by current research on GVTs and the experiences of students who participated in the X-Culture Project.

Cultural diversity in teams

Cultural diversity is often credited for better virtual team outcomes. Firstly, culturally diverse teams bring a wide range of ideas, skills, competencies, and worldviews to the table. They are not likely to dismiss a proposal as a consequence of groupthink. As a result, solutions provided by diverse teams are often more creative, analysis of the alternatives is more thorough, and first-hand country-specific knowledge is more comprehensive. However, research shows that diverse teams are infinitely more complex than homogenous ones. They often experience communication problems, such as misunderstandings and misinterpretations. It takes much longer for them to develop cohesiveness and reach a consensus. Diverse teams often need to spend a lot of time and effort on actively managing group processes to accommodate different cultural norms. Stereotyping sometimes makes work in diverse teams complicated. Additionally, diverse teams have difficulties developing trust, which is essential to smooth team functioning (Lowry et al., 2010). Teamwork expectations, such as team roles and their relations, distribution of work, and control processes, differ depending on the culture as well (Hinds et al., 2011). Cultural misunderstandings and subsequent conflicts were shown to have a negative impact not just on people who are directly involved in them, but other team members as well. Cultural disharmony of any kind signals to the group that beliefs and ideas from different cultures are incompatible. This in turn, disrupts group performance and has an especially detrimental impact on creativity (Chua, 2013). Therefore, it is essential that culturally diverse teams should pay attention to culture if they want to succeed.

Global teams operate virtually and have to deal with issues associated with the appropriate use of technology to facilitate team processes. However, attitudes towards technology use are culturally determined as well. Communication technology differs in the richness of communication it allows. Face-to-face communication is considered to be the richest media of communication, followed by videoconferencing, phone calls, emails, chat, and texts, which are considered to be leaner communication methods. Needless to say, lean communication media often makes it even more difficult to create a well-functioning team. When team members have never met face-to-face, never heard each other's voices, and know little about each other, the development of trust, a necessary condition for efficient team processes, is tricky. At the same time, lean media was reported to have a positive impact on some aspects of team performance. For example, member characteristics, such as age, gender, and status are less visible in virtual communications, and thus stereotyping becomes less of a problem. Additionally, the use of written communication levels the playing field for team members who have accents, or who do not speak English fluently.

Overall, academic research suggests that global virtual teams may achieve superior performance compared to homogenous teams. Yet, to achieve these results, they should rely on the active management of cultural diversity and virtual components of team functioning.

Common cultural misunderstandings and ways to deal with them

Research has identified the best practices of global virtual team building (Berry, 2011; Gibson et al., 2014). To simplify team interactions and avoid misunderstandings, teams are advised to agree on the following before work begins: (Daim et al., 2012; Nydegger and Nydegger, 2010).

- A face-to-face (FtF) team-building activity at the start of the project is essential for building team spirit

- Understanding technology that will be used by the team is a must for all team members and training should be provided if necessary.
- Early on, the team should create explicit start-up norms and expectations for all team members:
  - Decide what to do if a team member fails to contribute
  - Agree what to do if a team member thinks he/she is misunderstood or if he/she does not understand the message.
- Establishing easy, regular and frequent communication is essential. For this purpose, team members have to:
  - Establish regular team meeting schedule
  - Establish a timeline for responses
  - Establish and respect deadlines
  - Agree to clearly acknowledge receipt of other people's messages
  - Be explicit about their activities and thoughts
- Creating psychologically safe communication climate by being accessible, asking input, encouraging team members to communicate in a constructive manner goes long way to establishing trust. To this end, teams should:
  - Agree on what behaviors are and are not allowed
  - Be inclusive (e.g., addressing all messages to all team members)

These suggestions are aimed at creating positive attitudes among team members. They help them come to an agreement about team processes, their responsibilities, and how to foster an atmosphere of trust that helps teams to resolve problems and conflicts that arise in the process of working on the project. Below are some common challenges that members of GVTs mention, as well as the ways to deal with them. Most of these challenges have cultural explanations, which are discussed below. It should be noted that in most cases, these challenges can be mitigated, if not avoided, by following the team-building suggestions mentioned above.

Work-related attitudes and behaviors

An often-cited problem in GVTs is a lack of initiative or participation of some members. It is sometimes explained by the fact that people from high power distance and collectivistic countries, such as India or Taiwan, are more accustomed to receiving explicit requests from team leaders. Research shows that team members from collectivistic and high power distance countries find it difficult to adapt to new teams, unlike people from individualist cultures such as Australia, where membership in groups is more transient and calculated. Collectivist team members also have difficulty taking on leadership and accepting changing leadership, which is also consistent with their high power distance (Harrison, 2000). They are less active in group discussions, and they tend to agree with the suggestions of other team members more. An American student once commented that she often starts team discussions because no one else says anything. Right after she offers her opinion, the rest of the team immediately says that it's perfect; nobody ever criticizes her suggestions or contributes any alternatives. As one of the solutions to this problem, an attempt was made to create a shared document where every member had to contribute ideas anonymously. When soliciting the opinions of other team members, the student tried to use open-ended questions and non-evaluative statements. When it did not work, another explanation was considered. The student noticed that when the whole group "agrees" with her, she ends up writing the section of the report, since it was her idea. Once this option was considered, the student changed the tactics with the permission of the instructor and refrained from contributing during the following week, telling her group that she has a difficult exam and she will not be able to contribute to group work as much as before. Contributions from other members followed. This example suggests that sometimes multiple explanations to team members' behavior have to be considered.

Another issue often raised in GVTs is the importance of the project to some team members. It was noticed that people from masculine and individualist cultures are more focused on the project than members from feminine or collectivistic cultures, who are more concerned with group processes. The solution to this problem suggests a recalibration of expectations for both groups. For successful team functioning, both types of behaviors are important. While collectivists tend to have more favorable attitudes towards team processes such as trust, interdependence, communication and information sharing (Mockaitis et al., 2012), individualists are more task-focused and motivated by personal rewards. Research suggests that both excessive and minimal task focus in GVTs are equally harmful. Although minimal attention to the task at hand has an obvious negative impact on team performance, some non-task-related interactions are necessary (Shollen and Brunner, 2016). The beliefs of team members about the relative importance of work and non-work activities and behaviors need to be discussed during the team formation stage. As one possible suggestion, it was proposed that all team members should agree at the beginning of the project to reserve some time for group maintenance issues, and some time should be devoted purely to project-related interactions. Non-work-related communication can become a source of team conflicts, and people from collectivistic cultures tend to spend a lot of time and effort on non-project-related communication. During a recent X-Culture project, one of the U.S. students contacted his instructor, complaining that he will have to drop out of the project. When asked to elaborate, he explained that his team is getting along very well. They chat and text each other all the time. They discuss who eats what for breakfast, what classes they are taking, the weather, one of the team member's' new puppy, and so on. The student's frustration was palpable: he just wanted to get the project done, and get a good grade. His instructor had to help the student realize that people from collectivistic cultures spend a lot of time on relationship building needed for team trust, and non-task interactions are usually a big part of that. The student who got frustrated with the "small talk" of his teammates had to frame the experience as something broader than just completing the report. In the end, the U.S. student had to adjust his behavior to better fit into the group; reminding him about the part of his grade that was based on evaluations by his team members did the trick.

Another work-related topic discussed in GVTs is social loafing. Social loafing or free riding refers to situations when individuals extend less effort on team tasks than they do on individual tasks, unless their contribution can be identified and evaluated. Research suggests that social loafing is more common among team members from individualistic cultures. There are multiple causes for individual underperformance in GVTs (Furumo, 2009). While active team members usually report feeling trust and team cohesion, less active students tend to have less favorable team experiences. They either engage in social loafing or completely withdraw from the team. A possible explanation is in the level of involvement and identification with the project, as well as their individual ability to deal with conflict. When students are less involved in teamwork and experience conflict, they feel less motivated to contribute to the group project and engage in social loafing. Social loafing behaviors further increase when individual performance is difficult to identify. A suggestion for managing team processes would be to improve the team oversight of individual members and resolve conflicts as they arise. Individual responsibility for a particular part of the project can usually prevent social loafing. To ensure that social loafing will not affect the team's performance, it is advisable to make a couple of individuals responsible for every part of the project. The likelihood that each milestone will be met is then higher because if one person is not able to deliver, there is a backup. Setting up rules about what happens if a team member does not do his/her part was already mentioned as an important step in team formation. Good communication between all team members throughout the project is the key, and designing collaboration processes to minimize social loafing by making individual contributions easily identifiable is important (Zhang et al., 2011).

Holidays and time off is another issue many GVTs try to navigate. Some team members assume that holidays and breaks in other countries happen during similar times as theirs. Poor initial communication as to when some team members will not be available causes these problems. One of the U.S. students was fuming about the behavior of her Brazilian teammate, who disappeared from the project during Carnival week. Her main complaint was that the spring break is coming up, and no work will be done then. When asked if she told her teammates that she would not be available during spring break, she realized that it never occurred to her – probably as it did not occur to her Brazilian teammate to remind the rest of the team about Carnival.

Power relationships in teams

Instead of relying on hierarchical relationships prevalent in some organizational teams, many GVTs rely on peer-to peer interactions, which may cause ambiguity in expectations around the member roles and goals, weak leadership, competing lines of authority and poor delegation (Daim et al., 2012). To prevent this, ownership should be clearly and explicitly communicated, delegation communicated in advance, and intended results and outcomes clarified (DeRosa, 2009).

It was noticed that high power distance orientation may have a negative impact on team performance. Team leaders from high power distance cultures are less likely to assume cooperative stances towards other team members. In one of the X-Culture groups, a South Korean student who believed himself to be the team leader came up with his vision of the strategy for the client company. The rest of the team discussed his proposal, and it was decided that a different strategy that a majority of team members agreed with would be the team solution. Once the work was complete and the team submitted their report, the student in question went back, deleted the team report and substituted it with his original one. Such "authoritarian" behavior may not always be counterproductive: In another team, a student from France was determined to produce the best X-Culture report possible. She made sure that all her team would submit their work to her two days before each deadline. The team decided that it was easier to comply than to argue, and the report indeed was very good. However, the student responsible for team success received very negative feedback from her teammates.

Another cultural characteristic that has an impact on power relationships in a team is individualism/collectivism. Some studies have suggested that although managers worldwide use the directive as well as supportive behaviors towards their teams, managers from individualistic countries exhibit less of both behaviors compared with their colleagues from collectivist countries (Wendt et al., 2009). This means that individualists prefer to have a less hands-on approach to leadership than collectivists. The implication of this finding is that, to individualist team members, the more involved approach of collectivistic leaders might appear as too controlling, while collectivistic team members will perceive the less-involved approach of individualist leaders as lacking in authority or compassion. As a solution to these issues, joint decision-making processes should be encouraged to make sure all voices on the team are heard.

Face saving strategies

One of the common problems, widely recorded in communication with team members from Asian cultures, is saying yes when they mean no (Lockwood, 2015). In the situation when they do not understand the instructions of a team leader or request of a team member, they tend to agree out of fear of losing face, even though they do not know what specifically they agreed to. To resolve this issue, more nuanced communication is necessary. Instead of asking the teammate if he/she understood or is in agreement with the team decision, it is a good practice to ask the person to summarize what he or she will be doing or show them the example of what needs to be done. Wadsworth and Blanchard (2015) mentioned that providing examples of what the final product should look like was successful in reducing ambiguity and ensuring that the request was understood were. If a team member asks another to do something and provides an example of what the product should look like by screen sharing or email of the template, it reduces ambiguity and helps the person who has to accomplish the task to know exactly what's needed.

Language proficiency

Many English-speaking students complain about the language skills of some of their team members. Although all students participating in X-Culture have to confirm that they can speak English fluently, most of them overestimate their skills. Some students even use Google Translate in their everyday communications and team reports. Plagiarism seems to be at least partially related to this issue, since many non-English-speaking students feel that it is better to copy and paste someone else's work, not because they do not want to do their own, but because it sounds better. English-speaking students usually end up doing most of the editorial work on the reports, which is an issue that should be discussed at the beginning of the project when the team decides how to divide responsibilities.

Perhaps more importantly, language proficiency was found to be correlated with perceptions of power in team dynamics. Language proficiency can be a very divisive subject in virtual teams (Cohen and Kassis-Henderson, 2017). It can be used for self and other categorization and can lead to either status enhancement or marginalization of a team member (Lockwood, 2015). The asymmetries in common language fluency can contribute to "us versus them" dynamics and be detrimental to the formation of trust in global virtual teams. Language in global teams serves as a tool that empowers team members who are fluent in the common language, and disenfranchises those who are not. Team members who are fluent in English are likely to dominate the discussion and feel more confident in team communications. Language proficiency largely determines who contributes information to the team and who participates in decision-making more.

The use of acronyms, buzzwords, and slang is often discussed in cross-cultural communication literature as a cause of many misunderstandings within diverse teams, even among team members who know the language. Although students are reminded about it before the project, mistakes still sometimes happen. One U.S. student, who is a hard worker and a straight-A student, had the following experience in her X-Culture project. She was placed on a team of several Hispanic students, along with one more U.S. student from another university. The team reached the decision that she would be doing research on the market that their company should enter. After some discussion, the team settled on the EU. For the American student the fact that she was assigned to research the EU market sounded counterintuitive, because there was a Spanish student who probably knew a lot more about the E.U., but she decided to be a good team player and did the research. At a later point in time, she presented her thorough research of the European market to her team, and was told that her teammates that what they meant by the E.U. was Estados Unidos—the U.S.! Fortunately, the team had time to fix the problem. Overall, though, the story suggests that acronyms and other words we take for granted must be checked and double-checked and preferably not used at all. As a solution to the problem, careful encoding and decoding of information should be emphasized; students should remember to summarize what's being said, restate the points others made, and ask further questions when in doubt.

Another solution lies in relying more on written communication. Some research found that, although language proficiency differences lead to social categorization in verbal media (such as the telephone and Skype), they are not that prevalent in teams who use written media, such as email (Klitmoller et al., 2013). Written media allows students less proficient in English time to process information from others and prepare higher-quality contributions of their own. Thus, communicating in writing leads to better group dynamics high better quality of the group project. Misunderstandings related to written communication may also happen. The use of emojis, capitalization, and other means to enhance or emphasize the message or some of its parts is often misinterpreted cross-culturally. One of the U.S. students was very upset at her teammate and complained that she was constantly yelled at. When asked to explain, she proceeded to show email and text messages from her teammate where some words were capitalized, which she interpreted as yelling. It took a brief Skype session between the two to set the record straight—in fact, the other student was very shy and non-confrontational. He was capitalizing some words to make sure the main words in his message come across clearly.

Understanding of time

Culture has an impact on a variety of behaviors related to time, such as the importance of punctuality, the relationship between tasks and social time, the focus on the clock or event time, fast and slow paces of living and working, and the symbolic meaning of time, among others (Brislin and Kim, 2003). All time-related beliefs and norms have positive as well as negative aspects. For example, a fast pace of time has a positive impact on economic productivity but a negative impact on human health. An emphasis on social time has a negative impact on productivity but a positive impact on network development and group cohesiveness. The creation of time awareness norms in groups were found to mediate the effect of work planning on group performance (Janicik and Bartel, 2003). Explicit temporal planning helps groups coordinate their activities and complete their tasks more effectively. Temporal planning refers to group discussions about when certain actions will occur, how much time they will take, and other time-related considerations. Such discussions help form group norms and avoid a lot of misunderstandings. For example, the promptness of responses to teammates' requests was attributed to cultural differences (Holtbrugge et al., 2012). It appears to be an important issue in many X-Culture teams where people from more punctual countries (like the U.S.A.) complain about last-minute submissions done by their colleagues from less punctual countries (such as Brazil). The issue may be resolved by establishing a timeline for response (Daim et al., 2012). For example, in some X-Culture teams, the deadline for group member work submission is a couple of days before the due date so that the person in charge of the submission has time to receive all input and submit it on time.

Conflict resolution

Research suggests that out of the five conflict management approaches (avoidance, accommodation, competition, collaboration, and compromise), group performance is most positively affected by collaborative conflict management tactics (Chang & Lee, 2013). People with collectivistic orientations were found to utilize collaborative conflict management styles more often. On the other hand, Paul and colleagues (2004) have found that the higher the individualistic orientation in a virtual team, the less likely collaborative conflict management was to be used. The virtual teams with individualists tend to have a low tendency to pursue group interests unless their group interest matched self-interest. These teams were also less likely to resolve conflicts.

Conflict avoidance in diverse GVTs is also common. Team members who form collectivist cultures sometimes do not give accurate feedback to underperforming members. It is observed that on some teams, all members get the highest grade from their peers, no matter how much they contribute. The opposite is also true: in some X-Culture groups, students have been confronted by their teammates for trying to evaluate their contributions objectively. In one team, a person from a collectivistic culture demanded that as friends and teammates, they should support each other by giving everyone high participation grades. Although this behavior might help to build team spirit, it helps little with objective feedback of everyone's work. As mentioned earlier, successful teams usually have discussions before the project starts as to what the consequences are for not doing one's share of work. If collectivism is the cause of the problem, and some team members feel uncomfortable evaluating others harshly, an appeal can be made to other students to collaborate for the benefit of the whole team.

Another example of conflict avoidance is a situation where a team member stays quiet during the group discussion out of a desire not to contradict other team members. In this case, the team might address a quiet member of the team, but the invitation to contribute should use a more specific request. For example, White (2014) suggests that instead of asking if the person has anything to say, the question should ask specifically about previous relevant experience or knowledge the person may have. Of course, the problem with this approach is that the team members should know each other fairly well, which often is not the case in GVTs.

Cultural differences in decision-making

The decision-making process is often described in 5 sequential steps: problem recognition, information search, construction of alternatives, choice, and implementation (Adler, 1997). Situations where several people are involved in decision-making, are called distributed decision-making. When the decision-makers come from different cultures and have different assumptions about the ways, the decision-making process should be handled, reaching a team decision is challenging. Global virtual teams often experience difficulties with distributed decision-making processes and activities and struggle with problem identification, proposal making, and formulation of solutions (Zakaria, 2017).

GVT members differ on the level and form of their participation in group discussions that are aimed at construction alternatives and choosing between them. While participants from low-context cultures, such as Germany or the U.K., make proposals using a direct approach and question the proposals of others using more aggressive tones, high-context participants from countries like China question the strategy by concealing their intentions and seeking approval from others. Low-context participants make proposals based in their personal opinions and demand actions be taken, which reflects their task-oriented culture. They do not hesitate to reveal their views on the matter and identify issues and people with whom they disagree. This might be perceived as a very insensitive approach, but it's also straightforward; such proposals, clear, direct, and detailed, often generate positive responses and are easy to work with. People from high-context cultures tend to use lengthy high-context messages; their intentions and attitudes are harder to read, yet they often explain their position in a tactful manner. High-context participants present their opinions in a courteous and appreciative way, and may also achieve positive outcomes, although it will take them a little longer, which may irritate their low-context colleagues.

Team members from high uncertainty avoidance cultures (such as Japan) may have a different opinion on problem definitions and the types of alternatives that are being considered. Team members from collectivist cultures, on the other hand, might not be comfortable with making decisions individually and would much rather achieve consensus within the group first. Group members from collectivistic cultures where harmony is important might not want to share ideas that make them stand out from the group or are contrary to what other group members proposed. Group members from high power distance cultures may be reluctant to contradict the group leader. Although these differences do exist, they can be managed with proper communication within a team.

Cascio and Shurygailo (2003) suggest that an initial face-to-face meeting of the team members can be an important first step in making all group members agree to explicit roles, responsibilities, deliverables, and group processes, such as communication mechanisms, conflict resolution, etc. The first meeting is essential in helping team members not only become clear on some basic facts about each other's background but also their assumptions about the project, processes, working style, and motivation. Special attention should be placed on developing trust in the team, and positive interaction at the beginning of the project is the essential first step in this direction. The initial social interaction should be followed up by the establishment of the team's processes and norms. Trust is established by repeatedly delivering results that meet the expectations of teammates. It is essential that interactions are positive; therefore, the team has to agree on what the team members should do if they are not able to deliver on their promises. If team members know the process that should be followed in case they are not able to do what they agreed to, they will be more likely to communicate this to their team and work with the team on an alternative solution. Needless to say, the team has to have a norm that reinforces positive interaction without shaming underperforming team members. If this process is followed, the team will be able to manage the decision-making process in a collegial way, no matter their beliefs about the form different stages of the process should take.

Technology preferences and use

Research suggests that technology has had a generally positive impact on global virtual teams' communication and decision-making (Shachaf, 2008). Lean media, such as email and texting, decreases our ability to see nonverbal and social cues, and reduces verbal miscommunications due to cultural diversity, accents, and language proficiency. Non-English speakers are able to express themselves better through written communication. Culturally diverse teams were found to prefer written forms of communication such as email over more direct and "rich" communication media such as teleconferencing, Zoom or Skype because they decreased the "noise" in cross-cultural communication. This typically has a positive impact on team performance. For example, in some studies, the performance of diverse virtual teams was found to be superior to the performance of diverse face-to-face teams. Thus, the reductive capabilities of technology are beneficial for culturally diverse teams' processes and performance (Staples and Zhao, 2006).

Some studies showed that people from different cultures use communication technology differently. For example, people from low power distance cultures, such as Sweden or the U.S.A., tend to use communication technology to enhance the information access of team members. People from China and France, high power distance cultures, were found to use the same IT to monitor, record, and control the performance of team members, rather than to support collaboration (Hinds et al., 2011). Common agreed-upon rules of team interactions usually alleviate these differences, at least to some extent.

Patchy internet connections in some countries and preferences regarding the use of particular social media apps complicate matters in some cases. However, X-Culture students are usually very good at selecting options that are equally available and accessible to all their team members and teaching each other the technology they plan to use, if necessary.

Conclusion

Cultural problems in GVTs are numerous and vary on a case-to-case basis, as no two situations are exactly alike. One of the learning opportunities in X-Culture is the opportunity to identify cultural phenomena that affects the behaviors of people and develop personal strategies for dealing with these behaviors. Students should be reminded about the basic principles of managing culture in GVTs, which are building trust, open communication, active listening, slowing down, and political and religious restraint. This does not mean that the communications between team members should be "nice" at any cost, and negative emotions should not necessarily be suppressed. The positive impact of voicing frustration is that it signals to the team that something is not working, that the team faces challenges and needs to focus effort on overcoming them. As a consequence of bonding over the frustrating situation, teams should be able to discuss the common vision for the outcome of the project and team processes. If the team members do not share negative emotions, it will take them longer to figure things out. Respectful sharing of negative emotions builds the common feeling that the team is in it together, and everyone feels passionate about the project. The expression of negative emotions that should be avoided is interpersonal attacks when negative emotions are targeting individual group members (Ayoko et al., 2012). Disagreements are normal in any group; it's how to handle them that matters. Culturally, the intelligent model of collaboration (Janssens & Brett, 2006) states that global teams consist of culturally diverse members who have different assumptions about how to manage relationships and how to make and execute decisions. The main idea behind this approach is to create structural elements in GVTs that will not facilitate cultural consensus or integration but rather ensure the recognition that group members may not have the same beliefs or goals in life but still can contribute to the group project. Thus, "the challenge than in developing collaboration within global teams is not the development of and conformity to a homogenous team culture but the construction of a team culture that recognizes the differences among team members and allows them to coexist or to fuse" (Jannsens & Brett, 2006, p. 132).

References

Adler, N.J. (1997). International Dimensions of Organizational Behavior, 3rd ed. Cincinnati OH: South-Western.

Berry, G.R. (2011). Enhancing effectiveness on virtual teams. Understanding why traditional team skills are insufficient. Journal of Business Communication, v.48(2), pp.186–206.

Brislin, R.W., and Kim, E.S. (2003). Cultural diversity in people's understanding and uses of time. Applied Psychology: An International Review, v. 52(3), 363–382.

Cascio, W.F., and Shurygailo, S. (2003). E-Leadership and virtual teams. Organizational Dynamics, v. 31(4), pp. 362–376.

Chang, W.-L., and Lee, C.-Y. (2013). Virtual team e-leadership: The effects of leadership style and conflict management mode on the online learning performance of students in a business-planning course. British Journal of Educational Technology, v. 44(6), pp. 986–999.

Chua, R.Y.J. (2013). The costs of ambient cultural disharmony: Indirect intercultural conflicts in social environment undermine creativity. Academy of Management Journal, v.56(6), pp. 1545–1577.

Cohen, L., and Kassis-Henderson, J. (2017). Revisiting culture and language in global management teams: Toward a multilingual turn. International Journal of Cross Cultural Management, v. 17(1), pp. 7–22.

Crisp, B., and Jarvenpaa, S.L. (2013). Swift trust in global virtual teams. Trusting beliefs and normative actions. Journal of Personnel Psychology, v.12(1), pp. 45–56.

Daim, T.U., Ha, A., Reutiman, S., Hughes, B., Pathak, U., Bynum, W., and Bhatla, A. (2012). Exploring the communication breakdown in global virtual teams. International Journal of Project Management, v.30(2), pp. 199–212.

DeRosa, D. (2009). Virtual success. The keys to effectiveness in leading from a distance. Leadership in Action, v. 28(6), pp. 9–11.

Furumo, K. (2009). The impact of conflict and conflict management style on deadbeats and deserters in virtual teams. Journal of Computer Information Systems, Summer, pp. 66–73.

Gibson, C.B., Huang, L., Kirkman, B.L., and Shapiro, D.L. (2014). Where global and virtual meet: The value of examining the intersection of these elements in twenty-first-century teams. Annual Review of Organizational Psychology and Organizational Behavior, v.1, pp. 217–244.

Gonzales-Perez, M.A., Velez-Calle A., Cathro, V., Caprar, D.V., and Taras, V. (2014). Virtual teams and international business teaching and learning: The case of the global enterprise experience (GEE). Journal of Teaching in International Business, v. 25, pp. 200–213.

Harrison, G.L. (2000). Cultural influences on adaptation to fluid workgroups and teams. Journal of International Business Studies, v. 31(3), pp. 489–505.

Hinds, P., Liu, L., and Lyon, J. (2011). Putting the global in global work: An intercultural lens on the practice of cross-national collaboration. The Academy of Management Annals, v. 5(1), pp. 135–188.

Holtbrugge, D., Weldon, A., and Rogers, H. (2012). Cultural determinants of email communication styles. International Journal of Cross Cultural Management, v. 13(1), pp. 89–110.

Janicik, G.A., and Bartel, C.A. (2003). Talking about time: Effects of temporal planning and time awareness norms on group coordination and performance. Group Dynamics: Theory, Research and Practice v. 7(2), pp. 122–134.

Jimenez, A,., Boehe, D.M., Taras, V., and Caprar, D.V. (2017). Working across boundaries: Current and future perspectives on global virtual teams. Journal of International Management, v. 23, pp. 341–349.

Janssens, M., and Brett, J.M. (2006). Cultural intelligence in global teams. Group & Organizational Management, v.31(1), pp. 124–153.

Kelley, E., and Kellloway, E.K. (2012). Context matters: Testing a model of remote leadership. Journal of Leadership and Organizational Studies, v. 19(4), pp. 437–449.

Klitmøller, A., Schneider, S. and Jonsen, K. (2015), "Speaking of global virtual teams: language differences, social categorization and media choice", Personnel Review, Vol. 44 No. 2, pp. 270–285

Lockwood, J. (2015). Virtual team management: What is causing communication breakdown? Language and Intercultural Communication, v. 15(1), pp. 125–140.

Lowry, P.B., Zhang, D., Zhou, L., and Fu, X. (2010). Effects of culture, social presence, and group composition on trust in technology-supported decision-making groups. Info Systems Jounral, v. 20, pp. 297–315.

Lowry, P.B., Schuetzler, R.M., Giboney, J.S., and Gregory, T.A. (2015). Is trust always better than distrust? The potential value of distrust in newer virtual teams engaged in short-term decision-making. Group Decision & Negotiation, v.24, pp.723–752.

McLarnon, M.J.W., Taras, V., Donia, M.B.L., O'Neill, T.A., Law, D., and Steel, P. (2019). Global virtual team communication, coordination, and performance across three peer feedback strategies. Canadian Journal of Behavioral Science, v. 51(4), pp. 207–218.

Minton-Eversole, T. (2012). Virtual teams used most by global organizations, survey says. Found at: https://www.shrm.org/about-shrm/press-room/press-releases/pages/virtualteamspoll.aspx.

Mockaitis, A., Rose, E., and Zettinig, P. (2012). The power of individual cultural values in global virtual teams. International Journal of Cross Cultural Management, v. 12(2), pp. 193–210.

Nydegger, R., and Nydegger, L. (2010). Challenges in managing virtual teams. Journal of Business and Economics Research, v. 8(3), pp. 69–82.

Paul, S., Samarah, I.M., Seetharaman, P., and Mykytyn, P.P. (2004). An empirical investigation of collaborative conflict management style in group support system-based global virtual teams. Journal of Management Information Systems, v.21(3), pp. 185–222.

RW3 CultureWizard (2018). Global virtual teams are falling short of their potential. PR Newswire. New York, May 24. Found at: https://www.prnewswire.com/news-releases/global-virtual-teams-are-falling-short-of-their-potential-300654333.html.

Shachaf, P. (2008). Cultural diversity and information and communication technology impacts on global virtual teams: An exploratory study. Information and Management, v. 45(2), pp. 131–142.

Shollen, S.L., and Brunner, C.C. (2014). Virtually anonymous: Does the absence of social cues alter perceptions of emrgent leader behaviors? Leadership, v. 12(2), pp. 198–229.

Staples, D.S., and Zhao, L. (2006). The effects of cultural diversity in virtual teams versus face-to-face teams. Group Decision and Negotiation, v.15, pp. 389–406.

Wadsworth, M.B., and Blanchard, A. L. (2015). Influence tactics in virtual teams. Computers in Human Behavior, v.44, pp. 386–393.

Wendt, H., Euwema, M.C., and Emmerik, I.J.H. (2009). Leadership and team cohesiveness across cultures. The Leadership Quarterly, v.20, pp. 358–370.

White, M. (2014). The management of virtual teams and virtual meetings. Business Information Review, v. 31(2), pp. 111–117.

Zakaria, N. (2017). Culture matters. Decision-making in global virtual teams. CRC Press, Taylor & Francis Group, Boca Raton, FL.

Zander, L., Zettinig, P., and Makela, K. (2013). Leading global virtual teams to success. Organizational Dynamics, v. 42(3), pp. 228–237.

Zhang, L., Chen, F., and Latimer, J. (2011). Managing virtual team performance: An exploratory study of social loafing and social comparison. Journal of International Technology and Information Management, v. 20(1), pp. 103–119.

CHAPTER 9

Intercultural Challenges in Virtual Teams

ROBERT WARMENHOVEN, HAN UNIVERSITY OF APPLIED SCIENCE
FLORETIN POPESCU, HAN UNIVERSITY OF APPLIED SCIENCES

Introduction

Intercultural challenges are one of the most mentioned problems by people working with other people in a Global Virtual Team (henceforth GVT). In recent years, there has been an increasing interest in the issues that people, including staff and students, face while working in a GVT (Popescu and Warmenhoven, 2018). However, little attention has been paid to how to deal with these challenges in a practical way. Furthermore, there is a need for some training exercises to self-develop intercultural skills. This chapter intends to introduce some useful tools that might benefit teams to mitigate the challenges of working in cross-cultural teams.

The chapter is organized in the following way: the first section starts with an explanation of the cultural map introduced by Erin Meyer. This cultural map can be applied as a tool to learn more about intercultural differences within a GVT. The second section attempts to stimulate group dialogue using a group assignment that can be used in a GVT. The third section is concerned with an exploration of the intercultural sensitivity model of the American interculturalist Milton Bennet (2002). Bennet suggests that the development of intercultural sensitivity is not static, but a dynamic process divided into six stages, starting from a denial stage and ending with a certain level of intercultural competence. The final section comprises several assignments to enhance cross-cultural awareness and to speed up GVT team development.

The Better Son

An excellent way to introduce the complexity of intercultural challenges in virtual teams is to elaborate on the following anecdote to a group of virtual team members.

"A father living somewhere in the Atlas Mountains region in Northern Africa is sitting with his friends and are enjoying a relaxing moment in the living room. After some time, they are getting thirsty, so when the oldest son walks into the living room, the dad asks his son to get some water for him and his friends. Unfortunately, the son is in a hurry and tells his dad he is about to leave to go to the university because he has an oral-exam that he cannot miss. So he refuses to get water for his dad. Moments later, the second son walks in the living room. The dad asks the same question, can you get us some water? The second son responds positively and tells his dad that he will get them some water. He walks into the kitchen, but silently slips away via the backdoor to play soccer with his friends" (source unknown).

Who is the better son? Depending on your cultural background, you might say the first son, and you will disagree with people that state that son number two is the better son. This anecdote always leads to confusion and disagreement between people; they cannot agree with which son is the better son, because of their own cultural bias.

The main issue in this anecdote is that two values are contradicting: being honest versus showing respect. In some cultures, being honest is an essential trait, which is the opposite of other cultures, where showing respect to, in this case, your dad is of utmost importance. That you leave your dad thirsty is of secondary importance. Students who are at one side of this discussion don't understand the viewpoint of the other side; they are puzzled about the claim that the other son is the better son, and the debate about who is the better son always leads to a lively experience. It can be assumed that people that work in a global virtual team experience the same type of clash of cultural values, and therefore, working in global virtual teams is a challenge.

Intercultural problems while working in a Global Virtual Team

Numerous studies deal with cross-cultural communication problems while working in a Global Virtual Team. However, few writers have been able to able to come up with practical tools for dealing with the specific intercultural issues that people face every day while working with team members that are located all across the world. Below are two remarks made by students that participated in X-Culture. The students in question experienced difficulties with team members with different cultural backgrounds.

"Tim (from the Netherlands) and Andrew (from the UK) work together in a GVT on the task of writing an international business plan. Tim just finished reading the market selection part created by Andrew and is giving him feedback. In the Netherlands, it is highly valued if you are honest in your feedback, so he tells Andrew straight away that the introduction part is weak and that the market selection is incomplete and not done properly. Andrew becomes more and more silent during the conversation. At a certain moment, Andrew is irritated by the lack of respect shown by Tim and thinks Tim's behavior is arrogant. Andrew takes the feedback very personally and has the opinion that Tim does not like him. In the weeks to come, working together feels awkward."

"Anja (from Germany) participates in a global virtual student team (GVST) with students from Peru and Mexico. Progress is going fine, although according to Anja, the Skype meetings take too much time, and she is not happy with the lack of efficiency during these meetings. Pablo from Peru wants to start every Skype meeting with at least 20 minutes of small talk. Anja does not see the importance of small talk; some chit-chat for a couple of minutes is merely acceptable. She wants to talk about the coming deadlines as soon as possible, so she is pushing the others to get to the point straight away. After a couple of weeks, she notices that she is always the person complaining about the deadlines during Skype conversations and feels she became the "mother" of her team, always pressing others to start working. For Anja, working together in a virtual team is a terrible experience."

The names of the students have been changed to guarantee anonymity.

Tool 1: Reflection moment: "What was the issue?"

Think about your own experience working in a Global Virtual Team, or, if you have no prior experience, think about a situation where you had to deal with people from a different cultural background and reflect on the following questions:

1. What was the situation like, what happened? (Briefly set the scene, i.e. where and when)
2. What was your task, what was the aim, and what was your role?
3. What were the activities you had to arrange to complete the task
4. What was the final result? (Positive – Negative effect)
5. How well did you perform during the situation (give a grade 1(low) – 10 (high) to express your performance.
6. Were you able to connect with the other team members? (build rapport) (give a grade 1(low) – 10 (high) to express if you were able to connect.
7. Did you enjoy the experience working with this group? Give a grade 1(low) – 10 (high) to express the enjoyment

If you now elaborate and compare the three dimensional areas (performance-connection-enjoyment) you just reflected upon, what was the problem area you faced? Using these dimensions might help you understand the problem differently and will help you to focus on the aspect where the main problem is rooted. The interesting question is: what is the opinion of your group members? Will they come to the same conclusion as you? Or according to them, was the problem with another dimension?

Connection

Enjoyment   Performance

What are intercultural differences?

According to Geert Hofstede (1991), culture is learned behavior. We are all programmed through our upbringing or the socialization that happened during the interactions with, for example, the teachers and other children at our primary school. We learned cultural norms, values, and perceptions from our parents and everyone else that surrounded us during our childhood. Our parents taught us, again and again, to behave acceptably, praising us when we showed the appropriate behavior and punishing us when we did not. For example, the handshaking ritual is a cross-cultural deal-breaker. In some countries, a firm handshake is appreciated. In other countries, a firm handshake is considered aggressive, and a limp handshake is the only respectful handshake one should give. Alternatively, staring someone in the eyes during the whole conversation is, in some countries, a must-do; in other countries, it can be seen as very rude and intimidating. It is not difficult for most people to recall intercultural experiences, both good and bad that they have experienced. Nevertheless, as one American student once told me, she experienced more problems with her American team members than with the German, Peruvian, and Turkish students in her virtual team. This exemplifies the fact that sometimes, not only the intercultural background but the individual programming are the primary source for challenges in a virtual group. As an individual, you can always choose to act with the approval or disapproval of others in your group or to act as an individual keeping your own norms and values.

The Cultural Map

An inventive way to explain cultural differences is using the cultural map introduced by Erin Meyer (2014). According to Erin Meyer, success in our ever more globalized and virtual world requires new management skills to navigate around cultural differences. Furthermore, managers need the ability to decrypt cultures foreign to their own (Meyer, 2014). Many challenges that GVT members face have their root in the inability to understand these differences. When you cannot understand what is going on, it is even more impossible to deal with these challenges. Cultural programming often determines what someone views as acceptable behavior and what behavior is unacceptable. Knowing and respecting these differences is crucial in today's environment. Erin Meyer dismisses the confusion by providing a "culture map" for visualizing these differences. The model identifies eight essential problem areas marked by cultural differences and creates a scaled continuum for each area. Each of these eight scales represents critical dimensions virtual team members should be aware of. The eight scales are:

1. Communication: explicit vs. implicit
2. Evaluation: direct negative feedback vs. indirect negative feedback
3. Persuasion: principles first vs. application first
4. Leading: egalitarian vs. hierarchical
5. Decision making: consensual vs. top-down
6. Trust: task-based vs. relationship-based
7. Disagreement: confrontational vs. avoiding confrontation
8. Scheduling: structured-linear-time vs. flexible time

By studying the positioning of your own culture and the culture of your group members, the virtual teams will be able to understand how culture influences the collaboration within the group, which can help groups avoid painful situations, as described earlier in the introduction part of this chapter.

Communicating

This scale measures the degree to which a culture prefers **low or high-context** communication, a metric developed by anthropologist Edward Hall (1959). In low-context cultures (such as the U.S. and Germany), communication is precise and explicit. Repetition and written confirmation are appreciated for the sake of clarity. In high-context cultures (such as China, Japan, and France), communication is sophisticated, nuanced, and layered, and reading between the lines is expected. It can be concluded that this dimension adds an extra layer of complexity on top of every GVT. For example, some X-Culture students complain that their group members are too direct and insulting, while others make the opposite complaint, that students are too vague, or "Hiero is dishonest, he says yes, but means no." These differences in the preferred style of communication lead to tensions within virtual teams.

Evaluating

Often confused with the Communication scale, the Evaluation dimension measures something distinct: the relative preference for **direct versus indirect** criticism. The French, for example, are more

Anglo-Dutch Translation Guide

What the British say	What the British mean	What the Dutch understand
• I'll bear it in mind	• I will do nothing about it.	• They will probably do it.
• Please think about that some more	• It's a bad idea: Don't do it.	• It's a good idea: Keep developing it.
• I'm sure it's my fault, but	• It is your fault!	• It was their fault.
• I almost agree	• I don't agree at all.	•He's not far from agreement.
• That is an original point of view	• You must be crazy.	• They like my ideas!

Fig 9.1 Anglo-Dutch Translation Guide
Source: Student Material HAN-2010

high-context communicators than Americans yet are much more straightforward regarding negative feedback. Spaniards and Mexicans are equally high-context communicators, but the Spanish are much more direct than Mexicans when it comes to giving negative feedback. An excellent example of lost-in-translation problems is the quirky Anglo-Dutch translation guide. When the British say, "That is an original point of view," the Dutch will interpret this as "They like my idea!" However, the British actually mean, "Your idea is stupid!" Indirect cultures use down-graders like "maybe" and "pretty much" in their language when they give feedback; direct cultures prefer to use up-grade words like "clearly," "very," and "certainly." For example, in the United States, students will always be direct, except when they must give feedback. A lot of U.S. universities use the Hamburger approach. Feedback will start with something positive to show respect, and then the real negative feedback is presented. The feedback ends with something positive again to make sure the feedback receiver is not in tears after receiving the negative feedback, avoiding a painful situation.

Persuading

This scale measures the preference for principles-first versus applications-first arguments (also known as deductive versus inductive reasoning). Students from Germanic and southern European cultures usually find it more persuasive to express generally accepted theory before presenting an opinion or making a statement; American and British students typically start with opinions or factual observations, adding concepts later to explain their ideas. This difference can lead to problems in a virtual team with France and British students. Inevitably, students from France want to discuss the principles behind, for instance, country selection first, while the British student already selected a potential export market in a very hands-on way while leaning loosely on the theory.

Leading

This scale measures the degree of respect shown to authority figures, depicting a spectrum between the egalitarian and the hierarchical scale. The egalitarian group includes Scandinavia and Israel, whereas Russia, Nigeria, and Japan are more hierarchical in nature. This dimension builds on the concept of power distance, mentioned by Geert Hofstede (1991). Often, students mention "leadership issues" as a source of problems. For example, they complain that other students are overly passive, that they will only go into action mode when you give them a specific task, and that they show subservient behavior. To illustrate this point, consider that Dutch students expect collective decisions and prefer to continue talking until everyone is on the same page. This way of doing business can lead to problems with students that have a more hierarchical approach to decision-making. In contrast, other students might complain about having a dictator in their group, overruling all the joint decisions made.

Deciding

We often assume that the most egalitarian cultures in the world are also the most consensual (making a mutual decision) and that the most hierarchical ones are those where the boss makes top-down decisions. That is not always the case. The Japanese are strongly hierarchical but have one of the most consensual cultures in the world. Germans are more hierarchical than Americans but also more likely to make decisions through group consensus. This scale explores the differences between building group agreement and relying on one person (usually the boss) to make decisions (Meyer, 2014). To give an idea within, for example, X-Culture, decision-making, such as the decision of which company to focus on, or making promotional decisions as part of the marketing strategy, is essential. The student learns positively or negatively that in their GVT, different styles of decision-making are preferred.

Trusting

This scale balances task-based trust (mind-based) with relationship-based trust (following your heart). In a task-based culture, such as the United States, or the Netherlands, trust is built through group work: We collaborate well because we appreciate each other's work. In a relationship-based society, such as Brazil or Nigeria, trust is built by weaving personal, affective connections: We have laughed together and have come to know each other at a deep, personal level—so I trust you, we are friends. Because in essence, X-Culture works with virtual groups, relationship-based students face difficulties creating a meaningful relationship with other students because the whole project runs just for ten weeks. As a consequence, students feel disconnected from their GVT. A quote from the X-culture questionnaires exemplifies this: Julia (21): "... I personally have not enjoyed the project. There have been no personal or emotional connections to my teammates even though I have tried. By not seeing each other, I feel there is nothing...."

Disagreeing

In the Western world, scholars agree that the storming phase is a crucial phase in team development, and therefore, a little confrontation is healthy (Egolf, 2013). However, some cultures have different ideas

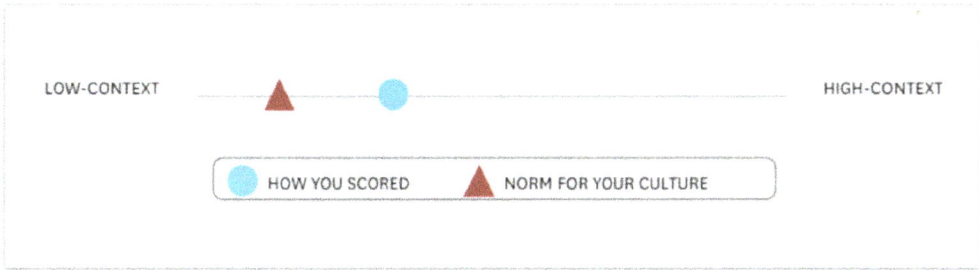

Fig 9.2 High-Low Context.

about how productive conflict is. People in Indonesia and Thailand view the public expression of disagreement as a weakness; an open confrontation is inappropriate and will negatively influence group harmony. However, workers in France and the Netherlands are quite positive about conflict and do not assume it will harm the relationship or has lasting effects. A Dutch student remarked that one of the Asian students in his group started to cry when he openly contested a decision made by her during a virtual meeting. His intention was not to make her cry; for him, it was only about this specific decision. However, his bitter, negative words were received as disrespectful and damaged the group harmony. He was advised to change his tone of voice in the future or otherwise leave the virtual group.

Scheduling

In the business world, it is common to use schedules and timetables, but in India and Kenya, people treat a schedule as a suggestion, and if new opportunities arise, the timetable can be altered quickly. Tasks are dealt with all at the same moment, and interruptions by other people are accepted and welcome. In contrast to Switzerland, The Netherlands and the U.S., in these countries, people typically stick to the plan. They prefer to complete one task before beginning with the following one. The weekly deadlines, as described in the X-culture instructions, work well for Dutch and German students. They see them as hard deadlines and start to complain to the other students when they do not deliver their work on time. The Scheduling scale measures whether you view time as linear or flexible, depending on how much value you place on structure or adaptability. It is based on the monochronic and polychronic distinction formalized by Edward Hall (1976).

How can your Virtual Team benefit from using the Cultural Map?

Start by plotting your personal score and your Country score using the eight scales. Via the website https://hbr.org/web/assessment/2014/08/whats-your-cultural-profile, you can do a free assessment to plot your score on the eight scales combined with your Country scores. The result will look something like Figure 1:

The next step is to compare your personal ratings with the other scores from your global virtual team members. Discuss the outcome using the suggested questions below.

Personal reflection

Reflect on the following questions:

a. Where are you (not) in line with your national culture(s)?
b. Reflect why/how come your score differs (personal views, experiences, other).
c. Can you come up with real-life examples that exemplify why your scores differ from the national score?
d. What personal strengths and weaknesses do you derive from this new insight?

Group reflection

During a (virtual) meeting with your GVT, compare the cultural map scores of all your group members by making a group profile.

a. On which two dimensions do you have the most significant similarities?
b. On which two dimensions do you have the biggest "gap" to bridge?
c. Can you recall a situation where the similarities helped to bridge differences within your group?
d. Can you remember an event or issue that created or widened the intercultural gap in your group?
e. How will this new insight into your culture influence your communication in the group?

X-culture Group Profile

Communicating	
Low-context	*High-context*
Evaluating	
Direct negative feedback	*Indirect negative feedback*
Persuading	
Principles first	*Application first*
Leading	
Egalitarian	*Hierarchical*
Deciding	
Consensual	*Top down*
Trusting	
Task-based	*Relationship-based*
Disagreeing	
Confrontational	*Avoid confrontation*
Scheduling	
Linear-time	*Flexible time*

---

f. What are the changes in your expectations towards your group members based on the outcomes of this assignment?

g. Define and agree on at least two thoughts that will stimulate positive communication in your group based on the outcomes of the test.

One of the outcomes of the cultural map is that you make it clear, in a visual way, that cultural differences within your virtual team exist. As a consequence, the group might feel the urgency to deal with these differences. At this stage, the Developmental Model of Intercultural Sensitivity (Henceforth DMIS) by Milton Bennet (2002) might give you some suggestions on how to develop the skills to overcome the intercultural differences in a virtual group.

The DMIS scale by Milton Bennet was created as a basic outline to illuminate the reactions that people have to cultural differences. The model consists of six dynamic stages: denial, defense, minimization, acceptance, adaption, and integration. The first three stages take an ethnocentric approach; this means you make your own culture as the point of reference. You evaluate opposing cultures through your own cultural lens. The latter three stages are ethno-relative, meaning you place your own culture within the context of other cultures. In the following paragraphs, the separate stages will be explained, and the suggestion is given how to use the DMIS.

Six DMIS Stages in Virtual Teams

Stage 1 Denial

In denial, stage team members are not aware of cultural differences that exist in their virtual group. They assume that within their group, there are no cultural differences: "All international students work in the same way as I do". Since individuals in this stage assume that cultural differences do not exist, they generally are disinterested in the background of other students and stick to the stereotypes they have internalized. This leads to the "Stupid Questions Syndrome," which asserts that that people know between two and four random facts about a particular country, and they will ask for confirmation about these facts during the first conversation with someone they have just met. An infamous question to Dutch people would be: "Do you always walk on wooden shoes?"

Quotes from students reflecting on their experiences in virtual groups:

"Jawal is a bit bossy, does not understand that because he is from India, he should not behave in this bossy way!"

"I do not like all these cultures in my group."

" I do not care about Chezi's home life,"

Suggestions:

The best way to overcome this stage is to learn more about other cultures in your group. Read a book about the history of that country; studying the Wikipedia of Zambia or Estonia might already give you a head start to get a first impression of your team members' countries. Attempt to establish a positive 'vibe' in the group. Do it in an entertaining manner, don't force people to learn about other cultures and definitely do not test them during the next virtual meeting, as your group members will resist and protest. At the end of this chapter, you will find the exercise "the Dinner table," a creative and fun activity to get to know each other on a deeper level.

Stage 2 Defense:

In the defense stage, individuals start to learn that differences exist in their group, but unfortunately, in a dualistic them-us way, they commonly come to the conclusion that there are only two cultures in the world: ours and all those others. Students start to realize or have already experienced that these differences might lead to problems. Sometimes in this stage, students feel threatened by the other cultures in their group. As a reaction, they will behave in a superior way: "the U.S. is the best" and will denigrate other team members: "you are from the jungle." The issue here is that they disregard the fact that there is a group problem and prefer to blame team members from another culture if a problem occurs. It can also happen that students will start to admire the different cultures and see their own culture as inferior, thereby downgrading their contribution to the group.

Quotes from students reflecting on their experiences in virtual groups:

"Unfortunately, there is racism in this group; it is difficult to work with racist people who have a belief of superiority."

"When you visit country X, you realize how great our own culture is."

Suggestions:

- Try to reduce your polarized perspective by emphasizing the similarities between you and them. Miscommunications between different cultures are possibly not so much caused by real differences but by the stereotypes, we have of each other. The assignment "Stereotypes," available below, might be helpful for recognizing the stereotypes you have of different cultures.
- Try to suspend judgment; for instance, by comparing your interpretation of your actions and event with those of someone you know well, but who tends to have different opinions (a fellow local student or co-worker, for example).
- Watch a foreign movie; you will learn a lot from watching scenes from another culture. Although the film might be difficult to follow, you do learn about values and norms in another culture. Additionally, it will give you a fresh insight into the verbal and non-verbal communication styles important in that culture. If possible, watch the movie with a student or friend with the same cultural background as in the film. Compare your interpretation and judgments: are they completely different? Start a dialogue about certain scenes that have triggered your curiosity. Stimulate yourself to leave your cultural comfort zone, and learn how to make sense of a movie utterly foreign to you. This is a proven way to open a whole new world for people in the defense phase of the DMIS-model.

Stage 3: Minimization

At this stage, students start to realize that cultural differences exist, but have the opinion that on a more human level, all people are the same. We see our norms and values as universal and interpret other cultures via our own cultural lens. Because of this, we judge what is right and wrong, good or bad, according to our norms. We want to help team members to be more like us. So if they adapt, cultural differences are minimized. When there is a problem in a virtual group, team members will complain that students do not behave like them or, alternatively, ignore the differences and thus reduce issues by choosing the easy way out.

Quotes from students reflecting on their experiences in virtual groups:

"Jing Jin is not very helpful, her English is weak, so we made her responsible for making up the tables and figures and the overall layout of the final report…"

"…I realized that student life in Germany and Japan are not so different. We both have much home-work and exams throughout the year."

Suggestions:

- Follow the golden rule, "Do unto others as you would have others do unto you." One practical way to improve communication with others is to imagine ourselves in their shoes. When we pause to think about how we might like to be treated in a specific situation, we build empathy for those actually in that situation.
- Learn more about your own culture, and reflect upon the norms and values that are settled in your mind. As a result, you will see that some of your personal views are not universal nor belong to your culture; they are the views that you have developed throughout your upbringing.
- Culture differs in how feelings and emotions are shown to others. How can you become more comfortable when other students express their emotions more or less strongly than you? Try not to react immediately. Check your own feelings first before responding. How do you feel about what the other person just said to you or the whole team? Ask yourself the question, "Why do I react in this way?" When you are clearer about your own emotion, you are able to communicate more effectively.
- Simply counting until ten might also do the trick sometimes.

Stage 4: Acceptance

At this stage, team members become aware that people in the world live in different environments, and as a result, intercultural differences exist. Students realize that, to paraphrase Trompenaars (2008), "Culture is the way a group solves a problem." Everywhere in the world, groups of people apply differ-ent problem-solving methods, and at this stage, students understand that their group members are not using an inappropriate way to complete a task, just a different way. Virtual team members start to admit that the more cultures present in the group, the better the results can be. Additionally, teams begin to recognize and appreciate the different ideas expressed in the group. However, in this stage, individuals still feel insecure about how to deal with these cross-cultural differences.

Quotes from students reflecting on their experiences in virtual groups:

"Working with people from a different culture is a challenge. But overcoming these challenges is great fun."

"After I realized that Amir's way of working of was very flexible, I followed his suggestions and accepted other changes too."

Suggestions:

When you are in the acceptance stage, the most important thing is to increase your cultural empathy. Try to see a situation from multiple perspectives. For example, take a look at the HSBC advertisement below. Three times the same picture appears, but the perspective is entirely different.

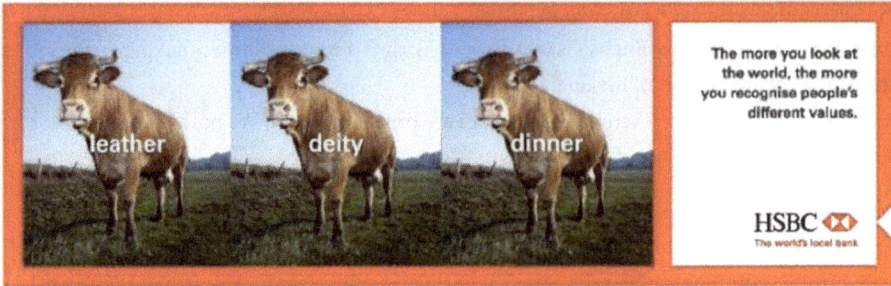

Fig 9.3 HSBC Ad.

- When working with people from other cultures, deliberately take more time before responding than you would do otherwise.
- Gestures may differ in meaning across cultures; it can happen that during a virtual meeting, your Brazilian group-member might misinterpret your okay gesture for a gesture with an insulting meaning. So, realize that the gestures used, along with their purpose, might be different around the globe. Discuss during the next virtual meeting if there are hand gestures that are insulting for your team members and should not be used.

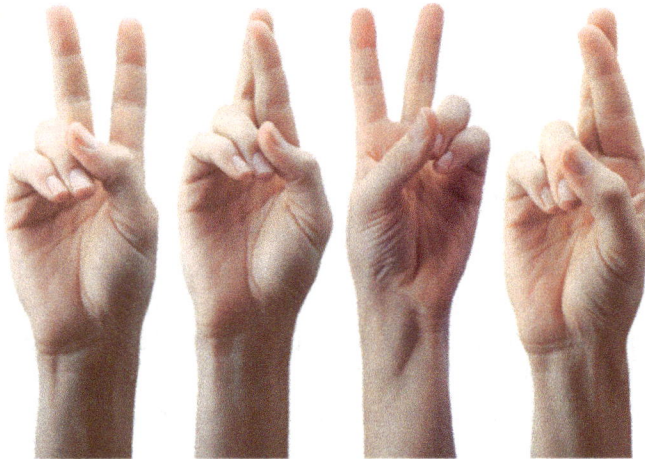

Fig 9.4 Picture Hand Gesture
Source: https://pixabay.com/photos/hands-fingers-the-gesture-victory-4451867/

Stage 5: Adaption

In the adaption stage, virtual team members have learned to understand situations and issues from different perspectives. What is the difference between the acceptance and adoption levels? Acceptance is on the knowledge level; adaption is on the knowledge and behavioral level. In other words, you know about cultural differences and can behave in a culturally respectful way, meaning that you are flexible in the way you interact and communicate with team members in your virtual group. Besides, when you have gained more experience in your interaction, you are no longer afraid to lose your identity because of the cultural traits you adapt to.

Quotes from students reflecting on their experiences in virtual groups:

"When we have a problem in our group, I try to figure out what the others are thinking."

Suggestions:

- Find out how verbal and non-verbal signals are used in one or more cultures that are relevant to you – through culture-specific books or conversations with people with a different cultural background.
- Keep on practicing flipping your point of view (reference shifting) to perceive problem situations from different angles using the cultural perspectives of others.

Imagine you are in the shoes of the group member you have an issue with. What might be the logic from that viewpoint? Can you come up with a third perspective as well? What will be the perspective of a fourth group member?

Stage 6: Integration

In the final stage, the integration stage, the individual student has developed a sense of him or herself as a valued member of two or more cultural groups. People at this stage can move in and out of different cultures. The student can take the best of their own and other cultures; they know their limits, and are not confused by them.

Quotes from students reflecting on their experiences in virtual groups:

"I learned so much... I consider myself an inhabitant of the world."

Conclusion

This chapter tries to decrease the impact and amount of intercultural issues within Global Virtual teams by introducing two models, the Erin Meyer cultural Map and the DMIS scale. The first model tried to explain cultural differences by adding the cultural map and its eight dimensions. The second model introduced the DMIS model. The DMIS model outlines the reaction team members can have when faced with intercultural challenges. Throughout this chapter, several suggestions and tools are given to deal with cultural differences while working in a Global Virtual Team.

One of the more important ideas that emerged from this chapter is that when working in a multicultural team, you should invest extra time to ensure that you understand everyone's work preferences and requirements. Furthermore, it was demonstrated that working in a GVT can cause more confusion and stress than working in a mono-cultural team, but on the other hand, it provides an excellent learning opportunity for people that want to improve their intercultural skills.

Additional assignment to develop intercultural skills

Assignment: Show and Tell your Dinner Table

Purpose: To share personal information with others

Instructions

1. In this activity, you will be sharing some information about yourself and your culture with others in the group. Share a picture of you having dinner in a standard setting, or share a picture of your birthday party.
2. Explain to others what they are looking at.
3. Ask each other out about the picture: the significance of the table settings, which is served first, why are you sitting there, what type of food, what courses are served? Are there any special rules and traditions? Where does the guest sit? Try to ask as many follow-up questions as possible.
4. What were the differences and similarities between the pictures you have seen?
5. Reflect on what you have learned about yourself and about others.

Assignment: Stereotypes
Purpose: To recognize stereotypes that you and others have.
Instructions:

1. From your own experience, make a list of commonly believed stereotypes about your own country. For example, people in the United States are rich. (As a group, you can choose to mention only positive or negative stereotypes for this exercise.)
2. Share these stereotypes with your group members.
3. Ask for additional stereotypes of your country from your group members.
4. Explain to each other how accurate these are stereotypes for your own country.
5. As a group, try to debunk all these stereotypes.
6. Reflect: How do all these stereotypes affect the way students communicate with each other?

Assignment: The story of your name
Purpose: To create an atmosphere of respect in the first virtual group meeting.
Instructions:

1. This is a simple method for helping people recall exciting stories about the other members of their group and, by doing so, create an atmosphere of respect.
2. Everyone has a story related to his or her name; in every culture, there are (unwritten) rules concerning the naming of a baby/child.
3. Ask each other to tell the story of their name(s) and explain how name-giving works in your culture. Explain exciting facts, stories, and the significant consequences if, for example, your Dutch parents called you Tiny Kox.
4. Maybe you are in a group with students called "Bald Eagle" or "The brightest color of the rainbow."

References

Bennet, J.M. & Bennet, M.J. (2002) Intercultural communication for Practitioners.

Egolf, D. B. (2013). Forming storming norming performing: Successful communication in groups and teams. IUniverse.

Hall, E. T. (1976), Beyond culture, Anchor Books, New York.

HAN, Student manual, "Training Personal Management", HAN, Arnhem, 2010

Hofstede, G. (2009). Geert Hofstede cultural dimensions.

Hofstede, G. (2001), Culture's Consequences, Comparing Values, Behaviors, Institutions, and Organizations Across Nations. Sage Publications, Thousand Oaks CA.

Hofstede, G., Hofstede, G. J. en Minkov, M. (2010) Cultures and Organizations, software of the mind. Intercultural Cooperation and Its Importance for Survival. McGraw-Hill, New York.

Popescu, F., Warmenhoven, R. (2018). Use of technology and virtual communication via global virtual teams at arnhem business school. In International Conference on Applied Human Factors and Ergonomics (pp. 239-248). Springer, Cham.

Meyer, E. (2014). The culture map: Breaking through the invisible boundaries of global business. Public Affairs.

Nunez, I., Nunez, R., & Popma, L. (2007). Intercultural Sensitivity. From Denial to Intercultural Competente.

Rosinski, P. (2003), Coaching across cultures, New Tools for Leveraging National, Corporate & Professional Differences, Nicholas Brealey Publishing, London-Boston.

Trompenaars, F. & Hampden-Turner, C. (1998), Riding the waves of culture: Understanding Diversity In Global Business, 2nd Edition, McGraw-Hill, New York .

What's Your Cultural Profile? - Typologycentral.com. (n.d.). Retrieved from https://www .typologycentral.com/forums/other-personality-systems/82478-whats-cul

CHAPTER 10

Dealing with Ethnocentrism in Global Virtual Teams

ERNESTO TAVOLETTI, UNIVERSITY OF MACERATA

NATALIIA KOCHKINA, TARAS SHEVCHENKO NATIONAL UNIVERSITY OF KYIV

1. Introduction

The concept of "ethnocentrism" was developed in sociology more than a century ago (Sumner, 1906) in order to distinguish between in-groups (those groups with which an individual identifies himself) and out-groups (those groups with which an individual does not identify himself). Its psychosocial nature opened the way to a wide array of applications in international marketing and international business, and it has been defined as "the universal proclivity for people to view their own group as the center of the Universe, to interpret other social units from the perspective of their own group, and to reject persons who are culturally dissimilar while blindly accepting those who are culturally like themselves" (Shimp & Sharma, 1987: 280).

In GVTs, individuals may cooperate with nationalities they are not familiar with, and in international student simulations, teams may even be allocated according to nationality in order to maximize teams' international variety. Therefore, the issue of "ethnocentrism" in GVTs is mainly nationality-based. Whether it is a nationality as citizenship or nation of birth or nation of residence or nation of study or the elected nationality, it doesn't change the fact that nationality is the main characterizing attribute of each member in a GVT.

The fact that the nationalities represented in GVTs may not be equal in size and in the level of representation makes the issue even more interesting, as does the eventual adoption of English as the official language.

Therefore, it is relevant to bring the issue of nation-based ethnocentrism into the open, in order to recognize it and deal with it properly. In fact, the first sign of ethnocentrism is its denial, which tends to be stronger if the community or the individual aspires to be international.

The US is a special case for the following reasons:

1. American English is by far the most adopted language in international business, world science, diplomacy, and cross-border cultural products;
2. Its economy is the largest in the world;
3. Its financial system occupies a very central role in international transactions and global FDI;
4. The US dollar is the most adopted currency in international trade;
5. Its military might influences geo-politics and it is not irrelevant as far as national confidence and international influence are concerned; its military spending ($643 billion in 2018) exceeds the combined military spending of the countries that follow the US in the list: China, Saudi Arabia, Russia, India, UK, France, Japan, Germany, South Korea, Brazil ($642 billion combined in 2018, International Institute for Strategic Studies); the quality of spending, with hundreds of military bases located in foreign nations and the focus on air defense and navy, increases its outreach and global influence;

6. It is the most influential nation in setting regulatory standards, and some of the most influential international institutions are located in the US: UN, IMF, World Bank;

7. It is the most influential nation in setting social standards due to the hegemonic role of some web companies (ex. Google, Facebook, Twitter, Netflix) who adopt policy regarding what can and cannot be published;

8. While some nations may have a larger domestic market and population, the US cultural industry (Hollywood, international TV channels, publishing houses, and magazines, to name a few) has been by far the most influential abroad since the end of World War II;

9. 25% of the top 500 corporations in the Fortune Global 500 list (2018) are based in the USA.

All of these factors have created a situation in which USA standards are confused or overlap with not well-defined "international standards." Therefore, the USA's ethnocentrism is both very strong and invisible and special for its size and outreach. In fact, it has been suggested that "globalization" looks like "Americanization," and the denial of that by US observers, due to other growing influences, reinforces the hypothesis that US ethnocentrism is taken for granted and tends to be confused with "international standards," making it very invisible. In fact, one often makes reference to English as the "international language."

Of course, ethnocentrism is not a US phenomenon only but involves every nation in the world. It gets bigger the less dependent the nation is on foreign culture or import/export.

Research on ethnocentrism in GVTs is limited (Knight et al., 2010) and suggests that international online collaborations do not have any statistically significant impact on ethnocentrism (Boehm et al., 2010). There is some statistical evidence that students scoring higher in ethnocentrism are less likely to enroll in international business and foreign language courses, and female students score higher than males in terms of the propensity to enroll in those courses (Grant & Wren, 1993), but travel abroad experiences and interaction with foreigners may not affect ethnocentrism scores (Neuliep et al. 2001).

This chapter aims at helping the members of a GVT to recognize and deal effectively with national ethnocentrism. It reports episodes of ethnocentrism and suggests how to address it.

2. Examples of ethnocentrism in Academia

2.1 Academic titles

Different nations have different rules for granting academic titles, Doctor and Professor being the most common). In the USA, the title of Professor is granted to the highest academic level of full professor, and the title of Doctor is granted to individuals holding a doctoral degree. In Italy, where the oldest university in the world, the University of Bologna, was founded—the very term university, universitas, in Latin, was coined at its foundation—the rule is different and more liberal: the title of Professor is granted to Associate Professors, Assistant Professors, and even High School instructors; the title of Doctor is granted to individuals holding a three-year bachelor's degree. Doctoral degree programs were introduced in Italy only 34 years ago, mainly as an educational path for academia; before that time, the academic career was based on post-graduate scholarships with no reference to a doctoral title. As many educational systems around the world have been going through a process of harmonization with the US model and as US universities become the leading ones in international meetings, it is common practice to create a parallel between US standards and "international standards." This can be disturbing for students and scholars coming from an academic tradition that is much older than the US one, and where the concept of the university itself was born. Nonetheless, in order to avoid the risk of appearing to be a less demanding higher educational system, Italian scholars feel obliged to adopt the most stringent US rule and drop their titles. An approach that is more sensitive to ethnocentrism should avoid these extreme measures and formulate possible symmetric solutions, such as dropping titles for all or allowing anyone to follow their own tradition. However, the opposite is true; Italians seem to believe that the perspective of US or German colleagues is something like: "there must be something wrong or sloppy in a higher education system that grants the title of Doctor to a bachelor and the one of Professor to an assistant professor or to high school teachers." There is not, indeed, a strong case for abandoning a centuries-long tradition for the sake of US conformism only.

2.2 University ranking

Academic ranking is critical in nations where some universities have much higher prestige than other universities. In the USA, UK, France, or Japan, being admitted to a high-quality university can dramatically change your career. This was not true in the tradition of some European countries, like Germany (Felix, 2016) or Italy, where national and centralized higher educational systems were intended to provide uniform quality in all universities. In the Italian case, the differences mainly depend on the economic and cultural environment in which the university is located, the disciplinary specializations, and other contingent reasons. The mobility of academic staff across the nation, a nationally centralized system of recruitment, the equal legal value of degrees (which essentially means that the public administrations cannot consider the value of a degree from the university X as superior to a degree of university Y) have produced a situation in which scholars are almost seen as employees of the national Ministry of Education, more than of the university in which they serve. In this system, some of the best academics are evenly distributed across universities, and the respective salaries are the same across the nation. Students' fees are nationally regulated, with most of the funding and rules coming from the central government. In this context, the university ranking is not as critical as in other nations.

These non-ranking traditions experience a serious disadvantage when compared to the hegemony-ranked cultures: either the less ranking-oriented nations enter the game of ranking, experiencing mediocre evaluations (due to the lack of a few richly endowed elite institutions that absorb most of the national resources in order to create concentrated excellence as opposed to widespread high quality) or they stay out of the ranking system and get marginalized in the international arena. The recommendation is to avoid the same ranking-based judgment in both ranking-concerned nations and nations that do not share the same ranking culture.

2.3 Language and academic style

The adoption of US English implies the use of addressing people by their first name, which is less typical of other cultures who tend to be more formal. In Italy, as an instructor, in an e-mail to a master's student whose name is Paul Smith, you would use the expression "Dear Dr. Smith" or "Dear Dr. Paul Smith." In the US, this would be a much more informal, "Dear Paul." Academic styles are on the move all over the world, but the adoption of US English in international settings brings with it the adoption of US habits and culture; this is taken for granted to such an extent that it goes unnoticed.

This adoption does not always move in the direction of more informal and less power-distance solutions, as the US system is less liberal than other higher education systems in the use of academic titles. What is constant in the method of change is the adoption of US habits.

In order to attract foreign students and in order to educate domestic students for an increasingly English-speaking international higher education market, most universities around the world have introduced courses in English. That limits the use of literature that is not in English and favors the adoption of English-written literature and textbooks. While the adoption of a common language favors global education and science, it reduces the variety and sources of literature and induces a process of transition to a language that, far from being "international," is simply the language of a restricted number of nations.

Many national higher education systems have also adopted an Anglo-Saxon three-tier structure (3-year bachelor's degree, master's degree, Ph.D.) in order to make their courses competitive in the international markets. This requires structural adjustments and the loss of long-lasting consolidated practices and traditions in the face of questionable advantages since what is successful in a given cultural tradition may not be appropriate in other contexts. Again, the constant is a process of convergence towards the US system.

The expression "smart casual" is assumed to be a neutral international expression, but it is not, and it is a convergence to a well-identified Western style.

2.4 Best practices and emulation

The process of convergence towards the practices of the US higher education system, in terms of the structure of courses, language, methods, and style, is justified by the success and the leading role of US universities. The point is that there is no evidence that such success is dependent on those practices (as it might well be a consequence of the hegemonic cultural and economic position of the United States in the world so that they would lead under multiple higher education models) nor that those practices would work in different cultural and economic contexts. Assuming that what works in the US would work anywhere else is a typical case of ethnocentrism. Such practices include the distinction between research universities and teaching universities, the creation of a few excellent universities as opposed to widespread high-quality universities, university governance and the 'steering at a distance' paradigm (Kickert, 1995; Marginson 1997), the role of private funding and private universities, the repartition of costs between tuition fees and government funding, and the elimination of the 'legal value' of academic degree in order to access the public administration. Far from being the adoption of the best practices, this is the emulation of the hegemonic power in a strive for isomorphism.

While the reported examples of ethnocentrism are not related to GVTs, they alter the perception of foreigners, especially in relation to systems that don't conform (yet?) to the "international standard." This is even more apparent in situations in which the project partner is not physically present.

3. Examples of ethnocentrism in cross-national comparisons

3.1 Debt (and credit)

It is very easy to fall into ethnocentrism when making reference to debt across nations. In Germany, the word "debt" is translated as "schuld," which also means "fault" and suggests a restrained attitude with reference to debt. In Italy, where the double-entry bookkeeping system was first introduced (the oldest European record of a complete double-entry system is the Messari accounts of the Republic of Genoa in 1340), there is more popular awareness that reducing debt implies reducing credit, as it functions as a mirror where a reduction of debt implies a reduction of financial wealth on the other side. It is easily forgotten that a banknote, while it is a credit for its holder, it is registered as a liability in the balance sheet of the central bank. The same is for the share of a company that is registered as a liability in the balance sheet of a company itself. If a significant amount of shareholders of a company start selling their shares, they can produce a financial impact on the company (as a decreased value of shares) that can be as serious as if the bank was claiming its money back; actually, credit can be granted for an agreed time limit (such as a ten-year loan) while shares can be sold at no notice. Therefore, while it is obvious that in business, an asset implies a liability, nonetheless, in some countries, "debt" is associated with a negative moral judgment. The sustainability of debt is also a matter of sustainability of credit, as an imprudent borrower needs an imprudent lender by definition. It is a sign of ethnocentrism to blame foreign recipients of credit while praising asset investments abroad, as one is impossible without the other.

3.2 Public Debt (and private credit)

The judgment on public debt is affected by national ethnocentrism and is contingent on an even stronger personal self-reference criterion. The main reasons for this are as follows:

1. Public debt cannot be assimilated to family debt for a number of reasons: a) family debt has to be repaid after a limited number of years while public debt can be rolled over indefinitely; b) the creditors of a family are not part of the family while, in the case of public debt, citizens can be both creditors and debtors, as the husband having a debt to his wife (the percentage of public debt detained by foreigners is in any case just a percentage, usually a limited one in rich nations); c) families do not levy taxes, print money or possess a currency; d) while a family with zero debt makes sense, a nation with zero public debt is in the long run a nation with zero public investment and that relies on private investment only; e) a family does not own a central bank and does not fix the interest rate to determine the cost of money, influence inflation, and pay negative real interest rate on its treasury bonds if it thinks this is the case (as it has been traditionally case of financially solvent nations like USA); f) a family doesn't have a central bank that can buy its debt (and so monetize it: the so-called quantitative easing) and keep it indefinitely in its balance sheet (or even cancel it, even if this is rarely made because this wastes for nothing the possibility of selling it back in order to control inflation). Despite all that, the silly comparison between national public debts and family debts is popular even in the business environment and brings with it the stigma associated with debt, depending on the national culture regarding debt.

2. The typical public debt to GDP ratio to compare national debts is meaningless if it is not associated with the quantity of the debt that is detained abroad, the currency in which it is denominated, the possibility for the nation to resort to its internal investors to substitute the foreign investors in case it is forced or wanted to do so, the real interest rate that is paid, the ability of the nation to influence financial markets and its central bank policy. Therefore, comparing the 104% public debt to GDP ratio of the United States to the 8% of Afghanistan or 180% of Greece or the 224% of Japan is a misleading exercise if it is not associated to other considerations and if other macroeconomic variables are not put into the picture.

Despite all that, it would be easy to report financial news reinforcing ethnocentrism and self-reference criteria on the basis of misleading comparisons of public debts and public debt alarms.

3.3 Why recommending a trade surplus is a sign of ethnocentrism

It is logical that it is impossible for every country to have a trade surplus at the same time unless we export to a different planet, as a trade surplus in one nation requires a trade deficit somewhere else. When a situation of unbalance is persistent, the currency of the nation that is in a situation of trade surplus appreciates (external adjustment), and its internal prices and salaries rise (internal adjustment), while the opposite happens in the country that is in the trade deficit. This is a perfect equation in an ideal world, but in the world, as it is, the unbalance can persist for a number of reasons: fixed exchange rates or a common currency, limited flexibility of prices and salaries due to market rigidity, immigration of low paid workers into the country experiencing a trade surplus, public spending in welfare as a substitute of higher salaries in the country experiencing the trade surplus, persistent movement of capitals (lending) from the country experiencing a surplus to the country experiencing a deficit and paying higher interest rates (a common currency and international bailouts favor the process). If the unbalance persists, policy intervention is needed to avoid the bankruptcy of the country experiencing a trade deficit, and with it the loss of credits of its lenders, but the distribution of the adjustment between the two countries can be determined by ethnocentric considerations. The country in the trade surplus might demand that all adjustment is made on the side of the country that is in a deficit, through reduction of its internal demand (mainly salaries, retirement benefits, and public spending), under the justification of the virtue of its export-led model. However, the opposite is also a valuable and less painful economic policy option, as increasing internal demand in the country experiencing a trade surplus can lead to higher salaries, retirement benefits, or public spending. In this case, the distribution of the adjustment will be dependent on the relative economic weight of the two countries and the relative economic weight of trade unions, but is frequently justified to public opinion under ethnocentric considerations, based on the supposed virtue of exports, forgetting that: 1) in a working market economy, growing exports should lead to higher salaries and higher prices and a rebalance of the trade deficit as a consequence; 2) that you cannot have an export-led economy if you don't have an import-led one on the other side, so instructing all nations to move in the direction of an export-led economy is illogical and unsustainable. In the long run, pursuing a constant policy of trade surpluses is a sign of ethnocentrism and shows little interest in both the sustainability of international trade and the fair rewards of domestic workers. If this is a persistent national strategy, intended to contain internal consumption and investment as much as possible in order to invest abroad as much as possible of what is gained through a positive current account, it can be qualified as "imperialism."

3.4 The United States of Europe as a sign of US ethnocentrism

The way many US observers read European politics reveals a high content of ethnocentrism. This is seldom revealed openly, but the implication is that European states are lagging behind the States in the process of building a United States of Europe similar to the United States of America. The states of North America have been faster in pursuing this objective, thanks to favorable conditions, better talent, and/or their lighter history, while Europeans are stuck under the weight of divisions and bloody history.

This parallelism is justified by the fact that many European politicians have been pursuing this objective actively since nineteenth century (Mazzini, 2009), and the Ventotene Manifesto in 1941 by Altiero Spinelli and Ernesto Rossi is probably the most famous manifestation (Vayssière, 2005). On the other side of the Atlantic, the involvement of the United States in favoring a closer union in Europe is both long-lasting and well documented (Aldrich, 1997). After World War II and until the '70s, this action was mainly aimed at keeping European allies linked together in a single market and avoiding the attraction of some states under the influence of the Soviet Union. Starting from the '80s, a common market with common rules and a politics-free competitive European frame, not influenced by the politics of single states, proved more favorable to US FDI in Europe.

That said, the idea of the European nations giving birth to a federal European super-state have never had either the political support of the majority of the European citizens nor any compelling reason rooted in political science (Majone, 2014). Actually, the world has been moving in a different direction, thanks to the spread of the rule of law in the relations between national states and thanks to the right of a people to self-determination as a cardinal principle in modern international law: there are 195 countries in the world in 2019, compared to 184 in 1980, 106 in 1950, 80 in 1937; and 67 in 1912. Therefore, there is no sign of consolidation of sovereignty across the world, despite the fact that many observers, climate change activists, and business leaders would like to see it happen. In fact, norms and limits to free trade imposed by states on international corporations have produced a sentiment among free-market economists and business leaders that is hostile to state proliferation and in favor of federations in order to contain public intervention: "[T]he existing sovereign national states are mostly of such dimensions and composition to render possible agreement (...). [P]eople will be reluctant to submit to any interference in their daily affairs when the majority which directs the government is composed of people of different nationalities and different traditions. It is, after all, only common sense that the central government in a federation composed of many different people will have to be restricted in scope if it is to avoid meeting an increasing resistance on the part of the various groups which it includes...There seems to be little possible doubt that the scope for the regulation of economic life will be much narrower for the central government of a federation than for national states" (Hayek 1948: 264–5).

Therefore, as the United States of Europe (or the far resembling proxy we have in the EU) are expected to be much more business-friendly than a high number of states with different regulations and tariffs, the United States of Europe project is highly appreciated by the global business on both sides of the Atlantic, both for ethnocentric reasons in the USA and for emulation of a hegemonic model in Europe. The idea of convergence to a USA model is almost taken for granted in the long run, as if it were just a matter of time, but a more careful and rational political analysis might suggest that this is far from definite or desirable as it reduces institutional variety and institutional innovation: "David Landes, the distinguished economic historian, has even seen in the political fragmentation of the Old Continent one of the roots of its later global dominance. By decentralizing authority, fragmentation made Europe safe from single-stroke conquest (...): 'Far from being stultified by the imperial government, Europe was to be propelled forward by constant competition between its component parts' (Landes 1998: 528). [...] 'Unity in diversity gave Europe some of the best of both worlds, albeit in a somewhat ragged and untidy way' (Jones 1987: 110)" (Majone, 2014).

The European Monetary Union follows the same line of thinking, a project built despite overwhelming and majoritarian criticism at the highest level of the economic profession (Jonung & Drea 2010; Feldstein, 1997; Thirlwall, 1998; Salvatore 1997; Dornbusch, 1996; Friedman 1997) as well as the most important piece of research commissioned by the EU in favor of it (Emerson, 1990, 'One market, one money', 1990) being criticized years later by the most senior economist leading it (Gross, 2017, 'One Market, One Money – A Mistaken Argument (post-factum)?'). Despite that, it went through, pushed by the ideological belief that the destiny of the European Union is to produce a political unity similar to the United States of America, while its highly negative consequences on EU politics and economics are still largely dismissed, denied, or not properly addressed to this day (Stiglitz, 2016; Mody 2018).

3.5 The perception of corruption

The most respected and adopted source of information for cross-national comparison of corruption is the Berlin-based Transparency International. Thirteen data sources were used to construct the Corruption Perceptions Index (CPI) 2018, but what they have all in common is that they are based on perceptions, and that ranking is based on cross-national comparisons:

1. African Development Bank Country Policy and Institutional Assessment 2016
2. Bertelsmann Stiftung Sustainable Governance Indicators 2018
3. Bertelsmann Stiftung Transformation Index 2017–2018
4. Economist Intelligence Unit Country Risk Service 2018
5. Freedom House Nations in Transit 2018
6. Global Insight Business Conditions and Risk Indicators 2017
7. IMD World Competitiveness Center World Competitiveness Yearbook Executive Opinion Survey 2018
8. Political and Economic Risk Consultancy Asian Intelligence 2018
9. The PRS Group International Country Risk Guide 2018
10. World Bank Country Policy and Institutional Assessment 2017
11. World Economic Forum Executive Opinion Survey 2018
12. World Justice Project Rule of Law Index Expert Survey 2017–2018
13. Varieties of Democracy (V-Dem) 2018.

It would be easy to deem it ironic that some nations with poorly transparent banking systems or fiscal paradises are in the first quartile - Luxembourg (9), Barbados (25), Seychelles (28), Bahamas (29), Brunei Darussalam (31), Botswana (34), Cyprus (38), Saint Vincent and the Grenadines (41), Rwanda (48), Saint Lucia (50) – while at least one G8 country is in the second quartile (we will not report who it is), but what is impressive is that such reporting doesn't take into account that perceptions and especially self-perceptions may be particularly distorted by the level of self-confidence or ethnocentrism of a country. This phenomenon is well-known and documented, but is ignored by the perception index; Olken (2009) illustrates the limitations of relying solely on corruption perceptions, whether in designing anti-corruption policies or in conducting empirical research on corruption, while De Maria (2008) reaches the conclusion that the most popular measure of corruption, Transparency International's (TIs) corruption perception index (CPI), is a flawed instrument, capable only of calculating vague proxies of corruption, and suggests that the index is oblivious to cultural variance and is business-centric in style and philosophy.

Andersson & Heywood (2009), in relation to developing nations, argue convincingly that the CPI contributes to the risk of creating a "corruption trap," as development aid is increasingly made conditional on the implementation of reforms that are impossible to achieve without that aid. On the negative and distorting effects of corruption perception indexes. also see Čábelková & Hanousek (2004).

If we cross-check perceptions with the largest corruption cases in business history, as it is possible to do by looking at the US Department of Justice's Foreign Corrupt Practices Acts, which pursues corruption cases all over the world, we find that the largest cases happened in countries that are very high in the ranking and whose citizens have a very high sense of patriotism and nationhood. Actually, the largest international corruption case reported by the US Department of Justice in relation to the Foreign Corrupt Practices Acts is by Siemens (paying penalties of $1.6 Billion in 2008), which is located in the same nation where Transparency International Secretary is headquartered. Siemens is also one of the seven corporations funding Transparency International.

In some national contexts, the flow of money between politics and corporations can be very high, due to the high cost of campaigning. In some low-context cultures, this is highly formalized, regulated, and transparent, and therefore legalized, even though many doubts persist in relation to the independence of the policymakers. In other national contexts, due to less codified traditions or different cultural attitudes, this is less formalized, less regulated, and less transparent, and scandals happen very often. Those scandals are then used by all parties as campaign tools. From a legal point of view, the difference between the two cases is clear-cut: in the first case, it is a legal, political donation; in the second case, it is corruption, and when it is revealed, it is headline news, but as far as the conditioning of policy is concerned, the difference is not as big as it is from the legal point of view. Kaufmann & Vicente (2011) speak of 'legal corruption in relation to the first case.

What we want to suggest is that the perception of corruption can be highly affected by ethnocentrism and national pride, but this is seldom highlighted by international agencies. International agencies are often located in those same countries, hold themselves in high esteem, and are more dismissing in relation to practices of less developed nations.

3.6 The perception of hard work

Some countries like Germany have a reputation and even a stereotype of being "hard-working," but OECD data and labor economics literature reveal a different story (Bell & Freeman, 2001): the nation is the very last one in OECD for average annual hours worked (defined as the total number of hours actually worked per year divided by the average number of people in employment per year). Some other nations with the reputation for working less, such as Greece, are at the very top or the ranking (tab. 1). The situation is, indeed, different for productivity, but productivity has nothing to do with working hard. A barista can wake up very early in the morning, produce a large number of espresso coffees very fast, and put them on the table; that would make him very "hard-working" while being unproductive as the coffee would get cold and would not produce sales. As this example shows, productivity actually depends not just of your effort and capital but also on the revenues you can generate for all sorts of reasons: size of the local and domestic markets, access to foreign markets and exchange rates are just two of the main variables affecting productivity. An investment banker in Luxembourg, on the opposite, can be highly productive moving capital from one investment to another despite any consideration regarding the number of hours worked.

Despite that, perceptions of hard-working (or their opposite) nations tend to be widespread and generate moralistic stereotypes.

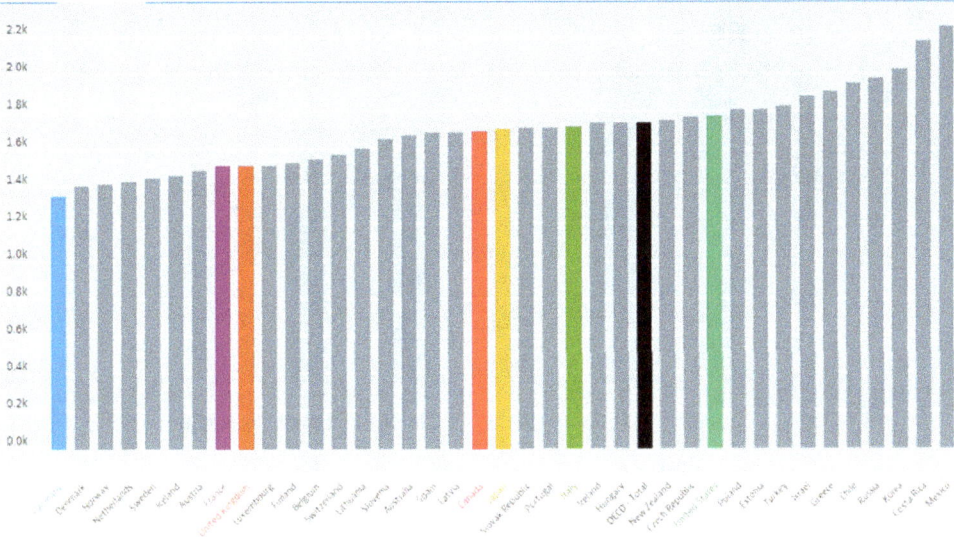

Table 1. OECD Employment Outlook 2018. The average number of hours worked per year per worker: https://data.oecd.org/emp/hours-worked.htm

4. Our empirical evidence from GVTs

To explore the influence of ethnocentrism on GVT activity, we conducted a survey of participants in the X-Culture project (Taras et al. 2012) at two universities in Italy (Macerata University - UNIMC) and Ukraine (Taras Shevchenko National University of Kyiv - KNU). There were 49 total respondents out of 105 (55 from KNU and 50 from UNIMC) project participants over the past two years. The survey was conducted online using Google Forms.[1] The results of the study were unexpected.

When asked which country respondents consider the most ethnocentric, the answers were distributed as follows (Fig. 1). The leader in ethnocentrism is the Russian Federation (36.7% of respondents). Interestingly, the Russian Federation was recalled with equal frequency by both the residents of Ukraine, which had been engaged in a territorial conflict with this country (34.8% of respondents) and representatives from other countries. The USA occupies the second position in terms of ethnocentrism (30.6%), and Italy unexpectedly climbed to the third position (24.5%). These results can be explained by the specificity of the respondents' sample from the Italian university, where half of the survey participants were not from Italy. Therefore, the students' responses reflected their first impression of studying in a new country, which was definitely influenced by cultural differences and was not always a manifestation of ethnocentrism. By and large, the study showed that young people usually do not quite understand

---

1 https://docs.google.com/forms/d/e/1FAIpQLSfdfJA8dl9JsDFpRryh-E_XwHusp-EVNfouOQ6ihm
EIRPqgJw/viewform?usp=sf_link

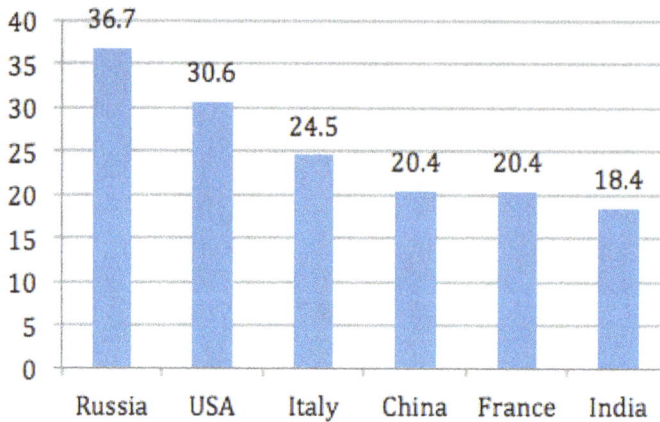

Fig 10.1 Countries that demonstrate the maximum degree of ethnocentrism
Source: compiled by authors based on the primary research

how ethnocentrism can manifest itself, as they often confused it with personal bad manners or gender discrimination. What is also interesting is that 15.3% of Italians consider themselves to be ethnocentric.

The fourth and fifth position in the rating of the most ethnocentric countries was divided between China and France. Moreover, the assessment of the degree of China's ethnocentrism is twice as high as that of Japan, another eastern country with a long history and strong cultural traditions. Despite certain political contradictions between Italy and France, not a single Italian considers France to be an ethnocentric country. India also showed high performance in the ratings.

Unexpected results were obtained on the opposite question (Fig. 2). Respondents consider the USA to be the least ethnocentric country (34.7% of respondents). Thus, the results for the United States were the most controversial. The second position of less ethnocentric countries is quite expectedly occupied by Canada (32.7% of answers), with the UK coming in third. Further positions with a small difference belong to Germany, the Netherlands, Norway, and Finland. As can be seen from the results, the conducted survey supports the idea that countries with a high level of individualism, according to Hofstede (2011), demonstrate the least degree of ethnocentrism.

20.4% of GVT participants came across ethnocentrism while participating in the project. This could concern both the participant and a member of a team, a groupmate, or a friend. In most cases, ethnocentrism manifested itself in the form of lowering peer evaluations during milestones, low respect in a chat, or ignoring opinions during discussions (Fig. 3). As noted above, respondents were often confused by trying to understand the essence of ethnocentricity. Telling their stories, they often talked about gender discrimination or personal offenses that were not relevant to the topic at issue.

However, there were also actual accounts of ethnocentricity, caused, in particular, by the level of proficiency in English, the official language of the project. The main initiators of such conflicts were representatives of English-speaking countries, primarily the United States. Below is a typical story of a group conflict caused by different levels of English proficiency:

"During X-Culture, most of the ethnocentrism came from US colleagues (possibly due to the language capabilities). Many opinions of Indian colleagues at the same time were ignored during the discussion."

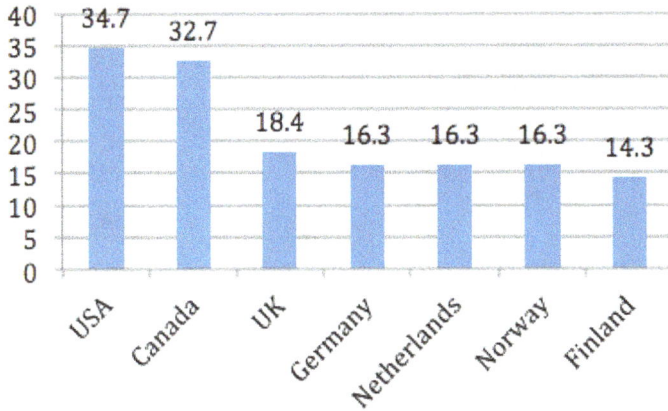

Fig 10.2 Countries that demonstrate the minimum degree of ethnocentrism

Source: Compiled by authors based on primary research

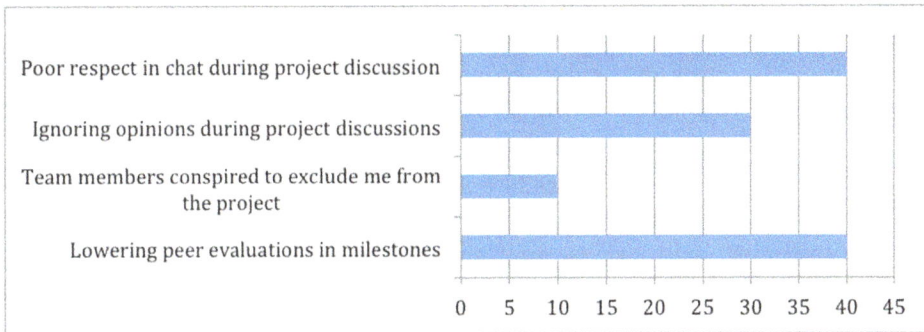

Fig 10.3 Forms of ethnocentrism manifestation in GVT

Source: Compiled by authors based on primary research

Respondents' views varied concerning the behavior of a person who has been targeted by ethnocentric attacks. 24% of respondents believe that a person should ignore such attitude and continue to behave as if nothing is happening. Every fifth respondent was ready to solve problems with the aggressor themselves. Interestingly, 78% of the people who chose this option belong to the Eastern European countries, namely Ukraine and Russia, which is evidence of the high autonomy and responsibility of such respondents. In turn, this is another confirmation of the need to re-evaluate the Hofstede cultural indices, particularly in terms of individualism/collectivism. Eastern European countries have long ago demonstrated much higher rates of individualism than in the Hofstede model.[2] In the case of ethnocentric behavior, 56% of respondents consider it expedient to seek help from other members of the group or tutors and project leaders.

---

2 https://www.hofstede-insights.com/product/compare-countries/

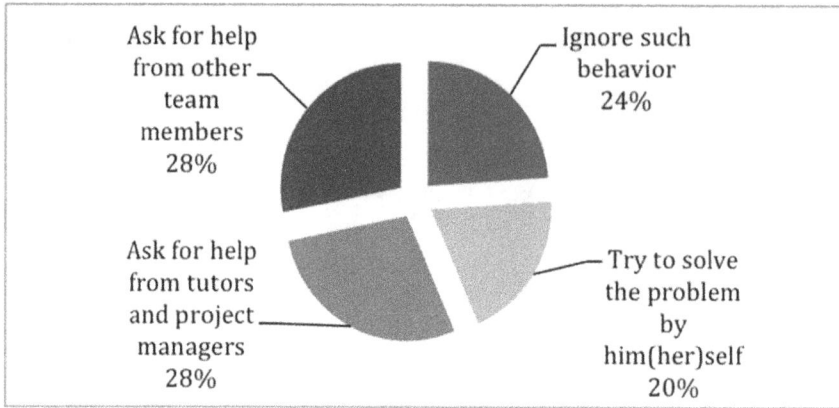

Fig 10.4 Reaction of a person who faced ethnocentrism in a GVT.

Source: Compiled by authors based on primary research

The survey participants appear to be quite tolerant in the matter of country sympathies and antipathies. 51% responded that they have no preferences regarding any country, answering the question: "Representatives of which countries would you like to work within a GVT?" (Fig. 5). The United States, Canada, Great Britain, Germany, and Italy scored 16.3% each. The choice of the first four countries is most likely due to rational motives, as the first three countries are English native speakers. Representatives of these countries can be useful in terms of writing and correcting text in English, the language of the international project under study. Germans are traditionally associated with responsibility and punctuality. A high grade received by Italians can be explained by their cheerful, sunny disposition, which can positively affect the team atmosphere.

When answering the opposite question, "Representatives of which countries you would NOT like to work within a GVT?" 71.4% of respondents said that they do not have prejudices about any country. Interestingly, ongoing local conflicts (in particular, between Ukraine and Russia) did not lead to an unwillingness to work together in the GVT.

The evidence is not conclusive because the sample refers to just two counties, and, in one case, some of the students had a long-lasting teaching experience abroad in just one country (Italy). Nonetheless, ethnocentrism is reported by 20.4% of students. By its own nature, ethnocentrism is denied and tends to be invisible, making it seem even more significant than 15.3% of Italians consider themselves to be ethnocentric.

5. Discussion and recommendations

Collaboration in GVTs and the subsequent lack of personal knowledge exacerbates ethnocentrisms, perceptions, and country-based stereotypes, as the personal interaction is, by definition, limited to web interactions, and the effective knowledge of partners is more limited than in traditional teams. The absence of personal contact also tends to emphasize other information, especially nationality. It is there-

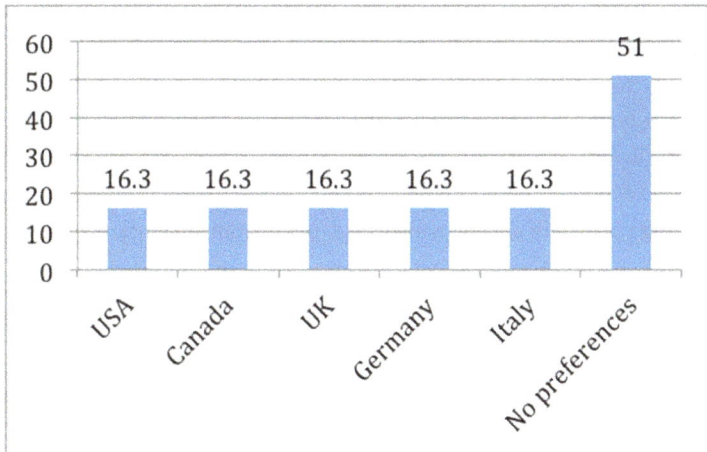

Fig 10.5 Most popular countries to deal with in a GVT
Source: Compiled by authors based on primary research

fore critical that members of GVTs are trained to refrain from the self-reference criterion (Lee, 1966) as a general rule and to compare their criteria with the criteria of other partners in the GVTs. A few examples and normative rules to follow:

1. Less fluent than expected partners in GVTs do not imply analphabetism or underdevelopment (on the contrary, if they do not speak fluently your highly important native language, then it is very likely that they are fluent in another one), and we cannot apply the same criteria we would apply to poorly-educated local residents.
2. The rules regarding academic titles, degree structures, and academic styles that we observe in other nations are not tolerated deviations from an "international standard" point of view: the fact that we use our language in international communication does not imply that our culture, rules, and institutions are the ones to be adopted, too.
3. There is no such thing as an international language or standard as they change across contexts and historical times.
4. The ranking of universities is not a sports ranking, as full comparability can be both impossible and undesirable, depending on local, national contexts and how open they are to 'international standards.'
5. Do not judge the economies of other nations based on a few variables your country is particularly obsessed with, and adopt an asymmetric approach: no debt implies no financial wealth on the other side; in order to have a trade surplus, you need a trade deficit somewhere else, and this cannot be sustained indefinitely in a non-imperialistic conquest-free economic world; zero public debt implies zero public investment in the long run; you cannot have an appreciation of your currency without a devaluation in other currencies (and vice versa).
6. Corruption is a complex social phenomenon to measure, and it is a global one: be aware of different institutional settings and problems in international comparability.

7. Challenge the assumptions you take for granted regarding institutional settings abroad, as what we take for granted tends to be especially invisible and can bias our evaluations.

8. Restrain from stereotypes on the media news and rely on data and data analysis.

9. There is a very high chance that you do not live in either the best country in the world or in the worst one, and different equally valuable social and economic settings are possible, out of any ranking logic.

10. Be open to learn and discover the culture of other nations and refrain from judging and ranking other cultures.

Although we may be sympathetic with the previous rules of thumb, experience tells us that ethnocentrism is highly invisible and frequent, including among international business operators, despite the many languages one can master or the foreign experiences he/she can have. Adopting Nick's rule in the Great Gatsby – "I'm inclined to reserve all judgments, a habit that has opened up many curious natures to me and also made me the victim of not a few veteran bores" (Fitzgerald, 1925) – and accepting its risks can be the best way to embrace open-minded and fruitful GVT cooperation.

References

Andersson, S., & Heywood, P. M. (2009). The politics of perception: use and abuse of Transparency International's approach to measuring corruption. Political studies, 57(4), 746–767.

Aldrich, R. J. (1997). OSS, CIA and European unity: The American committee on United Europe, 1948–60. Diplomacy and Statecraft, 8(1), 184–227.

Bell, L. A., & Freeman, R. B. (2001). The incentive for working hard: explaining hours worked differences in the US and Germany. Labour Economics, 8(2), 181–202.

Boehm, D., Kurthen, H., & Aniola-Jedrzejek, L. (2010). Do International Online Collaborative Learning Projects Impact Ethnocentrism? E-Learning and Digital Media, 7(2), 133–146.

Čábelková, I., & Hanousek, J. (2004). The power of negative thinking: corruption, perception and willingness to bribe in Ukraine. Applied Economics, 36(4), 383–397.

De Maria, B. (2008). Neo-colonialism through measurement: a critique of the corruption perception index. Critical perspectives on international business, 4(2/3), 184–202.

Dornbusch, R. (1996). Euro fantasies. Foreign Aff., 75, 110.

Emerson, M. (1990). One market, one money. Brussels: European Economy 44.

Feldstein, M. (1997). 'EMU and international conflict', Foreign Affairs, 76 (6), 60–73.

Felix, S. (2016). German students don't worry too much about university reputation. Times Higher Education, 28 April.

Fitzgerald, F. S. (2007) (first edition 1925). The Great Gatsby. Peterborough, Canada: Broadview Press.

Friedman, M. (1997). The euro: Monetary unity to political disunity. Project Syndicate, 28.

Grant, E. S., & Wren, B. M. (1993). Student Ethnocentrism: Its Relevance to the Globalization of Marketing Education. Marketing Education Review, 3(1), 10–17.

Gross, D. (2017). One Market, One Money – A Mistaken Argument (post factum). CHEPS Policy Insight, 5, 1–14.

Hayek, F. (1948). Individualism and Economic Order. Chicago: The University of Chicago Press.

Hofstede, G. (2011). Dimensionalizing cultures: The Hofstede model in context. Online readings in psychology and culture, 2(1), 8.

Jonung, L., & Drea, E. (2010). It can't happen, it's a bad idea, it won't last: us economists on the emu and the Euro, 1989–2002. Econ Journal Watch, 7(1), 4–52.

Kaufmann, D., & Vicente, P. C. (2011). Legal corruption. Economics & Politics, 23(2), 195–219.

Kickert, W. (1995). Steering at a distance: A new paradigm of public governance in Dutch higher education. Governance, 8(1), 135–157.

Knight, P., Freeman, I., & Butt, I. (2010). A Tri-Continental Global Collegiate Marketing Project-Reflections and Recommendations. Marketing Management Association Annual Conference Proceedings, 70–72.

Lee, J. A. (1966). Cultural analysis in overseas operations. The International Executive (pre-1986), 8(3), 5.

Majone, G. (2014). Rethinking the union of Europe post-crisis: has integration gone too far? Cambridge (UK): Cambridge University Press.

Marginson, S. (1997). Steering from a distance: Power relations in Australian higher education. Higher education, 34(1), 63–80.

Mazzini, Giuseppe (2009). "From a Revolutionary Alliance to the United States of Europe". In Steffano Reccia; Nadia Urbinati. A Cosmopolitanism of Nations. Princeton University Press. pp. 131–135.

Mody, A. (2018). EuroTragedy: a drama in nine acts. Oxford University Press.

Neuliep, J. W., Chaudoir, M., & McCroskey, J. C. (2001). A cross-cultural comparison of ethnocentrism among Japanese and United States college students. Communication Research Reports, 18(2), 137–146.

Olken, B. A. (2009). Corruption perceptions vs. corruption reality. Journal of Public economics, 93(7–8), 950–964.

Salvatore, D. (1997). The common unresolved problem with the EMS and EMU. The American Economic Review, 87(2), 224–226.

Shimp, T. A., & Sharma, S. (1987). Consumer ethnocentrism: Construction and validation of the CETSCALE. Journal of marketing research, 280–289.

Stiglitz, J. (2016). The Euro: And its threat to the future of Europe. Penguin UK.

Sumner, G. A. (1906), Folkways. New York: Ginn Custom Publishing.

Taras, V., Bryla, P., Gupta, S. F., Jiménez, A., Minor, M. S., Muth, T., ... & Zdravkovic, S. (2012). Changing the face of international business education: the X-Culture project. AIB Insights, 12(4), 11–17.

Thirlwall, T. (1998) "The folly of the euro", Window on Work, no. 4, pp. 4–9.

Vayssière, B. (2005). Le manifeste de Ventotene (1941): acte de naissance du fédéralisme européen. Guerres mondiales et conflits contemporains, (1), 69–76.

CHAPTER 11

Global Academic Virtual Teams versus Corporate Virtual Teams

BETTY JANE PUNNETT, UNIVERSITY OF THE WEST INDIES, BARBADOS

BELLA L. GALPERIN, UNIVERSITY OF TAMPA

TERRI R. LITUCHY, CETYS UNIVERSIDAD, MEXICO

LEMAYON L. MELYOKI, UNIVERSITY OF DAR ES SALAAM, TANZANIA

THOMAS ANYANJE SENAJI, KENYA METHODIST UNIVERSITY

ALI TALEB, MACEWAN UNIVERSITY

Summary of Key Points

- Most literature focuses on corporate virtual teams (CVTs); this chapter focuses on academic virtual teams (AVTs);
- Virtual teams of all kinds are proliferating, and this is true in academia as elsewhere;
- AVTs are similar to CVTs in some ways, but they are also unique in some aspects;
- Examples of CVTs and AVTs illustrate the characteristics of these teams and highlight the unique aspects of AVTs (membership, outcomes, cultural differences, reward systems, funding);
- Well established AVTs include GLOBE, LEAD, Best Practices in HRM, and X-Culture;
- Considering the unique aspects of AVTs, and our experiences working with such teams, we suggest best practices for AVTs;
- We also use the results of a survey of AVT members as input information on best practices;
- The main takeaways discussed are communication, technology, benefits, satisfaction, goals, relationships, leadership, collaboration, and information sharing.

Overview

Over the past twenty years or so, many academics and practitioners have, in some way, addressed the question, "What makes a virtual team succeed or fail?" Most of this literature has dealt with virtual teams that are associated with businesses/organizations or corporate virtual teams (CVTs). There is less discussion of the unique aspects of academic virtual teams (AVTs) and the best practices for these teams. In this chapter, we focus on AVTs, their characteristics, and approaches for creating and managing them to ensure successful performance. Virtual teams provide significant advantages—reduced travel costs, the enhanced possibility for team members collaborating on projects regardless of distance, and the ability to draw on the best talent from anywhere in the world. Our objective is to make practical recommendations for designing and managing AVTs. This has become even more relevant today in light of the Covid-19 pandemic, which has resulted in most academic activities moving from in-person to virtual. For example, in the summer of 2020, planned in-person conferences associated with groups such as the Academy of Management and the Academy of International Business were all conducted virtually. We expect that there will be more virtual collaboration in the academic world in the future, and understanding what makes AVTs succeed will be ever more important.

Corporate Virtual Tteams Versus Academic Virtual Teams

There are many definitions of virtual teams. Jessica Lipnack and Jeffrey Stamps (1997), the authors of Virtual Teams: Reaching Across Space, Time, and Organizations with Technology, described a virtual team as a group of people who interact through interdependent tasks guided by a common purpose. Many authors have said that virtual teams are project-focused and that virtual teams are often formed when the need arises and disbands when the task is completed (see Grenier & Mettes, 1995). This means that virtual teams are usually formed for a temporary period of time to implement a particular task, such as solving a specific problem or to work on new product development. To give an example, a virtual team was formed in the new product development division of the Whirlpool Corporation in the 1990s. The team included experts from around the globe, including the United States, Brazil, and Italy, who came together to develop a chlorofluorocarbon-free refrigerator in response to concerns about damage to the earth's ozone layer.

This team dynamic implies that there is little prior history, and that the responsibilities of each team member may change with each virtual team. For example, a person may be a leader in one virtual team and play a minor, supportive role in another team. The flexible nature of roles is crucial for the attainment of the objectives of a particular virtual team, and research suggests that the structures of virtual teams are typically non-hierarchical and decentralized (Savage, 1996). They are 'non-hierarchical' in that members may all be at the same level in an organization, and there is no superior-subordinate relationship; however, the role of the team leader is often a crucial one. This means that virtual team members often focus on lateral and informal information exchanges to accomplish their work.

In an attempt to better understand virtual teams, experts have outlined their key characteristics. Sze-Sze Wong and Richard Burton (2000, p. 341) from Duke University suggest that virtual teams have a number of characteristics, including: "(1) a set of culturally and organizationally differentiated members, who are (2) grouped temporarily, are (3) physically dispersed, (4) connected by weak lateral ties, and (5) engaged in performing non-routine tasks." To use the Whirlpool example, we see that the virtual team members came from different countries around the globe and were geographically dispersed, but they were from the same division and company. The virtual team was temporarily formed to develop a specific type of refrigerator, a non-routine task. Members of the team shared lateral ties because they were from the new product development division.

Virtual teams are sometimes not as clear-cut as the Whirlpool example, and teams may come in different forms. It is possible to have virtual teams composed of members who are geographically dispersed, but are culturally and organizationally homogeneous. For example, a virtual team at Walmart was composed of members from New York, California, and Arkansas (one company, one country). Wong and Burton noted, however, that some teams may contain members from different cultural and organizational boundaries, but they are physically co-located. In other words, members are from different backgrounds, but team members are close enough together (either physically or virtually) that they can talk to each other within seconds or minutes, rather than hours or days. For example, a team could be made up of members from Brazil, Canada, China, India, and Russia, all working from different offices in Toronto.

Eric McConnell (2012), a project manager who has worked on various projects in the software industry for over ten years and has taken a variety of roles on software projects and project activities, categorizes virtual teams simply into two groups: global virtual teams (GVT) and local virtual teams (LVT). In GVTs, members can be located in different countries and cities around the world. Employees can come from a variety of companies because their organizations are interested in collaborating efforts and resources (for example, people, technology, and/or money) in order to perform common outsourced projects and achieve shared goals.

A recent incident involving an investigation into the causes of two airplane crash tragedies in a span of five months illustrates how individuals from many different organizations may be affected by a particular event and thus come together virtually to identify and examine that event. The crashes involved the same model of plane, the Boeing 737 Max 8, thus affecting Boeing's reputation and affecting airline associations, aviation bodies, several governments, and passenger groups, insurance underwriters, among others. Data from the black boxes of the Ethiopian Airline Fight ET 302, which, in March 2019, was flying from Addis Ababa to Nairobi when it crashed, killing all 157 people on board, showed "clear" similarities with the crash of a Lion Air jet in October 2018 (Robison & Johnsson, 2019). This situation required a team of experts from different countries and organizations to work together to determine the causes of the crashes.

Local virtual teams (LVT) members usually belong to the same country and often the same company. The organization may be either large or small, and it has sufficient resources, namely technology, to encourage virtual teams and facilitate the organization of its employees into productive remote groups. Companies that have been successful at implementing virtual teams include: SAP, G.E., and IBM. SAP, the world's largest inter-enterprise software company, has more than 30,000 employees in 60 countries, and virtual team collaboration is critical to the company's success. G.E. employs more than 90,000 employees throughout the world and has invested in training its leaders and employees through virtual classrooms. IBM uses virtual meeting software and chat tools to enable more collaboration, even as team members work more autonomously during the hours that are best for them (Derosa, 2017).

This trend towards virtuality has increased during the Covid-19 pandemic, with many companies requiring that employees work virtually from home. Many employers who had not previously embraced the idea of virtual work have been essentially forced to experiment. News reports and informal conversations suggest that many companies are considering continuing the experiment once the pandemic is over. There seems to be a general agreement that the plusses of virtual work (at least some of the time) outweigh the minuses, although most people argue that some in-person meeting time provides real and important value.

We define an AVT as a team, usually made up of academics, working on scholarly pursuits, usually research, without physically meeting, and with the help of communication technologies. Academic relates to education and scholarship, virtual means it does not physically exist, and team implies an interdependent group of people linked by a common purpose. These teams are seen as collections of individuals who depend on each other, share responsibility for accomplishing outcomes, and see themselves (and are seen by others) as a cohesive body (note that AVTs often develop names for the team and its work). Although our focus is largely on professors and research, much applies to student teams working on projects, or any group working on research or other academically related projects.

AVTs are different in some ways from other virtual teams. The following discussion highlights characteristics that make these teams somewhat unique. We focus on AVTs that consist of professors rather than students, but student teams will find that many of the issues discussed apply to them as well.

Most AVTs are made up of members from different universities, colleges, schools, departments, and so on. These teams are not driven by specific organizational goals, and they may have loose parameters and unclear goals. In contrast, a typical non-AVT is made up of members of one organization (company, government department, a state-owned enterprise, NGO, and so on) or perhaps a few people working on a collaborative venture. The team is usually working on a specific project that has been identified by the organization(s). As such, the project will have well-defined parameters and outcomes, with rewards and sanctions associated with achieving these outcomes. In sum, non-AVTs have overarching organizations, while AVTs do not.

AVTs have goals and timelines that are self-imposed. There is often no organizational deadline to be met, nor organizational sanctions for not meeting goals and timelines. Self-imposed goals and timelines are easier to ignore than those that are set by someone else who has control over rewards and sanctions. Particularly in cases where there are conflicts between AVT goals and timelines and those of the primary workplace, it is natural that the primary ones will take precedence. We have often noted in our AVTs that when deadlines are not met, the "excuse" is usually something like "I had to finish grading," "the Dean asked me to head a special committee," "I had a problem with a group of students and had to meet with them several times," and other similar statements related to the group member's primary workplace. The trade-off is not hard to understand as the academic's Head, Dean, etc., is not likely to accept "I couldn't get my marks in because I had to meet an AVT deadline," while AVT members will accept the reverse.

AVT members can sometimes feel isolated and overstretched. The AVT project may have no particular relationship to the rest of her/his Department, Faculty, University, and so on. While members may be working closely within the virtual team, there may be no one "at home" with interest in the project and no one with whom to discuss issues that arise. Even successes may not be particularly relevant to colleagues at the home institution. The team member has selected the broader academic constituency over the more immediate one. If the other choice was made, colleagues might feel that you have chosen to work with others outside your primary institution and that, in some sense, you prefer this to work with those inside the institution. In one case, a Department Head questioned the value of a multiple-authored paper, particularly because the other authors were not from the home institution, and asked, "Shouldn't you be publishing with your colleagues here?" Another case arose when one of our members attended a promotion interview where the following comment was made: "You appear to be publishing a lot, but you are all over the academic space, in book chapters, journal articles, and special issues, and the Vice-Chancellor does not feel you are progressing." In this case, it appears a narrow research focus was seen as desirable. The diverse nature of AVTs, including different disciplines as well as organizations, cultures, and more, means that a narrow focus is unlikely, as members will have varying interests, which will be reflected in the project and its outcomes. The AVT member has to walk a fine line between what those deciding on promotion see as positive and what the AVT as a whole decides.

AVTs may not have access to the latest or most appropriate technology. These are not University projects in the normal sense, and funds may not be readily available for the most effective technology. AVTs often depend on small grants and even self-financing, and thus they may settle for what is available at low or no cost. Many grants do not cover access to technology on the assumption that the institution should cover this. In non-academic organizations, technology will be a priority for any virtual team because the project is seen as valuable in terms of profits, and ICT will be built-in to the overall resourcing of the project. Our experience with AVTs is that we rely on Skype, not because we think it is necessarily the best, but rather because it is essentially free. Many of our team members are situated in countries with limited infrastructure, and it is not uncommon to have technical problems during our Skype calls. These problems have included disconnection, degraded voice or video, and other quality issues; nonetheless, we make do because we have little choice.

AVTs are often long-term. Most are focused on research and may be designed as multi-year projects. This means that a long-term commitment is required from participants, and it may be challenging to maintain the commitment over time. Circumstances naturally change, and team members may also change. It has been our experience that team leadership, as well as membership, has to be flexible and that some people will want to continue throughout the lifetime of a project (and beyond into other projects), while others will want to join for a short period or specific aspect of the research. In some ways, the AVT becomes a process that incorporates a series of projects. During the, so far, ten-year duration of the LEAD project, some members have retired, others have accepted administrative positions, still, others have left academia. The current team make-up is quite different from what it was initially. We have published based on our specific research, but we have also published on more general topics and have moved from a largely academic focus to include developing teaching and training materials, such as textbooks.

AVTs are thus somewhat different from other virtual teams. These differences need to be taken into account when designing and managing an AVT. If these are considered at the outset, it is more likely that the AVT will be successful and achieve desired outcomes. The good news is that these challenges can be overcome, and most people feel there is real value in working with AVTs. One author commented, "There are many rewards to being part of an AVT. Not only do you work with interesting people from around the world on interesting projects, but you may be able to visit places you would like to visit. I have been to Peru and Brazil, Kenya and Ghana, thanks to two different AVTs." Yet another commented, "I have drawn very important lessons from leading scholars through AVTs and been able to co-author papers with eminent scholars, and this has enhanced my profile in academia."

Examples of Academic Virtual Teams

There are several well-established AVTs. These include the GLOBE team, the LEAD team, the Best Practices in IHRM project, and the X-Culture team. This is by no means meant to be a complete list, as there are many others that could have been included; however, these teams have written about their experiences as AVTs. These teams have carried out research projects over the past several decades, and although X-Culture is largely a cross-cultural student project, it does engage in a variety of research projects as well. Below, we briefly describe these teams.

Global Leadership and Organizational Effectiveness (GLOBE):

GLOBE is an organization dedicated to the study of the relationships among societal culture, leadership, and organizational practices. With more than 200 researchers from 62 countries studying more than 17,000 mid-level managers in the initial phases, the 2004 study is the largest and most prestigious study of its kind in the social sciences. In the latest 2014 study, more than 70 researchers collected data from over 100 CEOs and 5,000 senior executives in corporations in a variety of industries in 24 countries. This study demonstrated the considerable influence of culture on societal leadership expectations and the importance of matching CEO behaviors to expectations for leadership effectiveness. GLOBE is preparing to undertake a new phase of research ("GLOBE 2020"), while their most recent book, Strategic Leadership across Cultures: The GLOBE Study of CEO Leadership Behavior and Effectiveness in 24 Countries, offers essential reading for anyone studying or practicing in the fields of global leadership, cross-cultural leadership, international business, and organization studies. The results of the GLOBE studies have been used to inform leadership, business, and management practice in an increasingly globalized world (see www.globeproject.com).

Leadership Effectiveness and Motivation in Africa and in the African Diaspora (LEAD):

Following an in-depth study of the management and leadership literature, this group found that the theories and empirical evidence rarely reflected the situation in Africa and the African Diaspora. The project started in 2008 and continues to shape the understanding of the African view of effective leadership. The project comprises researchers from Africa (East, West, South, and North), North America (U.S. and Canada), and the Caribbean, with a core team and regional teams. Members are encouraged to volunteer and take the lead on output, and other members contribute while the team leader coordinates efforts considering various deadlines. The project started with an emic approach comprising of Delphi and focus groups, which led to the development of Africa-specific instruments that have been psychometrically validated and are now being used. The project still welcomes collaborators from Africa and across the world. LEAD outputs have been presented at a variety of conferences, papers have been published in journals, chapters have been contributed to edited books, and a book devoted to the project's early results was published in 2017 (see LEAD: Leadership Effectiveness in Africa and the African Diaspora, edited by Lituchy, Galperin and Punnett, 2017).

Best practices in IHRM Project (the experts.asu collaborations):

Housed at Arizona State University, experts.asu is the University's expertise profiling system that promotes research across all continents and is supported by the Arizona Board of Regents (ABOR) and the Arizona Commerce Authority (ACA). In this largely virtual community, researchers collaborate on academic research in various disciplines ranging from engineering, earth sciences, and medicine to social sciences. In this context, Von Glinow, Drost, and Teagarden (2002) looked at the IHRM practices in a ten-country/region sample.to identify best practices in IHRM. They found anomalies and counterintuitive findings, and through their "gap analysis" identified several universally embraced ethics or best practices. These findings made a significant contribution to research, and most notably, the researchers offer a solution to the methodology for conducting globally-distributed IHRM research. The findings signal new directions for those involved in managing within and across different cultures. Their work presents a compelling argument for understanding cultural contexts by seeking and establishing derived ethics (see VonGlinow et al., 2002)

X-Culture:

X-Culture is a successful global collaboration in International Business education. Professors from 140 universities in 40 countries take part in X-Culture every semester, which remains open to new additions. Students are put in global virtual teams of about six, with each member in a different country, and work on real-life international business challenges presented by real companies. No travel is needed, and all collaboration is virtual. The best students are invited to the X-Culture Global Symposium, where they meet their team members and top managers from the client company. Research is also a part of the

X-Culture project, and researchers are invited to participate in their "research hackathon" (https://x -culture.org/hackathon/). At the hackathon, attendees are placed together in a conference room at a quiet university campus, phones off, laptops on, and perform research for several days; including brainstorming paper ideas, research design, data analysis, results, and drafting papers. The end results are clearly defined paper ideas, polished study designs, initial results, initial drafts of papers, and new contacts and co-authors. X-Culture recently won Wharton's Re-Imagine Education Award in the Nurturing Employability category.

Having ourselves participated in AVTs, we can say that participation in such teams is rewarding in a number of ways:

- The ability to collaborate without having to travel, particularly where financial resources are limited,
- The opportunity to publish in prestigious journals, with well-known academics,
- Mentorship from leading scholars and researchers,
- Possibilities to learn and grow professionally,
- Simply getting to know others from different countries and backgrounds.

While there are clear benefits to participating in AVTs, there are also challenges. The diversity in these teams, along with the limited amount of physical interaction, can lead to problems where some team members have a different understanding of expectations. A particular concern is that some team members may not accept the importance of deadlines. These challenges can be mitigated by good team leadership; for example, the leader can track deadlines and remind participants of them. The team leader and core team of the AVT to which we belong have been instrumental in sustaining the momentum of our AVT. Limited funding for occasional face-to-face meetings is also a drawback because face-to-face interactions serve to resolve issues more quickly than emails or Skype calls. Governance is also an issue to be considered, and GLOBE, for example, has recently established a Board of Directors.

Some of the teams referred to earlier have described their experiences, the challenges faced, and the practices identified as contributing to positive outcomes (best practices), and we have personally discussed the experience of working within AVTs with colleagues. The following are some ideas drawn from these discussions.

Early in the development of the GLOBE project, one of the authors of this chapter asked the GLOBE founder, Bob House, about funding for such a large undertaking. She says, "I was expecting to hear that they had received some very large grant to allow them to address the major questions they were looking at," and goes on to say, "what I received was some of the best advice for all such teams." Bob House explained that it was very difficult to get major funding for such a project. He said that funds were limited in the social sciences and that competition for these funds was always substantial. He had chosen to apply for many smaller grants for pieces of the project, and to have research partners do the same. Many Universities have funding available, usually up to US$5,000-10,000, that is relatively easy to access. In the LEAD project, we have been fortunate to get a couple of somewhat larger grants, but we have also relied substantially on these smaller amounts. Paul Hayes (also of GLOBE) suggested setting up a committee with responsibility for finding funding, including writing grant proposals.

As well as issues associated with funding, Paul Hanges presents other suggestions in a presentation entitled Managing a Multinational Team: Lessons from Project GLOBE (www:// globeproject.com, 2019). He identified some other challenges associated with the project. Including its long-term nature, the large size and dynamic nature of the team, the virtual nature of communications, and the cultural differences of participants.

Paul Hanges says, "Choose your team members wisely," and based on our experience, we would certainly concur. The problem is that it is often impossible to tell who will be an effective team member until the project is underway. We have not yet solved this problem in our AVT, but it seems to be an area where more thought is needed—for example, it seems that the tasks to be carried out should be identified early on, and a determination made regarding who can take on those tasks. If skills that will be needed are not available among existing AVT members, then a special effort can be made to attract members with the required skills. We also believe that it is important to identify some way of getting rid of non-productive team members. This could possibly be done by having an "evaluation" subset of members who periodically review members' performance and report to the AVT as a whole.

A social contract for the team is often considered a hallmark of AVTs, with several people stressing the importance of such a contract. Hanges suggested developing one at the outset. He noted that the GLOBE contract was explicitly discussed, written down, and agreed to, but over time it meant different things to different people. This also has been our experience. We began by considering the development of a social contract as essential, but today we might favor a more fluid and evolving agreement. Interestingly, respondents to our survey did not give particular importance to social contracts.

It is important to build in milestones and tangible evidence of success to share with all members. From our experience, this is absolutely key to the well-being of an AVT. To be effective, this relies on some member(s) with good organizational skills to keep track of progress and outcomes. We have been somewhat less successful on the organizational front in some aspects of our own AVTs and now recognize that identifying a 'keeper of information' needs to be an explicit task. Unfortunately, it can be a mundane and rather thankless task, so perhaps, again explicitly, it needs to be rotated through the group. Another closely connected issue is keeping track of who is on the team, when they joined, what they have contributed, and so on. We have found this affects the appropriate recognition of contributions in terms of questions of authorship and the like. In our experience, the main project often leads to side projects involving only a subset of participants, and keeping track is complex. However, keeping track is essential, so again, there is a need for someone with organizational skills to agree to this responsibility.

Virtual communications, particularly in view of cultural differences, is a major challenge to be handled. Our experience suggests that most AVTs use English as the main language of communication, but there are cases where teams include members whose first language is not English. It may sound superficial, but we find that sensitivity to the communication challenges and cultural differences is actually what works. In these cases, the need for sensitivity should be discussed openly among all team members, and the potential difficulties acknowledged. For example, if English is used, those members who are less fluent may find it difficult to follow verbal discussions and to provide input. Slowing down the pace of communication may help, as well as specifically asking all members for input. Summarizing verbal discussions in writing and asking for written comments can also help. Team members should be encouraged to say essentially, "Stop, I am not following;" Hanges refers to this as the equivalent of a "stop the train emergency lever."

Special Issues and Best Practices for AVTs

AVTs present substantial benefits, including increased publication, more visibility, and enhanced prestige and collegial interactions. There are also several special issues that these virtual teams experience. These include membership, outcomes, cultural differences, reward systems, and funding. We briefly discuss each of these.

MEMBERSHIP

AVT membership is usually voluntary, and members are self-selected; they are not assigned by management/organization. The authors have all participated in AVTs, and this was always the case. Some of our universities encouraged this, but not always. As an example, one university devalued publications with multiple authors, which are the type of papers that AVT collaborations result in. AVTs often arise out of academic meetings, where a group of like-minded colleagues identify a similar interest and an opportunity to collaborate. This forms the nucleus of the AVT, which may then expand membership by inviting others to join. AVTs are thus usually made up of members from multiple organizations.

Outcomes

The "real" outcomes for an AVT may be publications, not project completion. In other organizations, getting the project done satisfactorily and on time is what matters, and is the basis for rewards/sanctions. AVTs look for opportunities to publish throughout the life of the project, and this can sometimes distract them from the project itself. For example, we had the opportunity to publish a book discussing early results, with team members contributing chapters. This seemed too good of a publishing opportunity to pass up, and we all happily agreed, but it meant that some aspects of the project were put on hold while we turned our attention to writing book chapters. In addition, members may agree to work on side projects, such as this chapter.

Cultural differences

Members come from different organizations and are likely to embody varying organizational and national cultures. A member's primary affiliation is their "home" institution. Each organization may have different priorities and strategies, as well as organizational values. This can mean that there is a clash of cultures within the AVT. For example, some universities value book publications, while others may place more emphasis on refereed journals, or public policy papers, and so on. Imagine members of an AVT, some arguing for a book, some for a journal paper, and others for a public policy paper. How does one decide? AVT members have to balance these conflicting demands.

Reward systems

Cultural differences imply varying reward systems. In academia, performance in some colleges and universities may be judged by the number and status of publications, while others focus on teaching, service to the institution, or service to the public. Consequently, each university will have different requirements. Those that emphasize research often have low teaching loads, where the focus is on teaching, itt is considered important to have more classes and interactions with students, and so on. The AVT itself does not usually have a reward system, per se. Members of the AVT work within the established reward system of their home institution. For example, those with high teaching loads have less time to devote to research, yet most AVT projects are research-oriented. There is also the challenge of linking a member's effort to output, such as with the order of contributors. This "reward" is particularly pertinent in cases where publication points for promotion are awarded on the basis of the order of listing of the authors on a paper.

Funding

AVTs are often self-financed. There may be funding available from some institutions, as well as from granting agencies, but this funding has to be identified and sought by individuals or groups within the AVT. This takes time, effort, and commitment from team members. Based on our experience, we each have to identify small sources of funds that we can access for "pieces" of the project. In the LEAD project, we conducted focus groups, and one team member secured funding for some Caribbean countries, another for Canada, and so on, while others contributed their own funds. The costs were not onerous; nevertheless, this illustrates the need for commitment from team members, given these types of demands.

The following table summarizes some of the typical contrasts between Academic Virtual Teams and Corporate Virtual Teams. Research-focused academic teams may be different from student-based academic teams on some factors.

Academic Virtual Teams (AVTs)	Corporate Virtual Teams (CVTs)
AVT members from different institutions	CVT members from the same organization or a group of organizations in a strategic alliance
Varied corporate cultures & rewards	Similar corporate culture & rewards
Research AVTs – varied ages, positions/levels	More similar ages, positions/levels
No direct compensation	Compensation tied to meeting goals
Focus on learning & knowledge	Focus on corporate objectives
Difficult to get rid of unproductive members	Can be removed or terminated
Research AVTs – longer term	Short to medium term, project-oriented
Shared, changing leadership	Designated leaders
Self-selected for personal growth	Assigned by superiors for strategic reasons
Self-funded/small grants	Corporate funding as required for tasks
Use of inexpensive available technology	Best technology for important tasks

The main focus in the table is on AVTs that are involved in research (i.e., professors). Student-based AVTS are likely to have younger members and may be quite similar in age and stage of academic level. Student AVTs are also likely to be relatively short-term, working together for one semester in most cases.

In summary, CVTs function within an organizational setting and structure and have the support, policies, procedures, and so on that are part of such a setting and structure. ATVs do not have these, and have to design their own supports, structures, etc. This generally means that CVTs are more planned, regulated, and controlled, while AVTs are more fluid and changeable. There are benefits and drawbacks to fluidity and change. The next section on Best Practices for AVTs seeks to make the most of the benefits while overcoming the drawbacks.

Best Practices

We conducted a survey on AVTs during 2018 with one hundred and fifteen respondents. Respondents were quite varied, with essentially an equal number of men and women, ages ranging from twenty-five to seventy-nine, and coming from a variety of countries and backgrounds. The survey asked about various facets of the AVT experience and the best practices for such teams. We draw on these survey results to develop the Best Practices presented next.

Frequent Communication is Important

Communication involves sharing relevant information amongst the team in order to keep each member abreast of current developments within the team, as well as on the progress of the AVT's activities. Respondents stated that their teams all interacted virtually on a regular basis, and over three-quarters of respondents said communication was the most critical factor for success. Interactions among the team members are especially important because they do not meet physically. Some respondents said that communications between at least two members occurred on a weekly basis (42% of those surveyed), while others interacted monthly (35%).

Technology is Critical for Communicating

Technology is one of the factors driving the proliferation of virtual teams, including AVTs. In the survey, 41% said that technology was important for the success of their AVTs. Teams used a variety of technologies. Over three-quarters of respondents used group forums and email distribution lists, followed by internet phone calls such as Skype. File sharing systems such as Dropbox and Google Drive were also used by more than half of the AVTs, as well as conference calls and social media. Most respondents felt their technical skills were excellent or very good/good. A survey by RW3CultureWizard (2016) found the most effective communication approaches for global teams were face-to-face meetings, conference calls, video-conferencing, and group emails/email discussion groups. Given the situation facing AVTs, these teams have to find the means of communication that works for them and can be supported by technologies and arrangements that members can access. In our research, members plan to meet at academic conferences to discuss progress in a face-to-face setting. Face-to-face opportunities are limited for AVTs, and they should be used every time they are available.

AVTs must Provide Benefits

The majority of respondents (86%) felt that the benefits of AVTs outweigh their challenges. Indeed, most people said they found the AVT to be very important to their productivity in terms of conference attendance, and publications and were satisfied with their AVT experiences. Respondents were most satisfied with goals (over 50%), relationships (47%), leadership (35%), outcomes (34%), and technology (30%). There are tangible benefits for participants, and the interactions with colleagues from other parts of the world result in AVT members who are more productive with the likelihood of increased motivations.

Goals are Important

Respondents (67%) felt that goals are critical for success. While goals are important for all types of virtual teams, they are more critical for members of virtual teams. Having a goal unifies the AVT and motivates members to exert the effort necessary to achieve the desired outcomes. To ensure that goals are acceptable to all members, they must actively participate in a dialogue to develop those goals, which includes setting milestones or steps for assessing progress toward achieving the goals. Specific, identifiable goals help members stay committed, disciplined, and motivated while they work as a virtual team. Clear goals are particularly important because AVT members are separated by large distances and working in isolation, and goals may be the only thing that gives them the motivation to complete a task.

Using the AVT that we are part of, the goals of the team are publications in journals or books, and two approaches have been applied to elicit consensus on the goals. The first is for a subset of interested members to respond to a "call for publication" (conference, journal paper, or book chapter). The second is to work on a specific research project and invite members to express an interest in being part of the research team. By registering interest, the member implies that they agree to the goals.

Build Sound Relationships

Our survey shows that the nature of the relationship that develops among AVT members contributes to the performance of the team (i.e., success or failure), and in reaching their goals. 66% of those surveyed stated relationships were important to the success of their AVT, and a large majority (93%) thought a good team member was "collaborative." Relationship building and regular chat sessions with all team members lead to greater satisfaction of the individual team members and better team performance. In AVTs, relationships may be hard to build because members do not meet face-to-face. Relationships can still be built through social team-building activities when opportunities arise. For example, team members may meet at a conference and have lunch or dinner together or attend a social event.

Ensure Effective Leadership

Like other teams, AVTs requires leadership, and the survey confirms that leaders play a role in the success of the team. Leaders of AVTs should demonstrate a transformational approach to leadership, that is, one that inspires, conveying a vision and passion for the projects that is contagious, and instilling energy and enthusiasm into team members. At the same time, the leader plays the role of a coordinator more than anything else. Proper coordination of tasks was stated as very important by 71% of the respondents. In AVTs, the leadership role may be shared among the team—understanding, caring about each other's situations, providing moral support, and helping to inspire members, as well as defining the vision of the AVT, is the responsibility of all team members. AVT members need to recognize that they are operating in a flat, not hierarchical, setting, and that all have to assume leadership roles by giving suggestions, volunteering to lead the production of publications, and recognizing mutual achievements within the team. The AVT leader should still retain the overall coordinator of the team. For example, the authors of this chapter work in an AVT, which has a leader and core team. Members of the core team often receive information from various sources about opportunities to publish and pass these on to other team members.

Collaboration and Information Sharing Leads to Success and Diversity is an Asset

The survey identified the attributes of a good AVT member. Collaboration was considered to be the most important, followed by sharing information, proactive engagement, providing useful and timely information, and being professional (all mentioned by over 85% of respondents). Slightly fewer mentions (over 75%) were given to caring about teammates, offering assistance, and having good social skills. The majority of respondents considered their AVTs to be diverse in terms of disciplines, countries, and cultures, and demographics such as gender, age, and career stage, and diversity were deemed useful attributes, as 80% felt the team had capitalized on it.

Summary

We discuss AVTs as an emerging phenomenon characterizing academic work. AVTs are described as distinct from non-academic or corporate virtual teams CVTs. AVT members usually work for different institutions; these may be located in different parts of the world and have different cultures. Some well-known examples of AVTs—GLOBE, LEAD, Best Practices in IHRM, and X-Culture—were briefly described. The findings of our survey on AVTs were used to identify best practices for AVTs and the factors that drive their performance and success, including goals, leadership, communication, relationships, and the team's membership makeup. The importance of understanding AVTs is likely to increase in the future, particularly given the impact of the Covid pandemic, which has resulted in decreased travel and in-person meetings.

References

Derosa, D. (2017). 3 Companies with High-Performing Virtual Teams. On Point Consulting. Retrieved from https://www.onpointconsultingllc.com/blog/3-companies-with-high-performing-virtual-teams.

Global Leadership and Organisational Effectiveness (GLOBE) Retrieved from https://www.globeproject.com/.

Grenier, R. & Metes, G. (1995). Going virtual: Moving your organization into the 21st century. Upper Saddle River, N.J: Prentice Hall.

Hanges, P. (2019) presentation entitled Managing a Multinational Team: Lessons from Project GLOBE (www:// globeproject.com, 2019). https://x-culture.org/hackathon.

Lipnack, J., & Stamps, J. (1997). Virtual teams: Reaching across space, time and organizations with technology. New York: John Wiley & Sons.

Lituchy, T. R., B.L. Galperin & B.J. Punnett (2017). LEAD: Leadership Effectiveness in Africa and the African Diaspora. New York: Palgrave Macmillan.

McConnell, E. (2012). Virtual Teams – Definition, Management and Benefits. My Management Guide, Retrieved from https://mymanagementguide.com/managing-virtual-teams-understanding-definition-management-and-benefits/.

Robinson, P., & Johnsson, J. (2019). Two 737 max crashes in five months put Boeing's reputation on the line. Bloomberg Businessweek, Retrieved March 13, 2019 from https://www.bloomberg.com/news/features/2019-03-13/two-737-max-crashes-in-five-months-put-boeing-s-reputation-on-the-line. www.rw-3.com/about-us.

Savage, C. M. (1996). 5th generation management: Co-creating through virtual enterprising. Dynamic Teaming, and Knowledge Networking. Butterworth-Hainemann, Boston.

Von Glinow, M. A., Drost, E. A., & Teagarden, M. (2002). Converging on IHRM best practices: Lessons learned from a globally distributed consortium on theory and practice. *Human Resource Management, 41*(1), 123-140. https://doi.org/10.1002/hrm.10023 Retrieved March 29, 2019 from https://asu.pure.elsevier.com/en/publications/converging-on-ihrm-best-practices-lessons-learned-from-a-globally

Wong, S. S., & Burton, R. M. (2001). Virtual teams: What are the characteristics, and impact on performance? Computational and Mathematical Organizational Theory, 6, 339-360.

CHAPTER 12

The Role of Cultural Values in Global Virtual Teams

Chinese Culture as an Example

DING-YU JIANG, NATIONAL CHUNG CHENG UNIVERSITY

CHIA-HUA (DEMI) LIN, NATIONAL CHUNG CHENG UNIVERSITY

1. Introduction

Due to the impact of globalization, global virtual team (GVT) members have to deal with cultural differences. We use a Chinese culture as an example to provide a framework for approaching this issue. You might have classmates from China or Taiwan, and you might have had the opportunity to interact with them closely; if you have not, however, the X-Culture project will provide you with an excellent opportunity to work with Chinese or Taiwanese people. China is an emerging global power and has been the world's most populous country for several centuries, and China and Taiwan both use the Chinese language and have similar cultural roots. Figure 1 shows the most populous nations on earth, with China accounting for 18.40% of the world's population. It is likely, therefore, that you will encounter Chinese team members when working on team-based projects during your work or studies. Here, we define Chinese members as not only people from China, but people who have been heavily influenced by Chinese culture. Figure 2 shows that China is the largest source country for international students in the United States, with a total of 369,548, and Taiwan is the seventh-largest.

Hopefully, you will enjoy the opportunity to work with Chinese team members. This chapter presents some of the differences and challenges that Western team members may experience when working with team members from China or from Asia in general.

Historically, Chinese culture, or Confucian culture, has influenced many Asian countries. You might know that numerous ancient Korean, Japanese, and Vietnamese books were written in Chinese. China has been the cultural center of East Asia for centuries, and Chinese culture, especially Confucian ideology, is still influential. It is helpful in maintaining family and societal stability by emphasizing family ties, personal social prestige, respect for authority, and hierarchy. Your Chinese team members might seem very friendly or even over-friendly in contrast with your Western colleagues since Chinese culture plays an important role in their behavior. According to Chinese culture, people tend to assume that strangers are above them in the hierarchy; for instance, a new acquaintance may be more knowledgeable or competent than you are, so you should be polite and humble. At the beginning of the project or during team building, Chinese team members might seem less confident and assertive than Westerners. That does not mean that the Chinese members will never be confident and assertive; they just show their respect from the beginning.

When you try to motivate your team members, you might say, "You did a great job!" Your Western team members would be pleased to hear your praise. However, your Chinese team members might be less positive; even worse, they might feel tense about being evaluated. Your Chinese team members will enjoy being recognized only when they truly trust you as a close friend. Why is there such a difference?

The Most Populous Nations on Earth

Estimated share of the world population by country (2020)

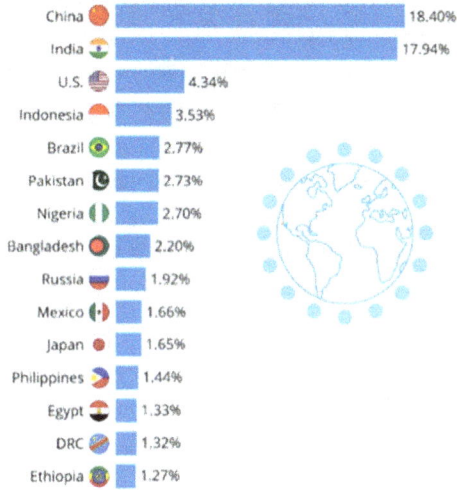

Country	Share
China	18.40%
India	17.94%
U.S.	4.34%
Indonesia	3.53%
Brazil	2.77%
Pakistan	2.73%
Nigeria	2.70%
Bangladesh	2.20%
Russia	1.92%
Mexico	1.66%
Japan	1.65%
Philippines	1.44%
Egypt	1.33%
DRC	1.32%
Ethiopia	1.27%

Source: IMF

statista

Fig 12.1 The most populous nations on Earth

Adapted from https://www.statista.com/chart/18671 /most-populous-nations-on-earth/

Where America's International Students Come From

International enrollment in U.S. higher education in the 2018/19 academic year

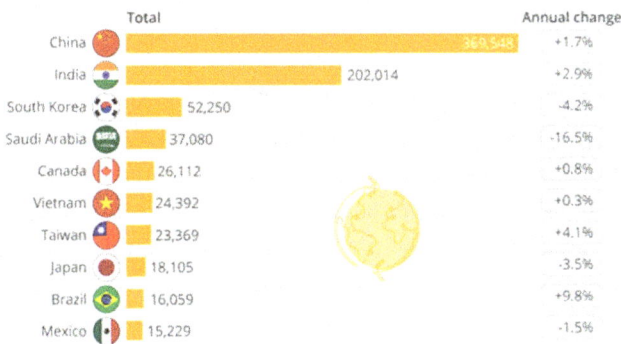

Country	Total	Annual change
China	369,548	+1.7%
India	202,014	+2.9%
South Korea	52,250	-4.2%
Saudi Arabia	37,080	-16.5%
Canada	26,112	+0.8%
Vietnam	24,392	+0.3%
Taiwan	23,369	+4.1%
Japan	18,105	-3.5%
Brazil	16,059	+9.8%
Mexico	15,229	-1.5%

Source: IIE 2019 Open Doors Report on International Educational Exchange

@StatistaCharts

Forbes statista

Fig 12.2 Where America's international students come from

Adapted from https://www.statista.com/chart/20010 /international-enrollment-in-higher-education/

Chinese culture emphasizes social role obligations, believing that one should behave differently and appropriately in different social contexts. For example, you should obey your parents' orders even if you do not agree with them, you should show your authority and dependability in front of your subordinates, and they should fully support your decisions without question. In a work situation, your Chinese team members might think that doing a job well is an obligation. People who are influenced by Chinese culture wouldn't take doing a well-done job as a laudable thing. If you say to your Chinese team members, "I enjoy working with you!" they will be happier than if you say, "You did a great job."

Cultural values shape individual behaviors in many respects. In this chapter, we focus on the three most common Chinese cultural values you may encounter during the X-Culture project. These cultural values focus on interpersonal interactions and might make your Chinese team member seem very different from your expectations.

These are the three Chinese cultural values we introduce in this chapter:

- Guanxi
- Face
- Harmony and avoidance of conflict.

2. Guanxi

Lee and Chen are both freshmen who meet at the welcome party of a Chinese community at the university. At the party, they find out that they are from the same town in southern China, and even went to the same high school. With this Guanxi—unique connection—they soon become good friends. Although they have different majors and take different classes, they go for lunch, hang out, and go to the gym together. They have known each other for just two weeks, but if you ask them, they will tell you that they trust each other fully and have each other's back.

2.1 What is Guanxi?

Guanxi is a term adopted from the Chinese word for a personal relationship and refers both to the relationship type and the relationship quality. Generally, Chinese culture educates people to be friendly to foreigners and to emphasize family values. Chinese people tend to maintain good relationships with others and are willing to provide favors to those acquaintances. Obedience and obligation are significant features of kinship relationships. Westerners, especially Americans, focus on individuality. However, Chinese people are more like nodes in a network. By building close relationships with critical nodes, you can extend your influence through your connections or Guanxi. However, after further interactions, you might find that Chinese people have two sides—one for acquaintances, and the other for close friends or family members.

In Chinese culture, appropriate interpersonal interactions depend on the Guanxi between the two people involved. Guanxi has multiple meanings, referring to the relationship type, relationship quality, and expected interaction patterns. When interacting with strangers, you should be polite, maintain some amount of psychological distance, and build the relationship by exchanging interests. When interacting with friends, you should be expressive and supportive, and when interacting with close friends or family members, you should focus on mutual needs, but primarily you should fulfill the other's needs to strengthen the level of loyalty between you. It is necessary to lower your ego and be aware of mutual obligations. Keep these interpersonal interaction patterns in mind, as Chinese people might have extensive interactions with various non-close-friends or strangers with little psychological or emotional involvement.

2.2 Why Guanxi could be a challenge

Even if you have a good relationship with your Chinese team members, it does not necessarily mean that you have Guanxi with them. When you interact with your Chinese team members, you should be polite in the beginning. Then, when someone provides you with a personal favor, it is a sign of their willingness to build personal Guanxi with you. If you do not give support in return, he or she will consider your response to be a rejection or a sign of immaturity. Once reciprocal interactions develop, trust will lead to friendship, the other person might start to share their personal feelings and private opinions, and you will be expected to share something in return. Chinese people are taught to be cautious in building relationships with others, and in a close friend relationship, a highly mutual interdependence is expected. When your Chinese team members share their personal lives, it is an indication that they want to build Guanxi with you. Most Chinese people want to make a good connection with others, even those they do not like. Take it slowly and try not to get stressed.

2.3 How to solve the problem

Chinese people use various activities to build and maintain Guanxi, such as gift-giving, regular interactions, or providing substantial support. If you want to develop Guanxi with your Chinese team members in the X-Culture project, you might need to be aware of their personal needs and wishes. Showing your understanding and concern will improve your Guanxi with your Chinese team members. You could also get to know your team members' hobbies and interests through Facebook and Instagram. Sharing mutual hobbies or having a pleasant conversation about hobbies will bring you a lot closer to each other and facilitate smooth cooperation.

3 Face

Ann and Megan have been best friends since they were roommates in college. In their senior year, they join a business case competition hosted by a famous food company, hoping to perform well in the contest and get a chance to earn an internship in the company. The competition asks participants to team up with students from a different college; therefore, Ann and Megan start to work with three other students on one of the competition tasks, a new product development plan. During their team meeting, they come up with a new organic energy drink as their product.

All team members are supportive of each other's ideas and thoughts until their discussion turns to the marketing strategy. One team member would like to focus on businessmen and women as their target customers. Another member suggests offering it to mothers with newborn babies, and yet another insists on targeting college students because they are most familiar with this target group. Ann proposes that they should maybe focus on all people who need energy; however, Megan immediately disagrees and says she thinks it is a bad idea. Ann gets so angry that she ends the team meeting and leaves the room right away. Later, in their dorm, Ann blames Megan for what she said at the team meeting. "I'm your best friend!" says Ann. "I was trying to save everyone's face! But you, as my best friend, you make me lose face in front of everyone!"

3.1 What is face?

You might think an open discussion is the best way to generate creative solutions. However, you might also be aware that Chinese people are reluctant to be direct and openly critical. Face is a form of social prestige, representing a person's social influence and public image. Thus, "having face" means you are an essential and influential person. "Saving someone's face" means not expressing an opinion in public if it might threaten someone's public image. "Giving someone face" has two meanings: one is to acknowledge someone's outstanding performance or contributions in public to help to promote their public image; the other is to do a favor for someone while expecting a return in the near future.

Why do Chinese people value their social prestige (face) so much? The answer is highly related to their self-concept. In some extreme cases, face is the essential element in Chinese people's lives. Chinese culture emphasizes that people should always be aware of others' opinions of them, and an individual's social prestige is more important than how people see themselves. Thus, Chinese people's self-esteem heavily depends on how others perceive and evaluate them. Receiving criticism or negative feedback in public will mean a loss of face for a Chinese person; therefore, they may block open group discussions to protect their face. Chinese people will feel less threatened when criticism and negative feedback are delivered in private.

3.2 Why face can be a challenge

Face may make your Chinese team members sensitive to any negative or even not-so-good feedback. They might respond defensively or withdraw from a group discussion. Face is strongly linked to one's personal sense of value in the Chinese context. Thus, a face-threatening situation will make your Chinese team members feel uncomfortable and frustrated. Especially in a GVT project, communication among members relies heavily on social media and telecommunication software and is mostly conducted through text messages. Without social cues or visible information, your Chinese team members might feel uncertain about how to behave "properly" to protect their face. A lack of confidence in communicating in English is also a key factor. You might find that your Chinese team members express their own opinions infrequently and conform to task assignments without any disagreement.

3.3 How to solve the problem

The importance of face to Chinese people is similar to that of clothes to human beings. Losing face is almost equal to being naked in public. This means that you should save a person's face in public by avoiding challenging them and leaving criticisms, sensitive questions, and negative feedback for private communication. They will recognize that you are saving their face in front of the team and will be more supportive of your decisions about the GVT tasks. From another point of view, your Chinese team members may never give you negative feedback; this might reflect your great work, but it could also mean they are just avoiding criticizing you in public to save your face. If you want to know your Chinese team members' genuine thoughts, you should ask them about their personal opinion of you in private, just like good friends, where they will feel comfortable giving you honest feedback.

4. Harmony and avoidance of conflict

Jack and Tom are classmates, and they have an excellent relationship. One day, Jack uses Tom's pen without his consent, and Tom is furious. However, Jack will not admit that he was wrong and will not return

Tom's pen. Tom tells their teacher about this matter, hoping she can help to deal with this situation. But the teacher doesn't criticize or correct Jack's wrongdoing; instead, she reminds Tom not to destroy the friendship over something so petty.

4.1 What are harmony and avoidance of conflict?

Face is not the only factor that makes Chinese people less aggressive in public. Chinese culture also highly values harmony, or avoiding direct conflict. Westerners have less emphasized the concept of harmony. However, this Chinese cultural concept may explain why Chinese people often choose to deal with matters harmoniously when facing conflict. Maintaining the harmony of interpersonal relationships is one of the most important Chinese cultural values.

Interpersonal conflicts are thought to threaten harmony, while harmony is the best way to make everyone feel safe and secure. Open arguments and expressions of emotion are considered immature behavior. Well-educated people should control their negative emotions and neutralize any conflict situation. Chinese people believe that a family with a harmonious relationship can achieve anything. They also think that getting the short end of the stick is not always a bad thing; you might even gain something from the loss. That is, maintaining group harmony is more critical than ensuring justice. When siblings or classmates get into an argument, a Chinese father or schoolteacher is very likely to punish both brothers or both students without asking why they are fighting. Breaking harmony is not allowed even when you are suffering.

Thus, Chinese people might feel pressure to express opinions that differ from others and tend to be less familiar or less skillful in dealing with conflict situations than Westerners. They might stay silent rather than speak up when they are mistreated. That does not mean that Chinese people will never fight back; it is just that Chinese culture emphasizes group harmony more than justice.

4.2 Why maintaining harmony and avoiding conflict can be a challenge

Culture affects people's perceptions of how to handle conflict. The Western individualistic culture emphasizes individual autonomy, the pursuit of personal achievement, and personal satisfaction. In contrast, Chinese collectivist culture regards interpersonal and social harmony as the most important values. The completion of work and the satisfaction of individual needs are secondary matters, and the individual's responsibility is to contribute to the collective benefit. In a collectivist-oriented culture, because the goals of the group are more important than the goals of the individual, people tend to avoid conflicts within the group, or cooperate more in conflict situations to maintain a harmonious relationship. Chinese and Western societies vary widely in their understanding of conflict resolution. Chinese people value harmony and avoid conflict, while Westerners regard interpersonal conflict as a healthy part of an interactive relationship. Such differences in cognition can cause communication difficulties and misunderstandings.

You might notice that your Chinese team members only offer supportive and positive feedback and always try to neutralize potentially conflicting interactions. If you believe that everyone should express their opinions freely and thoroughly, it might seem as though your Chinese team members are making communication difficult. As members are trusting and willing to cooperate, the level of group harmony rises. However, if you are the team leader, you might expect all team members to express their own opinions and give feedback on others' ideas. You might be a little frustrated with your Chinese team members' silence; however, they just want to ensure team harmony before expressing their personal opinions, especially in public. Even in a GVT project, where members are physically distant, your Chinese team members are still looking for a harmonious team atmosphere.

4.3 How to solve the problem

Harmony-oriented people have many strengths: they are cooperative, supportive, and work well in a team. However, harmony and conflict avoidance may make Chinese members unwilling to express their sincere thoughts. If group members experience unpleasant feelings in a group interaction, they may be reluctant to express their feelings because the harmony of the relationship is the primary consideration. Therefore, you may need to explain to your Chinese team members why conflicting interactions might be useful in critical decision making, and encourage them to express different opinions and focus on tasks rather than personal feelings.

The characteristics of the whole team will also affect the way members feel about harmony and dealing with conflict. Chinese team members may also make the most appropriate judgments based on their perceived background and social cues. If you are the leader of the group, try to build a pleasant team atmosphere that may encourage Chinese members to express their thoughts and opinions.

During team discussions, team members will share opinions and ideas and generate creative ideas through brainstorming. However, you may find that the Chinese members support everyone's views and do not put forward their ideas. Also, when a member of the group takes a strong stand, the Chinese members may give in to their persistence. If you are the team leader, one way to pay more attention to the Chinese members and show that they are free to give their opinions is to ask questions such as "What is your opinion on this matter?" or "I think your idea is excellent; can you tell us a bit more?"

5. Conclusion

In today's rapidly-changing environment, how to get along with people from various cultural backgrounds and different countries in the shortest possible time can be a formidable challenge. When team members encounter cultural conflicts, they must take the issue seriously. After all, in the era of globalization, teamwork requires not only great experience and knowledge, but also excellent learning ability and adaptability. It is important to tolerate and respect cultural differences while at the same time trying to minimize cultural conflicts. "Prevention" is better than "treatment," and trying to find a solution to a problem can waste a lot of time. Conflicts may also cause misunderstandings among team members, which can affect the atmosphere within the team.

In GVTs, members come from all corners of the world, with different educational and cultural backgrounds. Hence, learning to tolerate and accept different cultures is very important. "Putting yourself in others' shoes" is the main prerequisite for mutual understanding. The team will become more cohesive only after members' behavior and attitudes are gradually accepted with knowledge and awareness. Respecting and understanding different cultures are the core values of a cross-cultural team.

CHAPTER 13

Managing International Teams
How to Address the Challenges and Realize the Benefits of National Diversity in a Team

MARKETA RICKLEY, THE UNIVERSITY OF NORTH CAROLINA AT GREENSBORO

Summary of Key Points

- International teams are increasingly common in all levels of organizational hierarchy.
- Companies led by diverse teams are more profitable, but not all circumstances call for using an international team.
- National and cultural differences among team members activate differences in ways of thinking and in social categorization, allowing the team to leverage non-redundant information.
- However, cognitive and identity-based differences can hinder effective communication and fuel conflict, limiting process efficiency.
- International teams outperform homogeneous teams when:
  - The task is cognitive, complex, and indecomposable – as opposed to manual and routine.
  - The task requires innovativeness and creativity – as opposed to speed and efficiency.
  - The task involves problem analysis – as opposed to solution implementation.
- To realize the benefits of national and cultural diversity in a team:
  - Choose team members whose knowledge, skills, and abilities align with the problem.
  - Be mindful of team proportions to avoid the formation of subgroups, status differentials, power dynamics, and tokenism.
  - Assign a team leader with a global identity.
  - Allow the team to practice solving simpler problems together before tackling more complex problems.

If you were to look at the top management team of the world's largest steel company, ArcelorMittal, you would find that its seven members come from five different countries (ArcelorMittal, 2020). This may seem unique, but international teams are increasingly common. In fact, among firms belonging to the Fortune Global 500, 13% of CEOs and 15% of top management team members are foreigners (Ghemawat & Vantrappen, 2015).

This trend is also apparent among middle managers and project teams across a variety of industries. In Germany, the advertising team at Ogilvy & Mather's Berlin office has members of 14 different nationalities working on its marketing campaigns. At General Electric Aviation in the Czech Republic – which happens to be GE's only foreign location that designs, manufactures, sells, and services GE aircraft engines outside the United States – you would find 18 different nationalities among its 650 personnel. Overall, according to a recent study, 74% of respondents have worked with colleagues from other countries to improve business processes (EIU, 2009).

International Teams as Drivers of Performance

Companies increasingly view international teams as drivers of performance. Lenovo, China's largest PC maker and the company that acquired IBM's PC business in 2005, consciously combined different nationalities in its executive ranks. Andy Miller, who served as Lenovo's CFO from 2005 to 2009, makes the following observations about the composition of Lenovo's top management team: "We have the Eastern presence and Western presence—two very different cultures—and I think we can use that to our competitive advantage."

Research suggests that Miller's remarks regarding the performance benefits of international teams are spot on. Diversity in senior management teams is not only tied to increased business profits (Barta, Kleiner, & Neumann, 2012; Hunt, Layton, & Prince, 2015; Hunt, Prince, Dixon-Fyle, & Yee, 2019; Nielsen & Nielsen, 2013), but the magnitude of the performance increase is far from trivial. A study published by McKinsey & Company in 2019 of over 1000 large companies covering 12 countries found that firms ranking in the top quartile of ethnic/cultural diversity in the top management team were 33% more likely to perform above the industry median in terms of profitability than firms ranking in the bottom quartile. In the board of directors, the results were even more pronounced. There, the likelihood of performing above the industry median was 43% greater for top-quartile firms in terms of ethnic/cultural diversity in the board than for bottom quartile firms (Hunt et al., 2019). Unfortunately, causal studies have not been performed on the topic. However, the available correlative evidence provides strong support for a positive, economically significant relationship between international team diversity and firm performance.

So, how do international teams help drive value creation? Well, first of all, international teams do not always outperform homogeneous teams. The superior performance of international teams depends on whether diverse perspectives are salient for the task at hand. Team performance also depends on the selection of members and the overall composition of the team, because these have implications for the formation of factions within the team, or other power dynamics stemming from differences in members' relative status. Finally, team performance may also depend on the cultural and experiential background of the team leader, and on whether the team has had a chance to practice working together.

In the remainder of the chapter, we explain these issues in greater detail. We discuss when and why international teams can be expected to be most useful, and when they are unlikely to increase task performance. We will then offer recommendations on how to effectively assemble and manage an international team, in order to realize the performance benefits of national and cultural diversity.

The Advantages of International Teams

"Creative solutions don't happen by accident. They aren't enacted by lone geniuses – they come from diverse teams that work well together and optimize the right methods and behaviours" IDEO (Aycan, 2019).

Making use of differences in identity and cognition

What is it about international teams that allows them to outperform culturally homogeneous teams? International teams are powerful because they can activate both identity-based differences, such as those deriving from social categorizations, as well as cognition-based differences representing differences in ways of thinking (Page, 2017).

Different identities allow diverse teams to tap into deep social knowledge of multiple cultural groups, such as their social norms and cultural codes. In a business setting, the inclusion of multiple identity-based perspectives yields insights into how a diverse or foreign customer base may react to a product. For instance, an international marketing team is better equipped to calibrate product specifications to meet distinct, local market needs. Equally as important, international teams are more likely to successfully dissuade firms from offering products that are unlikely to satisfy customers in a region or country. For example, instead of creating an aisle display for Smokey Bacon Flavor Pringles with the message "Ramadan Mubarak," as the British multinational retailer Tesco did in 2015, an international marketing team may have recognized the inappropriateness of the marketing tactic, saving Tesco from a public relations embarrassment – as well as a bad couple of days for the company on Twitter.

Identity-based versus cognition-based differences: An example

To highlight the distinction between identity-based differences and cognition-based differences, and to arrive at a definition of each, let's consider a hypothetical example that introduces two different teams and their respective discussions while creating an advertising campaign for a new product.

The first team is multi-functional and is composed of engineers, accountants, and marketing experts. In that discussion, the engineers highlight the technical capabilities of the product, the marketers focus on previous campaigns' relative market penetrations, while the accountants remain focused on being under budget for marketing for the quarter.

The second team is multi-generational and is composed of members of Generation Z, Millennials, Generation X, and Baby Boomers. Here, the younger members of the team argue for using influencers and social media to market the product, while the older members of the team instead offer data on the market reach of a television commercial that runs during the halftime of the Super Bowl.

After reading the hypothetical example above, how do the two teams' approaches to solving the advertising campaign problem differ? Is there a difference in the kinds of information each team draws on and views as salient?

You may notice that the multi-functional team brings together different information, different patterns of thought and ways of thinking about a problem, as well as different higher-level mental models. We define these as cognition-based differences. These cognitive differences stem from members having different educational and experiential backgrounds.

The multi-generational team, in contrast, is drawing on identity-based differences, which represent modes of categorization and social knowledge of others belonging to one's in-group. People who share an identity (whether it is generational, racial, gendered, or based on any other social categorization) often share a common social character, such as shared values, attitudes, and characteristic ways of relating to others.

International team members can also tap into cognitive differences. Being from different countries, international team members were likely socialized differently, went to different schools, and were trained differently. Consequently, they have different information, experiences, skills, techniques, modes of perception, mental models, and approaches to problem-solving, which they can apply to solve complex problems.

When are international teams useful?

Given that international teams can draw on identity-based and cognition-based differences, let's explore when and why international teams can be expected to outperform homogeneous teams.

International teams are more innovative

Studies indicate that international teams are more adept at finding creative and innovative solutions (Jang, 2017). Thanks to their different cognitive approaches, international teams can access and pool a broad range of information sources, skills, and capabilities from among their team members. The team can then integrate the knowledge and develop creative solutions or innovative approaches (Stahl, Makela, Zander, & Maznevski, 2010). In a study of 7,615 firms participating in the London Annual Business Survey, researchers found that businesses run by more culturally diverse leadership teams were more likely to develop new products than were homogeneous leadership teams (Nathan & Lee, 2013). Similarly, international marketing teams developed more novel, meaningful, and valuable campaigns (Suh & Badrinarayanan, 2014). International teams are also quicker to arrive at innovative solutions. Milan Slapak, the CEO of GE Aviation Czech Republic, noted that having 18 nationalities in the business unit "makes innovation super quick" (Slapak, 2019).

International teams make better decisions

International teams also make better decisions. Decision-making is ubiquitous in the business environment. From hiring and staffing to resource allocation, policy changes, or strategic positioning, business decisions often have long-lasting consequences that can be difficult to reverse. Indeed, research shows that effectiveness in organizational decision-making is 95% correlated with firm financial performance (Blenko, Mankins, & Rogers, 2010). Improving decision-making outcomes is, therefore, of great interest to firms.

A recent study of 566 real business decisions made by 184 business teams shows that team diversity makes a great difference for decision outcomes. In particular, international teams make decisions that are, on average, 75% better than those of wholly homogeneous teams (Cloverpop, 2017). (Decision-making can be improved even more by increasing diversity further. Teams that were diverse along national, gender, and age dimensions made decisions that were 87% better than those of homogeneous teams (see Figure 1) (Cloverpop, 2017).

What could the reason for this be? Well, the ability to rely on multiple identities and multiple cognitive approaches allows international team members to bring different perspectives, experiences, and information sets to the table. This, in turn, helps people sidestep their own cognitive biases and see how a decision might play out in alternate contexts. Since team members have different individual experiences, they tend to focus more on facts, re-examine facts, process them more carefully, and maintain objectivity (Levine et al., 2014; Sommers, 2006).

Overall, international team members challenge inherent biases, they question groupthink and are thus more flexible in how they allow the group to approach business problems – leading to positive outcomes.

Fig 13.1 Decision-making by diverse teams (Cloverpop, 2017)

The Challenges of International Teams

In an ideal setting, companies would reap the benefits of diverse teams without any downsides. But in many cases, differences among individuals also hinder effective communication and fuel conflict, which limits process efficiency and inhibits performance. Diversity in identities and ways of thinking pose major challenges for effective communication and efficient collaboration in international teams.

Effective communication remains a challenge for international teams

Team friction stems from a lack of commonalities among international team members. When international diversity is high, team members must work to overcome both cultural and language barriers. These pose a substantial challenge, because they mean that team members lack a shared identity and meaning system.

Imagine collaborating on a project with a person where one or both of you are not communicating using your native language. In addition, you may both struggle to interpret the meaning of facial expressions, and you cannot ease tension through a shared sense of humor. You may also find that you disagree on acceptable behavioral norms. That's quite the handicap.

Studies examining international teams indicate that friction may appear very early during collaboration. Upon receiving an assignment, team members may not agree on the meaning of shared information (Gibson, 1996). Not only that, they may even disagree on acceptable norms regarding information sharing within the group and with outsiders (Goodman, Ravlin, & Schminke, 1990). Furthermore, they may have different expectations regarding how the work itself should proceed (Gibson & Zellmer-Bruhn,

2001). These issues may breed conflict and hinder fruitful collaboration. Indeed, decreased team efficiency is a significant drawback of international teams.

When are international teams not useful?

Given the problems that international teams face, when is it not desirable or recommended to use international teams? We address this issue next by focusing on which types of tasks and processes benefit
from international team members' access to an expanded set of identities and ways of thinking and
which do not (and why).

The type of task matters for exploiting the benefits of international diversity

It turns out that diversity in social knowledge and cognitive schema is useful in only a subset of tasks – in
cognitive, non-routine tasks, to be exact. Indeed, international teams outperform homogeneous teams
when the business problem is complex, multidimensional, and indecomposable (Page, 2017); in other
words, when the problem is too complex to be solved by any one individual and impossible to separate
into smaller, independent parts.

However, international teams do not outperform culturally homogeneous teams when the business
problem requires completing a manual, routine task (e.g., assembling pizza boxes at a rapid pace), a
cognitive, routine task (e.g., processing expense reports accurately), or a manual, non-routine task (like
ensuring customer satisfaction in catering a wedding). For tasks other than cognitive and non-routine
ones, the communication and efficiency costs of national and cultural diversity outweigh its benefits.

Categorizing types of tasks

Tasks can be classified along two dimensions: 1) routine versus non-routine, and 2) cognitive versus
manual (Autor, Levy, & Murnane, 2003).

To have a sense of the distinctions, let's first examine the manual dimension. Consider the types of
tasks taken on by a line worker assembling product components compared to a nursing home employee.
While both involve manual work, the line worker is engaging in routine work, while the nursing home
employee is repeatedly faced with non-routine problems and tasks.

Along the cognitive dimension, routine cognitive work can be exemplified by data entry work, while
non-routine cognitive work is akin to the work of a medical researcher (Autor et al., 2003). Interestingly,
non-routine cognitive work is the type of work that employs the greatest proportion of people and
where people earn the highest incomes (Dvorkin, 2016).

International teams are more effective during problem analysis than implementation

Where the company is in the problem-solving process also determines the desired level of national
and cultural diversity within a team. Problem-solving generally involves three distinct stages: (i) problem identification, (ii) problem analysis, and (iii) implementation.

In the first stage, the relevance of individuals' experiences for the task at hand is critical for accurately
identifying the problem that needs to be solved. In contrast, problem analysis benefits greatly from
diversity of thought. It is here, in the second stage, that companies enjoy the greatest benefits of team
diversity. However, when it comes to implementing the proposed solution, diverse teams are no longer

optimal. This is presumably because diverse teams struggle more than homogeneous teams to communicate effectively and collaborate efficiently (Ancona & Caldwell, 1992). Therefore, upon reaching the implementation stage of the process, homogenous teams are preferred.

In the next section, we turn to what managers and international team members can do to avoid pitfalls and reach their full potential.

How to Realize Gains from National and Cultural Diversity in Teams

Match the team to the problem

An essential component to leveraging the benefits of an international team is to match the people to the task at hand. Therefore, even before thinking about whom to select or how to configure the overall team, it is important first to consider this: what business objective is this team being asked to address, solve, or manage? Only once the goal is clearly defined can the organization choose team members whose knowledge, skills, and abilities align with the assignment.

Now, let's think through a few specific examples of projects that MNCs or companies that are seeking to become international commonly undertake and consider how the response team should be composed.

Entry into a new foreign market

While foreign markets offer opportunities for value creation and growth, firms that operate abroad often struggle to replicate the success they have in their home market. In fact, foreign market entry efforts fail more often than they succeed (Alcacer, 2015). Why? Well, in and of itself, every entry effort into a market requires making a series of difficult decisions such as selecting a location, determining when (and how quickly) to enter, choosing an entry mode strategy, and engaging strategic partners—among many others.

When expanding internationally, these decisions are further complicated by language and cultural differences, compliance and regulatory issues, as well as different customer preferences. Faced with an unfamiliar environment, even experienced executives fall prey to cognitive biases that limit their ability to process information effectively. These biases may lead to overestimating the size of the market, misjudging the relevance of the firm's resources and skills, or to underrating the competitive strength of local rivals already operating in the foreign location.

During the initial stages of foreign market entry, it is therefore important to tap individuals that are familiar with the way the company works, but who do not just see what they want to see. In other words, when configuring a team to accurately assess the viability of a foreign market and handle an initial market entry, companies should select people who are company insiders, but who can maintain an outsider's perspective.

One approach is to compose a team out of third-country foreigners – that is, people who are neither parent-country nor host-country nationals. Although they are company insiders, third-country nationals (TCNs) can scout a market and plan entry because they can maintain distance from both the dominant culture of the parent country as well as from the host country the firm is seeking to enter. Furthermore, the variety of perspectives they bring to the task allows a team composed of TCNs to notice salient differences in the host country's business environment and to evaluate how the identified differences could affect the firm's ability to operate profitably there.

Importantly, although TCNs notice differences, their previous international experience also makes them more comfortable, tolerant, and flexible when dealing with them. This ease in dealing with foreigners is an important asset when communicating or negotiating with potential suppliers, buyers, regulators, or other stakeholders in the new market who appear to behave in unexpected ways.

Member terminology in international teams

Because we will be discussing issues relating to cross-border operations, it may be useful to introduce and define relevant terminology.

A multinational firm is an organization with operations in two or more foreign countries. Multinational companies (MNCs) typically have headquarters, and these are located in the MNC's "home country" (sometimes also referred to as the "parent country"). This is the country where the company was established and where it is domiciled. An MNCs foreign operations are performed outside the MNC's home country in a "host country" (or "subsidiary country").

Therefore, when we talk about employees' nationalities, apart from discussing their specific country of origin, we can also classify them as being (i) "parent-country nationals" (PCNs) – a.k.a. from the country where the MNC is headquartered, (ii) "host-country nationals" (HCNs) – a.k.a. from a subsidiary country, or (iii) "third-country nationals" (TCNs) – a.k.a. from neither the parent country nor the host country.

In contrast, a team composed solely of parent-country nationals (PCNs) may wrongly assume that the business approaches, leadership styles, and behaviors that work well in the home market will also work abroad. Host-country nationals (HCNs), in contrast, are native. Therefore, a team composed of HCNs may not be sufficiently sensitive to the pain points a company is likely to experience when operating there.

A second possible approach is to configure a team composed of a combination of PCNs, HCNs, and TCNs, and allow the team to use their various perspectives and experiences to assess the foreign market. However, as we explain later in the chapter, differences in status among individuals in the team or the formation of subgroups in the team may hinder fruitful communication and collaboration. A mixed team needs to be composed with those challenges in mind.

Growing and managing foreign operations

Once operations have been established in a foreign market, the next task is to grow and expand the company's presence and market share. It is time to increase the proportion of HCNs on the team. HCNs who were not only born, but also raised, educated, and employed in their native country are very valuable to an expanding firm because they possess superior linguistic, economic, cultural, and institutional knowledge of the foreign environment (Tung, 1982). This deep understanding allows HCNs to effectively adapt to products and processes to meet the needs of the foreign market (Bartlett & Yoshihara, 1988). Appropriate adaptation, in turn, boosts demand for the product and fuels growth.

HCNs' host-country experience also makes them adept at navigating the local institutional environment (Gupta & Govindarajan, 1991). From helping the company figure out how to register new business entities, acquire requisite permits, or fulfill regulatory requirements, HCNs' tacit knowledge of their home environment is vital for overcoming the types of bureaucratic hurdles that would otherwise impede growth.

By virtue of being embedded in local social and professional networks, HCNs can also foster crucial connections between the firm and the local labor market. Importantly, the presence of HCNs signals legitimacy in the host-country environment (Harzing, 2001; Rickley & Karim, 2018). For example, having a local CEO as the public face of the company enhances acceptance and positive perceptions of a foreign firm's presence in the host-country environment.

Taken together, as firms strive to grow and effectively manage their foreign operations abroad, not only does the proportion of HCNs in the team need to rise, but the level of responsibility and leadership duties of HCNs ought to grow as well.

Product development for a foreign market

Developing a product to meet the needs of a specific market is similar to the logic introduced above for growing operations. Again, it is important to tap individuals with an in-depth knowledge of local demand preferences, regulations, and professional norms and who possess local network connections. At Sony and T-Mobile, for example, international teams are used to advocate for foreign customers' preferences through the product development, product introduction, and product adoption phases (Lyall, 2006). Research indicates that a team where one of the members shares the end user's ethnicity is 152% more likely to understand the end-user relative to when a member of the team does not (Hewlett, Marshall, & Sherbin, 2013).

Transferring product or process knowledge across borders

One of the greatest advantages of multinational firms is their superior capacity to transfer knowledge across country borders (Kogut & Zander, 1993). But the fact that it is easier to transfer knowledge within a multinational firm compared to between two separate firms in different countries doesn't mean it is easy. Effective knowledge transfer requires command of knowledge, familiarity with context, as well as motivation to succeed.

Because knowledge is transferred from person to person, MNCs need to tap individuals who (i) understand the knowledge that must be transmitted, (ii) can be trusted to transfer the knowledge in a predictable way, and (iii) have the requisite personal connections to foster knowledge exchange between the knowledge originator and the knowledge recipient.

In MNCs, these individuals are often PCNs, who "grew up" in the firm. Relative to HCNs or TCNS, PCNs can be expected to possess a deep understanding of organizational strategy, be aware of the firm's strengths (and be cognizant of the firm's weaknesses), understand linkages between systems, company history, legacy, and culture—and even be sensitive to company politics. As a consequence, they can be expected to know how the knowledge to be transferred fits within the organizational context, i.e., the goals of the organization as well as the organization's constraints.

For the purpose of knowledge transfer, PCNs are also considered to be trustworthy. Having been socialized in headquarters, they are thought to identify with the parent organization as a whole and with its objectives (Kobrin, 1988). This means that they can be expected to enact the dominant logic and strategy of corporate leaders in a predictable manner (Boyacigiller, 1990; Prahalad & Bettis, 1986). PCNs often have strong interpersonal ties to individuals in MNC headquarters, as well as to expatriates working in foreign subsidiaries. Close social ties enable the transfer of information and knowledge (Hansen, 1999).

Taken together, when tasked with transferring product or process knowledge, the team ought to have an increased proportion of PCNs (Gaur, Delios, & Singh, 2007).

Cross-cultural collaboration

When pursuing initiatives that require cross-cultural collaboration—like when a Hollywood studio partner with the Chinese movie industry to produce the next Chinese-American blockbuster film, or when NGOs from different countries join forces in their humanitarian efforts following a natural disaster—cultural misunderstandings and different ways of operating between the two groups can lead to frictions and delays that threaten the realization of the joint project. In these situations, including individuals that can cross divides and help build a common platform that helps the two sides understand each other can be the difference between achieving success or stumbling toward failure.

People with the ability to cross divides are called boundary spanners. In cross-cultural situations, multicultural individuals often effectively serve the boundary spanning role and are a great asset (Rickley, 2019). Multicultural individuals are people who have internalized two or more cultures. Based on their past immersive experiences, they can identify with multiple nationalities and leverage commonalities between them. By building upon commonalities between other team members, boundary spanners bridge cultural and linguistic boundaries, and facilitate the kind of intra-team communication and interaction between team members that is integral to a successful project outcome.

Be mindful of team proportions

In the previous section, we discussed strengthening or limiting the presence of certain types of individuals (PCNs, HCN, TCNs, multiculturals), and a logical question arises: what should the overall team composition look like? Indeed, there are a couple of aspects of team composition to keep in mind when assembling an international team.

Beware of the single, dissimilar team member

When composing a team, it may be tempting to create an "international team" by including a single, non-native member to an otherwise culturally-homogeneous team. However, this should be avoided. A solo member will often struggle to introduce new knowledge, to have ideas heard, and therefore to substantially influence group deliberations and decision outcomes. In practice, the benefits of having multiple perspectives to draw on diminish when one member is without support from the others. Being the odd one out can lead to being seen as the "token member," which can result in stereotyping and marginalization (Early & Mosakowski, 2000).

Subgroups can splinter a team into opposing factions

We just saw above how problems come about when there is a single, non-native member in the team. However, problems can also arise when multiple team members share a national origin. In that case, the international team may splinter into subgroups based on shared nationality.

Splintering can precipitate subpar communication and even conflict because it leads to the formation of "in-groups" and "out-groups." For example, in a team composed of Americans and Germans, American members may view another American as "one of us," but not have the same perception of German team members. Subgroup members tend to share and support in members' viewpoints and band together against out-members' ideas and proposals. Subgroup members may form factions and even "close ranks" to vote on issues as a bloc.

The splintering tends to more pronounced when a subgroup members' backgrounds align along more than one attribute (i.e., nationality and gender in common, or nationality and functional experience in common) (Lau & Murnighan, 1998), such as if in the hypothetical international team introduced above the Americans were also all marketing specialists, while the Germans were also all engineers. In these instances, the separation between the subgroups – also called a faultline – is stronger.

What issues does the formation of a faultline pose for teams? Simply put, subgroup formation inhibits a team's ability to listen to one another. Faultlines limit teams' abilities to effectively communicate information, accept the legitimacy of the information that is being transmitted, consider the validity of shared information in-depth, and integrate available information across domains. In essence, team faultlines constrain the benefits of diversity.

With respect to team composition, the risk of faultline formation is greatest in moderately diverse teams, where a limited number of different backgrounds are represented but where there are also commonalities between individuals. In particular, teams with subgroups of equal size or power may experience the greatest dysfunction, because they may perceive they are competing over a fixed amount of scarce resources. In contrast, homogeneous teams do not have enough differences among members for subgroups to form.

To avoid the negative consequences of team faultlines while retaining the benefits of multiple perspectives in a team, consider assembling a team with dissimilar individuals—in other words, a highly diverse team. Highly diverse teams do not have the opportunity to form subgroups because there are not enough similarities among members. Instead, the selected individuals may derive a team identity from their diversity, rather than from any similarity between individuals.

Address status differentials and power dynamics within the team

In addition to minding team proportions, another issue that may arise when composing an international team is relative status among team members. Nationalities can differ in perceived status, either broadly speaking or within a particular organizational context (Leslie, 2017). People from advanced economies may enjoy a high status relative to people from emerging economies, for example. Or, in the context of a headquarters-subsidiary relationship, individuals of parent-country origin may be considered high status, while people of host-country origin are considered low status. These status differentials and perceptions of high and low power can counteract the benefits of diversity because they inhibit information flow and integrative problem-solving. Low-status individuals can be disinclined to speak up, fearing that their contributions will be dismissed. Alternatively, low-status individuals may have trouble championing their solutions toward successful implementation.

Overall, to enjoy the benefits of international team diversity in contexts where status or power dynamics are in play, it is important to support and give voice to members who may feel marginalized because of their status. In these cases, team leaders also need to reinforce the importance of a single team identity.

Assign a team leader with a global identity

Indeed, team leadership is an important consideration when assembling an international team. The right leader can soothe the frictions that arise, while the wrong leader can further exacerbate them.

Studies indicate that one attribute that is particularly useful is for the leader to have a global identity (Lisak, Erez, Sui, & Lee, 2016). A global identity is earned through extensive international experience and interaction with people from different cultures. International teams benefit from globally-enlightened leadership in a range of ways, which, when put together, help them to realize the full potential of their national and cultural diversity.

First, leaders who have a global identity are more likely to identify with all the members of their international team. This means they act as bridge-builders between diverse members and foster better communication. An executive at L'Oreal characterized the abilities of people with a global identity as follows: "[They] have a kind of gymnastic intellectual training to think as if they were French, American, or Chinese and all together inside them" (EIU, 2013). Second, leaders with a global identity act as role models, as they guide, mobilize, or even inspire the members of their team toward sharing and considering different sources of knowledge. Third, they encourage and foster shared goals.

In sum, leaders with a global identity can convey a sense of inclusion for all team members, regardless of any member's country of origin. They can effectively diffuse us vs. them mentalities. For them, everyone is treated as part of the "in-group." This is important, as it unites subgroups through an inclusive workplace culture.

Overall, by recognizing and framing diversity to be an asset instead of as a problem to be overcome, team leaders with a global identity are well equipped to extract the benefits of national and cultural diversity in a team.

Practice solving problems together

Finally, international teams get better at working together through practice. By first working on simpler problems, nationally diverse members can build up to attacking more complex problems. Practice allows team members to become familiar with one another's communication styles, work behavior and to recognize each other's strengths as well as each other's blind spots. Another important component of working together effectively is to build interpersonal trust. Oftentimes, this is done more easily in more informal or social settings, where team members can get to know one another as people, instead of just as colleagues.

References

Alcacer, J. (2015). Competing globally. In R. Casadesus-Masanell (Ed.), Core Curriculum: Strategy: Harvard Business Publishing.

Ancona, D. G., & Caldwell, D. F. (1992). Demography and design: Predictors of new product team performance. Organization Science, 3(3), 321–341.

ArcelorMittal. (2020). Executive officers. Retrieved from https://corporate.arcelormittal.com /who-we-are/leadership/group-management-board

Autor, D. H., Levy, F., & Murnane, R. J. (2003). The skill content of recent technological change: An empirical exploration. Quarterly Journal of Economics, 118(4), 1279–1333.

Aycan, D. (2019). 4 common missteps on the road to innovation. Retrieved from https://www.ideo .com/blog/4-common-missteps-on-the-road-to-innovation

Barta, T., Kleiner, M., & Neumann, T. (2012). Is there a payoff from top-team diversity? McKinsey Quarterly(April).

Bartlett, C. A., & Yoshihara, H. (1988). New challenges for Japanese multinationals: Is organization adaptation their Achilles Heel? Human Resource Management, 27(1), 19–43.

Blenko, M. W., Mankins, M. C., & Rogers, P. (2010). The decision-driven organization. Harvard Business Review, June.

Boyacigiller, N. (1990). The role of expatriates in the management of interdependence, complexity and risk in multinational corporations. Journal of International Business Studies, 21(357–381).

Cloverpop. (2017). Hacking diversity with inclusive decision making. Retrieved from https://www .cloverpop.com/hubfs/Whitepapers/Cloverpop_Hacking_Diversity_Inclusive_Decision _Making_White_Paper.pdf

Dvorkin, M. (2016). Jobs involving routine tasks are not growing. On the Economy. Retrieved from https://www.stlouisfed.org/on-the-economy/2016/january/jobs-involving-routine-tasks -arent-growing.

Early, P. C., & Mosakowski, E. (2000). Creating hybrid team cultures: An empirical test of transnational team functioning. Academy of Management Journal, 43, 26–49.

EIU. (2009). Leveraging the power of global innovation. Economist Intelligence Unit.

EIU. (2013). The rise of multicultural managers. Economist Intelligence Unit.

Gaur, A. S., Delios, A., & Singh, K. (2007). Institutional environments, staffing strategies, and subsidiary performance. Journal of Management, 33(4), 611–636.

Ghemawat, P., & Vantrappen, H. (2015). How global is your C-suite? MIT Sloan Management Review, 56(4), 72–82.

Gibson, C. B. (1996). Do you hear what I hear? A framework for reconciling intercultural communication difficulties arising from cognitive styles and cultural values. In M. Erez & P. C. Early (Eds.), New perspectives on international industrial organization psychology (pp. 335–362). San Francisco: Jossey-Bass.

Gibson, C. B., & Zellmer-Bruhn, M. (2001). Metaphors and meaning: An intercultural analysis of the concept of teamwork. Administrative Science Quarterly, 46, 274–303.

Goodman, P. S., Ravlin, E. C., & Schminke, M. (1990). Understanding groups in organizations. In L. L. Cummings & B. M. Staw (Eds.), Leadership, participation, and group behavior (pp. 323–385). Greenwich, CT: JAI Press.

Gupta, A. K., & Govindarajan, V. (1991). Knowledge flows and the structure of control within multinational corporations. Academy of Management Review, 16(4), 768–792.

Hansen, M. T. (1999). The search-transfer problem: The role of weak ties in sharing knowledge across organization subunits. Administrative Science Quarterly, 44(1), 82–111.

Harzing, A.-W. (2001). Who's in charge? An empirical study of executive staffing practices in foreign subsidiaries. Human Resource Management, 40(2), 139–158.

Hewlett, S. A., Marshall, M., & Sherbin, L. (2013). How diversity can drive innovation. Harvard Business Review, December.

Hunt, V., Layton, D., & Prince, S. (2015). Diversity matters. Retrieved from http://www.mckinsey .com/business-functions/organization/our-insights/why-diversity-matters

Hunt, V., Prince, S., Dixon-Fyle, S., & Yee, L. (2019). Delivering through diversity. Retrieved from http://www.mckinsey.com/business-functions/organization/our-insights/why-diversity-matters

Jang, S. (2017). Cultural brokerage and creative performance in multicultural teams. Organization Science, 28(6), 993–1009.

Kobrin, S. J. (1988). Expatriate reduction and strategic control in American multinational corporations. Human Resource Management, 27(1), 63–75.

Kogut, B., & Zander, U. (1993). Knowledge of the firm and the evolutionary theory of the multinational corporation. Journal of International Business Studies, 244(4), 625–645.

Lau, D. C., & Murnighan, J. K. (1998). Demographic diversity and faultlines: The compositional dynamics of organizational groups. Academy of Management Review, 23(2), 325–340.

Leslie, L. M. (2017). A status-based multilevel model of ethnic diversity and work unit performance. Journal of Management, 43(2), 426–454.

Levine, S. S., Apfelbaum, E. P., Bernard, M., Bartelt, V. L., Zajac, E. J., & Stark, D. (2014). Ethnic diversity deflates price bubbles. Proceedings of the National Academy of Sciences of the United States of America, 111(52), 18524–18529.

Lisak, A., Erez, M., Sui, Y., & Lee, C. (2016). The positive role of global leaders in enhancing multicultural team innovation. Journal of International Business Studies, 47, 655–673.

Lyall, K. (2006). How to improve your new product success rate. Market Leader, 34(3), 47–51.

Nathan, M., & Lee, N. (2013). Cultural diversity, innovation, and entrepreneurship: Firm-level evidence from London. Economic Geography, 89(4), 367–394.

Nielsen, B. B., & Nielsen, S. (2013). Top management team nationality diversity and firm performance: A multilevel study. Strategic Management Journal, 34(3), 373–382.

Page, S. (2017). The Diversity Bonus: How Great Teams Pay Off in the Knowledge Economy. Princeton, NJ: Princeton University Press.

Prahalad, C. K., & Bettis, R. A. (1986). The dominant logic: a new linkage between diversity and performance. Strategic Management Journal, 7(6), 485–501.

Rickley, M. (2019). Cultural generalists and cultural specialists: Examining international experience portfolios of subsidiary executives in multinational firms. Journal of Management, 45(2), 384–416.

Rickley, M., & Karim, S. (2018). Managing institutional distance: Examining how firm-specific advantages impact foreign subsidiary CEO staffing. Journal of World Business, 53(5), 740–751.

Slapak, M. (2019, 5/24/2019) GE Aviation in the Czech Republic/Interviewer: M. Rickley.

Sommers, S. R. (2006). On racial diversity and group decision making: Identifying multiple effects of racial composition on jury deliberations. Journal of Personality and Social Psychology, 90(4), 597–612.

Stahl, G. K., Makela, K., Zander, L., & Maznevski, M. L. (2010). A look at the bright side of multicultural team diversity. Scandinavian Journal of Management, 26(4), 439–447.

Suh, T., & Badrinarayanan, V. (2014). Proximal and distal influences on project creativity in international marketing teams. International Marketing Review, 31(3), 283–307.

Tung, R. L. (1982). Selection and training procedures of U.S., European, and Japanese Multinationals. California Management Review, 25(1), 57–71.

CHAPTER 14

Good Coaching Could Change the Game
How GVTs Could Be Coached Effectively

ABDULRAHMAN CHIKHOUNI, MOUNT ROYAL UNIVERSITY

APRIL BEAURIVAGE, MOUNT ROYAL UNIVERSITY

Each organization has its own culture and structure, and there is a need for people from within the organization to direct less informed or new employees to the proper way of doing business. In some organizations, there are units or individuals dedicated to supporting the work of other units that need more resources and guidance. Typically, in large multinational companies, there are support and coaching units that provide guidance and training through a proactive service to support teams and ensure effective decision-making. The support unit provides coaching for teams to obtain a level of expertise on topics such as scheduling, cost management, and data quality check. This enables teams to track and execute projects in a controlled matter. When it comes to X-Culture, students can rely on the coaching program to solve challenges that face them during the project. Similar to the support unit in large companies, the coaching program uses coaches who undergo months of practical training, learn effective feedback through hands-on methods, and develop manuals to provide feedback and advise teams.

Many students start the X-Culture project feeling excitement mixed with a sense of exploration. However, due to the nature of the project, which brings people from different countries together and has them virtually work together, some students start to face challenges either due to their readiness to tackle such a project or due to the composition of their team and miscommunication. Fortunately, X-Culture provides some help to ease the situation through the coaching program. This chapter will explain the importance of coaches and support units in organizations generally and, more specifically, in X-Culture. Furthermore, we provide some recommendations for how teams can benefit from utilizing these expert resources, and include team-based examples through X-Culture projects and the corporate environment.

To better understand coaches in X-Culture and corporations, it is essential to first identify the terminology difference between an X-Culture Coach and the regular perception of a head coach of sports teams. X-Culture Coaches support and do not lead. Coaches, as defined by X-Culture, are "former X-Culture project participants who showed excellent performance, scored high on Cultural Intelligence, Emotional Intelligence, and Technical Literacy tests. They also showed care and creativity in their comments and produced excellent-quality business proposals." As mentioned, X-Culture coaches are experienced with the program and understand what a professional report should look like. Each semester, when new students compete by writing business reports for challenge companies, a new group of X-Culture participants becomes coaches.

Why Are Coaches Important?

We will explain the importance of coaches in the corporate world and the X-Culture context and examine the similarities between the two. To do this, the authors interviewed three informants from a Canadian multinational company that has a designated supporting unit within the organizational structure. The support unit was created to be a channel of communication from skilled coaches to project teams. The unit acts as a center that shares tools and serves as one consistent voice. Similar to X-Culture, the unit is constantly improving through ongoing cycles of people, processes, and tools. During an interview with the informants, the importance of coaches came up as a crucial factor for the success of project teams. Coaches are important to businesses because they ensure best practices are harnessed and communicated back to teams to ensure their success. The following were outlined for the importance of coaches:

1. Act as a trusted knowledge center to ensure project teams have the tools, training, and human connections required to deliver successful projects and to bridge the gap between different project areas
2. Provide on-demand training for new team members
3. Monitor and inform about streamlined guidelines, rules, and regulations
4. Direct project teams to the right contact to solve specific issues within the organization.

Coaches are seen as trusted knowledge centers who help teams bridge their knowledge gaps and encourage them to learn the suitable tools and processes. For instance, many teams are not well-informed about how to develop financial metrics for their reports, which is essential to prepare professional reports that could be presented to executives. To solve this issue, a specialized group within the support unit functions as a guide to help project teams using financial metrics in their reports.

Coaches and support units provide training on demand for new members for tasks that are not usually discussed during typical training sessions. Through speaking with a spokesperson, it was discovered that the Canadian company uses many internal reporting software programs, and the usual training does not properly inform new employees about all of the software. Therefore, new members need more allocated time to learn the processes from the support unit. Experts will spend time showing how the tool works in a systematic process.

Coaches are important as monitors and a source of guidance for rules and regulations. For instance, the support unit in the Canadian company was heavily involved in setting up specific standards for an external consultancy that, due to a lack of knowledge, does not accurately follow the rules. If problems arise, the coach will try to solve the problem, but if it persists, they will direct the situation to the proper leaders who can solve the problem. Moreover, coaches will create action items to ensure important deadlines are met.

From interviewing a key leader of the support unit, a specific statement came up a few times, which was: "If we cannot answer your question, we know who could." Effective coaches should know where to direct project team members when they are unable to answer specific questions or do not have the specific skill sets to solve an issue. When a new member is assigned a project and is unsure of where to turn to, the support unit can advise on a proper contact point. In X-Culture, for instance, there was a case where a coach was supporting a team where a male member was sending inappropriate messages to a female member. He showed no intent to do the report and expressed violent intentions. Because the Coach was not experienced with sexual harassment cases nor had the responsibility to lead a case such as this, the coach re-directed the case to the X-Culture Administration team and was able to direct the affected student to the right contact within the organization.

Coaches in X-Culture play similar rules that support team performance in the context of companies, and below, we will show how the abovementioned four rules of coaches apply to the context of X-Culture.

Point 1: Coaches in X-Culture serve as a trusted knowledge center because they have completed the same report for a different client, and therefore are familiar with the report format and the requirements for the weekly deliverables. They have attained a high score on their final report and were trained in theoretical topics, including conflict resolution methods, free-rider handling, and plagiarism. To improve the capabilities of coaches, they undergo a 17-week program designed to provide additional training and coaching experience to enable them to help X-Culture students. One of the authors worked as a coach and a head coach in X-Culture, and she experienced the role of coach as a trusted knowledge center. For instance, she was trying to help a group to explain the choice of a target country for expansion, but she realized that the team had not provided sufficient research to show how their selected destination was the right fit for the challenge company. As a result, the team performed more in-depth research and adjusted the report accordingly. This simple readjustment at the time of submission saved the team from realizing their error later, which potentially would have resulted in them submitting a weaker report than they would have intended.

Point 2: Students competing in X-Culture complete a report that is evaluated by many professors around the world, who outline errors and areas of improvement. As coaches have previously competed in the project, they are aware of mistakes found in reports. They can ensure that students are not making the same mistakes by providing on-demand training for students. As an example, the report requires students to complete a framework called SWOT analysis for the client company they have selected. The student can contact their assigned coach for proper training on how to conduct a SWOT analysis, and the coach will be able to address whether or not the framework has been used effectively or if the students need to research further to improve their report.

Point 3: X-Culture coaches are aware of the guidelines, rules, and regulations students must abide by when completing their report. With a two-month deadline that includes weekly submissions on top of each student's personal lives, it becomes difficult to keep up with deadlines. Students can ask coaches to clarify tasks needed to be completed and their respective due dates. Also, reviewing this information with a coach may save a team from making some simple mistakes that might affect the quality of the report. In addition to due dates, handling conflict situations is another primary topic related to rules and regulations related to X-Culture. It is discovered that the most common types of interpersonal issues include free-riding, coordination problems, and negativity. A coach has the responsibility to ensure students are following rules that do not promote conflict situations between teams, such as bullying or free-riding. As a previous coach, I was assigned a case where two students were assumed by their team to be free-riders, but after contacting the two affected students and collecting some information about the date of the first contact, and the details of the absent team members, I realized that the whole problem was about communication, not free-riding. After sorting out the issue of communication, the team functioned properly until the end of the project.

Point 4: X-Culture coaches can redirect students to the right contact within X-Culture. Coaches will be the first contact point for students and will most likely be the only contact point. They will act as an intermediary between students and the Head Administration. Coaches can help with almost all of the students' needs, except for technical problems and the rare cases of harassment that need to be handled by a higher administrator skilled in that area. It is difficult for a student to reach the administrative team. One must understand that all X-Culture participants are busy individuals, often with full-time jobs or educational studies. Therefore, when a problem arises, it is almost always directed towards a coach to handle, and 9 out of 10 times, a coach will answer a problem. However, if there is an off chance a coach does not have the proper resources to solve the task, they know exactly where to direct it to within X-Culture.

As a final remark, it is important to reiterate that coaches enjoy helping students and appreciate X-Culture. The Coaching Program itself was initially designed in response to students who had previously competed and enjoyed the project and were seeking a way to stay a part of X-Culture. Coaches simply love being coaches. As each semester progresses and a new group of students become coaches, the program improves. Previous coaches are asked to provide feedback to the program to ensure the successful continuation of future coaches. The support unit in the aforementioned Canadian company similarly advances their unit with a new cycle of experts who join the team. After coaches within the team have built up their expertise and helped improve the unit, new coaches will join with an understanding of people, project teams, and execution needs. The drive to help others and to keep a professional relationship are key motivators for coaches when joining the support unit. Each new round of X-Culture coaches brings new skills and expertise to the program, all with the same burning passion for X-Culture and the goal to support X-Culture students.

Coaches, Not Nursing

It is essential to distinguish the common misconceptions about the purpose of coaches. As mentioned during the interview of an expert from the support unit in the Canadian company, there existed a case where a project team approached the unit in the hope for them to do work for the team instead of seeking direction. The case involved migrating documents through online software, a task that needed to be completed by the project team due to reservation rights of the documents. The team expected the support unit to complete the task, but the unit was able to redirect the team and show them the process instead of doing the task for them. The example shows how coaches should not be used to lead teams but instead to support them.

As discussed earlier, a typical coach, such as a sports coach, is different than an X-Culture coach. A sports coach will lead the team and provide answers for the team to reach success. However, in X-Culture, the coach will not lead but instead support. They will not offer a final answer but rather a direction. A coach should not be approached to correct errors or solve problems but instead used to seek feedback. Feedback does not include writing a section of the report for a team or correcting grammatical errors, but instead providing the right direction on an area of the report that needs improvement. A common description used by X-Culture of a coach is to "mentor who provides feedback or directs students to the right resources, but does not run the team or do its work. The teams are responsible for completing their own projects, making their own decisions and meeting deadlines."

Typically in organizations, coaches are not expected to lead the group but to provide direction and feedback. One of the contacts in the Canadian company described teams approaching the unit for direction on new processes related to stewardship reporting and supply chain management. They sought to gain validation on their work and feedback for the team to execute in front of a leadership team professionally. Sometimes the unit will receive requests that are not aligned with the coaching concept and instead expect the expert team to complete a task for them, as mentioned earlier. Another example involved a project lead who owned a project artifact and was tasked with coordinating the artifact at a leadership meeting. However, the support unit specifies that they are not part of the team, and ownership of work needs to be aligned with the project team members. Therefore, the project team had to lead the artifact and use the unit only as a supporting member.

Teams should utilize coaches as a source of feedback. Often, a coach can be a helpful source to improve the report as they are an external person, not a part of the team. They will identify unclear sections that are not supported properly and are poorly formatted. The goal of the feedback is to improve a team's performance and to strengthen the ideas a team has to present. Some team members approach coaches with the expectation that a coach can help add to the report, finish a chapter, or even collect data for the project. That high level of expectation could be due to a miscommunication regarding the role of coaches or merely an act of desperation on the part of some team members after losing the hope from being free riders in their team; therefore, they approach coaches looking for someone who can fill in the gap. X-Culture participants need to keep in mind that coaches are not their team members.

As one of their responsibilities, X-Culture coaches are continually providing feedback to teams. The first stream is through weekly feedback. Coaches are tasked to challenge companies, then assigned to review a certain number of reports with four to five other coaches. Through this, teammates who are inspired by X-Culture and are responsible and intelligent often spend hours debating and discussing the best approach to feedback. They are dedicated to ensuring each team succeeds through the feedback provided. As a previous coach, my fellow coaches and I evaluated 30 reports each week. Out of 30, there were only 2 or 3 reports that were close to perfection but still needed readjustments with simple tasks such as poor formatting. That being said, every report we analyzed could be improved, and this states the importance of weekly feedback when adjusting a report.

The second approach to feedback that coaches provide is through assigned cases. If a team directly asks for a coach, the coach will be contacted and assigned to a team. Students should utilize this source, as coaches enjoy being assigned feedback cases and the chance to help motivate a team to succeed personally. In this case, however, teams should not wait for coaches to provide answers for them or lead them in a step-by-step approach to complete the challenges. Instead, this source should be used as a way for the team to develop their problem-solving skills with an outside source providing feedback. Examples of feedback offered by coaches could include the formatting of the project, the accuracy of information about the client company, proper citation, etc.

On a final note, coaches are not technical people, managers of the challenge companies or X-Culture. Coaches are unable to help cases involving technical problems where surveys may close earlier than the due date, submission errors, or email technicalities. They do not have specific access to details or information about challenge companies any more than students do. Additionally, they are not full-time employees of X-Culture and are often students who are studying full-time. Coaches are not group team members, and there should be no expectation for them to contribute to a teams' report. In the end, coaches do not have answers but instead, have experiences and ideas. X-Culture's challenges are not standardized tests. There are no right or wrong answers, only more or less effective ideas, and teams should utilize coaches to help display brilliant ideas in their final report.

Communication with Coaches

Communication involves two parties, the sender and the receiver, and for effective communication, the message must be understood by the receiver. When introducing culture into the communication model, the sender and receiver are influenced by different experiences and influences that may change their perception of the intended message. When discussing the topic of communication with the Canadian company, we found that communication is a key topic related to the effectiveness of the support. The primary form of communication was identified as electronic, through email. However, this was also described as the most misunderstood form of communication, as messages may be missed due to email overload and time differences, misinterpretation of tone, and unclear instructions.

One specific member of the support unit described her struggle with time zones and cultural differences when communicating with teams offshore and how it directly impacted deadlines. She required information for budget forecasting but received no response in time for the data deadline. The resulting impact was an unnecessary variance in the budget forecast numbers because of the lack of data from the offshore team. Furthermore, this impacts timelines and results in extended deadlines for all teams involved. The support unit emphasized that good communication is maintained through good stakeholder management across all departments and that over-communicating is better than under-communicating. Additionally, communication is also virtual, as the support unit is centralized from the head office and often faces virtual challenges from offshore teams, which is not the case in face-to-face communication.

X-Culture is specifically focused on virtual collaboration, making communication an important topic to address. It is essential to set the rules of communication between group members, but also to set standards between the communication of teams and coaches. Moreover, coaches could help students develop better communication techniques with their group members. Coaches can answer questions such as how to connect with team members on what platforms, language barriers, and how to contact a coach as teams work through their report. When coaches are trained through theoretical training and have also experienced communication problems are previous competitors, they can use this knowledge to help teams.

Coaches can recommend communication streams for students to use with one another and also with coaches directly. Often having two sources is best, one for immediate communication such as WhatsApp or Facebook Messenger, and another for the discussion and ideas of work like Google Docs or Dropbox. Additionally, when discussing with a coach, it helps to connect through a different source than email for more immediate answers, if the team chooses to do so. This method helps to increase communication between a team and coach and decreases the risk of false or incorrect information being transferred through multiple people within a team by one person relaying the information. A method the Canadian company uses to increase communication between teams and the support unit is to utilize meeting room services through Skype calls. Project teams can host a call and ensure they are connected with the support unit, which increases the communication between the two teams, especially when working with a project team remotely.

Besides communication platforms, teams also may struggle with language barriers. With X-Culture participants located from all over the globe, students may have different proficiencies in languages. X-Culture contains a large number of English speakers, and non-native English speakers may have more difficulty understanding what specific tasks or team members are asking. The spelling or pronunciation of certain words may be difficult to understand. This may also apply to coaches who are trying to discuss with team members who may not realize what a coach is referring to. In this case, if a coach is not confirming that the message is received clearly by the team, the team should not be afraid to ask for more clarification.

Concerning the Canadian company, it was described that the support unit often deals with communication barriers due to the size of groups. They described that there may have been fluctuations in the number of project teams that are assigned to a coach to support. Members of the support units will have anywhere from three project teams consisting of five members each to over forty teams. Because of the changes in project team numbers, the coach and support unit must find ways to effectively communicate and to clarify that the team understands the support they are receiving.

The company example includes a case involving two support unit members. The first member was assigned only two project teams and was able to effectively communicate with the teams each week by holding face-to-face meetings and directly asking if they understood what was being taught. On the other hand, the other support member dealt with over forty project members and was unable to meet with each one personably, leading to him using email as a baseline. Because of this, the assigned coach was unable to understand if the team was effectively receiving the information he was providing and progressing with their project work. It requires more effort from the support members to ensure that the team is not afraid to ask for more clarification or questions.

A great deterrence to communication in virtual teams is time differences. Teams with members from around the globe deal with significant time differences, which can affect meetings, the transmission of information across members, and the completion of weekly assignments. Often when some members of a team are discussing a specific matter, another team member is sleeping and therefore missing the discussion. Moreover, when there is a problem that arises in research or analysis, it might be the case that the person who needs help is unable to find an available person to ask immediately. This is also applied to coaches who have trouble discussing with students from different time zones. Emails are not received and sent back for hours, sometimes delaying progress for days. A possible method discovered by previous coaches and students who have utilized the coaching program has suggested that it is helpful to utilize a platform besides email for constant communication. Email is sometimes seen as inefficient for immediate discussion; therefore, the use of another source is suggested for constant communication with students. The Canadian company is utilizing Skype Messenger as an immediate form of communication between a support unit member and a project team, as emails are often lost due to communication overload because of time differences.

To further discuss how best to communicate with a coach or support unit, a provided list of what teams should do and not do is shown below.

Teams should:

- Contact a coach as soon as possible. Coaches have the responsibility to respond within 24 hours of the submitted request.
- Share incomplete reports with coaches. Teams should not be discouraged from submitting a report that is not yet complete. Coaches can help teams no matter what the state of the report.
- Ask questions. Coaches are there to help teams succeed. If there is a section of the report that is unclear or that a team does not understand, a coach can help solve the problem.
- Be clear on what the ask is of the coach or support unit. Teams should have a clear goal of what they are seeking out when looking for support to obtain the most viable answer.
- Be persistent if you do not hear a response after a prolonged time. Often, coaches and support teams are busy or unable to answer immediately due to time differences or other external

factors. However, once Coaches are aware there is a request and communication has been made, allow time for them to respond.

Teams should not:

- Hesitate to contact the virtual coaching program for support. The coaching program was implemented to ensure students can ask X-Culture for help.
- Assume coaches or support units know every solution to your problems. Although they are trained with specific skill sets, they are continually learning from supporting teams and may not immediately know a direct answer.
- Contact the X-Culture Admin to ask questions on report deliverables. The admin team may take time to redirect you to the coaching program. Students are encouraged to contact the coaching program for help related to report writing.
- Ask coaches to write the report. Coaches will review and provide feedback to a report only.
- Expect coaches to respond immediately or be available at your convenience. It is important to note that although coaches are tasked with helping teams, they may be unable to answer a request immediately or be available at any time. This is due to different time zones or other differing country factors.
- Ask all questions near the end of the term. Coaches will help as much as possible, but it benefits both parties if questions are asked continually throughout the progress report and not saved until the very end before the submission deadline.
- Ask to change deadlines. Coaches do not have power over deadlines. They are enforced to ensure teams are making progress with reports.
- Not submit the weekly report and wait for their coach to provide feedback after 24 hours of submitting the report for review.

How to Benefit Most From Coaches

After discussing the purpose of coaches, common misconceptions, and how best and when not to communicate with coaches, the topic of how to benefit most from coaches arises. The first way to benefit from coaches is simple: contact them. Do not be afraid to reach out to a coach. Coaches are also students, which can make it more comfortable to share concerns with them rather than with the administration. The X-Culture Coaching Program was created to support teams, similar to the support unit in the Canadian company being created to fill in a gap in allocated resources towards teams. Creating the first step of contacting the support team drives coaches with a confirmation that what they are doing has a true purpose of helping teams.

Secondly, be specific about what you are asking a coach. The most likely type of question asked of a coach includes feedback and suggestions for report development. However, teams that submit requests must be specific on what feedback they are looking for, whether this is regarding certain parts of the report or the entirety of it. One of the informants of the Canadian company explained that support requests that relate specifically to learning processes receive more attention from the supporting unit. The more information provided by a team when seeking help, the more specific a coach can be with their feedback and help to fix the problem.

Another way to benefit most is to ask as early as possible. Students should contact coaches continually throughout their report or immediately when a problem arises. This will help students to understand the project better and to receive immediate answers to problems. The support unit often deals with break-in work, which is defined as teams who approach a coach for help at the last minute versus being proactive and asking early. A specific example involved a team that did not seek help from the supporting unit to review a report presented during a leadership meeting. The project team sought out the support of the unit only hours before the meeting occurred, which required the unit to piece together a quick cohesive answer to their question. The supporting unit advised the team that they should have been informed earlier so they could have prepared the project team better in front of an executive board.

Additionally, feedback is not the only reason students or project teams may approach coaches, as their questions may also be related to communication conflicts, time zones, technical problems, and any other potential problems that may arise. However, using coaches as feedback is a great outlet to look over a team's report. Teams that utilize coaches are seen to perform better and report higher levels of satisfaction.

A recommended way to benefit most, which is not utilized by all teams, is to stay in contact with a coach throughout the semester. Typically, after a case has been resolved or after five days, a coach will depart from the case and work on another. However, this does not need to mean the termination of communication between the assigned coach and the team. Teams have the option to continue speaking with the coach to receive feedback or other matters. This also creates a relationship between the coach and the team, a factor many coaches include as a reason that being a coach provides them satisfaction. Creating a student-coach interaction instead of simply doing paperwork provides a more enjoyable experience for a coach. The support unit emphasized the importance of keeping a professional relationship with project teams, especially with vendors who are external to the organization. By maintaining a positive attitude and supporting them through various changes and processes, the project team can be more successful and motivated to try their hardest. Additionally, the support unit can identify how best to improve teams by maintaining a long relationship and understanding their needs.

Lastly, students and coaches are asked to be direct with one another. If a student feels their feedback is too generalized, not related to specific facts or observations, does not provide guidance, or is inconsistent, the student should inform their assigned coach to improve their feedback and help the team succeed. Additionally, if a coach is showing a lack of respect or neglects to respond to a team, teams have the option to contact the Administration or seek another coach. However, sometimes teams may not agree with a coach's feedback or take it negatively. It is important to note that coaches are providing truthful feedback for a team to succeed and never intentionally plan to deceive a group.

There are sufficient resources available on the X-Culture website (xculture.com) and materials provided by the coaches to ensure all students succeed in their experiential learning experience with the X-Culture. The coaching program has been designed to ensure further support is available for students that enable them to deliver quality reports but also have a successful learning experience with X-Culture. Whether it is X-Culture's coaching program or a support unit in a corporate environment, there are coaches trained with the expertise to help teams succeed. They are motivated individuals who seek to help teams, and should be sought out by teams for a multitude of reasons, whether it be feedback-driven or suggestions on their work.

CHAPTER 15

Known Problems in GVTs and Best Ways to Address Them

The X-Culture Experience

VAS TARAS, THE UNIVERSITY OF NORTH CAROLINA AT GREENSBORO, X-CULTURE, INC.

A danger foreseen is half avoided.

Knowing What to Expect

Working in global virtual teams (GVTs) is challenging. Many things can and will go wrong. Knowing what can go wrong allows us to prepare for the challenges, and knowing what to expect greatly improves the chances of success.

The X-Culture research team has been studying the challenges experienced by the members of international teams and experimenting with different strategies for resolving these challenges. Based on years of research, we now know reasonably well what can go wrong and what strategy works best to resolve each type of challenge.

This training module provides a summary of the most common challenges and best practices for dealing with these challenges.

Time-Zone Differences (reported as a challenge by 76% of all GVTs)

Global Virtual Teams (GVT), by definition, are "global." The GVT team members are located around the planet, which means they are in different time zones.

First and foremost, time-zone differences make it very difficult to schedule a live conversation among all team members. Our research shows that hosting live meetings in Skype, WhatsApp, or Google Hangouts is extremely important, especially in the first days of the project. Even a single Skype call significantly improves team dynamics and performance. However, time-zone differences make it hard to hold such live teleconferences.

We will describe the issue in much more detail in subsequent training modules, but briefly, the biggest challenge GVTs face is the lack of interpersonal contact. Without live meetings, team members do not know each other personally and perceive each other as just a name (i.e., John Smith) on the computer screen. Sometimes, team members do not even know if their team members are male or female. As a result, they never develop the rapport and social ties that hold a team together, which include a sense of belonging and a sense of social obligation to one another. No amount of email or instant messaging can replace a few minutes of actual live conversation.

Time-zone dispersion makes it hard to find a time for live teleconferences that work for all team members. Not only does this deprive the team of the opportunity to get better acquainted with the team members, but it also leads to a sense of dissatisfaction with the team members who cannot join the conversation or with the team as a whole.

Secondly, global dispersion of the team members makes communication in global virtual teams very slow. If you are in the U.S. and you send an email to your team member in Japan, the person is likely sleeping and will not see your message until it is the next day for you. When the reply is sent, you will likely be sleeping, so you will not see the reply until two days later. As a result, team members are rarely able to exchange more than 2–3 messages per week.

In and of itself, this is not a big challenge. However, combined with the self-serving bias and difficulties of observing performance in GVTs, this may lead to a major problem. Let us explain.

People are acutely sensitive to injustice. We do not get upset because of a small salary; we get upset if our salary is smaller than that of others. We do not get upset if we must do a lot of work; we get upset if we do more work compared others on the team. If we feel someone is making more money or working less, we tend to try to restore justice by working less. The thought becomes, "I am not going to work hard if he's not working hard. If my pay is less, I am going to work less."

Most GVT members are very reasonable and know that if someone is slow to reply to their messages, it is probably because of the time-zone differences. However, it is common that there is one team member, let's call him Jack, who interprets the delays as a lack of effort on the part of the team member in a different time zone.

Jack has no way to directly observe how hard the other team members are working. So, when Jack emails his team member in Japan and does not receive a reply for 3–4 days, he assumes the team member in Japan is not working hard. Jack feels that this is unjust, gets upset, and decides it is not fair that he should work hard when someone on the team is not working hard and does not even reply to Jack's emails for several days. Jack tries to even out the situation by working less.

Now, there is really a team member (Jack) who is not working hard. So, it is very likely that more team members will find it unfair that they are doing their share, but Jack is not. One by one they, too, reduce their effort. The more team members get upset and reduce their effort, the more likely that the remaining team members will also give up and stop working. Why should they give full effort when several other team members are not working hard? It's not fair. This way, a simple technical challenge becomes a major interpersonal crisis.

Such a situation happens much more often than one would expect. 76% of the team's report challenges are due to time-zone differences, and our data suggests that in about 28% of teams, this initial time-zone problem leads to much bigger conflicts later.

Best Practices

There is no easy way to solve the root cause of the inability to communicate live, which would require moving all team members to the same time zone.

However, teams that try harder to create personal relationships and have at least occasional real-time conversations via Skype, WhatsApp, Viber, Facebook, Zoom, or Google Hangouts tend to greatly improve their team climate and performance. Even if only a few team members can join the teleconference, such an approach speeds things up. If all team members cannot join at once, it is a good idea to have several teleconferences with 2–3 team members each time, so that all have participated in the live teleconference at least at some point.

To facilitate such meetings, Doodle is an excellent free tool that makes coordination and scheduling easy. It automatically adjusts the schedule for time zones and had several other useful functions.

Our research shows that recording the live meetings and sharing them with the team members who could not attend live aids them as well. There are several add-on programs that allow recording Skype or Facebook calls, but YouTube Live has a recording function embedded in the default options. YouTube Live works just like Google Hangouts, but it has a few extra options, such as recording the meetings or streaming it live on YouTube. A training module on online collaboration tools provides more details.

Other scheduling and coordination problems (reported by 71%)

Related to the previous challenge but unique in a few important ways is the challenge of scheduling. Often, team members have difficulties scheduling meetings even if all the team members are in neighboring time zones. Sometimes, team members may want to co-edit documents in Google Docs at the same time, have a meeting among two of three team members, or decide on important deadlines.

It may be a real hassle for global virtual teams to find a time that works for all team members for a teleconference or to vote on an issue. Sending emails back and forth takes time and often leads to much confusion.

Best Practices

It works best when the team uses Doodle to find a time that works for everybody or to get everyone's vote on the issue. More on how to use Doodle can be found in the training module on online collaboration and coordination tools.

Email overload (reported by 56%)

When teams rely on email-only communication, they often end up with dozens or even hundreds of emails that are difficult to follow and are full of redundancies and conflicting information.

The problem is exacerbated by the tendency of some team members to copy all or reply all even if the communication concerns only two team members. The problem here is not that there are too many emails, but that team members stop paying attention to emails. They see one, two, three emails that are copied to them but do not concern them, and they stop paying attention to subsequent emails from their team members. Our surveys show that 82% of GVT members say that they missed important correspondence from their team members because they did not recognize the important message in a flood of irrelevant correspondence.

Lastly, emails are not a very good way to keep track of prior correspondence. On the one hand, emails usually contain earlier messages in the email body (when you reply, the original message is also recorded). However, each time a team member replies, another email message is created. A few days of actively discussing an issue via email creates dozens of messages in everyone's email account, making it difficult to find the one that you are looking for, or the one with the attachment you need, etc.

Best Practices

It works best if the team creates a Facebook, WhatsApp, Viber, Skype, or a similar group (group call) and has their team conversations there, instead of relying on just email. In addition, a Google Docs file can be used as a discussion board. This way, all correspondence is permanently saved, and it is easy to review the entire conversation. This makes it easier to find earlier messages, an approach that is especially useful when some team members miss parts of the conversation and want to review the record later.

Better yet, teams should consider using online collaboration tools such Trello, Slack, or Basecamp. They are much more functional than Facebook, WhatsApp, or Viber, and the time invested in learning how to use them is well worth it. Most of these platforms are inexpensive and usually have an extended trial period sufficient for the duration of the X-Culture project.

Lastly, it is always a good idea to separate the communication medium by the purpose of the conversation. It is best to have a discussion related to a co-edited document in the document itself. For example, if the team uses Dropbox to co-edit Word files, the comments pertaining to certain points in the document can be made directly in the document using the Comment function. This way, it is easy to locate the issue directly in the document, leave a comment, reply to a comment, and delete the comment when the issue has been addressed. A conversation about non-task related issues is best had on Facebook or WhatsApp.

Conflicting copies of the document in email attachments (reported by 46% overall, reported by 92% of GVTs that used only emails to share files)

When teams rely on email attachments to co-develop the team report, it may be hard to track which attachment is the latest version of the file. Commonly, someone will make edits in an older version of the file and the team ends up with conflicting copies of the document. Merging those files may be a real challenge. This leads to lost time and frustration, and usually undermines motivation to continue.

Also, it is a very common occurrence that a wrong file is attached, or the sender realized the file needs a little update after the file had been sent. Unfortunately, once the email has been sent, it is impossible to access the attached file and replace or correct it. So, the sender has no choice but to make the necessary minor correction and then send a new email with a new attachment.

Best Practices

It is never a good idea to share files via email attachments. This is simply an ineffective, outdated practice.

Dropbox is by far the best and most convenient tool for sharing and co-developing files. It solves several major problems, including:

- Multiple copies of the file: Only one copy of the file is in the shared folder and is accessible to all team members. Changes are made directly in that single copy of the file, thereby avoiding the confusion of multiple conflicting file copies.
- After-send file corrections: When a team member is done with the file and wants to inform the team that the file is ready for further editing, the team member can simply send an email or make a note in a discussion group. If the team member later realizes the file needs a few more corrections, it is easy to go directly to the file and make those additional corrections. There will be no need to inform the team, as the team will see the latest (and only) version of the file.

Files in Dropbox can be accessed from a computer, smartphone, or tablet.

The greatest advantage of Dropbox is that it saves all older versions of the file. For example, if at some point there is a need to access a week-old version of the file, Dropbox allows for doing so. It keeps in the memory all the edits made to the file and allows users to go back in time and restore earlier versions or undo latest changes. By default, Dropbox keeps the last 90 days saved in its memory, but professional accounts allow for tracing all prior versions of the file up to a year back, and with a more expensive subscription, the time restrictions can be removed completely. Everyone at least occasionally makes errors or deletes important parts of the file; Dropbox allows for restoring the pre-error version of the file.

The only shortcoming of Dropbox is that it does not allow for simultaneous co-editing of the file by two or more people. If multiple people open and edit the same file at the same time, Dropbox creates two copies of the file. It does inform both users that someone else is also using the file, and therefore, it is easy to spot the problem before multiple copies are created. Still, this sometimes leads to confusion and the need to merge the file copies later.

Google Docs solves this problem by allowing multiple users to co-edit the file at the same time. One user can see another typing new text into the file in real time. The only problem with Google Docs is that it is an in-browser tool and thus lacks some functions offered by self-standing applications such as Word, Excel, or Power Point.

There are several other documents sharing and co-editing platforms, such as OneDrive or iCloud.

Calendar differences (reported by 32%)

Members of Global Virtual Teams come from countries that have different holidays and academic calendars. One person's business day may be someone else's holiday, which often disrupts the team's flow and leads to unexpected delays.

The issue is especially relevant when the holidays coincide with the deadlines. For example, the U.S. Thanksgiving holiday is often very close to the final deadline for the X-Culture Project during the October through December round of the project. Since most teams have two U.S.-based team members, this often creates a major problem for the team.

The challenge is that if the team is sufficiently diverse, it is impossible to fully account for these calendar differences. No matter how much the deadlines are moved, there will be always someone on the team whose off days/holidays will conflict with the deadlines.

Best Practices

The only way to deal with this challenge is to plan. It is a very good practice to ask all team members to share when they will be on a holiday or unable to participate for other reasons. If the team is informed ahead of time, then it is usually easy to rearrange the workload so that the team member's absence won't affect the workflow.

It is also a good idea to assume that your team members are not familiar with the holidays in your country. Even huge international holidays like Christmas or New Years may not be celebrated in some countries and your team members may not realize that you will be off on those days.

The same applies to holidays like Ramadan or Diwali that are very big in some parts of the world, but completely unknown in others.

Language proficiency differences (reported by 31%)

In truly global teams, most team members will have different native languages. Thus, no matter what working language the team chooses, it will not be the native language for most team members, and they will not be perfectly fluent in it. This may lead to communication difficulties. Furthermore, it is likely that any writing undertaken by team members who are not fluent in the working language will be poor.

We conducted extensive research on the effects of language proficiency on team dynamics and performance, and here are some notable findings.

First, GVT members tend to greatly overestimate the challenges related to language differences. Before they start working in GVTs, 85% of the X-Culture project participants expect language difference to be a "big" or "very big" challenge. However, after the project is over, only 31% say the language was a "big" or "very big" challenge.

Second, a difference in the language proficiency tends to be a bigger problem than low language proficiency. That is, teams where everyone is proficient in the working language, or teams where everyone is not very proficient in the working language, tend to not see language proficiency as a problem. The complaints about language proficiency as a factor that negatively affect team dynamics and performance come primarily from teams where some team members are very proficient, and others are not proficient.

In other words, teams where the average language proficiency is relatively low still write good reports. However, when the team members vary on their language proficiency skills, this creates dissatisfaction. Team members who are more fluent in the working language tend to blame their less fluent colleagues for the difficulties the team may be experiencing, often unjustly.

Third, often non-native English speakers blame their low proficiency in English for their low performance. For example, people who tend to plagiarize (copy and paste work of others), when confronted, often say they did it because their English is poor and they thought it did not make sense to write the piece on their own in poor English when a much better piece could be copied off the internet. Likewise, people who do not actively participate in team discussions tend to explain their lack of participation by their low English proficiency.

Our research shows that working language proficiency differences have a much weaker effect on the actual quality of work than the effect they have on team climate, which in turn may damage team performance.

Another notable observation is that, based on peer-rated language proficiency, students from English-language countries are not always the highest-rated. When we ask the X-Culture participants to evaluate the English proficiency of their team members and then average those scores by country, the U.S., U.K, Canada, Australia, and the like do not always appear on the top of the list of the 40+ countries that participate in X-Culture each semester. Even if some of the students in these countries are foreign students, it is still very unlikely that they are not fluent in English, as studying in these countries at the university level requires a certain level of language proficiency. The fact that countries where English proficiency is objectively higher are not always the highest-ranked suggests that personal biases and perceptions affect language proficiency evaluations.

What appears to be happening is that when the team is working well or a person is liked by the team members, the person still gets good ratings on this criterion even if that personal working language proficiency is low. In contrast, when a team experiences conflicts or other difficulties, team members tend to search for reasons. The self-serving bias is a tendency to attribute failures to external causes. Instead of blaming ourselves, we tend to assign blame to factors we do not control. Low working language proficiency among other team members becomes a convenient excuse for why the problems in teams are not "my own fault", but rather the result of "something I cannot change". As a result, even though the fact that some of the team members may not be very fluent in the working language may not be a big problem, we tend to exaggerate its role and effect on the team dynamics and performance. The rationale in this case is, "I am a hard worker, I did my best, we would have done so great if it was not for those few team members who could not even speak English."

Best practices

It is wise not to rush to blame performance deficiencies on the working language skills. Poor English skills are

a convenient excuse, but the true cause may well lie in a lack of effort. This applies to both team members who justify the lack of their participation in discussions and/or the poor quality of their writing on their poor English, as well those who justify conflicts and other problems in their team on the poor working language skills of some of their team members.

The truth is that if the team members who are not perfectly fluent in English but work hard, language is not such a big obstacle.

It works best if the team members who are not fluent in English are assigned tasks that do not require them to produce finished written pieces. For example, they can be assigned to search for information and literature, perform coordination tasks, submit the reports, and possibly write initial drafts of some report sections. Team members who are more fluent in English, in turn, should be assigned to do more writing and possibly the final copy editing of the report.

Cultural Differences (reported by 78%, but objectively a problem in only 12% of the teams)

Members of GVTs differ from team to team in many ways. They come from different cultural backgrounds, and their values, attitudes, traditions, working, and communication styles are different. They are taught and evaluated by different instructors, so they likely have different levels of skill and different understandings of the task.

All these differences are often referred to as "cultural differences," although technically it is a mix of various types of differences (e.g., institutional, economic, etc.), and culture is only part of that mix.

Our research shows that, before the project starts, the clear majority of GVTs expect cultural differences to be a challenge (78% choose "big" or "very big" challenges). Remarkably, after the project is over, the percent of GVT members who indicate that cultural differences presented a "big" or "very big" challenge drops to 12%. Instead, GVT members share that technical issues, such as time zones, low subject knowledge, and the like were a much bigger challenge.

GVT members love to complain about cultural differences. We often hear, "he is like this because he is Indian," or "she is American and therefore she is like that." Similarly, GVT members commonly say they were misunderstood, disrespected, or mistreated because their team members did not understand their culture.

However, further research almost always shows the problem was something else, such as a lack of commitment, poor technical skills, or just personal circumstance. For example, if a team member is not contributing, plagiarizes, is confrontational, shy, or disrespectful, GVT members tend to attribute these tendencies to culture. However, when we test whether people from a particular country tend to display these tendencies more than people from other cultures, almost always the results come in negative, suggesting that the issue was a matter of personality or particular circumstances and that national cultures (or institutions, for that matter) are not to blame.

This is not to say that culture does not matter. Much of X-Culture's research focuses on culture, and it is clear that cultural differences do affect team dynamics and performance. However, the effect is less significant than many people expect.

One of our papers recently presented at the Academy of International Business analyzed the effects of about a dozen different distances and differences on team dynamics and performance. Specifically, we tested the effects of the following differences:

Personal diversity

1. Age diversity
2. Gender diversity
3. Working language skill differences
4. Technical skill differences
5. Personal value differences
6. Cultural intelligence differences
7. Psychic (perceived) differences among the cultures represented on the team.

Institutional diversity

1. National variety (number of countries on the team)
2. Economic variety (GDP/capita; PPP)
3. Difference in HDI (Human Development Index)
4. Difference in economic inequality (Gini)
5. Difference in corruption
6. Difference in civil freedom
7. Difference in percent women in parliament
8. Difference in religiosity
9. Difference in national cultural values
10. Geographic dispersion (x1K km)
11. Time-zone dispersion (hours)

In summary the study found:

First, most of these distances and differences had only a small effect on team process and performance. The correlations were in the 0.1–0.2 range, which indicates a rather weak effect (the distances/ differences explain only 1% to 4% of the variation in team dynamics and performance).

The only notable exception was the perceived distance (explained about 17% of variance in the team dynamics, correlation 0.41). Differences in working language skills and technical skills also had a relatively strong effect (explained about 9% of variance in the team dynamics, correlation 0.31). However, even these more significant factors affected only the team dynamics (team satisfaction, conflicts), but not the quality of the team report.

Second, different types of distances affected different types of outcomes:

-NS indicates that the effect is likely to be negative but less strong or non-significant.

+ NS indicates that the effect is likely to be positive but less strong or non-significant.

Team Effectiveness

	Task outcomes	Psychological Outcomes
Personal	(-) NS	(–) - *Less communication* - *Conflicts* - *Less satisfaction* *Reasons:* • Communication challenges • Out-group prejudice • Less similarity-attraction
Institutional	+ + *More creative* + *Better business proposal* *Reasons:* • Variety of perspectives • Variety of knowledge pools and resources • Interactive learning	+ NS

Diversity appears at the left, spanning the two rows labelled Personal and Institutional.

Fig 15.1 Team Effectiveness.

Personal differences had a negative effect on team dynamics and hindered communication, created more conflicts and reduced satisfaction.

In contrast, institutional/national differences had a positive effect on the quality of team output. More diverse teams produced better business proposals.

Best practices

It works best if a team tries to turn cultural differences into opportunities. Team members come from different backgrounds and have access to different pools of knowledge and ideas. It is likely they have access to different libraries and different professional networks. When teams are different, brainstorming tends to be particularly effective and more creative ideas are generated. Thus, communication and idea exchange is key in diverse teams.

Rather than assigning different report sections to different members and letting them work independently, team members should communicate frequently, use brainstorming and discuss key decisions whenever possible.

Don't dismiss the ideas of others just because they are different from yours. Learn from each other. The more different ideas you have on the table, the more likely you are to have a solution that is the most creative and effective.

Lastly, if problems arise, do not rush to blame them on cultural differences. The issue could be simply a result of different personalities, a lack of effort, or an inadequate skillset. Assigning blame to cultural differences provides an excuse not to try to work it out. You can't change someone's culture; however, recognizing that the problem may not be cultural, and thus can be solved by working harder or communicating more, gives a chance at improving performance.

Free-Riders (93% of the teams report having at least one "free-rider," but only 4% of all team members are true "free-riders.")

We have an entire training module devoted to the issue of "free-riding" (a.k.a., shirking, free-loading, social loafing). Here is a summary.

In any team, there is a chance that some team members have a busy work schedule, family obligations, or get sick. As a result, these team members don't actively participate in the project. Some may send an email or two at first and then disappear; some never send any messages. This is called "social loafing" or "free-riding." It is a common problem in teams in general, and especially in global virtual teams where team members have not met each other in person and have not developed the close social obligations (friendship) that tend to improve participation in traditional collocated teams.

Studies report that up to 30% of the members in corporate global virtual teams tend to be free-riders, that is, they do some work but do not meet expectations of their team.

Our data shows that in X-Culture, on average, there is one team member per team whose participation rate is below expectations (does something, but less than expected by the team). Approximately 3% of all trainees (one per 10 teams or so) don't participate at all and are excluded from the project.

In most cases, the "missing" team members turn up toward the end of the project. After all, they need to get a grade for their course. This situation creates more problems, as most of the work is done by then and the team no longer needs the help of the "missing" team member.

Best practices

It works best if team members do the following:

- First, try to foster close social ties among your team members. Studies show that spending only a few minutes asking team members about their interests, hobbies, studies, work experience, and interesting facts from their lives helps a lot and leads to a noticeable improvement in team commitment.
- Right at the start of the project, discuss what each team member is expected to do and what happens if they don't perform. Better yet, develop a Team Charter that clearly states the roles and tasks of each team member and what the team will do if a team member doesn't do his/her share or work.
- Keep sending emails to the "missing" team members every few days even if you never hear from them.
- Every week you will be asked who on your team is not actively participating in the project. Make sure to provide the names of the "missing" students. The information will be used to identify problems and help resolve them. In cases when nothing helps, and the "missing" team member doesn't participate, the person will be excluded from X-Culture.
- Don't wait too long. If after several days, you don't hear from a trainee or two, start working on the project with the trainees who replied to your emails. Keep sending updates to the "missing" students, but don't wait too long for them. Just do what you can with the available resources.

- If you never hear from your missing team members, despite your best efforts to get in touch with them, or their input remains very limited, give low peer evaluations to the "missing" students. Their poor performance will be reflected in their course grade.

Lack of leadership, difficulties with workload distribution and team coordination (reported by 42%)

With no formally appointed team leader and no prior experience together, some teams experience challenges due to a lack of leadership. Everyone is waiting for someone else to tell them what needs to be done and how. Time is running out and the team is not making any progress. Frustration builds and team members start blaming each other for the problems.

There are many reasons your team members may be reluctant to take initiative. For most of them, this is the first time they have worked in a virtual team and the first time they have worked with people from different cultures. For most of them, English is a foreign language. They may have difficulties communicating or are just shy to start a conversation. Most of them don't have prior leadership experience. Some team members come from cultures where modesty is valued, and they may be worried that if they try to assume a leadership role they will be perceived as too aggressive or inconsiderate.

Best Practices

The best advice we can give to an individual team member is that the process works best if you personally take initiative. Don't be afraid to take the first step. If you see that something is not done right, just send your team members your vision for how things should be done. If nobody knows what needs to be done, simply send your suggestions for who should do what. Don't be pushy, just say: "I see we have a problem here, why don't we do the following…" It is likely that your teammates are as lost as you are, and they will appreciate that someone is finally taking a leading role. It's better to try and fail than to never try. If someone else is trying to manage your team, be supportive.

Poor quality of work from some team members (hard to quantify, but most teams have at least one team member whose work quality is unsatisfactory).

GVT members come from around the world. Just like in corporate global virtual teams, X-Culture team members vary in terms of their skills and experiences: some have excellent skills and work ethics while others don't. For most of your team members, English is not their first language. Some have received better training than others.

It is very likely that just like in real business teams, some of X-Culture GVT members will not be skilled enough to do a good job. Our research shows that in 72% of the teams, at least one team member prepares a report section that is so weak that the other team members will have to redo it. It is also possible that a team member may not complete his/her work at all (happens in 26% of the X-Culture teams). For example, a team member may get sick right before the final deadline, or simply not complete the work for no particular reason. This happens in all kinds of teams, including business teams at top firms.

Worst of all, the team members will likely learn how poor the work of some of some of the team members is only a few days before the final deadline. Until then, the team assumes everyone is working hard and will produce a good report section. Then comes a surprise: one section is missing or is of very poor quality and there is no time to re-do it.

Best practices

It works best if GVTs do the following:

- Don't wait until the last day and just hope that everything will work out. Check the work of your team members regularly.
- Use Dropbox or Google Docs to store all your team's work from day one. This way, you can always see everybody's work progress and intervene if somebody is underperforming.
- It is also a good idea to assign two students to each task. Doing this will not only stimulate the exchange of ideas and improve the quality of the work, but will also provide a backup if one of the team members doesn't do his/her work.
- Some teams also assign one team member to be a backup, whose job is to just stand by and wait until something goes wrong. When it does (and something will go wrong), this will be the team member who will pick up the slack.
- Lastly, it is always a good idea to assign one team member to be a coordinator, whose job is to frequently check the work of each team member, detect problems early, and if needed re-assign workload so that the problem is addressed before it's too late.

Plagiarism

(Report draft: 32% of the teams have a similarity rate above 15%, suggesting plagiarism; Final report: 6% of the teams have a similarity rate above 15%, suggesting plagiarism)

It is common that when the report draft (due one week before the final deadline of the project) is submitted to TurnItIn.com, the team discovers that the work of one or more team members contains plagiarism.

This often happens in corporate virtual global teams as well. In some countries, attitudes towards copyright and intellectual property are rather relaxed, and some people just don't know or don't care that plagiarism is a serious problem.

Additionally, some students' English is poor, and they feel that it is better to copy and paste somebody else's work than to do their own writing.

The problem is that by the time the team learns that part of the report was plagiarized, it is often too late, and there is simply no time to redo it.

We devote an entire training module to this important issue. Here are just a few quick tips on the best ways to prevent or resolve the problem if it happens.

Best practices

It works best if you do the following:

- Discuss your team policies about plagiarism early on so that every team member knows plagiarism will be caught by TurnItIn and will not be tolerated.

- Check the work of your team members regularly to detect problems early on.
- Submit your report draft early: you can submit your work to TurnItIn at any time, including several weeks before the deadline. However, you can submit your work and test it for plagiarism only once. Hence, it would be wise to submit your work only close to the deadline when it is finished.
- If there are team members whose English is very poor, it may be a good idea to not assign them to do any writing, and instead, task them with collecting information or helping with coordination.

Failing to harness the power of team (observed by researchers in 74% of the teams, but only 11% of the teams recognized it as a problem).

The value of teamwork is in the exchange of ideas, discussions, brainstorming, checking each other's work, and correcting mistakes.

GVTs bring together people from around the world. It is a mistake to waste this opportunity to interact and put diverse minds together.

One of the biggest mistakes a team can make is to divide the questions among the team members so that each team member answers one or two questions, and then simply combine the sections and submit the report without the team members reading each other's work.

Notably, although this is a widespread problem, only a very small portion of the teams recognize it as an issue. When we point out that what the team has done is not the best strategy and present the evidence that a different strategy has been shown to be more effective, most teams still ignore the advice and keep doing what they were doing.

We devote an entire training module to the issue of crowdsourcing and creativity in GVTs and large groups. Here is a summary of best practices:

Best practices

Experience shows that the best reports are produced when teams rely on collective wisdom. One of the more successful strategies is described below. You can use a different process; this is just an example of a successful plan of action that addresses some of the shortcomings of the commonly-used strategy of dividing the workload by questions

1. Once the client organization is selected, each team member generates ideas for answering each question. This can be done in a teleconference using Skype, on a Facebook Groups discussion board, or using a Google Docs file where all questions are listed in a text document and everyone can write down their thoughts and comment on each other's input. The discussion can be open and go on for several days.
2. Only after all questions have been brainstormed and initial ideas have been gathered, the team divides the tasks among the team members.
3. It works best if the team appoints one of the team members as a coordinator who regularly checks the work of others and sends reminders when needed. The team also appoints one member (usually a native English speaker) who does the final copyediting.

4. Each team member's work is stored in Dropbox or Google Docs and everybody is required to regularly read the work of everybody else and provide feedback.

5. Once the final draft of the team report is put together, every team member reads the entire report, makes corrections and adds comments and suggestions for further improvement. It works best if a single copy of the document in Dropbox is co-edited by the entire team using MS Word's Track Changes or Google Docs (see instructions at the end of this document for how to use these tools). This way, all suggested revisions are visible in one document.

CHAPTER 16

The Art of Effective Feedback

VAS TARAS, THE UNIVERSITY OF NORTH CAROLINA AT GREENSBORO, X-CULTURE, INC.

What is feedback?

The term "feedback" is used to describe the process of providing evaluation, comments, and suggestions on prior work or behavior.

To put it simply, an individual or a team completes or performs a duty and submits the product to you for a review (feed). The feedback gives reviews the work or observes the behavior and provides an evaluation, comments, and suggestions (feed-back).

A big part of being a supervisor, colleague, or coach is providing your subordinates, colleagues, or trainees with feedback.

The X-Culture GVT coaches will be asked to provide feedback on a regular basis. First, they will be evaluating and providing feedback on the work submitted by the teams (weekly deliverables). Second, often teams approach coaches directly and ask to review and provide feedback on their report draft or particular ideas they are considering including in their business proposal. Third, the coaches will also observe behaviors and interactions of the students within and between teams, and may be asked to provide comments and suggestions based on their observations.

Why and Why Not?

It is important to understand why (and why not) you provide feedback.

You are NOT providing feedback to:

- Show you are the boss;
- Show off how smart you are;
- Tell someone how incompetent they are;
- Complain about problems;
- To make someone feel good or bad.

You have only ONE goal: To ensure that the performance improves in the future.

This is very important and bears repeating: The main purpose of feedback is to ensure performance improvement. This means that sometimes, coaches need to restrain their urge to criticize, complain, or give correct answers.

So, before you say anything, ask yourself if what you are about to say will improve performance in the future. Likewise, after you say anything, ask yourself if what you said is enough to improve future behavior?

Feedback giving has been extensively researched and there is a wealth of knowledge accumulated on what works and what does not.

This training module provides a summary of approaches to feedback giving that have been scientifically proven to provide the necessary awareness, motivation, and guidance to greatly increase the chance of future performance improvement. It also provides a review of the approaches to feedback giving that seem reasonable, but have been shown to impede improvement and instead lead to resentment and dissatisfaction, undermine motivation and actually reduce the chances of better performance in the future.

Specifics of X-Culture

The principles of effective feedback giving are largely universal. Methods that have been scientifically shown to work tend to work in all situations regardless of who provides and who received the feedback, such as:

1. Boss-subordinate;
2. Subordinate-boss;
3. Colleague-colleague (friend, peer);
4. Judge-contestant;
5. Coach-trainee.

However, the X-Culture project has several unique features that must be taken into account to maximize the positive impact of feedback.

X-Culture does not neatly fit in any of the five models listed above.

X-Culture students are not your employees and you are not their boss. They do not depend on you and do not have to obey to you, as a subordinate would obey a leader. However, your input plays a great role and has a huge impact on their bosses (professors, X-Culture admin). So, you are comparable to an assistant boss.

X-Culture students are not your colleagues or peers. You are also a trainee in the X-Culture project, but your status is higher than theirs. So, you are essentially a senior colleague.

You are a coach and they are trainees, but you are more than just a coach to them. You are also a judge of their work as competition contestants. Your evaluation of their work impacts their performance evaluations, grades, and chances of winning the competition, but you do not fully determine the outcome. Your evaluation is just one of the data points used to select the winners of the completion. So, you are a coach who is also a judge.

Lastly, the students will also be evaluating your performance as a Coach and feedback provider and their feedback will have an impact on your ability to successfully complete the X-Culture GVT Coach training. Every week, the students will be asked to comment on their experience receiving help from coaches and provide feedback on your work. So, you judge them, but they also judge you. It is a two-way street.

Thus, the X-Culture model is a combination of the boss-subordinate, subordinate-boss, colleague-colleague, coach-trainee, and judge-subordinate models.

Also important to keep in mind is that:

- Just like with most business decisions, in X-Culture there are often no right and wrong answers to the challenge questions.

For example, if a team recommends a certain new market or market entry mode, there is usually no way to objectively know that this recommendation is correct or wrong; it is not as simple as 2+2=4. Sometimes, you see an answer that is clearly bad or clearly brilliant. However, most of the time, you will be looking over an acceptable business proposal with no way to know for sure if it is economically viable or not.

The only way to know would be to implement it and see if it works or not, which is practically impossible. So as with any business plan or business idea, we must rely on the quality of supporting arguments. The quality of the work can often be only determined based on: (1) how clearly the idea is presented and (2) how convincing the supporting research and arguments are. Thus, the task is to not so much to tell if the team is "right" or "wrong," but to encourage them to try to improve further.

- Just like many employees often don't care about the outcome and do just enough not get fired, some X-Culture students do not care whether their business proposal will help their clients grow their business. These students simply want to get through the project with as little effort as possible and get a passing grade. You will usually see right away who is really trying their best to help their client, learn through the process, and strengthen their resume to maximize chances of getting a good job down the road. It is a good idea to challenge and push these students to do as good of a job as possible. However, if you feel a student just wants to get through and get a passing grade, try to help them learn and grow, but do not get upset if they do not appreciate your effort and do not follow your advice. Most of them will be trying hard, but some just want to get a good grade with minimal effort.

- X-Culture is designed to resemble a real corporate environment as much as possible. However, for most students, X-Culture is part of a college course for which they paid a lot of money (college tuition). They see themselves as customers rather than employees, and unlike employees, students often feel entitled to a good experience. They feel our team (including coaches) is obliged to make their experience as pleasant and fun as possible. Of course, our role is to give them a realistic preview of what it is like to work in a real corporate global virtual team on a real business consulting project, which may or may not be fun and pleasant. It is rare, but sometimes you will encounter students who feel that you owe them, who do not realize you are not an employee of the university they paid money to and that the university did not hire you to help them succeed. So, if you encounter a lack of appreciation, take it professionally, do not get upset and use it as a learning opportunity for yourself.

Barriers to Giving Feedback

Often, it is not easy to provide good feedback. Studies show (Hesketh & Laidlaw, 2002) that the following are common barriers:

- A fear of upsetting the recipient of feedback;
- A fear of doing more harm than good;
- The recipient of feedback is resistant or defensive when receiving criticism;
- Feedback being too generalized and not related to specific facts or observations;
- Feedback not giving guidance on how to rectify behavior;

- Inconsistent feedback from multiple sources;
- A lack of respect for the source of feedback.

All of these present challenges, but these are surmountable obstacles. With the right training and experience, one can overcome these issues.

The Anatomy of Feedback

Ultimately, feedback is a combination of the evaluation of past work or behaviors and suggestions for improvement. Good feedback informs the quality of the current progress, and how it can be done better in the future.

We commonly differentiate between "positive" and "negative" feedback.

"Positive" feedback is aimed at identifying successful strategies and behaviors and encouraging to perpetuate them in the future.

"Negative" feedback is often referred to as "constructive" feedback. The logic here is that the negative feedback is aimed at helping improve future performance. It helps to "construct" or "develop" better future performance. Pointing out the good helps and often is necessary, but it is not enough to improve. Unless we point out deficiencies, we cannot expect an improvement in the future.

Thus, most studies provide this "formula" for feedback:

Feedback = How You Did + How You Could Do Better

The Understood and Unknown Knowns and Unknowns

When the military plans their operations, they create a matrix of knowns and unknowns. This allows them to plan their missions with a better understanding of what they know and what they do not and, thereby, be better prepared for uncertain situations.

	Knowns	**Unknowns**
Knowns	Known knowns Things we know we know e.g., the terrain where the operation will be taken place: we know it will be in a forest and we have maps.	Known Unknows Things we don't know and we know we don't know them e.g., the weather: we know we don't know if it's going to rain, so we plan for uncertainty
Unknowns	Unknown knowns Things we will encounter and understand, but we don't know that yet. e.g., we know how the enemy is communicating and we understand that system, but we don't know yet this is what they are using.	Unknown Unknowns Things that we will encounter that we won't understand, but we don't know that yet e.g., the culture of the enemy we know and don't think is different and unknown to us, but we will soon find out and won't know what to do about it.

A similar model can be used to when providing feedback. The feedback receiver may or may not

1. Be aware of the problems or performance deficiencies; and
2. know how to fix the problem.

Essentially, we are dealing with a 2x2 matrix like this:

		AWARE OF THE PROBLEM	
		YES	NO
UNDERSTANDS HOW TO FIX THE PROBLEM	YES	Knows there is a problem, and knows what to do about it The student/employee just does not care. To do for the Coach: MOTIVATOR Motivate to improve.	Does not know there is a problem, but if they knew there is a problem, would know what to do about it The student/employee wants to do better, just doesn't know there is a problem. To do for the Coach: JUDGE Just point out the problem.
	NO	Knows there is a problem, but does not know what to do about it The student/employee knows the work is no good but needs help with fixing the problem. To do for the Coach: TEACHER Motivation and direction for improvement.	Does not know there is a problem, but even if they knew there is a problem, would not know what to do about it The most difficult case: The student/employee is not aware of the problem and wouldn't know how to fix it. To do for the Coach: JUDGE & TEACHER Point out the problem, provide motivation and direction for improvement.

Depending on the case, the focus may have to be more on pointing out the problem, or on motivation to fix it, or on teaching how to fix it, or all of the above. More likely than not, motivation will likely be part of the equation.

The X-Culture Model of Effective Feedback

At X-Culture, we find the basic feedback formula to be insufficient for effective feedback. It is too mechanical and does not take the human component into account. The X-Culture formula for effective feedback also relies on the research in psychology and recognizes motivation as an important component of effective feedback.

Feedback = How You did + Motivation to do better + How you could do better

That is, our research shows that it is not enough to simply tell a person how good or bad the work is and how it could be improved. Effective feedback also motivates the person to do a better job next time.

Extrinsic and Intrinsic Motivation

Extrinsic motivation stems from external factors, such as rewards or punishments. For example, people may be motivated to work harder/better to earn money, to win a prize, to get a good grade, or to avoid being fired or get a bad grade.

To increase extrinsic motivation, X-Culture coaches cannot offer any direct rewards or punishments. However, they can remind the students that poor performance may result in a bad grade, while good performance may lead to winning the X-Culture competition and the associated rewards and benefits. This reasoning can provide extrinsic motivation to work harder. Furthermore, they can emphasize that more effort invested in learning and performance now will improve their chances of getting a good job in the future. Conversely, failing to do a good job now may reduce the chances of a successful career in the future.

Intrinsic motivation stems from personal interest to do a better job. For example, people may be motivated to work harder because they like the sense of professional development and accomplishment, the satisfaction of doing a good job, the excitement of completion, and the fun of working with other people and enjoying their company.

To increase intrinsic motivation, X-Culture coaches should try to create a positive environment and trust, induce the sense of self-efficacy and belief in one's ability to grow and accomplish great things, and cultivate a sense of excitement and fun.

Expectancy Theory

In the context of coaching, expectancy theory is very relevant. Expectancy theory says that people only work hard if they feel that their effort will lead to desirable outcomes. Studies show that in a competition, people work hard only if they feel they have a chance to do well in the competition. If it looks like they have lost the chance to win, people often just give up.

For example, in contests that involve a contestant ranking, the closer one is to the top of the rank, the harder they tend to work. Even those who actually were doing poorly, when told they are moving up in rank, will start working hard. Conversely, even those who were doing well, when told their ranking is very low, would greatly diminish their effort. In fact, the highest effort is always observed among the top contestants who feel they really have a chance to win the competition.

The same is true for the low end of the ranking. People who believe they can lose (or be fired, or receive a low grade) if they do not improve their performance usually improve, but only if they believe the extra effort will help them avoid the punishment.

So, the job of a Coach is not only to point out an error and explain how to fix it, but also to instill a belief that the effort invested in fixing the problem will pay off and make a difference.

The Best Practices of Feedback Giving

Be specific

Generalizations do not help. Simply knowing if the work is good or bad does not explain why it is good or why it is bad, and thus it makes it hard to know what to do in the future to keep up (or improve) the good performance. The feedback must clearly identify what action is expected in the future to make or keep the quality of work high in the future. The best way to do this is to avoid generalities and instead focus on specific technical problems.

Ineffective Feedback	Effective Feedback
Great job.	Your use of references helps make the argument look more convincing.
This is not very good.	The sloppy formatting of your report makes it look unprofessional.

Focus on behaviors that can be changed, not on the person

If you praise effort instead of intelligence, you increase intrinsic motivation and provide a template to follow next time to improve performance. If you tell the feedback receiver that they are smart or creative, it makes the person feel good about herself, but it does not improve their motivation to work harder. In fact, it can lead to the opposite reaction: "If I am so smart and creative, I do not have to work hard."

You should praise effort, and focus on doing, not being.

Research shows that children who get praised for their natural ability tend to ask how their peers did on the same task. So, they worry about how good they are compared to others.

In contrast, children who get praised for effort tend to ask how they can do better next time, which is much more constructive: doing and trying, not being.

Ineffective Feedback	Effective Feedback
You are so smart.	You explained this point very clearly and convincingly.
You are so creative.	You developed a novel solution to the problem.
You don't know what you are talking about.	It is hard to follow your line of argument; the structure of your report needs to be more logical.

Remove emotions, focus on technicalities

Negative feedback often causes the feedback receiver to get upset, defensive, and become non-receptive to the feedback. It is very important to make the feedback highly technical and to use as little emotion as possible. Try not to use emotionally charged words like "good" or "bad," and instead use more neutral technical terminology.

Ineffective Feedback	Effective Feedback
Your explanation is bad.	Your explanation is not clear.
This argument is weak.	This argument is not supported by credible references.

When criticizing, suggest alternative behaviors

Studies show that people are most likely to take action when the call for action is accompanied by a plan. The more detailed the plan, the more likely people are to take action.

For example, in studies where people are invited to donate money or complete a survey, the response rate increases more than two-fold when, in addition to the invitation, there is a clear step-by-step guide for how to do it (e.g., just follow these steps: click on this link, select "donate", select the amount you want to donate).

Ineffective Feedback	Effective Feedback
Your argument is not convincing.	The argument is not convincing. To support it, find 2–3 statistics that illustrate your point, add them in your paper, provide citations to your sources.

Do not overload

Studies show that when people are presented with too many options, they stall. For example, in the context of online clothing shopping, people presented with too many color options are less likely to buy the item than when there are just a few colors to choose from. Likewise, when inviting people to buy an investment plan, people presented with more than 3–4 different investment plan options do not buy any. It is just too hard for us to process more than 4–7 points, and people \ put off the decision and do not take action.

Good feedback focuses on a few (1 to 4) key problems and suggestions. More may seem like a good idea, but it will likely result in the feedback receiver not following any of them.

Ineffective Feedback	Effective Feedback
Your report suffers from many deficiencies. Your formatting is very poor. You made many typos. You do not cite your sources and when you cite them, your referenced style is wrong. Some of your arguments are hard to follow. Your paper is too long. Also, you use the wrong font size and spacing.	I see a number of problems, but the biggest issues that you should focus on citing your sources and trying to make the paper a bit more focused and shorter.

Explain the impact on the client

It is better not to say that the work is simply bad or the arguments are confusing, or that you personally do not like it. Instead, try to explain how this may be seen by the client.

Ineffective Feedback	Effective Feedback
You have some interesting ideas, but the way you present your supporting arguments is very confusing. I could not understand what you were trying to say.	You have some interesting ideas, but I am afraid the client may not see them as such because your logic is not explained clearly. If you want a busy client to see right away the value of your ideas, they must be presented in a very clear and convincing manner.

Provide examples, models

People learn best from examples. Do not just point a problem or suggest a way to fix it, but also give an example, when possible.

Ineffective Feedback	Effective Feedback
Your recommendation for Germany as the best new market for the client is not convincing because you do not explain why you recommend Germany. Provide a good supporting argument.	Your recommendation for Germany as the best new market for the client is not convincing because you do not explain why you recommend Germany. Provide a good supporting argument. For example, if you believe Germany is a good market because it has many buyers who can afford the product, cite the country's GPD/capita and income.

The Feedback Sandwich

A good barber, before shaving his client, first puts some shaving cream on the client's cheeks.

You want to first talk about something positive before criticizing the work. This will relax the feedback receiver and create a friendlier and more trusting atmosphere.

It is also a good idea to finish up with some praise and encouragement. The positive tone induces motivation.

This is known as the "feedback sandwich."

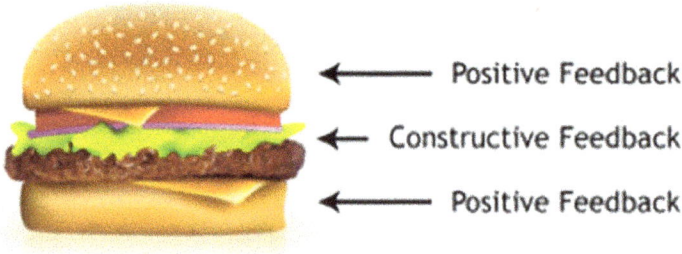

Fig 16.1 Feedback Sandwich

Ineffective Feedback	Effective Feedback
The way you present your supporting arguments is very confusing. It is hard to follow your line of reasoning.	Your work has many strengths, such as novel solutions to the problem and very professional formatting. However, the way you present your supporting arguments is very confusing. It is hard to follow your line of reasoning. It also helps that you provided graphs to illustrate your points.

Types of Feedback Provided by X-Culture Coaches

1. Personal requests for feedback: X-Culture teams can ask for feedback on their work by sending samples of their work to Coaching@X-Culture.org or submitting tickets through the XCRM system (separate module for training on XCRM). We usually receive only a few requests of this kind throughout the project, although the numbers can go up towards the end of the project as the teams are finishing up their reports.

   In this case, a pair of coaches will be assigned to the case and asked to review the team's work and provide personalized feedback. The coaches will take a day or two to review and provide feedback on this particular work sample (email directly back to the team, save a copy for the Coach Portfolio).

2. Group feedback: Every week. The teams submit their weekly deliverables on Sunday. The data is processed and distributed by the Coaching Director to the coaches for evaluation on Monday. The coaches have until Friday to review and evaluate the deliverables and provide feedback.

   Throughout the project, the weekly deliverables typically have one or two pages of initial notes and materials on that week's question. Some teams may have a more finished version of their work that spans 3–5 pages, but most of the time, these are relatively short submissions.

   One week prior to the final deadline, the teams submit full drafts of their reports, which are usually 20–30 pages in length.

   Lastly, the final reports are submitted at the end of the project and these documents are usually 15–35 pages.

   The coaches will not be providing personal feedback on the weekly submissions, report drafts, and final reports. Rather, the coaches will be asked to provide feedback on that week's submissions in general.

   This feedback will, essentially, start with, "I have read 50 submissions this week, and here are my impressions, comments, concerns, and suggestions…"

Feedback Structure:

- General impressions (0.5 to 1 pages);
- A review of most common problems and errors, including problems with formatting, presentation, and the actual recommendations. For each common problem, there will be an example, possibly with a screenshot, an explanation of why this is a problem, and suggestions for fixing the problem (2–3 pages);
- A review of interesting solutions, with examples and explanations for why these are interesting solutions;
- Any other comments and suggestions.

The general feedback to the entire cohort also allows us to be more detailed, review more typical problems, provide more examples, etc. If coaches had to provide this sort of feedback to every team, it would not be possible to say more than a few sentences, as more would require too much time.

To ensure that the feedback will be provided promptly, we will use a two-stage approach:

1. From the very beginning, the coaches will be given access to the last semester's submission (deliverables, report drafts, and final reports). The deliverables are very similar every semester. Students make the same mistakes, propose the same solutions, etc. Therefore, a few weeks before the corresponding deliverable is due, the coaches start with reviewing and providing feedback on last semester's submissions.

2. The Head Coaches will review this preliminary feedback and the coaches will use the feedback to further "polish" their feedback.

3. When this semester's teams submit their deliverables (Monday), the coaches will be asked to review these latest submissions and see if their feedback needs to be updated to address changes that may be present in this semester's submissions. The coaches will submit their final updated feedback to the Program Director (Friday).

4. The feedback from different coaches will be integrated and shared with the students as a consolidated, neatly-formatted PDF file.

References

Hesketh, E. A., & Laidlaw, J. M. (2002). Developing the teaching instinct, 1: Feedback. Medical Teacher, 24(3), 245–248.

Valcour, M. (August 11, 2015). How to Give Tough Feedback That Helps People Grow. Harvard Business Review, https://hbr.org/2015/08/how-to-give-tough-feedback-that-helps-people-grow

Porath, C., (October 25, 2016). Give Your Team More-Effective Positive Feedback. Harvard Business Review. https://hbr.org/2016/10/give-your-team-more-effective-positive-feedback

CHAPTER 17

Global Virtual Team Counseling

VAS TARAS, THE UNIVERSITY OF NORTH CAROLINA AT GREENSBORO, X-CULTURE, INC.

C ross-cultural counseling, conflict resolution, and teamwork facilitation is a very large and complex topic. Fully mastering this art would entail reading many books, taking many courses, and gaining extensive practical experience.

However, by reviewing the materials provided in this training module and completing the practical phase of the X-Culture GVT Coaching Program, you will gain a deep fundamental understanding of these issues.

Typical Issues

There are several interpersonal and administrative challenges that members of work teams can encounter. International and virtual teams have the added layer of complexity introduced by the cultural differences and geographic separation of the team members.

Most commonly, teams struggle with problems caused by free-riding (some team members not doing their share of work), communication difficulties, coordination challenges, the struggle for leadership within the team, workload distribution and ambiguity with claiming credit for work done, all sorts of problems stemming from cultural differences and stereotyping, differences in working styles and worth ethics, and institutional differences. Additionally, teams face common interpersonal conflicts and misunderstandings that can happen among people in most situations.

Serious conflicts, bullying, and sexual harassment are very rare, but we see one or two of those cases every semester, too.

Coaches Learning About a Problem

The role of the coach is to spot those problems and intervene in a professional and developmental manner.

There are two channels through which the coaches can learn about a problem and be assigned to a case.

1. The project participants can ask for help and counseling by sending a request to our XCRM System. This can be a request from a team or from an individual team member. In some cases, it is a direct request for help; in others, it is just a complaint that gives us a hint something is wrong, and help may be needed. Any case that requires an intervention will be reviewed, and a coach will be assigned to resolve it.

2. Every week, the project participants complete a weekly progress survey. The last question of each survey asks the team members to describe their experiences last week. Many students

provide no comments or just say a few words like "everything is good," while some students provide more detailed comments. The Coach Coordinator will be monitoring these comments for signs of conflicts and problems that may require an intervention. If a problem is detected, a coach will be assigned to investigate it further and see if a more substantive intervention or counseling may be needed.

The coaches will also be asked to review those comments, primarily to stay informed about the team dynamics and progress the teams are making, but also to review the comments for possible hidden calls for help.

Ultimately, it will be up to the Coaching Program Director, who will assign coaches to cases. The goal here is to ensure that every case receives due attention while keeping the workload evenly distributed across the coaches.

The Principles and Purpose of Team Counseling

It is important to understand several key principles of team counseling:

1. **There is usually no right or wrong**.

    Interactions among work team members are not an exact science. In most cases, all team members try their best within their personal abilities and circumstances. When something goes wrong, it is not because someone is "bad", but rather because people have different understandings of the task and situation, different obligations and resources, and/or different levels of skills and abilities. Rarely will you see cases when someone does or says something that is clearly inappropriate and could be labeled as "wrong". In most cases, there is no "guilty" party. However, in conflict situations, people almost always tend to see the other party as "wrong" or "guilty."

2. **Self-serving bias**.

    People have conflicts and misunderstandings all the time. Usually, it is because somebody makes a mistake or fails to communicate his/her intentions or reasons. It is very upsetting for us to realize we did something wrong. In fact, when a person realizes he/she made a mistake, this realization leads to a great deal of mental suffering. Many researchers argue that over the course of evolution, humans have developed a propensity for self-serving bias (a.k.a., self-serving attribution bias). We tend to attribute failure to others, and success to ourselves. When something goes wrong, we tend to believe it is somebody else's fault, and when something goes right, we tend to believe it is because we personally did a good job. This way of thinking is deeply hard-wired into our brains. We do not make the decision to think this way; it just happens. Even if it is obvious to others that the failure was clearly caused by our actions or lack of skills, we usually genuinely believe it was somebody else's fault or just a result of unfortunate circumstances. Likewise, in cases of success, we tend to see our role in the successful outcome as much larger than others do. Studies show that this tendency is not even psychological, it is biological; our brain is literally structured to operate this way. In studies that used FMRI, it has been observed that when people are presented with evidence that the problem was actually caused by their behavior or decisions, their pre-frontal cortex (the part of the brain that is responsible for higher reasons) literally shuts off and stops processing the information.

3. **Limited visibility of effort**.

In teams in general, but especially in global virtual teams, it is hard to see what other people are doing. As a result, team members always overestimate the amount of the work they do personally and underestimate the amount of work done by the other team member. If we do know about the work completed by the person, we assume the person did do the work. And since I know how much I personally do, and I do not see (and thus do not know) how much others do, I tend to assume that I work much harder than others.

In X-Culture, every week, we ask every team member to estimate what percent of work completed last week was completed by each team member. That is, out of 100% of the work completed last week, what percent was completed by the person who is answering the question, and by each other team member. With an average team size of about 6, it would be expected to see about 17% of work assigned to each team member. However, this is not the case. In evaluations of the work of others, we see an average of about 12-14%, which is close to what is expected, but still a few percentage points below the mathematical average. This tells us that we tend to underestimate the relative amount of work done by others.

However, in self-evaluations, the average is around 30%, which means that people overestimate their own contribution by about a factor of x2. In fact, if all self-evaluations are added for a team, we usually see a total of close to 200%, even though we would expect to see 100%.

From our interviews with the study participants, we do not believe this is caused by people deliberately lying and trying to make their performance look better. They appear to genuinely believe they work harder than others, likely because they simply are not aware of how much work others do.

4. **The counselor is not a judge**.

Given these cognitive and administrative constraints, a Coach cannot be in a position to judge who is right and who is wrong. The job here is to help the parties to come to a peaceful resolution of the conflict situation. It is almost guaranteed that all parties will retain their original convictions that they did nothing wrong and the issue was the other party's fault. However, with the proper counseling, they can still leave the situation satisfied, wiser, and better equipped to prevent a similar conflict in the future or resolve it more effectively if it still happens.

Let me reiterate: the role of the coach is not to determine who is right and who is wrong, but rather to defuse the conflict, turn it into a learning opportunity so it does not happen again, and help the team return to being productive and happy.

5. **They usually don't need advice, but just want to be heard**.

It is also important to understand that in most cases, team members involved in the conflict will not expect a decision, a judgment, or a solution to their problem from the coach. Most of the time, people are reasonable and have reasonable expectations. What they want is to know that the higher authority (the boss, the coach, the project coordinator, or even just another person) knows about the situation, knows the person is doing everything they can to successfully resolve the problem, and perhaps that another team member(s) are not doing their share.

So, in most cases, all a coach needs to do is to listen, show understanding, ask to continue trying to resolve the problem, and assure that we will continue to monitor the case, and if it gets worse, we will intervene. In fact, in most cases, it is preferred that this is all a coach will do, as a more direct intervention is often unnecessary or even undesirable.

The Reasons for Conflict

Counseling and conflict resolution is much easier when the counselor understands the root causes of conflict. The truth is, it is extremely rare that one of the parties involved in the conflict acted in bad faith. It is possible but extremely unlikely that the conflict was caused by malicious intent or mental illness. More likely than not, the conflict is due to:

1. **Parties having competing interests** (about 10% of the cases in X-Culture).

   Sometimes, our interests and goals may be competing or even mutually exclusive.

   For example, if we are stranded on an island with a limited supply of food, your interest is to have the food for yourself and my interest is to have the food to myself. As the amount of food is a fixed value, our interests are at odds.

   In organizations, we may be competing for the same position. In the context of X-Culture, your interest may be to win the competition, while mine interest is simply to get a passing grade.

   There may also be a difference in values or beliefs. One person may value harmony and the other completion. One person may believe individual interests should prevail over the interests of the group; another person may put group interests first. These differences can cause conflicts because we want different things.

   The way to resolve this conflict is to help the parties to clearly communicate their goals and interests to one another. If the goals are mutually exclusive, it may be impossible to find a perfect solution, but the clarity will help reach an acceptable compromise.

2. **Parties have different information** (about 70% of the cases in X-Culture).

   Usually, the conflict is caused by different information available to the parties involved in the conflict. We simply do not know what the other party wants or does, so we make assumptions. Those assumptions are often wrong, which causes conflict.

   For example, a team member did not do his/her part of the work, so I assume the person is lazy and incompetent. However, my perception of the situation and the person would be very different if I knew that the person had problems at home or in another project, was sick, or did put in the effort but simply did not have the skills to do the work right. Even more often, this type of problem can be caused by the other party not realizing how important it was to complete the task on time. In their culture or system, it would be OK to be a little late or to do a little less. If I knew this, I would be less upset, and probably would have planned for it to prevent the problem from happening.

   The key to preventing and resolving this sort of conflict is communication and transparency. As long as both parties share all the information they have, they can find a way to resolve the conflict.

3. **Parties process the information differently** (about 20% of the cases in X-Culture).

   Sometimes it happens that all parties have the same interests and the same information, but they process this information differently. People may rely on different experiences or simply have different cognitive skills.

   For example, team members may disagree on the best answer to a particular question, such as the best new market entry mode. They all want to come up with the best solution, and they all have the same information; however, one team member may be better informed or more skilled than another, so they may come to different conclusions as to what the best decision is. This may lead to an argument or even a conflict.

The way to resolve this conflict is, again, through communication. The parties should not only share with one another what they know but possibly even educate one another as to how they arrived at a conclusion and why their method is the best.

The X-Culture Counseling Model

Based on the premises and concepts listed above, we recommend that you follow the subsequent steps when helping a team to resolve a conflict or address a challenge:

1. Contact the person who expressed concern or requested help, and then asks for more information. Focus on listening and being empathetic. Do not give any advice and do not jump to conclusions yet.

    In most cases, no further steps may be needed other than assuring the person that you (the X-Culture Admin team represented by you, the coach) is aware of the situation and is ready to intervene if such a need arises.

2. If Step 1 is not enough, and if appropriate, contact other concerned parties (other team members, possibly even their instructors) to collect more information. Again, focus on listening and being empathetic. Do not try to make the decision for them, but rather help them make the decision or resolve the conflict on their own.

3. If Step 2 is not enough and a decision must be made, focus on helping the parties exchange information about their interests, knowledge, and understanding. Help them understand what is causing the conflict, reach an agreement, and develop a plan for the future (things they will do or stop doing to prevent this sort of problems in the future, etc.).

4. If Step 3 is not enough if the conflict persists or escalates and a higher authority must make a decision that potentially involves punishing one or more parties (e.g., demand an apology, exclude someone from the project, etc.), contact the X-Culture Admin to work out the appropriate course of action. We will have to involve instructors at this stage, and it may get much more complicated.

5. Keep notes of your observations and steps as you are interacting with the conflicting parties, and write a case summary when the case is closed. Try to be as detailed as possible, not only describing who said and did what and how the issue has been resolved, but also your understanding of the problem and your recommendation for GVT members, Coaches, and Instructors to prevent or resolve situations like this in the future.

Other Special Cases

Here is a useful review of some special cases from Harvard Business Review. The full text can be found here.

These cases are not always applicable to X-Culture, but the Coaches may encounter them in their future careers and thus may find this information useful.

When Talking to Someone Who Has the Tendency to Cry

"When the other side attacks you, your instinctive reaction [may be] to attack right back, to 'fight fire with fire' and 'give them a taste of their own medicine'…. More often, however, this strategy lands you in a futile and costly confrontation. You provide them with justification for their unreasonable behavior."

Aim to stay calm while standing your ground. Be willing to shut down a meeting that is not productive or professional. Say things — in a neutral, composed voice — like:

- "I need to have a conversation with you. I need you to lower your voice."
- "I need you to take a deep breath, or we will have to reschedule this. This is not constructive."

Let them know you appreciate the strength of their convictions, but you can do without the yelling.

Reiterate your good intentions and let them know you want to hear what they have to say after they've taken a moment or a night to calm down.

When Talking to Someone Who Gets Defensive

The participant might say things like, "You've misunderstood. They've got it all wrong. You clearly don't understand." These are tactics to avoid having a constructive dialogue.

In this case, call the person out on not listening and encourage him to do so, or say something like:

- "I see this as your responsibility—let's talk about why you don't see it this way."
- "When you blame someone else, you become the victim, which isn't helpful to you."

When to Address the Bigger Issue

If the participant's behavior is a recurring pattern, you should address the person's reactive tendency head-on. You might say something like, "I notice every time we sit down to discuss feedback, you get [upset, angry, defensive]. I have your best interests at heart. What can I do to help you receive feedback with more openness? And here's what I need in these interactions." Break the vicious cycle of avoiding difficult feedback conversations. Says Castelda, "Be careful not to stew on things or bottle things up. Give constructive feedback as things come up. It ends up being smaller."

Emotional reactions can put us on opposite sides of the table with the other person. By focusing on good intentions, preparing with integrity, and calmly and effectively responding at the moment, we can move to the same side of the table and help the other person grow.

Practical Examples for Common Workplace Situations

Source: Office Vibe

Please refer to the online article for more details.

These cases are not always applicable to X-Culture, but coaches may encounter them in their future careers and thus may find this information useful.

Focus On the Behavior, Not The Person

I noticed you haven't shown up for the last two team meetings. I'm worried that you missed some important information. Can we meet to discuss what you missed?

This is better than saying something like "You obviously don't care about this team since you don't show up for the meetings."

A Participant Seems Disengaged

If a participant is disengaged, you'll want to figure out if something is bothering them, so you'll want to:

- Show them you're noticing/looking out for them
- Tell them how it makes you feel
- Offer help

Here's what you can say:

I noticed you don't seem as happy as you usually do, and obviously, that makes me feel like I'm doing something wrong.

Is everything okay? I think if we met once a week to make sure everything's going okay, you'd be much happier.

A Participant Didn't Deliver a Project On Time

Terrible, but there's not much you can do about it. No point in getting mad, just make sure that this doesn't happen again. Everyone needs to be accountable for their work, so when giving feedback about this, you'll want to:

Highlight why this is important

- Motivate them for next time
- Offer ideas to improve

Here's what you can say:

The project wasn't delivered on time, do you have any idea why?

As you know, we're trying to get everything organized for the new website, so if you're late on a project, it slows down the rest of the team.

We'll just make sure that for next time, you have more time and resources to finish on time. The new website is going to be sick! I think for next time, what you could do is schedule blocks of time maybe one day a week to make sure that you're not overloaded with work towards the end.

I tried that on my last project and it made a huge difference.

An Employee Was Rude To a Coworker

Ideally, everyone on the team works well together and collaborates smoothly, but a tension between coworkers is a natural thing that occurs often. You want to put a stop to this one quickly.

- Explain why you're talking to them and not the coworker
- Don't blame, listen to their side
- Offer advice

Here's what you can say:

Stacey asked me to have a chat with you about something you said earlier, I don't think she was comfortable saying anything, so I offered to do it.

I'm curious, can you let me know what happened? I'm assuming it was a misunderstanding, but of course, I want us all to get along.

If it was me, I'd wait until the end of the day and then apologize to her, maybe ask to go eat lunch together to talk about it.

An Employee Doesn't Get Along With Anyone

This situation is a bit more troubling, but again, you'll want to focus on the behavior rather than the person.

- Be straightforward
- Offer ideas for a workaround

Here's what you can say:

I just wanted to let you know that I've gotten a few complaints recently from some people on the team.

I wanted to chat with you directly about it to see if there was anything we can do. It might be because you're stressed, but I think when you raise your voice it sometimes rubs people the wrong way, which might be why they're perceiving it as rude.

I wonder if working from home one day a week might help with some of the stress that you're feeling.

An Employee Doesn't Take Initiative

When you're giving feedback about this one, remember to:

- Tell them how it affects you
- Offer help and advice

Here's what you can say:

I notice that you're not taking as much initiative as you used to. That makes me feel like I did something wrong. Did I say or do anything recently to upset you?

An Employee Has Poor Time Management

Time management is a tough thing to get right and is a constant process of optimization, but if it's becoming a problem, then you'll need to give them some feedback. When you're giving feedback about this one, remember to:

- Tell them how it affects the team
- Offer tips

Here's what you can say:

I've been noticing that you weren't able to manage your time for the last three tasks.

Other people on the team weren't able to get their work done, and so it created some issues for other departments. We'll figure out how to get it fixed for next time, though.

I used to have that problem too, but then I discovered a tool to help with that. Personally, I use a tool called RescueTime, it's been a lifesaver.

I'd recommend trying it and seeing how you can optimize your time.

References

Su, A.J., Harvard Business Review, Sept 21, 2016, How to Give Feedback to People Who Cry, Yell, or Get Defensive, https://hbr.org/2016/09/how-to-give-feedback-to-people-who-cry-yell-or -get-defensive

Shriar, J, Office Vibe, Jeb 2, 2016, 8 Detailed Examples Of Giving Employee Feedback, https://www.officevibe.com/blog/employee-feedback-examples

CHAPTER 18

Organizing and Leading Instructional Webinars

VAS TARAS, THE UNIVERSITY OF NORTH CAROLINA AT GREENSBORO, X-CULTURE, INC.

We Do Not Have All the Answers (Yet)

Webinars and video conferencing have emerged as very effective modes of training in the modern workplace. As an international collaboration, virtual office, flexible work hours, constant travel, global freelancing, and crowdsourcing have become ubiquitous, the opportunities to meet face-to-face in a physical office are vanishing. In most modern organizations, organizational members are dispersed across various geographic locations, making face-to-face meetings often impossible.

However, in the past several years, many tools have been developed that allow for a virtual meeting in a form or a teleconference or webinar. They cannot fully replace some of the benefits of a face-to-face meeting, yet at the same time offer several new benefits that cannot be offered by the traditional face-to-face format.

Teleconference and webinar technologies are developing rapidly. The first systems were introduced about 15 years ago, but good free or inexpensive tools did not appear until about five years ago. In the past two-three years, the number of highly functional tools exploded, with several dozen viable options offered every year.

X-Culture has experimented with several teleconferencing and webinar tools. Namely, we have extensively tested the following webinar platforms:

- YouTube Live (formerly Google on Air)
- Webinar Ninja
- Webinar Jam
- Blackboard Collaborate
- WebEx
- Adobe Connect
- GoToMeeting/GoToWebinar
- Zoom Meeting/Zoom Webinar

The purpose of this training module is to share X-Culture's experience with webinars: what works, what doesn't, and what we don't know yet.

Video Lecture vs. Teleconference vs. Webinar

Although all of these formats rely on video as an information delivery and exchange, there are notable differences between teleconference, webinar, and video lectures.

A video lecture is pre-recorded and allows only one-way communication. It allows virtually unlimited time to prepare and edit the video. The video file can also be downloaded prior to watching so that internet bandwidth and connection stability are not a constraint. This allows for delivering the training material in the highest quality possible, in terms of the content and the quality of the picture and sound.

A teleconference is more of a conversation. All participants have equal roles in the sense that everyone can communicate at any time. It is usually a small group of up to ten people who are effectively sitting around a virtual table and talking. There is no need for a passive audience, attendance tracking, or a recording of the meeting; people simply meet and talk.

A webinar is a purposefully instructional event that divides the participants into presenters and audiences. One or more participants are on a virtual stage delivering the content like a professor or speaker, while the rest of the participants are in the virtual audience absorbing the information and possibly occasionally engaging with the presenter and other audience members, akin to students in a classroom.

A video lecture or teleconference may require pre-registration, but this is not always necessary. A webinar usually requires an advanced registration (often paid), and may involve a calendar reminder and some other steps.

Special Requirements for Video Lectures, Teleconferences, and Webinar

The technological and administrative needs and the format of the pre-recorded video lectures and teleconferences are relatively self-evident.

Video Lecture

A video lecture requires the ability to record multiple takes of certain segments of the lecture, making it possible to alternate between the lecturer and the materials the lecturer wants to show. That is, sometimes the audience sees the face of the lecturer, and sometimes the lecturer may display a chart, a picture, or video clip, or record their screen as they demonstrate a certain procedure. Numerous software packages allow for recording the speaker, embedding pictures or video clips, or capturing the presenter's computer screen and creating professional-looking videos. A search for "movie makers" will render dozens, if not hundreds, of free or inexpensive software packages suitable for this task.

Camtasia is probably the most powerful package for creating video lectures. Unlike other video makers, Camtasia has been specifically designed for this purpose, and has many useful features that meet the needs of this type of video.

Teleconference

A teleconference usually has only several requirements. First, it should deliver high-quality video and audio. Second, it should allow for an easy connection/login. Third, it should also allow for instant messaging, file sharing, and screen sharing. There are many tools that satisfy the first two of these criteria, notably Skype and Google Hangouts, as well as Viber, WhatsApp, Zoom, and the like.

The third requirement is a little trickier. Skype (as well as Viber, WhatsApp, and the like) requires that all teleconference members have the software installed on their computers. It works extremely well when all participants have the software and are typically always on, making it very easy to call one another, add more participants to the call, create permanent caller groups, etc. However, as surpassing as it may seem, there are still many people who do not have Skype.

Thus, joining the teleconference requires that they first install the program, create the account, and add all the participants to their contacts, which can take 15-20 minutes just to join the call. Skype is now experimenting with direct call links that allow joining the call in a web browser without installing the software, but this approach presents other inconveniences and is not a perfect solution.

Google Hangouts and Zoom do not require that all participants have the program installed on their computers. The meeting host, who must have an account, can generate a link and send it directly to the meeting participants. The meeting is essentially happening inside a web browser and thus does not require an installation of the software. However, it does still require an installation of a plug-in. It takes only a few seconds to a few minutes to install the plug-in, but occasionally the users have firewalls or security software that prevents them from running the script. This can result in frustration and delayed meetings.

Webinar

Because webinars are attended by a large group of participants (sometimes thousands) and the roles of the participants are different, webinars are much more complex than video lectures or teleconferences.

The following the requirements that cannot be fully satisfied by teleconferencing software such as Skype or Google Hangout.

1. *Large audience*

    Software such as Skype usually limits the number of participants to about 10, which is not enough to satisfy the need for serving a much larger webinar audience.

    Google Hangouts (YouTube Live) allows for live YouTube streaming and, therefore, a virtually unlimited audience size. However, this solution only allows for passive watching and lacks many other essential webinar features.

    Zoom Meeting allows up to 100 active participants in a meeting. This is best for round-table meetings and webinars. Zoom Webinar (costs extra) allows for a virtually unlimited passive audience and up to three active presenters, which is ideal for most webinars.

2. *Ease of access*

    With an audience of hundreds or even thousands, it is guaranteed that some attendees will have difficulties accessing the webinar. Even if it is only one in ten who have problems, this can still mean many frustrated audience members – and a lot of work for the webinar admin to resolve those problems. So, generally, any tool that requires the audience members having to create an account and install special software is not a viable option, as too many users will have difficulties with creating accounts or installing the software.

    This is particularly true for mobile devices. In a teleconference, all participants are generally highly motivated members of the organization who are committed enough to go through the hassle of installing a program on the computer or an app on their smartphone. However, webinar attendees tend to be much less motivated and committed. If they cannot access the webinar in a few seconds, many will give up and not try harder. Also, because the webinar participants do not feel the same responsibility to attend the webinar, many of them will not bother to access it from a computer, but rather will try to do so from their smartphone. This means an app must be downloaded and installed, which deters several potential participants.

    Thus, good webinar software is one that allows one-click access to the webinar. Ideally, the system sends an email with a link, and all the attendee must do is click on the link and access the webinar instantly.

3. *Registration*

Registration is usually needed to track who attended the webinar. First, it is often necessary to know how many people are expected to be in the audience, and often it is helpful to know who those people are to tailor the content of the webinar to their needs. Second, the webinar organizers, for example, a professor or supervisor, may want to offer academic credit or a merit badge for participation in the webinar and thus must know not only who registered for it, but also who attended the event.

Thus, the system must allow for easy registration and keep a record of who participated in the webinar.

Ideally, the webinar organizer must be able to send out targeted invitations to a group of students or organizational members. Therefore, the webinar access link must have the name of the person encoded in it so that the attendee does not even have to provide his/her name. With just a click on the link, the system automatically recognizes the user, and the username can be easily matched with the user profile in the webinar organizer's database.

Even better, the system should allow the attendees to register using their Facebook login. This way, the system can capture their demographics and interests, thereby providing the webinar organizer with the necessary information needed to tailor the event to a specific audience.

Here are preferred registration protocols based on the webinar audience

Known users (e.g., students, employees, etc.)

1. The webinar organizer has a roster of expected attendees and sends invitations to all users on the roster.
2. The invitees receive a customized email addressed to the person on the roster (e.g., Dear John) and a personalized webinar access link.
3. To access the webinar, the user clicks on the link and is taken directly to the in-browser webinar. The system automatically recognizes the user's name.
4. During the webinar, the system tracks the number of minutes the user was in the virtual webinar room, his/her comments, and other actions.
5. After the webinar is over, the system generates a list of attendees so that the webinar organizer knows who exactly attended the event.

Unknown users (e.g., happy to invite anyone)

1. The webinar organizer announces the webinar on a webpage, Facebook, or through other means
2. Interested users click on a "Claim your seat" link.
3. The link opens a registration form where the user provides his/her name, email address, and possibly more information.
4. The user may also be offered to choose a preferred session if the webinar is offered multiple times.
5. Alternatively, the user may be offered to one-click register using their Facebook profile, in which case the system also captures the demographics and other information available to the public provide on Facebook.
6. After "Claiming a seat," the user receives an email with the personalized link, and the process follows steps 2-5 from the sequence for Known Users.

4. *Payments*

Sometimes, the webinar organizers may want to charge for participation in the instructional webinar or may want to allow the webinar attendees to buy certain products or services during the webinar.

There is nothing wrong with webinar organizers or speakers being compensated for their efforts, and oftentimes paid registrations may be necessary to raise funds to invite speakers or to prepare valuable content.

Also, sometimes it may be necessary to charge a different price depending on the status of the attendee. For example, certain groups (organizational members, alumni, or subscribers) may need to be allowed to attend webinars for free, while everybody else may need to pay. Furthermore, the price may need to vary depending on the region.

5. *Multiple presenters and multiple admins in multiple locations*

It is often necessary to have multiple presenters who are in different countries (e.g., the webinar host and one or more invited speakers who join from different locations). It may also be necessary that multiple people have the right to launch the event, mute and unmute speakers, share the screen and administer the event otherwise.

Many systems allow only for one presenter or one admin, which can create problems if multiple speakers need to be invited or if the main webinar admin loses the internet connection and a backup is needed.

6. *Reminders*

Once the users are invited/registered for the webinar, the system should allow the users to put the event on their Outlook or Google Calendar. This can be done automatically or through a one-click "Add to Calendar" option.

Furthermore, the system should remind the users about the webinar at a predetermined time (e.g., 15 min before the webinar begins) by sending a reminder email or by triggering a calendar alert.

7. *Awaiting*

If a user accesses the webinar earlier, the system should indicate how much time is left until the webinar start and, possibly, offer a pre-webinar video lecture so that the users are entertained while waiting for the event to start.

8. *Raising hands and engaging in the discussion*

While it is generally enough for the webinar attendees to passively watch the webinar and the interactions between the presenters, it is often desirable that the attendees can engage in discussion with the presenters, ask questions, provide comments, etc.

If the number of attendees is very large, it may not be possible or desirable to give everyone an opportunity to talk whenever they feel like saying something. Ideally, all attendees will be muted, but if they want to ask a question or comment, they should be able to "raise their hand," and the webinar organizer should be able to unmute their microphone and webcam so that they could be seen and heard. After the question has been asked, the webinar organizer should be able to mute the user again.

Additionally, the webinar attendees should be able to comment or ask questions in writing through an Instant Messaging or Comments window. Ideally, they should be given a choice to leave a public comment (visible to all webinar attendees) or a private comment (visible only by the presenter to whom the question is addressed).

9. *Subgroups*

It is often desirable to allow the webinar attendees to break up into small groups and have a live discussion within their groups. This is especially useful if the format of the webinar requires practicing certain skills or exchanging ideas in smaller groups.

10. *Polling*

When the audience is very large, the most efficient way to engage with the audience may be via polling. The presenter may ask a question, and the audience should be able to easily provide their answers or vote on an issue. This way, a large group of people can express their opinion or show their knowledge without the need to give time to everyone to express themselves.

11. *End-of-Webinar Actions*

After the webinar is over, it is often desirable to be able to send a Thank You Note to the attendees, ask them to rate the quality of the webinar and provide feedback, give them an opportunity to sign up for the next webinar in the series, buy a product, sign up for a newsletter or opt-out from the future correspondence.

12. *Recording*

Usually, it is necessary to be able to record the webinar so it can be shared with those who could not attend the event live.

Webinar Solutions We Tried and What We Learned in the Process

X-Culture has tried all of the major webinar platforms. Here is what we learned in the process:

1. Most webinar platforms require a software installation or cumbersome registration. For example, Blackboard Collaborate, Adobe Connect, WebEx, and the like work best with closed groups, such as students enrolled in a particular course or employees at a particular organization.

2. Many webinar platforms are designed to deliver lectures, and thus the focus is on the slides, not on the speaker. Currently, most platforms allow for alternating between the picture of the presenter and the slides, but some still prominently display the slides with the speaker appearing only as a very small picture somewhere in the corner. These are not the best solutions when an interview-style webinar format is preferred.

3. Most free platforms such as Google Hangout/YouTube Live do not allow for easily inviting large groups, managing registrations, tracking performance, and keeping other administrative records.

4. The systems that have good functionality when it comes to invitations, registrations, and participation tracking tend to be designed for commercial applications. GoToWebinar or WebEx work very well but often require too many steps when it comes to registration.

5. Several webinar platforms allow organizers to charge for participation. However, they all use third-party payment processors, which makes the integration of payments quite a hassle. It is doable, but not with just a few clicks; setting up the pay-for-participation option may take several hours.

6. Additionally, better systems tend to have a hefty price ($50-$500 per month, depending on the max allowed number of users and unlocked features). Some, like Webinarjam, only allow an

annual subscription (about $1,000) and offer no free trial period (although it is possible to cancel the subscription within two weeks for a full refund).

7. Most providers offer multiple types of accounts. Some have a free account that allows a limited number of participants (for example, up to 10) and limited duration of the meeting/webinar (for example, up to 40 minutes), with the prices at around $20 to $500 per month depending on the functionality and the size of the audience. Usually, a package at around $50-70 per month should be sufficient for most needs (an audience in the hundreds, unlimited session duration, opportunity to record the session, etc.).

8. While Skype is extremely intuitive and essentially operates as a phone, a more advanced system requires a considerable investment of time in learning how they work. Be prepared to spend a considerable amount of time on first selecting the system that will satisfy your needs and then the many hours of learning how it works.

9. All systems are not perfect when it comes to video and audio quality. Even the most expensive systems often freeze, lockout participants, and have other technical problems, especially when the number of presenters is large. However, Skype and Zoom seem to offer the best quality. Surprisingly, such big-name providers like WebinarJam, Webinar Ninja, and GoToWebinar, and WebEx offered rather a poor video/audio quality, whereas Skype and Zoom were nearly perfect, based upon several tests of each system.

X-Culture's Free Choice

After trying several different products, X-Culture was using YouTube Live (former Google On Air) for a long time. In 2017, we also purchased a Zoom Webinar subscription.

YouTube Live is a very easy-to-use option. It is essentially a Google Hangout with the option of live streaming of the webinar on YouTube to a large audience and recording the event. Also, it is free and offers good video and audio quality.

YouTube live offers several huge advantages. First, it does not require any registration. The users just click on the link and instantly watch the event on YouTube. There is even no need to install a plug-in.

Second, it automatically creates a recording of the event and posts it to YouTube. This way, the recording of the event is ready to be shared almost instantly, with no rendering required. You can still go into your YouTube account and edit the video (trim, add background music, etc.). The recording can also be downloaded as an MP4 file.

Third, it allows for passive users to click on a presenter link and join the webinar room live to ask questions or engage with the presenters. Additionally, the attendees can leave comments below the YouTube video.

At the same time, YouTube live does not provide good functionality when it comes to registering for the event, sending reminders, keeping track of attendees, and keeping other administrative records.

YouTube Live allows for only one admin who can start the recording or mute/unmute speakers. Occasionally, one person may create the event, but another should administer the event later—and switching roles is not easy on YouTube live, other than by sharing personal login information.

YouTube Live does not allow for the restriction of the audience. Theoretically, anyone can watch the webinar if the person has the YouTube link. In fact, the system will even alert all YouTube channel subscribers about the event—and sometimes, we do not want the event to be open to the public but be restricted only to, for example, current X-Culture participants. However, designating the webinar as "unlisted" makes it virtually impossible for others to find it, unless they follow you. So, it is highly improbable that completely external people will attend your event if you do not give them the event link.

X-Culture's Paid Choice

X-Culture also now has a premium webinar account with Zoom. It allows us to have meetings with up to 100 people or have a webinar with a passive audience of up to 5,000 people.

Most of the time, we prefer the meeting format. Hardly ever do we have more than 100 people in attendance, so it makes sense to give them all an opportunity to "be in the webinar room." The only downside of this approach is that if people do not mute their microphones, sometimes the meeting is interrupted with annoying background noises. However, the software allows us to easily mute people who are not presenting, so this is not a big problem.

Also, Zoom meetings have an option where only the active speaker is displayed, meaning that the person who is speaking is shown on the entire screen, while those who are listening to a shown as small thumbnails. Unfortunately, this process has to be managed manually, which with a large group can be a bit hard. In comparison, YouTube Live automatically switches to the person who is speaking, which gives a bit less control but works better.

Zoom Webinar allows for up to three presenters at the same time. Usually, this is enough: one host, one speaker, and one audience member who joins to ask a question or make a comment. It is easy to invite any of the audience members to the webinar room, so once the "visitor" is done talking and another person wants to ask a question, it is easy to kick out one person and add another to the webinar room. A more expensive subscription allows for more presenters, but three has been shown to be a sufficient number.

Zoom is also very comprehensive when it comes to registration. Once a meeting it set up, it allows the host to either send personalized invitations or share a generic link. Once people click on the generic link, they are asked to provide their name and email. After registering, the person receives a personal webinar access link (also emailed) and a link to add the event to the calendar (very useful for reminders). Unfortunately, Zoom does not allow for an automatic reminder to be sent by email at intervals such as 24 hours, 1 hour, and 10 minutes before the event, but such reminders can be sent to all registered participants with one click, so it is not a large problem.

Zoom also allows for branding. Your company logo and background graphics can be added to the registration page and the registration confirmation email.

With Zoom, asking questions in writing is possible through the chat function, with customizations such as sending them to all participants or just some participants, breaking up into groups, raising a hand to ask a question, polling the audience, sharing the screen, showing slides, and more. It also allows paid participation, although setting it up may take some time.

Probably the best part is that Zoom also allows attendees to join the meeting/webinar via computer, smartphone app, and phone (by dialing a telephone number). It is the only truly universal platform.

Webinars Organized by the Coaches

X-Culture Coaches can choose to organize their webinars in YouTube Live or use the X-Culture Zoom Webinar account (login, password, and step-by-step guidelines will be provided on an as-needed basis).

CHAPTER 19

Principles of Crowdsourcing and Problem Solving in Large Groups

VAS TARAS, THE UNIVERSITY OF NORTH CAROLINA AT GREENSBORO, X-CULTURE, INC.

This training module is prepared based on the X-Culture's research into problem-solving by large groups. A brief overview of our work in this area is presented in this TEDx talk: https://youtu.be /DfNUz2qlQkY

What is crowdsourcing?

The topic of crowdsourcing is relatively new. The technology, which enables a large group of people to collaborate, has only been available for the last 10-15 years. Thus, nobody has the definitive answers yet on how to organize a large group of people so that they produce the best solutions. The X-Culture coaches are expected to know the principle of crowdsourcing and working in large teams. This exposure will give you a better understanding of the work designs we are testing in the X-Culture project. Additionally, such understanding will make the coaches more effective when advising Global Virtual Teams on the best ways to organize their workflow and coordination.

Here is what the X-Culture team has learned so far.

Two heads are better than one, especially if the second head is that of an expert. Therefore, when a solution to a difficult problem is needed, business owners and managers often turn to consultants. Consultants are thought to add expertise that applies specifically to the problem being faced.

Under the traditional business consulting model, one or a few experts typically tackle a given problem. Depending on the scope and size of the problem, a single expert or a small team of experts is usually invited to review the problem and develop a solution. Sometimes, several consultants may be assigned to work on the problem, but even if they represent a large consulting company, the team rarely exceeds 3-4 experts. In other words, the consulting industry traditionally relies on consultants with specific knowledge or a small closely-knit expert team to solve problems.

A few other characteristics of the traditional consulting model are noteworthy:

1. The problems tend to be solved in secrecy. Non-disclosure agreements are very common, even if the client has no reason to demand that the case be kept confidential. As a result, the experts working on the case are often unable to discuss it and receive insights from their colleagues or even partners in the same consulting firm.
2. The consultants working on the case tend to be alike in terms of their education and demographic profile, as well as their geographic location and professional and social circles.
3. The consultants are usually selected for the job based on a "good enough" basis. That is, on the one end, the client reviews a list of available consultants and selects one (or a firm) who seems to offer the necessary expertise at an acceptable price. On the other end the consultant (or the firm) rarely passes on a contract if there is at least some fit. As the client does not have perfect

information about available consulting experts and the consultants rarely refuse an opportunity to take on a new project, the expertise-needs match is usually "good enough" but rarely perfect.

4. Once the consultants are hired, their pay is guaranteed, usually at a fixed amount agreed upon before the project starts or at a fixed rate per billing hour. In some cases, a profit-sharing component may be part of the compensation package to provide additional motivation to develop an effective solution. In all these cases, however, the consultants are guaranteed compensation, even if the final solution is not a good one.

Evidence mounts, however, that under the right conditions, crowds consistently produce better solutions than those offered by individual experts or small expert teams; under the right conditions, size and diversity beat ability. A review of decades of research into the power crowds at solving complex problems is provided in books such as "Wisdom of Crowds" (Surowiecki, 2005); "We are Smarter than Me" (Libert, Spector, & Tapscott, 2007); "Crowdsourcing" (Howe, 2007), "Wikinomics" (Tapscott & Williams, 2008), "Here Comes Everybody" (Shirky, 2008); "Cognitive Surplus" (Shirky, 2010), and "Re-Inventing the Discovery" (Nielsen, 2012).

A large body of evidence from experimental studies has strongly suggested that under the right conditions, a crowd will consistently outperform experts. We had seen that with Wikipedia when a large group of mostly amateurs effectively killed the expert-based encyclopedia industry; with Linux and other open-source software creating products that are in many respects superior to those offered by such industry leaders as Microsoft or IBM; with Apple's App Store, that increased the availability and quality of applications exponentially; or with Goldcorp, that transformed itself from a near-bankrupt into one of the world's most successful gold mining companies by opening its geological survey data and getting better input from the crowd than from expert geologists.

So what are the conditions under which crowds will consistently outperform experts at developing better solutions? They relate to the task itself, the crowd characteristics, and the process used by the crowd to solve the problem, namely:

The Task

The problem must be complex. You do not need a crowd to tie your shoe. A simple task like tying a shoe will always be performed faster and more effectively by a single person. However, a crowd is likely to outperform experts at solving complex problems that require diverse knowledge, skills, and connections that a single expert is unlikely to possess or have access to. The more complex the problem, the greater the crowd advantage.

The problem must require an innovative solution: An experienced accountant will always be more efficient and more effective at preparing a routine tax return. However, when a creative approach is needed, the expert's experience with producing route solutions would not be of much help. Often, the most innovative solutions are presented by people from completely unrelated fields, using methods that have never been applied before in the subject area. Innovation requires a diversity of ideas, and crowds offer such diversity.

The Crowd

The crowd must be large and diverse: Pooling similar sets of skills and knowledge does not add value. An assembly line may work better when identical workers repeat identical tasks over and over again, but the creative synergy comes from diversity. The resource-based view suggests that an organization can be comparatively more effective when it has resources that are valuable, rare, and cannot be easily imitated or substituted (Barney, 1991). Thus, to be effective and to ensure access to a wide range of skills, resources, and ideas that an expert cannot have, imitate, or substitute, a crowd must be large and diverse in terms of demographics, professional backgrounds, geographies, and social ties.

The crowd must have basic qualifications: Usually, a large and diverse crowd ensures that at least some individuals in it have the basic qualifications to tackle the problem. However, crowds are most effective when they are pre-selected to meet certain qualification requirements. Individuals who are completely incompetent in the subject are not likely to offer valuable, rare, substitutable resources (Barney, 1991) but will only add coordination cost.

The crowd must be able to engage in flexible terms: The best person for the job tends to work "somewhere else." However, the best person for the job may not always be available for a full-time engagement in a crowdsourced project. The crowd members are unlikely to have the time to review and keep track of all aspects of a complex project, and even revolutions rely on the group and semi-involved supporters. Thus, a crowd can work only if the project is split into small independent tasks. The platform must allow for flexible engagement so that the crowd members can contribute in small increments when it is convenient for them (Fisher, 2012).

The Process

The process must allow for the exchange of information: As noted earlier, the early crowdsourcing models were built around the hope that if the crowd is large enough, someone in the crowd will offer a good solution. However, crowdsourcing can do much more than just find the best person for the job. The true value of crowds is in the synergy that allows the crowd to produce a solution that its smartest member could not produce working individually. Social learning is the foundation for collective intelligence (Bonabeau, 2009). Social learning theory postulates that systems can increase their productivity by providing opportunities for learning by observing and imitating others (Albors, Ramos, & Hervas, 2008). Thus, a properly designed crowd collaboration allows the crowd members to learn from one another, build upon ideas of others, and tap previously unavailable resources (Marjanovic, Fry, & Chataway, 2012). Working together, we generate more and better ideas than working separately. 1+1 can truly equal more than 2.

Feedback must be part of the process: In addition to learning from one another, crowds are more effective when they receive frequent feedback on their work (Wooten & Ulrich, 2017). Unlike full-time employees, crowd members tend to have limited information about the progress of the project, and often do not see how their work fits in the larger picture (Dow et al., 2011). Regular feedback from project organizers and peers aids social learning and allows crowd members to stay informed, not veer in wrong directions, waste time, and lose interest in the project (Liu & Carless, 2006; Nadler, 1979).

Coordination is critical to avoid overload: The amount of information and communication generated by the crowd and the complexities of interactions among the crowd members can become overwhelming. To facilitate social learning and resource management, the crowdsourcing platform must facilitate coordination among the crowd members, including processing, sorting, rating, and sharing their input, comments, and ideas provided by the crowd members (Marjanovic et al., 2012).

The crowd must be motivated: Lastly and most importantly, one of the reasons why the early crowdsourcing platforms struggled was their inability to motivate crowd members to come back and keep contributing to the project (Dahlander & Piezunka, 2017). The early models tended to rely on the winner-takes-all incentives, where only the author of the winning idea receives a prize (Alstyne et al., 2017). The winner-takes-all model discourages idea sharing, thereby hindering social learning. Furthermore, if the crowd is large, winning the competition is as hard as winning a lottery but requires a huge investment of time and resources. As per the expectancy theory, as the chances of receiving the reward decrease, so does the motivation (Nadler, 1979). Not surprisingly, after the initial excitement subsides, volunteers see their chances of winning the award are minimal and stop contributing. Thus, the incentives must not be limited to a prize for only the winner. Many smaller prizes and recognition for smaller achievements, as well as other benefits such as an opportunity to interact with interesting people, gain the respect of the professional community, and the certification of achievement that participants can add to a resume, can increase motivation (Fixson & Marion, 2016; Wenger, 2000).

Business consulting is uniquely suited to be outsourced to crowds.

The task: The problems that businesses bring to the consultant are always complex and require an innovative approach; otherwise, they would be solved in-house.

The crowd: Unlike natural sciences and technology, business is a more general field. Most people, by virtue of being employees and consumers, have at least some understanding of staffing, compensation, marketing, and other functional areas of business. There are also more people with education in business-related fields and business experience than scientists or engineers. Therefore, statistically speaking, there are more people to form a large and diverse crowd for solving business challenges than for solving advanced science or high-technology problems.

The process: Where we fall short is the process. There is ample evidence that a large and diverse crowd of amateurs with basic qualifications using the right process may beat experts, but the optimal crowd-working process for solving business challenges has not been developed. We know the Wikipedia or Linux models will probably not work in the context of business consulting, but what will?

Unfortunately, answering this question is not an easy task. To put different crowdsourcing models to a test, particularly in the context of business consulting, the researcher must have a large enough crowd. It is one of those cases when an experiment conducted in a small sample cannot be generalized to a large crowd. Crowds are not just large teams. A crowd is fundamentally different from a team not only in terms of size, but also in terms of membership, reward structure, motivations, interdependence, coordination, communication, and many other aspects. The dynamics in a team or a workgroup is qualitatively different from that in a crowd. The relationships may not generalize to larger groups, and thus experiments conducted in small groups are unlikely to advance our understanding of crowds.

Furthermore, the nature of the business challenges is fundamentally different from the challenges of writing an encyclopedia or a piece of software. Therefore, using crowds that are already assembled to write encyclopedia entries or computer code will not help in studying business-consulting crowds.

The X-Culture research team is unique in that it does have access to a qualified crowd and a set of real-life business clients with real-life business challenges to explore the comparative effectiveness of various approaches to crowdsourcing in business consulting. With about 4,000 graduate and undergraduate students and non-student participants from over 100 universities and organizations in 40 countries on six continents, our crowd is huge, demographically diverse, geographically dispersed, and consists of members who all meet basic business qualifications.

We set out to test the pros and cons of different crowdsourcing models and contribute to developing one that will do to the business consulting industry what Wikipedia did to the encyclopedia industry.

Crowdsourcing Models

The potential of crowdsourcing has been recognized for a long time. Strictly speaking, voting is a form of crowdsourcing and has been used for thousands of years in national policy and leadership decision making. However, the use of crowdsourcing in other areas is only now gaining momentum. Below is a review of successful crowdsourcing projects with a description of their different models, pros and cons.

Workless Crowd Work

The simplest models of crowdsourcing do not require any work from the crowd. Instead, the crowd's resource surplus aids the project. A successful example of this approach is Folding@Home. This Stanford University project utilizes the idling capacity of hundreds of thousands of home computers. Individuals interested in contributing to the project only have to install simple screensaver software on their personal computers. When not used by the owner, the computer starts running protein-folding simulations for Folding@Home. Hundreds of thousands of individuals volunteer their computing surplus to the project, and their regular home computers do work that is beyond the computing capacity of even the strongest supercomputers. This may not be a case of the crowd versus experts, but is still a good example of a crowd of personal computers outperforming a supercomputer. The crowd (personal computers) works only in their spare time and still beats the expert (supercomputer).

Crowdfunding is another form of crowdsourcing where the crowd, rather than one or a few professional investors, contributes funds or other resources to business startups, social, or art projects. As with the computing surplus pooling, the individual contributors are not expected to invest any effort in the project beyond simply sharing their financial resources. There are dozens of crowdfunding platforms, such as Kickstarter, Fundageek, Sellaband, and many more. Two basic models are used: the funds can be invested for an expected return, much like it works with venture capital, or the funds could be contributed for the cause with no expectation of direct return on investment. President Obama's 2008 presidential campaign, which raised $750 million dollars from small donors, is a good example of the latter.

Participating in such crowdsourced projects does not require any work in the traditional sense; one only contributes idle resources to aid the project leader or principal investigator's efforts. Strictly speaking, it is not an expert-versus-crowd model but rather an expert-aided-by-crowd one.

Prediction Markets

Prediction markets are a form of crowdsourcing where a voting-like approach is used to optimize decisions and make predictions. The most primitive version of this approach is described by James Surowiecki in "The Wisdom of Crowds." The book opens with a story from a country fair where the event attendees could, for a small fee, cast their guesses for a weight of an ox in one of the exhibits. The person whose guess is the closest to the actual weight gets the money contributed by the other voters. Although none of the voters were able to correctly guess the bull's weight, the average of the guesses was precise to a pound. The crowd, Surwicki touts, was smarter than any of its individuals. Similar results can be observed in jellybean count contests that are regularly run at festive public events.

Prediction markets (a.k.a. information markets) are effectively futures markets that sell securities representing bets on future events, such as the outcomes of elections or the future prices of stocks. One wins if one's prediction turns out accurate and loses if not. The prediction markets have proven to be remarkably accurate. For example, Iowa Electronic Market, one of the oldest and most known prediction markets, is also famous, among other things, for predicting the outcomes of presidential elections more accurately than a poll or expert predictions.

Unfortunately, prediction markets work only if the crowd bets real money, which may be illegal in locations where gambling is banned. Without real money at stake, experiments show, the bettors are not sufficiently motivated: they forego careful analysis, take unjustified risks, and produce inaccurate predictions. Furthermore, prediction markets are very sensitive to groupthink. Communication among the crowd members tends to reduce the variety of opinions. The opinion of leaders skews the crowd's perceptions, which introduces a systemic bias and undermines the quality of the prediction. Additionally, the application of the prediction market model to crowdsourcing is limited in the sense that it only works for making predictions regarding simple outcomes. It cannot be used to develop the complex solutions that are typically required in business consulting projects.

Volume-Based Models

The success of more recent crowdsourced projects tends to stem from the volume of individual contributions rather than their size or quality. Just like with information markets, under this model, a large number of small and seemingly insignificant contributions often translated into high levels of quality and precision of the average or overall contribution.

One of the most ambitious and probably most known crowdsourcing projects is Wikipedia (www.Wikipedia.com). By soliciting small bits of input from millions of amateur contributors, in a matter of a few short years, Wikipedia surpassed Encyclopedia Britannica in terms of the number, up-to-datedness, and often quality of the entries. The success of Wikipedia is, to a large extent, in its ability to compartmentalize work. A meaningful contribution does not require knowledge of prior developments and can be made in as little as a few seconds. The ease and convenience prompt millions of people to add new or revise existing Wikipedia entries, with many contributions as small as correcting a typo or adding a reference.

Another big advantage of the Wikipedia model is the fusion of consumption and creation. Any consumer can easily become a creator. It takes literally one click (on "Edit") for a Wikipedia reader to become a Wikipedia writer. With hundreds of millions of unique daily readers and the ease of making additions or changes, it is no wonder that improvements to the product are made with staggering frequency. Errors are spotted and corrected right away, and multiple conflicting corrections tend to converge around the most complete and accurate form quickly.

Galaxy Zoo uses a similar model (www.galaxyzoo.org). It was launched by an Oxford graduate student, who was frustrated with his inability to classify for his dissertation the 900,000 galaxies photographed for the Sloan Digital Sky Survey. After trying to complete the task himself, he quickly realized it would take him years to classify the necessary number of galaxies. With the help of a friend, he created a simple website that allowed "citizen scientists" to view the Sloan Digital Sky Survey images of galaxies and classify them on several characteristics (type, color, etc.) using multiple-choice scales. Although some classification may be incorrect, by comparing entries from different individuals, the mode (most frequent) classification tends to be remarkably accurate. Thousands of people interested in astronomy participated, completing the original task in a few short weeks. As of today, millions of celestial objects have been classified. In the process, several important discoveries have been made by project participants, such as discoveries of new types of galaxies and other phenomena and over a hundred scholarly papers published.

Similar projects include Seafloor Explorer (www.seafloorexplorer.org, over 2.4 million ocean floor objects classified by citizen scientists), Planet Four (www.planetfour.org, a Mars mapping project where amateurs help NASA classify and catalog images beamed by Mars explorers); and eBird (www.ebird.org, millions of bird observations submitted and cataloged by amateur bird watchers, numerous discoveries in biology, climatology and other fields). Zooniverse (www.zooniverse.org) is an umbrella platform that hosts dozens of projects that crowdsource observation classifications to aid in the detection of planets, study the behavior of penguins, chimps, worms, orchids, sun spots, asteroids, and much more.

The largest project of this kind is Google's use of CAPTCHA to digitalize millions of books. CAPT-CHA (Completely Automated Public Turing test to tell Computers and Humans Apart) is a type of software that uses simple tests, such as indistinctly written words or characters that pop up on online login and payment sites, that one must recognize to prove that they are a human and not a program trying to access the site. Google's project involved scanning millions of books page by page and running them through text recognition software. However, even the most sophisticated programs have difficulties recognizing some words. So, the problem words were added as the second word to CAPTCHA scribbles. The first word was a known one, but the second word is the one that the text-recognition software had problems identifying, so people transcribing these words as part of the CAPTCHA test were inadvertently helping Google digitalize books. As of today, over two billion people have contributed to this text recognition effort (many multiple times), making it the largest collaboration project in human history.

All these projects rely on the ease of contribution: in each of these projects, one can start providing input in seconds (e.g., reviewing and classifying images, recognizing words, or watching a live video stream and recording patterns or behaviors of interest). The contributors do not need to be familiar with prior developments, as each contribution is completely independent of the rest. In the case of CAPT-CHA, the contributors may not even know they are aiding the project. Although each contribution is typically insignificant, millions of such amateur contributions propel projects far beyond the abilities of small expert teams. Moreover, millions of amateur eyes reviewing millions of images are more likely to spot interesting things and make discoveries than a few dozen expert eyes, if only because of larger processing capacity due to a much larger number of eyes. For example, one of the contributors to the GalazyZoo had difficulties classifying a strange green object. After alerting the community of the issue, it was eventually confirmed the green blob is, in fact, a new class of galaxies. No scientist or team of scientists can compete with crowds on tasks like this, as the number of eyes and time invested tends to be more important here than the expertise, at least at the initial stages when spotting is more important than explaining.

In projects like this, an expert can better perform each small task that the project is comprised of. However, these cases are all about volume, and crowds beat experts on volume every time. Moreover, because volume often translates into quality, because the mode (most popular) choice of a hundred amateur-submitted classifications is often more accurate than a single expert-submitted classification, the crowd is likely to beat experts on quality, too.

Unfortunately, the Wikipedia and Galaxy Zoo models only work well for projects where work can be easily compartmentalized; that is, when the project can be split into small, completely independent tasks. Similar models applied to, for example, writing fiction books failed. Co-editing a novel requires that all contributors are familiar with the entire storyline, so the work cannot be broken into small independent bits. Even a small contribution requires a significant initial effort of reviewing prior chapters, so only a few take parts in the project, and still, the result is often a collection of disjointed writing pieces.

Typically, a business solution requires a good understanding of all aspects of the challenge and prior developments, so it is not always easy to split the project into small independent tasks and crowdsource it using the Wikipedia model.

Brute Force Competition

Another form of volume-based crowdsourcing is what we call "brute force competition." It is similar to the previous model in that its success depends on broadcasting and a large volume of contributions. However, the quality of individual contributions plays a critical role here. It is a simple competition model designed to deal with the fact that "the best person for the challenge works for someone else." It is usually prohibitively expensive to attract and retain the best talent, and, at times, it is impossible to know what talents are needed to successfully resolve the challenge. Accordingly, the challenge can be broadcast through a variety of channels in hopes of finding the person capable of devising the best solution.

The Goldcorp story, as told in numerous publications on crowdsourcing, is a good example of how this model works. In 1999, this Canadian gold mine company was on the brink of bankruptcy. It owned thousands of acres of land where geological surveys indicated a presence of large deposits of gold, but the company geologists failed in their attempts to locate the gold. After attending a seminar on crowdsourcing at MIT, the CEO of the company decided to post all its proprietary geological survey data and invite "virtual prospectors" to identify most promising mining sites. A move like this was unheard of in the mining industry, which is notorious for being very secretive. Geological survey data determines the price of the land, the valuation of the company, and ultimately the mining company's financial success, so naturally, this information is never shared.

The prize fund of $575,000, to be paid to the authors of the most accurate predictions, attracted over 1,500 prospectors from 50 countries. Surprisingly, many of them were not geologists, but some of the best suggestions came from people from seemingly unrelated fields, such as statisticians and mechanical engineers. The results exceeded all expectations. Eighty percent of the new promising sites identified by the crowd turned out to yield substantial quantities of gold, totaling several times what Goldcorp projected to find in the area. Just one year after the crowdsourcing experiment, Goldcorp's revenues increased 170 percent, cash flow grew 1,180 percent, and profits soared from $2 million to $52 million, soon turning the company from being nearly bankrupt to a major player in the gold mining industry.

Another successful application of this model is InnoCentive, a crowdsourcing company that launched Eli Lilly in 2001. Clients seeking help in chemistry, computer sciences, math, entrepreneurship, and other fields can broadcast their challenges to the InnoCentive website and offer a prize for the best solution, usually ranging from $10,000 to $200,000. Individuals can submit their solutions, and the best solution gets the prize. The participants are people from all walks of life. Most have full-time jobs, often in unrelated fields, but review InnoCentive challenges for fun and participate if they find something interesting that complements their hobby. Some are professional scientists looking for new challenges and an additional source of income. Broadcasting the challenge and inviting the crowd to solve it not only greatly improves the chances of finding a solution but also reduces cost by removing the costs associated with retaining in-house staff and covering the associated payroll, equipment, and utility costs.

Idea Jams, such as IBM's regularly organized Innovation Jams (www.collaborationjam.com) are a variation of this model. They attract tens of thousands of participants who submit ideas for new products, business ventures, fixes for known problems, and predictions of yet-unknown problems and challenges.

The evidence strongly suggests that the brute force crowdsourcing model can be very effective. If the crowd is large and diverse enough, there is a high probability that someone out there has a better solution than that produced by in-house experts. However, it has a serious limitation. Because the crowd members do not communicate among themselves, they cannot learn from each other. As a result, the brute force crowdsourcing model is limited to the peak performance of the best individual in the crowd. Under this model, the only reason the crowd beats the in-house experts is that there is a better expert in the crowd than those in-house. The brute-force model hinges on the premise that as long as a large enough number of individuals submit their solutions, one of them will be better than what can be produced in-house. Because many solutions are developed simultaneously, the development time can also be significantly shorter than a sequential in-house trial-and-error approach. By offering the compensation only to the winner, many submissions can be attracted at a low price, making the model economically feasible.

Despite its potential, the brute force crowdsourcing model misses out on the synergetic potential of crowdsourcing. Under this model, 2+2 still equals 4. The crowd does not offer a better solution than what could be offered by its best member. In a sense, it is recruitment rather than crowd work model, perhaps with the added benefit of a shorter development time and lower cost to the client. The true value of crowdsourcing lies in idea exchange, in social learning that yields a final product that is better than the product any individual member of the crowd could develop working individually. The models described below utilize this added benefit of crowdsourcing.

Open Source

A step up in complexity is found in open-source software development projects such as Linux, Firefox, or the Apple App Store. Much like under the Wikipedia model, the workflow is highly modularized. To make a valuable contribution, one does not have to be familiar with all prior developments. The software code is developed on a modular basis, using a common coding language.

Apple's App Store is an example of a highly compartmentalized crowdsourcing platform. Individual app developers do not have to be familiar with other apps to make a valuable contribution. The modules (applications) are finished products that work independently of other programs contributed to the App Store.

The interdependence is higher in projects like Linux or Firefox. The individual software modules are designed to complement the rest of the code and can rarely be used as self-standing, fully-functional software products. Individual apps in the App Store can thus be compared to individual buildings in a city. The city offers numerous synergies, but each building can be used independently. Software modules in Linux are more like Lego blocks that can be assembled into larger structures as needed. A missing or malfunctioning block may render the entire system unusable, while each piece by itself is not a complete finished product. In fact, the individual modules of Linux are more like raw clay chunks rather than finished bricks: existing modules that can be and often are further modified by the end-user.

Compared to volume-based crowdsourcing projects such as Galaxy Zoo or Wikipedia, open-source software development has a higher start-up and coordination cost. First, the qualification requirements are much higher. One must learn the coding language and understand the software kernel before one can start making valuable contributions. Second, an expert must review individual contributions for compatibility and functionality before they can be added to the system. Unlike Wikipedia, where a low-quality individual entry does not affect the rest of the product, a bug in an individual module may crash the entire open-source system. However, with the proper coordination and quality control process, the crowd often creates a product superior to what can be created by experts.

The big advantage of the open-source model over the brute force model is that it offers synergy stemming from collaboration. Although the contributors may never communicate directly, by allowing them to build upon the work of other crowd members and modify and reassemble the existing modules in new ways, the final product is often better than what any individual crowd member could produce working individually. Each contribution provides a stepping stone for the next one, so in theory, the peak performance of the crowd is not limited to the peak performance of its best member, but a sum of peak performances of its members. This can exist as a huge step forward from the brute force model.

Democrowd

The "Kasparov versus the World" chess game played in 1999 on Microsoft's MSN Gaming Zone platform is a good example of what we call a "democrowd" model. A crowd of over 50,000 from 75 countries played against the world champion and the highest-ranked chess player of all time (at the time of the game). Each party had 24 hours to make its moves. The crowd relied on online discussion boards to discuss their moves. The crowd's moves were determined by popular vote. Even though Kasparov was by far stronger than any member of the World team, and even though Kasparov was reading the crowd's discussion boards and thus was fully aware of their thinking and intentions, which gave him a huge advantage, the crowd nearly won the game. If it were not for a rigged vote at move 51 that gave Kasparov a big advantage, the crowd of amateurs would have likely beaten the world champion. Individually, none of the World team members would have had a chance against Kasparov. Together, using the democrowd model, they nearly defeated him.

The democrowd model combines the volume, information market, and open source collaboration models. It benefits from a huge number of initial ideas submitted by the large and diverse crowd. The brainstorming proceeds with heated discussions, critique, and improvement of the initial suggestions until several most promising ideas are collectively developed by the crowd. A discussion board is reminiscent of the open-source software kernel that allows everyone to "speak the same language," thereby enabling collaborations among the many crowd members. Often, the final ideas are different from those in the initial pool. No one could come up with the best idea on one's own; it could only be developed collectively. Finally, the best decision is selected by a popular vote, as is done in the information market model.

The democrowd model retains all the benefits of the earlier-described models, although it has some limitations. On the one hand, at the initial brainstorming stage, individual contributions may be small and not require a significant effort, nor awareness of other developments, which encourages participation. On the other hand, there are no safeguards against low-quality contributions. The discussion can quickly become crowded with useless suggestions and comments, which makes coordination difficult and may lead to frustration and the departure of many participants. The voting helps shed inferior ideas and focus on the best options, but it often happens too late to remedy the problem fully.

Competitive Collaboration

The competitive collaboration crowdsourcing model increases the synergetic potential of the crowd by not only allowing but strongly encouraging the crowd members to review the work of others. As the crowd learns from and builds upon the ideas of their collaborators, novel ideas are found. A good example of this model is the MatLab Central programming contest that was held semi-annually between 1998 and 2012. The tasks usually required developing a program code for solving such problems as sorting objects on a list of characteristics or finding the shortest route along with a random set of landmarks. The code that completes the task most efficiently wins. Thousands of programmers took part in MatLab contests. The code submission would be immediately published and could be freely reviewed by other contestants. Moreover, the code would be automatically tested and ranked for accuracy and efficiency. This way, the best solutions would be immediately identified.

The first submissions tended to be rather weak. However, as the contestants reviewed and tweaked each other's work and resubmitted it with improvements, the quality of the top-scoring solution rose rapidly. The contestants would become obsessed with staying on top of the rankings, often taking time off from their jobs or school to stay focused on the task. One would often submit a winning code just to see it resubmitted with a minor improvement by another coder minutes later and thus has to go back to the drawing board to devise a still better solution.

In a sense, the model encourages plagiarism, albeit simply copying the work of others would not help. An original improvement is needed every time to get ahead. The only way to stay high in the ranking is to constantly monitor and learn from competitions' contributions while innovating beyond the last-best solution at the same time. This competitive collaboration process yields synergy: the final solution tends to be not only hundreds of times more efficient than the first workable solution but also many times better than what the best of the crowd members could devise on his/her own, without the opportunity to review and learn from other submissions. The real-time testing and ranking of the submitted solutions allows for the weeding out of low-quality submissions and focusing on the most promising ones.

Theory: Why Can Crowds Beat Experts?

The notion that a crowd can beat an expert at solving a business challenge is counterintuitive. As per the example provided earlier, a large crowd of random individuals cannot compete with a world-class nuclear physicist at designing a nuclear reactor. However, there is reason to believe that at some types of tasks, a crowd with a good collaboration process can outperform an expert, even if the expert greatly exceeds every single member of the crowd in terms of skills and knowledge. Under the right conditions, diversity and size trump ability.

Volume

First, the size and diversity of the crowd provide several big advantages. If a project can be compartmentalized into small, simple independent tasks, and if each small task only requires generic skills and has a low setup cost, the crowd will beat experts simply because of the crowd's larger processing capacity. GalaxyZoo, with its simple, standardized multiple-choice classification interface, is a good example of how a large enough crowd can classify galaxies much faster than a single expert can.

Furthermore, according to the law of large numbers, an outcome, however unlikely, will happen if the number of trials is large enough. As the size of the crowd grows, the probability of an outlier who just happens to have an excellent solution to the problem increases. If the crowd is large enough and there is a system in place to identify good solutions, there will be an outlier who will submit a solution better than that submitted by an expert.

Quality from Volume and Diversity

Although compared to an amateur, an expert, by definition, produces better quality work, a crowd of amateurs can outperform experts even in terms of quality. The popular TV show Who Wants to Be A Millionaire illustrates this tendency very well. The players can seek help from a friend, presumably selected for his/her knowledge and erudition, and from the audience, a random collection of spectators. Astonishingly, the audience (crowd) is correct 98% of the time, whereas the friend (expert) only 55%.

The reason the crowd consistently provides more accurate answers than the experts is the crowd's size and diversity. If even a small percent of the crowd knows the correct answer, the crowd will give the correct answer. Suppose the question has four possible answer choices. Under the random answer scenario, each answer then is expected to receive 25% of the votes. Now, suppose 5% of the crowd knows the correct answer. Then, the remaining 95% will vote randomly, while the 5% will vote correctly. The result will be 28.75% for the correct answer and 23.75% for each of the three remaining incorrect answers.

If the crowd is diverse enough, the errors will be randomly distributed, and if the crowd is large enough, the standard error will be small enough to give a detectable advantage to the correct answer. Mathematically, in a diverse and large crowd, even if only 1% of the crowd knows the correct answer and everybody else guesses randomly, the crowd will give the correct answer.

On simple tasks, such as classifying galaxies using a standard multiple-choice scale, the numbers do not have to be large to ensure accuracy. For example, it is likely that a large percent of amateurs will correctly classify the direction in which a spiral galaxy is spinning (clockwise or counterclockwise) and its color. Thus, asking only three or four amateurs to classify each galaxy and recording the most popular classification usually ensures a correct classification. Even if the majority provides wrong answers, if those answers are randomly distributed among the available options, and a sizable minority chooses the correct answer, the model will always be the correct answer.

More Quality from Diversity

Outsourcing problem solving to a crowd is like sending thousands of ants in all directions to look for food. If there is food out there, one of them will find it and show it to the colony. However, the important condition is that the ants go out in different directions. Even a million ants going far and searching thoroughly, but going in the same direction, are likely to fail.

The diversity of the crowds ensures searching in all possible locations. Experts of high ability tend to be homogeneous in terms of their knowledge, way of thinking, and access to resources. They are trained at the same places; they apply the same perspectives and heuristics. When working as a team, they may also be susceptible to groupthink, which further narrows their viewpoint. However, most problems, particularly in business, do not succumb to a single heuristic, and require a variety of perspectives. Innovative solutions require diverse collective intelligence. Identifying new opportunities requires searching in previously unsearched places. Experts are like super-ants who are exceptionally good at searching for food, but they are few and going in the same direction. Crowd members may be no match to experts, but they are many and searching everywhere, including where experts would never search because their paradigm says there is no food there. The clear majority of the crowd members will, of course, fail. But if the crowd is large and diverse enough and if there is a good solution out there, someone is bound to find it and, thus, the crowd will return a good solution. The collective intelligence based on the size and diversity of the crowd has a good chance to outperform deep, but narrow expert intelligence.

Social Learning

The innovation process tends to follow a punctuated equilibrium pattern. The initial solution produced by an expert is likely to be significantly better than any of the initial solutions proposed by the individual crowd members. The expert is also more likely to further refine that initial hunch and further increase the gap between the quality of final products produced by an expert versus that produced by an amateur. The expert may even have one or a few breakthroughs along the way that greatly improve his solution.

However, social learning shifts the balance in favor of the crowd. While no amateur in the crowd may be capable of a revolutionary invention, by learning from one another, by exchanging ideas, by accessing each other's information silos, crowds are capable of building upon each other's strengths and achieve remarkable heights. An idea proposed by one crowd member may give an idea to another, and breakthroughs are more likely. The snowball quickly grows, feeding off the many snowflakes collectively added to the mix.

Brainstorming sessions are a good demonstration of this process. The crowd often runs out of ideas and sits silently for a while. Then, someone throws in a new idea, and that idea triggers a cascade of new ideas from the crowd. When that line of thought is exhausted, there might be another pause, until someone's new idea triggers a new cascade of contributions. The dynamics when working on more complex problems are the same. When it seems the crowd is stuck and cannot advance beyond a solution, someone proposes a new idea or identifies a new opportunity that propels the entire crowd to the next level of problem understanding. The progress may be gradual for a while, as the crowd is stuck at making only marginal refinements to the new working solutions until someone else comes up with a new breakthrough idea that yet again punctuates the equilibrium and brings the crowd to the next level.

Most crowd members, working individually, would never reach certain levels of understanding of the challenge. However, many may be able to offer a breakthrough idea when the working solution is stuck at that high level. The innovation process tends to follow the punctuated equilibrium path in both experts and amateurs. However, the diversity of the crowd, the crowd's access to more different pockets of knowledge that may offer breakthroughs at different stages of the idea development allow for more punctuations and, thus, a superior final solution.

It is important to note, however, that communication is the key to "punctuating" the innovative process in a crowd. The crowd can learn from its members and raise itself a step up only if the members of the crowd learn from each other and feed off each other's ideas. If the process allows for effective information exchange, diversity trumps ability.

Multi-Purpose Module Architecture

Lastly, crowd work allows for a "second-level" innovation. Particularly in open-source projects, each individual block would be created using the advantages described above. Namely, a large and diverse crowd will approach the challenge from every possible angle, bring a variety of ideas, create a large collection of modules, and collectively improve them in a series of punctuated breakthroughs and gradual evolutions. By leveraging the potential of its size and diversity and with the right process in place, the modules designed by the crowd may already be better than those designed by an expert. However, the crowd can then have an endless stream of ideas for assembling those existing modules into new products. Again, because of the crowd's size and diversity, chances are it will come up with more useful combinations than an expert can dream of. Furthermore, as the new structures are assembled from existing blocks, the new architecture is likely to spur new tweaks and additions, further improving the variety and quality of the final products.

To conclude, an expert is, by definition, more capable than an amateur is. However, a crowd of amateurs can greatly exceed the peak performance of its individual members. Due to a large volume of initial ideas and subsequent improvements aided by the crowd's size, diversity, access to different resources, social learning, and modular architecture, a crowd can offer a solution far superior to what its smartest member could develop individually and quite possibly, superior to that developed by an expert.

The Crowdsourcing Tradeoff Wheel

As reviewed above, in a complex system such as a crowdsourcing platform, many factors are at play and often at odds with one another. For example, as the crowd gets larger, coordination costs increase. The more crowd members engage in discussion, the more noise there is in the system and the harder it is to identify truly valuable contributions. Drawing on the social learning theory (Bandura & Walters, 1963) and the expectancy theory of motivation (Lawler III & Suttle, 1973), we have identified eight such tradeoffs. Figure 1 shows how they fit together. The competing factors can be aligned along two dimensions: Synergies vs. Costs and Crowd vs. Platform. Every opportunity for synergy comes at a cost. Every input from the crowd must be matched by resource contribution from the platform. The competing factors create two diagonals that determine crowd's effectiveness, efficiency, and cost: Resources and Process.

Resource tradeoffs

- Crowd size increases the number of solutions but at a greater cost of coordination.
- Diversity can lead to more creative solutions, but it creates conflict.
- Qualified solvers can make valuable contributions, but they are costly to attract.
- Flexibility allows us to make contributions quickly when it is convenient for the solver, but it reduces engagement.

Process tradeoffs

- Feedback helps steer the crowd in the right direction, but monitoring progress, processing and evaluation of the intermediate deliverables, and providing opportunities to interact with the client or other appraisers are costly.
- Competition that identifies and rewards the most creative ideas and comments increases motivation to contribute such ideas, but it also leads to social waste, because the time and effort spent on solutions that did not win are lost.
- A process that promotes idea exchange and communication aids creativity via social learning, but it can also undermine creativity by generating groupthink (Janis, 1982; Turner & Pratkanis, 1998).
- A process that encourages more comments and contributions leads to noise in the system, which makes the identification of valuable contributions harder.

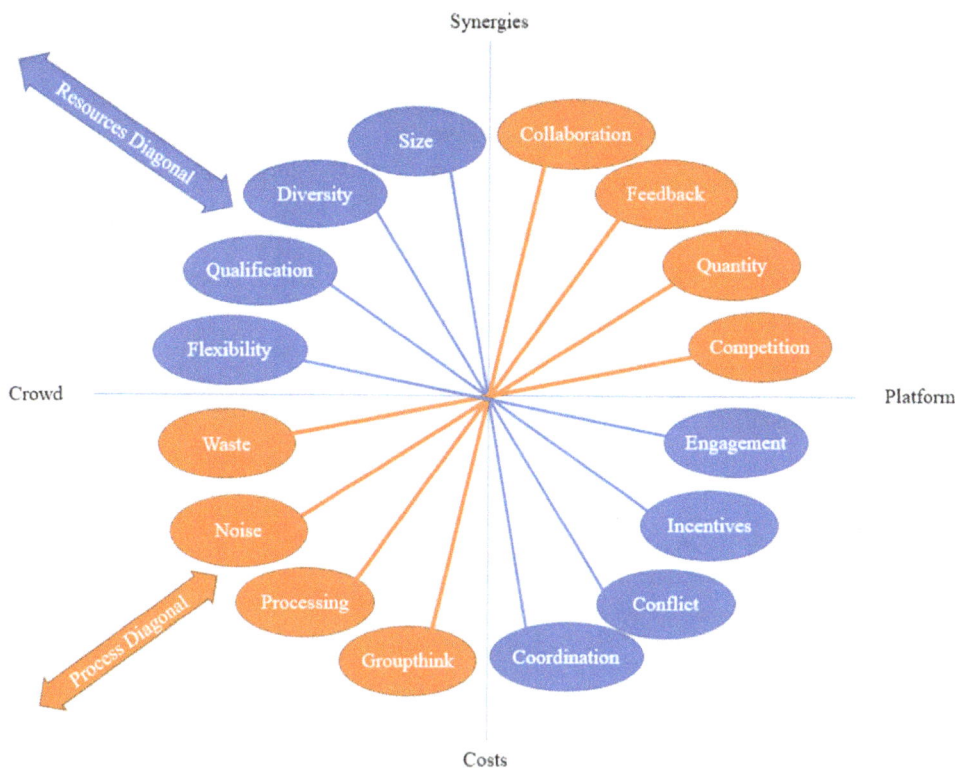

Fig 19.1 Trade-off wheel of crowdsourcing problem-solving

X-Culture Research

X-Culture is currently conducting a series of tests to evaluate the comparative effectiveness of various crowdsourcing and large group collaboration models.

The present study intends to take our understanding of the potential of crowdsourcing beyond anecdotes. There have been several successful crowdsourcing projects, but there have been even more failed ones. We know of instances when crowds outperformed experts, but can they consistently deliver superior results?

We intend to test the comparative effectiveness of several models of crowdsourcing experimentally, as well as compare the performance of a crowd under various conditions to the performance of experts.

Rather than projects that rely merely on the volume of contributions, we are particularly interested in a crowd's ability to solve complex business challenges that require innovative approaches and unconventional thinking. If the initial evidence is correct, if the crowd with a good crowd work process indeed can consistently beat the experts, the crowd-based approach can do to the business consulting industry what Wikipedia did to the encyclopedia industry.

Sample

The study will be conducted based on the X-Culture platform. Over 900 diverse teams comprised of 4,500 individuals from 40 countries on all 6 continents take part in the project semi-annually. Most of the participants are graduate and undergraduate students, but there is a sizable group of non-student participants. The crowd is very diverse in terms of age, gender, nationality, culture, residence, areas of study, and other characteristics. The task is a consulting project that requires finding a solution to a real-life challenge presented by a real business. The work design is identical to that used in the real workplace in terms of how the consulting teams are formed and managed, the team members communicate with one another, and performance is tracked and evaluated. The motivation structure is also like that in the real workplace and involves a possibility of real monetary compensation in the form of post-market commission, as well as such benefits as opportunities for career advancement (internships, job offers to participants who offer the best solutions).

Experimental Conditions

The comparative effectiveness of the following crowd work models will be experimentally tested. Carried over the period of two seasons, the size of the X-Culture sample allows for a large N (100+) in each experimental condition to ensure the necessary reliability of the findings.

Control conditions:

1. **Expert:** Several experienced experts will be hired to complete the same task for control purposes. As their solution can still be shared with the client, their effort will not simply be for experimental purposes. Two sub-conditions could be tested:

   a. Expert star: experienced experts working individually
   b. Expert team: experienced experts working in small teams of 2-3.

Experimental conditions:

2. **Brute force:** Many solutions developed by amateurs.

   a. Working individually, no communication among individuals
   b. Working in independent teams; communication within teams, but no communication across teams.

Natural variation in quality is expected. Most solutions are expected to be weak, but due to the law of large numbers, some solutions are expected to be very good, possibly with the best solution superior to that produced by the expert condition.

3. **Optional Open Source:** The workflow is broken into a series of weekly milestone assignments. The work completed for each milestone is freely shared with all project participants. The project participants can use any work produced by other project participants.

   To ensure fairness in performance evaluation and compensation, each individual milestone submission (from an individual person or team) is graded and weighted equally in the total grade. Thus, while participants can greatly improve the quality of their final business solution by borrowing ideas from other submissions, they can receive a high overall grade only if they show excellent performance at each milestone. In other words, the overall grade depends not so much on the quality of the final report as on the marginal quality of each milestone submission. The milestone submission evaluations will only be shared with the authors of the submissions.

The expectation is that by reviewing the work of others, learning from it, and getting new break-through ideas inspired by hints in the work of others, the best solution produced by the crowd will be better than the solution produced by an expert.

4. **Forced Open Source:** Same as #3, but instead of simply giving access to the work of others and hoping the crowd members will take the time to review it under this condition at each mile-stone, each project participant will receive five submissions and be asked to review and evaluate them. To ensure a thoughtful review, the quality of the feedback will also be evaluated. The eval-uations of each submission will be shared with the group.

Incorporating the forced review and evaluation of the work of others at each milestone is expected to provide the following benefits:

- The project participants will review the work of others (social learning);
- The instant evaluations of each milestone component will provide a way to identify the best submissions, thereby helping to get through the clutter to the most valuable pieces of information.

The expectation is that forced review and instant ranking of the milestone submissions on quality will aid social learning, thereby increasing the frequency of breakthroughs (punctuations between equilibriums) and, ultimately, the quality of the final product.

5. **Survival of The Fittest:** Same as #4, but at each milestone, the most promising solution is selected and becomes the working version for the next round for all project participants. To reduce the chance of an error, the 5-10 best solutions (top 1-2%) may be selected at each stage, and the project participants will be required to choose one from the few they like the most and continue working on that version.

The expectation is that forcing the crowd to drop inferior solutions early on and focusing on the few most promising lines of work will aid overall progress and improve the quality of the final product.

Also, using the crowd's evaluations of the milestone contribution to select the submissions that will advance to the next level, this model adds the prediction market element. Evidence accu-mulated by studies of prediction markets suggests that a crowd is very good at predicting which solution holds the most promise. Adding the information market component to the model will only strengthen the final product.

To ensure the fairness of the performance evaluation, the overall project grade will be based on the quality of marginal contributions at each milestone. An additional bonus may be offered to the teams whose milestone solutions advance to the next round. This way, a project participant who submits high-quality work at each milestone will receive a high overall grade even if none of his/her intermediate submissions made it to the next round. At the same time, a project participant will receive a low overall grade if his/her marginal submissions were of poor quality, even though his/her final product is expected to be of high quality thanks to the forced survival of the fittest system.

6. **Pruning:** Same as #5, but instead of advancing only the top 1-5% of ideas to the next round, the bottom 10-20% is "pruned" while the remaining 80-90% advance to the next round. This way,

the focus shifts from selecting the very best ideas and disregarding the rest of the teams to getting rid of the worst ideas while letting all other ideas stay in the game.

This approach solves two major problems of the Survival of the Fittest model:

First, more ideas will remain on the table, thereby reducing the chance that some good ideas will be discarded prematurely.

Second, gentler pruning will reduce dissatisfaction. No team will likely be happy to learn that their ideas are so bad that they must abandon them. Under the previous model, up to 95% of the teams will get this disappointing news. Under the Pruning model, only the completely hopeless cases, the underperformers, will be dropped.

The expectation is that forcing the crowd to drop inferior solutions early on and focus on a few most promising lines of work will aid overall progress and improve the quality of the final product.

Based on the 80-20 rule, getting rid of only the worst 20% will allow for the elimination of 80% of the wasted effort, thereby leaving more time and resources to pursue more promising venues.

7. **Individual-Team-Individual-Team (IT-IT):** The biggest but very common mistake GVTs make is to distribute the workload by question: one team member does Question 1, another team member does Question 2, and so on – all with the hope that at the end of the project, the team will copy and paste the individual sections into one coherent document.

Not only do most of the teams later learn that the work completed by the different team members is drastically different in terms of style and quality, and pasting it all into one document creates a very incoherent report, but also, some team members simply do not do their work and there is nothing to copy and paste. Most importantly, such an approach leads to the waste of the most valuable resource a team has: collective wisdom and collective creativity. If the team members do not collaborate, the best the team can produce is the work produced by the individual team members.

The IT-IT model forces the team to go further and produce work that no individual team member could produce working alone.

It splits the workload into several blocks (3 in X-Culture experiments), each lasting two weeks. In week 1 of each block, all team members are required to complete and submit the task individually. In week 2, the team members are required to share their individual submissions, review and debate the different competing ideas, and then collectively develop one final team submission. The team can select one best individual submission, create a combination from several individual submissions, or develop a completely new submission building upon the ideas developed individually.

The logic is that by forcing each team member to answer each question individually first, they will come to the subsequent group discussion with a better understanding and proposals. This will provide more ideas to choose from. Furthermore, the team members will be more vested in their own original ideas and thus will be more likely to engage in a constructive debate and argument rather than support the first idea presented by other more active team members.

This approach may take more time but also has the potential to produce much better results.

Additional Experimental Conditions

1. **Competition:** The crowdsourcing is organized as a competition with a leaderboard, prize for the winner, and elements of gamification. The expectation is that the competitive element, the

prospects of winning (or losing) will make the process more exciting and provide the incentive to work hard.

2. **Collaboration:** The crowd has an opportunity to collaborate across teams and individuals, including by means of a discussion board, sharing and commenting on each other's work, and the opportunity to see and build upon the work of others. The expectation is that the collaboration opportunity will facilitate idea exchange and improve the quality overall.

3. **Hybrid:** A combination of collaboration and competition where there is still a leader board and a winner, but also an opportunity to collaborate. The expectation is that the competition element will provide the incentive to do better, while the collaboration element will provide an opportunity to do better.

Crowd types:

1. **Composed of individuals:** Many individuals work independently as a crowd, although communication is possible or even forced as per experimental conditions listed above.

2. **Composed of teams:** Many teams of 5-7 diverse individuals working in largely autonomous teams, although cross-team communication is possible or even forced as per the experimental conditions listed above. The expectation is that the team arrangement will further encourage communication (if only within the team), thereby aiding social learning, as well as by allowing greater specialization (dividing up the workload so that the smaller project tasks best suit individual team members, rather than one person completing all components of the project as in the individual arrangement).

3. **Expert + Crowd:** The crowd works in collaboration with an expert. The crowd generates ideas, proposes solutions, and an expert uses the input to produce a final clean version of the solution. The expectation is that the crowd will provide all the benefits of social learning and access to different sources of information and resources while the expert will ensure the quality of execution.

Preparing for the Theory Test

On the Theory Exam, the coaches will be asked to show their understanding of the basic principles of crowdsourcing and large group collaboration, including the nature of the problem, examples of successful crowdsourcing platforms and methods, the types of models being tested by the X-Culture team, and the logic behind each of them.

Additionally, the coaches are welcome (but not required) to review additional literature on the topic. Google Scholar is an excellent source of quality research.

For the final reflection paper, coaches can choose to propose more crowdsourcing and collaboration models, as well as use their own observations to discuss which of the models appear more promising.

Likewise, coaches can choose to develop additional or better text-based training modules, record video lectures, or prepare live webinars that address this topic.

And as always, if you see any typos, poor language, or have other suggestions for improving this document, please share your corrections.

CHAPTER 20

Dealing with Student Aversion to Team Projects

SUSAN GODAR, WILLIAM PATERSON UNIVERSITY

Whenever businesses are asked about the soft skills they are seeking in new professional hires, they put "teamwork capability" at the top of their lists. Currently, almost all project work is done in teams. While there may be some jobs that are best done by a sole worker, they are becoming scarcer every day. Employers now anticipate that the college graduates they hire will have team experience in both face-to-face and virtual spaces; the expectation is that these new hires will have learned to play well with others in the various milieu. The problem is that, as soon as I announce that we will have a "team project" this term, the groans start.

Teamwork is different and more complex than solo work. A team has been defined in the literature as a temporary grouping of individuals with complementary skills who are working toward a common goal with similar amounts of dedication. Two of the elements of that definition, complementary skills and similar amounts of dedication, are prerequisites for the formation of trust in a team. Students are frequently averse to team projects because of their prior experiences with dysfunctional teams where trust was never built.

Trust and Teamwork

When virtual teams were initially being used in academia, a large body of research identified trust among team members as critical to team success. That position on the importance of trust has not changed in the 20+ years since the first research was done. If team members do not trust one another, they will be unlikely to share ideas, listen to the ideas of others, and stay engaged with the team. Global virtual teams used in education require the rapid development of trust, called swift trust (Crisp & Jarvenpaa, 2013), because of the timeframe, i.e., the semester/term, in which their projects are conducted.

To give the students practice with teamwork that they can take into the workplace with them, many courses include a team project. If I ask students who "likes" team projects to raise their hands, I am lucky to get 10% of the class with hands above their heads. When pressed to explain how the team project in another class was very unsatisfactory and caused them to lose trust in their teammates, they usually say:

- It took more time than doing it myself,
- A few people took over the whole project and wouldn't tell the rest of us what was going on,
- Nobody else on the team did any work, or
- It was too hard to find meeting times because our school and work times didn't mesh.

It is important to recognize that any of these reasons is likely true (Liu, Tulare, & Pierce, 2018). It often does take longer to work with others on a project than it does to churn out the said project in one night by oneself. After all, one must talk and come to an agreement on a course of action when one has partners. Decisions must be reached on both process and content. It is sometimes also the case that you will need to spend extra time explaining the project to other team members who missed a class, have a lower level of language ability in the discipline, or are slower to grasp concepts. When those things happen, a team project does, as the first point says, take more time and result in a loss of trust in the other team member's abilities.

The second and third points are often mirrored images, depending on whether you are an "in group" or "out group" member. Sometimes one or two students with very high marks in a program will commandeer a project to preserve their overall grades. They are afraid that the other less academically proficient or less motivated teammates will somehow ruin the project and hurt their final mark for the class. This then becomes a self-fulfilling prophecy: because the others in the group are not kept abreast of the status of the project, they become Free Riders, taking advantage of the efforts of others without participating in the project. Then, the few who worked either solo or in a small clique claim – rightly – that nobody else did any work. This result leaves both sides, the doers and the non-doers, unhappy with team projects. They have decided that teamwork leads other people to be untrustworthy about completing a fair share of the work product.

The fourth issue, about difficulty in finding mutually agreeable meeting times, can be especially problematic for part-time students, students engaged in activities like sports or campus groups, and working students. If a team member consistently misses meetings or is hard to reach, they will not be a trusted member. It can be a very vexing problem when there are time differences among teammates, i.e., in geographically distributed team projects.

Trust Across Borders

Adding the layer of a Global Virtual Team (GVT) project with students from multiple countries on a team brings more concerns and can cause an increased lack of trust:

- There is no casual socializing, which reduces the information you have about the others,
- Traditional cultural and social norms do not exist because participants come from other cultural backgrounds, and
- You cannot directly observe the amount of time and effort your teammates are putting into the project. Often, your first clue about a problem comes too late in the project.

All of these can cause a lack of trust within the team.

When teams develop internal trust, the students have a very different attitude toward team projects. Thus, while many of my students offer reasons against team projects, within a class there are students who will talk about their positive experiences with those projects. They will offer reasons like:

- With more people, we had more ideas,
- We could distribute the workload,
- We ended up with a better or more complete project than one person could do, and
- I was able to know more people in my class.

Especially if diverse teams are created and supported, students can generate better solutions to projects that require creativity or analysis. They will have more input from different viewpoints. In teams, also, the work need not fall onto one person's shoulders, but can be spread out. A teamwork task can lead to social bonding. Students can meet and have experience working with a variety of people. They can learn how to deal with personality differences and differing perspectives on a problem. Those positive outcomes are more likely to occur when teammates trust one another.

When we use GVTs in our classes, we tend to be particularly interested in students learning about other countries and perspectives. Of course, we want students to learn the content of the course, e.g., some basic information on international marketing or finance. However, we also think that much learning will take place in informal discussions and working through team problems with students from other countries. In fact, in a class, the final output, a presentation, results of a simulation, etc., is usually secondary to the experience of working across borders with people from different world views.

How to Foster Trust

Professors must utilize methods that will facilitate an increase in trust within each team so that it can function. While recognizing that a student may have had bad experiences in the past, we need to turn the downsides mentioned by the "no to teamwork!" group into positive outcomes. How do we set up a project where students will have a good experience working with their team members and not come away with the attitude that "all people from country Y are _____" [fill in your own negative word here!]? Coupled with this is a need for speed. Students must be helped to develop swift trust to accomplish their project within the confines of an academic semester/term.

Most researchers agree that three major things must take place before the team starts its work if we want the team to develop internal trust and therefore succeed. The team must be put together carefully, its members must be trained in some basics of teamwork, and there must be time for the participants to learn about their teammates. Often, none of these things are done. Instead, we tend to randomly assign students to teams or let them pick their own teammates. Then, we presume that they will know the ways to make teams effective, even those with students from multiple different backgrounds. We do not convey to them the importance of some casual socializing to make the work run more smoothly. In other words, we do not lay a foundation upon which trust can be built. We tend not to follow up after the team starts working together with continued training. This makes it highly unlikely that the teams will succeed.

Although we are using various types of multi-country exercises to prepare our students for the global workplace, we should also recognize that there can be some significant differences between academic exercises and those in industry. If we want to minimize the differences, there are specific courses of action we can take. These actions, too, should serve to reduce student aversion to teamwork projects, as they make the process more transparent for students and take away some of the reasons for students to be concerned that their work will not receive proper recognition. In the following sections, I discuss the three areas in which action must be taken and offer recommendations on how to increase intra-team trust in each area.

Setting Up the Teams

When a company is putting together a team to work, on a new process for handling customer complaints, for example, they do not simply assign people to it at random. Rather, they select people who have the requisite complementary expertise and skills in handling those complaints. This selection process is hard to duplicate in an academic team as students come with a narrower set of learning experiences, making it harder to assemble a team with truly "complementary" skills.

In large team projects involving multiple participating schools, the size of the student pool and the shortness of the academic calendar make it very difficult to spend much up-front time in putting teams together to maximize diversity. The recommendations below would be the optimal choices in setting up teams. Of course, one of the advantages of a multinational team project, even if it only involves students from two countries, is that it is a diversified team by its very nature.

The factors to consider in creating an optimal team come from the literature on GVTs and are supported by the elements in a program called Comprehensive Assessment of Team Member Effectiveness (CATME). CATME is the result of a U.S. National Science Foundation grant to faculty members in Purdue University's School of Engineering for the development of a computer program to improve assigning students into teams, and was released in 2005 (Layton, Loughry, Orlando, & Moore, 2007). In my classes, I put together teams based on marks in prior courses, students' evaluations of their "dedication" to the project, and overlapping time availability for teamwork. (See CATME.org for more information.)

There is a debate about putting together a mixed-ability group of students, i.e., those with differing marks in prior courses or different levels of dedication to success. The argument advanced by some who believe in putting together teams of students with differing motivations is based on the belief that less-prepared or dedicated students will "up their game," learning from or adapting to the better or more dedicated members on their team.

There is, however, no proof that students will be able or willing to do that. Rather, this type of intra-team diversity may be the root cause of students' negative experiences in prior teams. If a better student is already stretched for time, she is unlikely to want to spend that time bringing others "up to speed" about the course content, technology, etc. Instead, it is much easier for her to "hijack" the project and complete most of it herself, particularly if she feels her course marks are at stake. Similarly, a less-dedicated student is unlikely to commit more time simply because his peers do. This may force the student into being a free-rider on the project. When these chains of events happen, they destroy trust within the team. This leads to Recommendation 1: Instructors should attempt to put together teams with similar course marks and similar commitment toward the exercise.

As an instructor, you should be aware that this recommendation will result in some truly wonderful deliverables at the end of the team project and some really bad ones. The teams of good students will produce better results. In my experience, the payoff is that all students are happier with this arrangement. Whether the team was high or low achieving, they all report that everyone did the same amount of work and that they felt that their ideas got a fairer hearing within the team. The resulting presentations/papers/etc. were considered by the participants as really "teamwork," as opposed to the work of one or two members. This more homogenous assignment of personnel to teams also most accurately reflects a business approach where people are put on teams with others who have similar levels of interest in the success of the project.

In X-Culture, for example, the required grading scheme for professors is that the project must comprise at least 20 % of the student's final grade. This is an attempt to make the project equally significant for all participants. We must recognize, though, that some students are more grade-responsive than others. Therefore, an instructor may want to add screening questions about the amount of time students have available and are willing to devote to a project.

The instructor must also decide about other factors to consider in constituting a team. For example, it may be advantageous to have single-sex teams or require that a team have a minimum percentage of males or of females. The purpose of minimums is to prevent one person from being excluded or ignored based on gender bias.

In a global virtual situation, language and writing skills are also a consideration. It is likely, based on research in the corporate arena, that the person considered most fluent in the language used by the project will do more work. Others will defer to his or her presumed expertise. If there is a common second language, i.e., Russian in former Soviet countries and French or Spanish in former colonies, insider cliques may form and block out other ideas.

The overall message then is that care must be placed in putting together teams. Assembling high-performing teams for a project is difficult, whether in business or in academia.

Training for Being a "Team"

While I am sorting out who will be on what team, I also need to start helping students un-learn the habits of their prior bad experiences and build upon their prior good experiences so that trust can be created rapidly. Simply assembling people into a group does not make the group a team. They need to learn how to behave as a team. For the most part, in their previous experiences, they have been grouped, given a task, and left to figure out the rules of teamwork. Somehow, we assume that they already know how to be teammates. But, in my experience, they do not. If they cannot do this when operating in a face-to-face class with people they see frequently, it is even less likely that they have the skills to be teammates with students who are from another country.

Suppose that you handed a group of people an Australian football and told them to figure out the actual rules of play. If they had never seen a game before, they would not even have an idea of where to start. What sort of actions with this football are legitimate? Must you use only your feet? Are there particular positions or roles that various members of the team should play? How do you score a game? For what actions might you be penalized... the list goes on and on.

Being on a well-functioning team, whether for Australian football or for a course project, requires training in the rules of the game. While each team will develop their own strategy to solve the task given them, they need to learn general principles of teamwork (Holmer, 2001). There are a number of free resources that a professor can use to start the discussion about establishing norms of behavior on a team. A Google search on "working in teams" and "team norms" will yield a very large number of sources that can be used in class or made available to the student via computer links. Recommendation 2: Instructors should include instruction on how a team develops its norms.

Students should be encouraged to develop no more than five norms as more become difficult to follow. Specifically, the norms should cover the following areas:

- Frequency, duration, and attendance of meetings
- Means to ensure that all voices are heard
- Delegation and commitment to completing tasks
- Definition of "agreement" on project directions
- Other areas of importance to the specific project.

The group should also decide how to deal with transgressions from these norms. For example, what if a member misses a meeting or a series of meetings? How will the group handle that? Being very clear upfront about how the team will work serves to increase trust.

Learning About Others

Beyond the general rules about operating as a team, we must set up ways for students to develop trust in their teammates. Without trust, the experience of working with students from different countries and cultures will be a disaster. Since our main objective in using these teams in our classes is to give students the opportunity of working across borders, it is especially incumbent upon us to give assistance in developing trust and in students' learning about the countries and cultures of their teammates. This means that space must be created within the project for the students on a team to get to know one another (Darics, 2019). Recommendation 3: There must be built-in mandatory socializing time.

"Mandatory socializing" sounds like an oxymoron. We usually think of socializing as optional. In a F2F class, it happens automatically. Students arrive in a classroom before the class starts or stay afterward and talk with one another. But in GVTs, that does not happen without active intervention. Research has shown that trust can be created rapidly, i.e., "swift trust" (Crisp & Jarvenpaa, 2013) if informal discussion among team members starts before the project is launched. It may be useful to develop conversation-starters, e.g., a list of questions that students can answer and share with others on their team, a brief biography, or even posting pictures of their pets. Throughout the duration of the course, opportunities must be built-in for conversations beyond the scope of the project to occur. This may involve collecting and monitoring email exchanges, establishing intermediate tasks in the project that require input from all members, and/or communicating with another professor if her/his student is non-responsive to the team.

Summary

Although many students bring tales of prior bad experiences with team projects, we have the ability to create a situation in which students develop trust in their fellow teammates and have a successful project. By thoughtfully assembling the teams, providing real instruction on how to operate as a team, and giving student participants the opportunity to engage in casual non-project conversations, we better prepare students for the global virtual business world in which they will be working.

References

Crisp, C. B., & Jarvenpaa, S. L. (2013). Swift trust in global virtual teams: Trusting beliefs and normative actions. Journal of Personnel Psychology, 12(1), 45–56.

Darics, E. (2019), Talking a team into being in online collaborations: The discourse of virtual work. Discourse Studies, 21(3):237–257.

Holmer, L. L. (2001). Will we teach leadership or skilled incompetence? the challenge of student project teams. Journal of Management Education, 25(5), 590.

Layton, R.A., Loughry, M.L., Ohland, M.W., & Rico, G.D. (2010). Design and validation of a web-based system for assigning members to teams using instructor-specified criteria. Advances in Engineering Education, 2(1), 1–28.

Liu, Y., Tulare, W., & Pierce, J. (2018). Straight from the horse's mouth: Justifications and Prevention Strategies provided by free riders on global virtual teams. Journal of Management and Training for Industries, 5(3):51–67.

CHAPTER 21

Preparing Students for the Global-Virtual-Team Based Projects

KAREN LYNDEN, THE UNIVERSITY OF NORTH CAROLINA AT GREENSBORO
TIM MUTH, FLORIDA INSTITUTE OF TECHNOLOGY

Global Virtual Team (GVT)-based projects present a host of benefits, along with challenges and issues to deal with throughout the project. This portion of the book is structured as a guide or "checklist" of what to expect, and what to do in order for the team to perform. Throughout, we will share stories based on real experiences, a variety of perspectives, and suggestions on how to best work through similar challenges that come your way.

- Section 1: Language differences
- Section 2: Culture and location differences: getting to know your teammates
- Section 3: Tips for creating success: Before, during, and, after the Global Virtual Team Project experience

Section 1: Language Differences

Working on a Global Virtual Team with teammates from around the world, you will most likely encounter "non-native" language speaking and writing teammates. This section exists to assist readers in approaching these dynamics with a spirit of openness and flexibility from the perspectives of the native-language speaker and non-native language speaker.

Every project should provide a requirement of the specific language (verbal and written) that it is expected for all team members to use throughout the project. In academic and in professional environments, the professor/employer will specify this requirement. If the language requirement is not clearly communicated, it is the collective responsibility of the team to clarify the requirement. If the rule is flexible, the team will need to set the communication standards from the very start that best fit the team's collective language skills.

Below are a few scenarios to consider when working with teammates with diverse language skills. For the sake of clarity in offering common and constant examples, we will assume the required communication language for the following scenarios is (American) English. The abbreviation "ESL" will be used often in this section, which stands for "English as a Second Language."

Please note, as the following section is reviewed, that the reader can also flip the "country" scenario to be any language as a "first language" (Spanish, Mandarin, Russian, etc.), and the scenarios below can apply in those translations contexts as well.

Scenario #1: Nearly everyone on the team is NOT Native-English-Language (speaking/writing)

There is one native speaker on the team, and four other team members are each proficient at the minimum required language requirement as ESL team members. This is one of the most common GVT language proficiency scenarios.

Possible Complications: Team members could assume the one native speaker would be the best "lead copyeditor" or "team leader," and miss the fact that one or more of the other team members would be a much stronger project planner and/or editor of the project.

Suggestions

Encourage a project structure that allows co-editors and divides leadership between a variety of project components, and select experts for each part of the project based on skills, knowledge, enthusiasm, work ethic, and other important factors, not just on language proficiency.

Find ways for everyone to have a voice and break through the language barriers. Often, ESL teammates are more proficient in speaking the language than at technical writing. Find the best ways to communicate ideas for each person, and use the available online tools to connect (free video conferencing, leaving voice messages, translation tools, etc.).

Scenario #2: Everyone on the team is Native-English-Language (speaking/writing)

The team is comprised of all Native-English-Language students. This is going to be simple! Our team consists of members from the USA, Canada, India, UK, and Australia. It's just a matter of the best editors on the team serving in the final stages as copyeditors of the final work. Easy! Right?

Possible Complications: This scenario might be one of the least complicated regarding language barriers, yet a few unexpected complications might arise, particularly in the copyediting process. Copyediting should unify a variety of authors' unique writing styles (a complex task on its own), yet this optimistic scenario does not account for variants in the English language.

The English language is often divided into three major dialects: British Isles, North America, and Australasia. Within these three, there are over 150 English dialects, each expressing different pronunciations, vocabulary, grammar, and spelling. To make things even more interesting, consider that the category above notes one of the three main categories as "North America," which is comprised of two countries, The United States and Canada. Canadian spelling combines British and American spelling rules. For example, French-derived words that in American English end with -or and -er usually retain British spellings (ex: color, center), but American spellings also commonly appear.

Additionally, teams with members across two or more dialects of the same language may find the use of certain vocabulary words or expressions is communicated "more formally" or use "antiquated" terms compared to more modern terms.

Based on the above scenario, the team will encounter differences in the way dates and times are expressed. Is it May 8 at 7 pm or 8 May at 1900? Regarding temperature and measurements, are we using the metric system or imperial system? It is 32 degrees outside—does this mean we are going swimming at the beach or ice-skating on the lake today? Expressions of financial terms are also caused for confusion (currency, periods vs. commas in separating thousands or cents, whether the financial symbol is placed before or after a numerical figure), and so on. The financial symbol for the "thousands separator" could be different in a number of countries (period vs. comma), such as expressing a client's quarterly billing:

German expression: US $ 400.456,50

English expression: US $ 400,456.50

In the most minor of mix-ups, a spelling change needs to be made. The most complicated of misinterpretations among these "English" speaking societies, however, can result in giving the wrong directions and measurements. It is not as easy as we might initially assume.

Suggestions

These details are presented to open your mind to the consideration that there will be differences, even among the same "primary/native language" speakers. Make no assumptions and follow the rules of the project you were provided (UK English, American English, and so on to guide you with spelling editing tools, expression of currency, and measurements). Edit often and with professional kindness. Be sure to share feedback respectfully while being mindful of your tone in communicating suggestions and corrections. Use the comment feature in your editing tool to explain in detail why a change is recommended.

Scenario #3: Everyone on the team is NOT Native-English-Language (speaking/writing).

Nobody on the team is a native speaker based on the project language requirement, yet all team members are proficient at the minimum required language requirement as ESL team members.

Possible Complications: This scenario might be the least complicated regarding "teamwork" barriers as everyone might be under the same language challenges, yet consider the following details. Copyediting should unify a variety of authors' unique writing styles, a complicated task on its own that also must account for ESL variables from contributing authors across many countries, so achieving this task will be a great accomplishment. It is rare that an individual would be asked to be a final editor of a non-native-language project, so this is one more accolade to incorporate on a resume or note in a job interview. This is a unique experience.

Suggestions

Consider approaching the project with at least two main co-editors to give multiple perspectives on interpreting and translating the work of all co-authors in order to develop one cohesive product. Being able to do this with other ELS team members should give all participants a great understanding of how to complete this successfully on future academic and professional projects. Consider utilizing library services (university-sponsored writing centers, etc.) for assistance in your approach to the editing process. To repeat the advice provided in another scene in this section, edit written work often and "with professional kindness." Use the comment feature in your editing tools to explain in detail why a change is recommended. If the work is edited throughout the project, all members of the team will likely develop greater editing skills, hone their personal writing style throughout the project, and become more comfortable with receiving feedback from each other and developing trust. Teammates will better understand each other's skills and hopefully increase each other's understanding of how to provide well-received and clear feedback.

Native Speakers Learning to Appreciate Non-Native Speakers

How many languages can you fluently read, speak, and write? If you have had the benefit of taking even an introductory-level course in another language, you likely can appreciate the difficulty of reading and speaking a new language, much less writing in another language on an academic, university-level project. If you do speak and write multiple languages proficiently, reflect on the time and effort it took for you to reach this level of skill, and acknowledge and appreciate the journey others are taking.

Translations tools. These are mostly helpful! Google Translate is a terrific resource, but it can't catch everything. Using this tool can bridge language barriers, yet sometimes the translation is inaccurate. In one online translation tool, someone (speaking English) in Australia would like to thank a new friend from Thailand (Thai language) for a "flower garland necklace," yet in the message received in translation, the thank you is for "a wagon wheel!" Many things can be understood through context and an understanding of the intended message, yet some things are simply a miss. The key is to be kind to each other, and for formal writing, use a native language writer to proofread the work to catch any details that were "lost in translation."

Activities to consider:

Listen. Develop an ear and appreciation for a new language: Watch a current movie and listen to music from a teammate's native language; gain an appreciation for the differences and similarities in expression and tone of language through a number of opportunities.

Share. Is there a movie, song, poem, you would recommend in your native language to share with others?

Learn. Learn a simple greeting or a phrase to show respect and interest with your teammate's language. This can be a simple way to show thoughtfulness and acknowledge that team members native language.

Editing. When editing the written work of others, look for the big ideas, and refine the spelling and grammar after a full read of the teammate's work. At times, the wording of translated text can be a bit awkward, more formal, or more "extravagant" than typically stated in academic or business writing, perhaps with antiquated words used in place of more modern phrasing. Learning to edit and communicate the ideas of others in a unified voice is an assignment to be taken seriously, and carried out with great respect for other team members. The editors will have a very valuable experience to note for future projects, as this skill is one that must be practiced and applied for mastery.

Section 2: Culture and location differences: getting to know your teammates

The Value of Diversity

Gaining a broader perspective by understanding the views of others is important, and being on a global team gives you the unique opportunity to get a genuine glimpse into the everyday experiences of others, what is trending in current culture in thoughts, politics, fashion, economics, and entertainment (just to name a few topics). You will have the opportunity to learn more from your teammates regarding norms for communication and "doing business in" standards in other locations. The statements above are expressed as "opportunities" because the unfortunate truth is that many people on a global virtual team really miss out on these aspects because they are focused on the task to the point that these unique and genuine exchanges with their teammates do not happen. Therefore, please do heed this warning, and be sure to take time to observe and ask questions to get to know your teammates and their perspectives and views.

Consider this a great opportunity to share perspectives on what everyday life schedules, culture, and business practices look like. Sharing perspectives will add to each other's personal knowledge and views, as well as developing a new team viewpoint toward finding creative solutions and new ideas.

Reminder: you are working with real, live people! Avoid treating the experience as a task with faceless components, and really get to know people right from the start. Make relationship-building a priority. When else have you had such a diverse group to work with? While you might feel that you don't have time for these exchanges, if you truly want to succeed and complete the best project possible, you must take the time to get to know each other and learn from each other's unique culture and environment. Below are several suggestions on ways to more specifically learn more about your teammates' culture and countries.

Activities to consider:

Add everyone's time zone on your computer and smartphone. It will be interesting to see how your schedules sync up (or do not) right from the start of your team formation. It might also help with everyone's understanding that the midday message you send and expect an answer to in a few hours was received by a teammate that just went to sleep, and they won't see the message until after they wake up, get ready for the day, and read your request. All in all, this may be 10 or 12 hours later, or even longer if they have to go to school and or work before reviewing your message. Setting expectations for communication is a critical step that should be completed at the start of the project. Also, remember the positives of being dispersed across time zones! In this situation, your team has the unique benefit of working and responding to needs and deadlines 24/7. Additionally, not everyone has to work weekends or late nights, or any other times that might be deemed inconvenient or difficult. With time zone dispersion, teams can work through demanding deadlines and communication schedules, all while sharing and shifting the burden of working on days or times that are challenging.

Note differences in national holidays, academic and other calendar differences, and add these to your personal calendar. One example might be a teammate in China not realizing that a teammate in Colombia, regardless of their religious affiliation, might not get much done the week associated with Easter Sunday, as many businesses and universities have a vacation for multiple days around this holiday. In Italy, there are specific weeks in the summer where many businesses operate with a reduced staff or even close as a traditional time for a summer holiday break. A United States teammate might celebrate Thanksgiving as a long-weekend holiday in November, whereas a teammate in India might not have in mind that the United States teammate is not going to be available to work on the project during that time as it is a country holiday that is not on the minds of others around the world when planning for conference calls and deadlines. These are just a few examples to highlight the importance of being aware and talking through personal schedule availability throughout the project timeline. Be sure to explore all of the positive ways to capitalize on your team's regional and cultural diversity. For example, your team will gain local knowledge of cultures, traditions, festivals, celebrations, and holidays that might not have been known to many on the team before they shared these unique regional details. These insights can offer your team a competitive advantage and insights.

Learn about your teammates' home countries. Subscribe to country national news feeds and read country overviews. Though there are many good resources to consider, two examples are:

- BBC country profiles http://news.bbc.co.uk/2/hi/country_profiles/default.stm
- Quintessential country guides http://www.kwintessential.co.uk/resources-types/guides

Listen. Listen to music (popular and even traditional/folk music on free services such as YouTube). Listen to the language of others on your teams even if you are exclusively communicating in a bridge language such as English and try the languages (many universities offer a no-cost basic language app online service).

Look. Search each teammate's university on Google Maps and see what the city center looks like from "street view." Are the cars smaller or larger in that area of the world? More or fewer motorbikes, pedestrians, or public transportation? What side of the road do people drive on?

Are there distinct architectural differences? Are road signs different? Do advertisements look different in other countries and regions outside your own?

LIVE connections via video chat. Take a few minutes for every call with some "getting to know you" activities. Past teams have shared stories of great ways students used collaboration tools to share a bit more about themselves. Here are just a few examples of one-minute live video chat activities before you get into the business of the day:

- What's in your refrigerator?
- What does your apartment/dorm look like?
- What does your desk look like, and how would you describe it?
- Show one object of meaning to you from your home or office and describe it.

One of our students shared an outstanding way to do this. On an initial Skype call, each team member showed their living space, the inside of their refrigerator & cabinets, played local music and displayed the outside scenery. This created an immediate connection as the students discussed favorite foods, music, activities, sport, and other topics.

Time zones and syncing up. As mentioned in section 2, consider adding everyone's time zone on your computer and smartphone. This will help each team member become more mindful of the differences in each other's daily schedules. Early in the team formation process, it is important to identify what time zones are associated with each team member, and determine how schedules sync up. It might also help with everyone's understanding of the "lag" between sending a message to a teammate and a reasonably expected timeframe for a reply.

For example, a team member in Calgary, Canada, sends a message at 9 AM to a teammate in Nairobi, Kenya. The teammate in Nairobi receives that message at 6 PM and reads the message two hours later, immediately after coming home from work at 8 PM. She thinks about and prepares a response, sending the reply as soon as possible the next day, after her first-morning break at 10 AM (Nairobi time). This has been a 13-hour wait for the team member in Calgary, who is anticipating a reply. If the team member in Calgary is not considering the time zone difference, she might have been waiting all "business day and through the night" for a reply (in the Calgary-time mindset). This could give the Calgary-based team member the perception that the Nairobi-based teammate is not communicating in a timely fashion. Next in this cycle of time, let's assume that the "morning" message from the Nairobi-based teammate will come to the teammate in Calgary at 1 AM (who is sleeping now). Upon waking at 7 AM, the Calgary-based team member replies immediately at 7:01AM and might believe they are giving a great impression by sending an "immediate reply" just moments after waking up. However, here again, there has been another large gap of many hours in time for the other teammate waiting for the response. Being mindful of how time zones relate to one another will not only spare "hard feelings" with thoughts that team members are not quick to reply, but these time differences can offer advantages by having staggered hours to cover tasks and responsibilities.

Another section of the text will cover in detail a number of helpful GVT communication tools, yet to close this section we would like to briefly mention two helpful (and no-cost) resources:

- Doodle: Polls and meeting planning surveys, with the automatic time zone conversion for all respondents for scheduling purposes. https://doodle.com/
- Time and Date's "The World Clock Meeting Planner:" Displays multiple time zones side by side for schedule planning and understanding time differences. https://www.timeanddate.com /worldclock/meeting.html

Additionally, it is important to talk about personal schedules and not make assumptions about "best times" for communication simply based on time zones. For example, some team members will prefer working on nights and weekends, while others will need to work early in the morning until noon because of a "second-shift" (late afternoon through evening) work schedule. Likely, most of the time your team will communicate asynchronously (not at the same time), yet these tips can help with coordinating deadlines and planning for synchronous communications where team members will join a chat, video call, or other live meeting at the same time.

Section 3: Tips for creating success: Before, during, and after the Global Virtual Team Project experience

In this portion of the chapter, you will find tips for professors and instructors to use when getting their students ready for and working on a Global Virtual Team (GVT) project.

Starting the Journey: getting ready for the TRAIL

Begin with the end in mind. Show the students examples of past reports. Discuss the "good" and "bad" aspects of these reports. Explain best practices from past projects (e.g., writing a team charter, getting an early start, assuring that everyone contributes, completing a final edit, etc.) and ask the students for their suggestions.

Talk. Discuss important concepts and use interesting articles and cases to begin the conversation. We have our students read articles on the Global Mindset through Harvard Business Review (HBR) articles. Recommended HBR titles we have had success with include: Managing Yourself: Making It Overseas (HBR, 2010) and Join the Global Elite (HBR, 2018). Students also take a simple Global Mindset inventory included in the above-mentioned "Managing Yourself: Making It Overseas" HBR article. This activity brings us to discuss the importance of Global Mindset when working on a GVT project and discusses what students can do (now) to improve their Global Mindset. Many college libraries subscribe to many publication sources, and in this particular case of HBR articles, our students can access these resources without cost. These resources can be found on the HBR website or through your university library. Ask your librarian for details on your possible university subscription for these resources. Some are no cost, others have fees. Typically, cases need to be purchased individually.

Read. Introduce students to readings such as Distance still Matters (HBR, 2001) and discuss how they can use the CAGE (culture, administrative, geography, and economic) analysis. Assign a case study to help students learn about the challenges of international expansions such as Ruth's Chris: The High Stakes of International Expansion (HBR, 2006). The students enjoy this case because they understand the business (steak restaurant) and it is a simple assignment (select one foreign city/country, they are not currently in, for a future expansion and recommend a mode of entry). As stated in both points in this section, "talk" and "read," by having shared cases and examples to relate to as a class community, these examples can be used to explain and relate to unique aspects of the "GVT project experience" and bring together theory and practice with shared references and a common vocabulary.

Anticipate. We ask our students what issues they expect to encounter in the GVT project and challenge them to provide a practical solution. The most common issues they mention are: language (unable to understand their teammates), team zone differences (I'm sleeping when they are awake), motivation (they won't do anything and I will have to do all the work myself), and expectations (I want to get an "A" on the project and my teammates just want to do as little as possible). You may not be able to "solve" all the issues ahead of time, but we find that our students feel more comfortable about the GVT project after having a chance to express their concerns.

Inspire (through past student stories). We tell our students that this may be their best college learning experience (and we firmly believe it) and reassure them that the experiences they gain from the project will overshadow the issues they face. We tell stories about past students and their positive experiences. In one case, a student completed the project and, after graduation, went to play professional basketball in Ukraine. A few months later, we received a picture of the student, wearing his basketball uniform, meeting his Ukrainian GVT teammate prior to a game.

Motivate. Review training material with your students, and afterward, have them take a simple Readiness quiz. To motivate your students, have the quiz count as a portion of their project grade.

Link. Link the good and bad of the GVT experience to real-world dynamics in the workplace that students will encounter. Be open and tell students there will be challenging parts of the project. For example, in a past project, we had a student on a team in which several students could not get along. It was a constant drama, and the students started using inappropriate and offensive language to one another. We eventually resolved the problem and believed these students learned as much from overcoming their personal conflicts as they did from the GVT project. We feel this reflects some of the real-world interpersonal issues they will face, and that learning to overcome them is a valuable skill. Remind students that everyone wants to be treated with respect. Don't minimize student concerns and let them know they can always come to you with their concerns.

Other Considerations. Class size and teaching mode (face to face, online, hybrid) will have an impact on how you prepare students for the GVT project.

The Golden Rule. We remind our students that everyone wants to be treated with respect, and they should keep this is mind when dealing with their teammates.

During the GVT Project

Consider employing the following components throughout the span of the project:

Team Charter. At the beginning of the GVT project, we strongly encourage our students to work with their teammates to establish a simple team charter. The charter should cover: roles (team leader?), communication methods (text, e-mail, phone, etc.), communication frequency & time (daily, weekly, take into account time zone differences), team promises (complete assigned work on time), and conflict (how to resolve any issues that may arise). It really is an important activity, and everyone needs to agree to the parameters of this living document.

Below is a short checklist of suggested items to include in a Team Charter:

- Require at least one video call to start the activity
- Together, review the project timeline; the project objectives, and main components

- Discuss individual interests, strengths, skills, areas of inexperience or weakness
- What technology will you use at different stages of the project?
- What is the expected turnaround time for messages? What should be done if this expectation is not met? How does the team move forward?
- Will you have a daily, bi-weekly, or weekly video or voice call? Will it be with the entire team or sub-groups? What time and dates can everyone agree on from the start of the project?
- Establish roles and have cross-trained and partners on a task. This can be complementary work and also a way to be sure nothing is left undone if a teammate does not deliver the expected work. Caution against dividing up the work without collaboration. This seems like an easy way to divide work, but what often happens, in the end, is a patchwork of ideas that might contradict each other, uneven work in sections, and missing sections.

- Review examples of good and poor team charters and take from those examples ideas to create an excellent charter for your team
- Consider the discussion of the peer evaluation system and how to use this exercise to provide feedback and help peers understand expectations and performance along the way. As with all surveys and feedback tools, comments can be the most helpful part of the process. By providing honest and professional feedback, you can help a team member that is having trouble.
- How will you handle non-performers? Again, discuss the importance of honest, candid peer evaluations.
- No assumptions: Discuss things we take for granted: how will our everyday lives and environment affect our ability to be responsive, meet due dates, and fully participate in the project?

Continuous relationship building: We encourage our students to take time to personally learn about their teammates (how are their lives the same and/or different than ours?).

Surveys: Every week, have each student complete a short, simple survey. This serves two purposes: to identify if the student is actively involved in the project (missing two consecutive surveys is a bad sign, upon which it is necessary to follow up with the student) and if there is team conflict. Encourage comments, as scores can be difficult to interpret, even if a scale is provided.

Team conflict: Always work with your students to see if the conflict can be resolved within the team. If not, be prepared to step in. In our experience, we have learned there are at least two sides to every situation. Don't believe or disbelieve the first story you hear. If necessary, you should communicate with the GVT project administrator and other professors involved. It is important to guide students toward self-resolution. However, some situations such as reported bullying and sexual harassment should be evaluated and addressed by the appropriate authority figures outside of the team.

Non-participation: 2–5% of teams will have the unfortunate dynamic of a "non-performer" on the team. It is very important for the instructor not to overreact, all while understanding that this is a great concern for the members of the team that are performing together. Encourage the team to continue to attempt to communicate with the non-performer and seek to find the root cause of the non-performance issue. Sometimes things are not what we assume, and the initial reaction of thinking the non-performer just doesn't care about the project or is lazy may not be the case. The root cause could be internet connectivity issues, energy disruptions (can be common or irregular, depending on the part of the world), or a team member consumed with a significant family or personal emergency. We encourage you to keep working to understand why that team member is not performing/communicating and use it as a learning experience from every possible angle. It is useful to consider how you would address this in a work environment or as a team leader/manager at work. A very clear team charter that expresses performance and communication expectations is helpful. Additionally, honest peer evaluations throughout the project timeline, rather than just one at the conclusion of the project, can serve as a helpful intervention opportunity.

The Goal: Throughout the project, continually stress your "goal" for the project. In some cases, it might be a complete report; in others, it may be the experience of working on a GVT. This helps the students balance their desire to earn a certain grade versus learn from the experience.

Grades: Yes, we know grading is difficult due to many factors. In our experience, we try to break the grade into many components (complete survey, peer rating, report, reflection paper, quiz, etc.) and have the grade reflect both individual and team performance. There is no 100% absolute recommended grading method. Finding a balance that brings together evaluating the course learning outcome mastery and evaluating contribution effort is key. Using 360 or peer evaluations can be a very useful component of grading a team project. The project grade must be a large enough % of the final grade in order for your students to take it seriously and to invest enough time to complete the project successfully. If this will be a multiple-week project, we suggest the project grade account for at least 20% of the final course grade.

After the GVT project

At the conclusion of such a dynamic and demanding project, it is important to help students debrief and get the most out of the experience through reflection. This is a way to celebrate accomplishments, share individual experiences, and process how the GVT experience relates to the student's professional career. Below are a few examples we have seen professors use with great success.

Reflection paper: Have your students write a short reflection paper (how did their team operate? what did they learn? What didn't work? suggestions to improve the project in the future?)

Class discussion: Since we believe the project itself is an important learning experience, we take one class for the students to share their reflection papers and experiences. For some students, this was the most valuable learning experience.

Post-test or post project survey: If there were pre-tests or surveys administered, consider providing a post-assessment and discuss any changes/differences in results, assumptions, knowledge, and perceptions. Typically, students enjoy non-graded individual assessments and comparing their own results. The best results for these types of individual assessments can be found when the assessments are private (between student and professor only and ungraded). This creates a safe atmosphere where students can answer questions honestly, not fearing judgment or comparison. Students might offer their reflections on these assessments in a class discussion, yet this would be at their own comfort level.

Celebrate: Regardless of the level of mastery, a class after the project is completed could be dedicated in part or in whole to a celebration ceremony with certificates, recognitions, and speeches. Take photos and make the moment memorable, as everyone has learned so much through positive experiences and challenges. Part of this ceremony might include mini-poster sessions of each student's experience or one-slide PowerPoint presentations.

Activities like this will help students further process the academic experience in meaningful ways by expressing higher-order thinking skills (analyze, synthesize, evaluate).

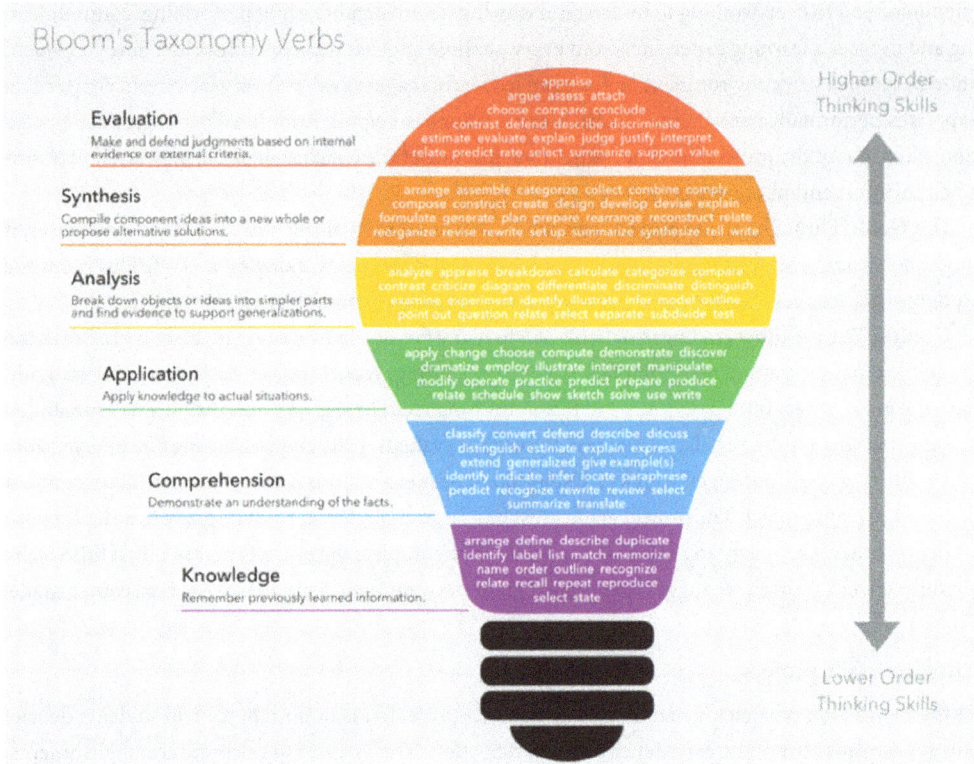

Fig 21.1 Bloom's Taxonomy Verbs.

File: Bloom's Taxonomy Verbs.png. (2018, May 22). Wikimedia Commons, the free media repository. Retrieved 15:33, June 29, 2019 from https://commons.wikimedia.org/w/index.php?title=File:Bloom%E2%80%99s_Taxonomy_Verbs.png&oldid=302484024.

References

Alon, I., & Kupetz, A. (2006). Ruth's Chris: The High Stakes of International Expansion. HBS No. **906A34**. Boston, MA: Harvard Business School Publishing.

BBC Country Profiles. (2013, January 24). Retrieved June 29, 2019, from http://news.bbc.co.uk/2/hi/country_profiles/default.stm

Bloom's Taxonomy Verbs.png. (2018, May 22). Wikimedia Commons, the free media repository. Retrieved 15:33, June 29, 2019 from https://commons.wikimedia.org/w/index.php?title=File:Bloom%E2%80%99s_Taxonomy_Verbs.png&oldid=302484024.

Use of image (rights are granted): Fractus Learning (https://commons.wikimedia.org/wiki/File:Bloom's_Taxonomy_Verbs.png), https://creativecommons.org/licenses/by-sa/4.0/legalcode

Bowen, D., Mansour, J., and Teagarden, M. (2010). Managing Yourself: Making It Overseas. Harvard Business Review. https://hbr.org/2010/04/managing-yourself-making-it-overseas

Ghemawat, P. (2001). Distance Still Matters: The Hard Reality of Global Expansion. Harvard Business Review. https://hbr.org/2001/09/distance-still-matters-the-hard-reality-of-global-expansion

Kwintessential country guides. (n.d.). Retrieved June 29, 2019, from http://www.kwintessential.co.uk/resources-types/guides

Unruh, G. and Cabrera, Á. (2013). Join the Global Elite. Harvard Business Review. https://hbr.org/2013/05/join-the-global-elite

CHAPTER 22

Grading Student Work in Team-Based Experiential Projects

DARIA PANINA, TEXAS A&M UNIVERSITY, MAYS BUSINESS SCHOOL

1. Introduction

Grading student work is an essential part of teaching. Not only does it help instructors assess student knowledge and progress, it also serves as a feedback tool for the students, focuses their attention on learning outcomes, and motivates them. Designing the grading rubric for team-based experiential projects involves multiple challenging decisions due to the experiential nature of the projects and the dynamics of teamwork. Experiential exercises are different from other assignments that students might encounter. They are focused on the process and designed to facilitate learning from experience, sometimes to the detriment of the quality of the final product.

Additionally, the group dimension of such assignments presents a further complication for grading and assessment since group outcomes may and probably should be assessed in multiple different ways. The greatest challenge for instructors grading experiential group projects is to design the assessment in a way that captures a diverse set of outcomes. Thus, there is the need to collect a variety of performance measures – on an individual as well as a group level. This chapter reviews some considerations, and best practices instructors might take into account while designing grading rubrics that reflect their teaching objectives, whether these are cross-cultural competencies, group processes, use of business knowledge or technical skills, or all of the above.

To design a fair and effective grading system, the following questions should be considered: What is being evaluated: product, process, or both? Who assigns grades: instructor, students, or both? Should student grades be based on individual or group performance? Depending on a group project, these questions might be answered differently. Yet, there is a general consensus among educators that a combination of different grading approaches is perceived as the fairest and accurate way to assess students' performance on experiential group projects.

What is assessed: Product, process or both?

The purpose of team-based experiential projects is to give students a realistic experience of working in teams solving real-life problems. The ultimate goal is to provide the students with a valuable experience. Thus, the grading of work products should be balanced against the broader goal of evaluating students' learning from experience (group processes). Although combination grades seem to work best and are preferred by students and instructors alike, computation of these grades can get very complicated. Recent studies suggest that the simple methods of combining the instructor's assessment of the group product and peer assessments of individual contributions work best (Zhang and Ohland, 2009; Guzman, 2018).

The combination grade reassures students that the group report (product) will not be the sole determinant of their grade, and other indicators of their performance (process) will also be taken into account. Ultimately, students that are too concerned about their grade for the final report will miss the opportunity to benefit from the experience as much as the project might allow.

The primary reasons to combine an assessment of the process with the assessment of the product is based on the need to ensure procedural fairness due to the following considerations:

- National culture and national differences in education systems should be considered for the global teams. Project grading is not equally important to all global team members. There are institutional and attitudinal differences towards grades in different countries. For example, U.S. students are extremely concerned about their grades, because GPA is an important metric that employers use in the recruitment process. Additionally, due to the high cost of education in the U.S., a failed class has serious financial consequences since it has to be re-taken and paid for. Similar situations are reported for other countries with similar education systems (Strauss et al., 2014). In other countries, students are not as concerned about their grades because potential employers are primarily focused on whether the student obtained the degree, rather than their GPA. Additionally, in many schools, the costs of education are low and there are policies in place that allow failing students to retake the final examination for the course without extra pay. As a consequence, such students might not be as concerned about their final grade on the project as some of their teammates.
- Language proficiency plays a role in the relative distribution of tasks in a team and the overall quality of the final product. For example, Strauss and colleagues (2014) found that the attitudes regarding group grades varied between students in multicultural teams based on their native language. Students whose native language was English felt that other team members drag their grades down by not contributing the same quality of written work as them.
- Different instructors have different expectations of student performance. While some students may be concerned about the final quality of the group project because their grade heavily depends on it, other students may not be particularly concerned about the group outcome because their instructor essentially gives a completion grade for the assignment – as long as students completed the project, they succeeded.
- Additionally, the experiential group project may account for a different portion of the overall grade in different courses. It is desirable that multiple instructors who pool students together for a group experiential project coordinate accordingly and agree on a common weight for the project in the overall grade.
- Finally, in some group experiential learning projects, students of different levels end up working together because it is not always possible to match the students exactly based on an academic level due to the differences in education systems. Clearly, expectations for undergraduate and graduate students differ, and this presents additional challenges in terms of disparities in expectations regarding the final group report.

For these reasons, placing too much emphasis on the group product is counterproductive. The answer to the question of what should be assessed, product or process, is both. The decision about the relative importance of the two elements in the rubric should be based on the teaching objectives of the class. For lower-level classes, the process will carry more weight, while for upper-level classes, students might be expected to produce group reports of a certain quality, even if they are working in challenging conditions.

Should students be evaluated based on individual or group performance, or both?

Assigning group grades (e.g., the same grade for all team members) and individual grades (e.g., assigning individual grades to students based on their individual performances on the project) are both practiced in higher education. Both of these methods have their positive and negative attributes (Kagan, 1995).

The arguments often mentioned to justify giving the same grade to all members of a group are:

1. In the real world, teams are rewarded based on their collective contribution, and individual contributions are often not recognized.
2. Social skills are important to potential employers, and a group grade signals the ability of the team members to manage team processes effectively.
3. Group grades motivate students to work on their cooperative skills, while individual grades may undermine group cohesiveness and lead to less cooperation.
4. Assigning the same grade to all group members signals to the students the importance of working together.

Arguments in favor of assigning individual grades are equally compelling:

1. Group grades are not fair because they are a function of team composition rather than the contributions of a particular student.
2. Group grades may undermine motivation because they reward slackers and demotivate high achievers. Giving the same grade for a group project is often resented by the students who experience free riders on their team or for a variety of reasons that have to do with a disproportionate amount of work. An individual performance assessment reduces the impact that social loafing has on other students' grades.
3. Group grades do not reflect individual contributions and thus violate individual accountability. For this reason, some schools have policies preventing instructors from using group grades. This can even be to protect against court challenges because grades are often the basis for various important decisions that affect students, from scholarships to admissions to programs and universities.

Therefore, the answer to the question of which grades—group or individual—should be used is both. Part of the final grade should take into account the individual contributions of students to prevent free-riding, yet, to encourage cooperation and teamwork, group grades should also be included in final grade calculations. The students also prefer grading procedures that combine group and individual assessments of performance (Hoffman, 2001).

Who assigns grades: Instructor, students, or both?

Instructors are well equipped to grade the product of teamwork. They are in the position to go through the group report and assess the thoroughness of research and analysis done by the group and/or individual students, as well as the quality of their conclusions and recommendations. However, assessing the process should involve student input, since instructors are not aware of the group dynamics and history. Due to procedural justice considerations, students like to have a say in the assessment of their team members. Thus, peer evaluations represent a valuable addition to the overall grade a student receives for the group project. Finally, research shows that self-assessments are poor indicators of performance and should be avoided (Zhang and Ohland, 2009; Guzman, 2018).

2. Possible Experiential Group Project Outcomes.

Since the ultimate purpose of the group experiential project is not only to test the students' knowledge and skills, but also an experience designed to help students learn, a variety of indicators are necessary.

Individual Performance Indicators reflect the effort and learning outcomes of the individual students, irrespective of the performance outcomes achieved by their teams. Teams usually vary in terms of the level of motivation, effort, and skills teammates bring to the project. Thus, to eliminate stress associated with the lack of control over the team outcomes, a fair grading system should reflect individual contributions. It might be argued that individual indicators should constitute a considerable part of the final grade for the project.

- Many group experiential learning projects involve pre-project training, pre/post-project surveys, as well as intermittent surveys throughout the project. These surveys are important as indicators of student learning (as in the comparison between pre/post-project attitudes and knowledge), as well as a source of the student feedback on the general progress of the project in a particular team. These tasks are commonly evaluated on a pass/fail basis (a student passed the pre-project training or not; completed a survey or not; contacted other team members or not). Assessing the quality of response is not always feasible. The common complication in the grading of these tasks is the situation when a student clearly did not make a good-faith effort. An argument can be made that unfinished tasks should be marked as missed assignments due to their importance as a source of data for student evaluation and possible future research.
- In addition to assignments that students complete by themselves, their individual performance indicators should reflect the feedback of their team members:

  i. The percent of work done is one of the commonly-used indicators of individual effort, which is an assessment by the rest of the team. An instructor has to decide how to deal with the complaints of the students who disagree with the assessments done by their teammates and argue that they did more than the team gives them credit for. Usually, the team evaluation of individual member's contribution should be taken into account, unless the student presents some evidence of malicious intent by other group members.

  ii. Peer rankings provide another important indicator of a student's participation in the team project. Peer rankings may be influenced by interpersonal team dynamics. The most common student complaint is a low peer ranking because one or more of the team members gave them an unreasonably low score due to some personality incompatibilities. Overly inflated peer rankings are also common, but students never complain about them. Usually, most groups tend to give all group members good scores unless some serious problems in the teamwork arise. Thus, the unfavorable peer ranking is a signal of team dysfunction that was caused by the assessed student, and it should not be ignored. Below are a few examples that show how teams provide feedback to underperforming students. In one team, an overly ambitious student wanted her team to succeed. She was constantly reminding her teammates about deadlines, volunteering to help with their parts of the project, spending a lot of time editing group reports, but got a bad peer rating at the end. Thus, even though she invested a lot of time and effort in the project, she alienated the rest of the team and failed on the peer assessment part of the grade. Another student did his work diligently but refused to socialize with his team when they were discussing non-project-related issues. He got very poor rankings as well. It might be argued that both students failed to realize how to work with their team members in a successful way and their peer rankings reflected that. At the same time, someone who is not overachieving in his/her contributions to the group work, but is a supportive and positive group member can often get a perfect score from the rest of the team. Overall, though, there seems to be a correlation between peer ratings and other indicators of individuals' performance. Therefore, peer feedback should be considered as a small part of the overall student grade.

Group Performance Indicators

Arguably, the most important indicator of performance in the project is the final report produced by the group. Two approaches to grading the team reports are common. According to one view, the final report is viewed as a team project. All team members are ultimately responsible for the team outcome, and all team members get the same grade for the report. Some degree of team member interdependence, to ensure that students are motivated to work with their teammates, is necessary. At the same time, the grading scheme should allow high-performing students to get a good grade, even if some of their teammates perform poorly. After all, even if one student on a team has particularly exceptional skills and a high motivation to do well, the quality of the team report might be dragged down due to a lack of skills, lack of commitment by other team members, or faulty team processes. As a way to resolve this problem, the instructor needs to collect information on which student was responsible for which part of the team report. If the data on what specific parts of the report each student worked on is available, it is possible to put a heavier weight on the individual performance of the report. Instructors have a variety of options that range from giving grades based on each student's part of the project to grading based on the team project as a whole. As a possible solution, it seems to be a good idea to give each student the same grade based on the quality of the overall group report, with a possibility of grade correction for individual students in extreme cases (e.g., one team member did not submit his portion of work, and the team project is missing an important component or several team members have a very poor command of English and the report is lacking in quality because of that). For example, all instructors grading X-Culture group reports assign grades for each section of the report. Students are required to specify which sections of the report they were responsible for. Thus, if the part of the report a student was responsible for is written better than the overall project, an instructor can correct the student's grade in some circumstances.

- The group report quality might be assessed in terms of:
- Quality of data on the company/industry/country
- Logic and flow of the argument,
- Quality of data analysis
- Quality of the work cited
- Neatness and visual appeal
- Form of data presentation.

When students who participate in group experiential projects come from multiple schools or are led by different instructors, each instructor grades group reports submitted by teams of their students. This means that multiple professors evaluate every group report. Instructors must grade the reports using standardized report evaluations to allow for the easy integration of team report evaluations.

- Group report size is another relevant piece of information. Project reports can range from just a couple of pages to more than 50. It is essential to give the students at least some guidelines regarding the desired report size. However, all else being equal, longer and more thorough reports should be rewarded. The grading of overly long reports is a bit more complicated: longer does not necessarily mean better. Therefore, certain space-expanding tactics, such as the reproduction of pictures, figures, and tables that do not contribute to the quality of the report, should be taken into account.

3. What if a student fails the project?

Reasons for failure might differ. Some students fail the assignment due to legitimate reasons, such as illness or some other physical inability to participate in group activities. Some students drop out of the project because of problems with other group members. Finally, a very small proportion of the students fail the project due to a lack of effort on their part.

In X-Culture, students may be allowed to vote underperforming teammates out of their teams. A student loses his/her place on the team if he/she gets unsatisfactory peer ratings for two weeks in a row. They then get a chance to be reassigned to a different team. In practice, it seldom happens because for a student to get an unsatisfactory peer rating, the team members have to be almost unanimous in their assessment. Usually, there are always students who will assign a good or at least average grade even for the least deserving students in the spirit of team harmony and cooperation.

Clearly, the students deserve a different treatment depending on their personal situation. While the last group might well deserve to fail the project completely, the first group clearly needs a chance to make up for the missed work. The middle group presents the most complicated case since it is sometimes difficult to determine whether the student's failure was their fault or due to the actions of other group members. Although the instructor has to make the decision on a case-by-case basis, it is advisable to give a student the benefit of the doubt.

The alternative assignments are usually used to make up for the failed group experiential project. Students may be asked to complete the project individually, following the same sequence of steps the groups are following. Grade assignment in this case should be based on report quality & quantity. However, the student will not get a full grade for the project due to non-participation in a global virtual team. Thus, the grade the student will receive will only reflect the achieved outcomes.

4. Grading of Activities Related to Experiential Group Project

Many instructors augment the experiential group projects with a few assignments that help students prepare for the project or allow them the opportunity to reflect and process their experiences. These assignments can also be considered as a part of the project and can be graded. Below are three main types of assignments that might accompany an experiential group project and make the learning more meaningful and impactful.

- Activities in preparation for the project: Group experiential projects are difficult due to the complications of managing team processes. In global teams, an additional complication is presented by cultural differences, the need to pick and use appropriate communication technology, and complications arising from time management issues associated with team members being dispersed through different time zones. Therefore, it is a good idea to prepare students for the experience. X-Culture pre-project training is mandatory to all students, and it involves all information students should be aware of before they start the project, such as project timeframe, weekly deliverables, technology choices, and best practices. Grading of such training is usually done on a completion basis. Supplementing this training with assignments that help students better understand the processes, pitfalls, and best practices of teamwork would boost student learning. Therefore, pre-project training should be supplemented with research and readings on the subject of global virtual teams. As a possible assignment before the beginning of the project, students may be asked to research academic literature in a particular field, such as global virtual teams or team processes in general. The instructor can also assign some review articles for students to read and discuss in class. This activity sensitizes students to the things they are about to experience and gives them some suggestions as to how some of the pitfalls may be avoided. Student papers and presentations of the research should be graded as a pre-project activity.
- Activities during the project: Once the project is underway, students participating in group experiential exercises will encounter multiple problems and difficulties in their teams. To support their reflection and problem solving, some class assignments can be implemented. Students may be asked to brainstorm tricky issues and situations. Good practice involves asking the students at the beginning of the class to provide examples of the problems they are facing. The concerns and problems they bring up can then be used as material to organize debates in class, followed by the writing of reflection papers. Another group project that may be used in addition to the X-Culture experience involves dividing students in class into groups based on their company selection. Students who share the same 'client' then get to compare their solutions to important parts of the project. For example, in a strategy class, teams of students who work in the same company can make presentations about strategic choices their company is making and the solutions different virtual teams suggest. The class then can discuss the pros and cons of proposed solutions and decide on the best course of action for the company. The students can then take this information to their virtual teams while they continue working on their reports.
- Activities upon the completion of the project: At the end of the project, a debriefing exercise is very effective. The students should be encouraged to step back, think about their experience and consider what they have learned from it. At this stage, the class discussion may be in order, which should be preceded by the assignment of individual reflection papers. Depending on a student, their learning preference, and their specific experience with the project, the learning outcomes will be different. Therefore, the grading of reflection papers should be done with care and leniency.

As another possible post-project activity, the students may be asked to design assignment rubrics for the next cohort of the students participating in the project. The assignment will require students to think about what are their learning outcomes and come up with a way to measure them fairly. This exercise can also be treated as a way to provide student feedback on grading the project.

Lastly, some instructors are experimenting with more innovative assignments that facilitate reflection. As one of the possibilities, the visual project is used. Instructors notice that sometimes students struggle to verbalize specific learning outcomes they might experience. In this case, an assignment can be employed that requires students to present their experience with the group project visually. The pictures are then discussed in class and compared. The list of possible learning outcomes is created as the result of class discussion. Needless to say, this is a very creative assignment that students particularly like. Besides, it avoids a common social desirability bias, when students list learning outcomes their instructor was talking about throughout the semester.

5. Example of a Group Experiential Learning Project Grading Recommendations

Below is the example of grading recommendations provided to the instructors who enroll their students in X-Culture: experiential group project that involves global virtual teams of students working on developing internationalization strategies for real-life companies.

To ensure that all global virtual team members are equally committed to participating in the project, all participating instructors have to comply with few grading rules:

- The X-Culture project must account for no less than 20% of the overall course grade
- Peer evaluations should account for no less than 30% of the X-Culture project's grade
- Every milestone should be included in the project's grade

The recommended values for each project component are as follows:

Performance Indicator	Recommended Value
Individual:	
Completion of the pre-project training	Must pass to enroll
Weekly progress reports, 10 total @2% each, submitted individually by each student (completed fully and before the deadline)	20%
Post-project survey (completed before the deadline, % questions answered, check for response non-randomness);	Must be completed to receive project grade/ mark
Peer evaluations (as evaluated by the other team members in terms of effort, intellectual contribution, help with writing the report, coordinating team efforts, other comments), reported weekly and post-project, an average of all.	40%
Team	
Quality of the team report (as rated by the professors)	40%

These are suggested guidelines, and it is up to individual instructors to decide which components of student performance to evaluate and how much each component should be worth as long as instructors follow the three rules mentioned above. This ensures consistency in expectations for the students throughout the project.

Conclusion

In conclusion, grading experiential group projects should be taken seriously, since "…testing and grading are not incidental acts that come at the end of teaching but powerful aspects of education that have an enormous influence on the entire enterprise of helping and encouraging students to learn" (Bain, 2004, p. 150). This approach to grading suggests that the students need to understand how they will be evaluated before the beginning of the project. A structured grading rubric is essential for explaining expectations and helping students improve their performance by focusing their efforts on specific aspects of the task (Burke, 2011). To be effective, rubrics should provide detailed breakdowns of points to be awarded for each learning outcome, be it the final group report or elements of the group process.

Experiential group projects have multiple outcomes, some of which should be measured on the individual and some – on the group level. Thus, to fairly reflect the multitude of learning outcomes, the grading rubric should include a variety of different measures and sources of performance data. This chapter suggested just a few common criteria often used to assess student performance in experiential group projects. The decision of which of the suggested measures to use in the assessment largely depends on the nature of the experiential project and its learning outcomes.

References

Bain, K. (2004). What the best college teachers do. Harvard University Press, Cambridge, MA.

Burke, A. (2011). Group work: How to use groups effectively. The Journal of Effective Teaching, v.11(2), pp.87–95.

Guzman, S.G. (2018). Monte Carlo evaluations of methods of grade distribution in group projects: Simpler is better. Assessment and Evaluation in Higher Education, v.43(6), pp. 893–907.

Hoffman, J.R. (2001). All together now? College students' preferred project group grading procedures. Group Dynamics: Theory, Research, and Practice, v.5(1), pp.33–40.

Kagan, S. (1995). Group grades miss the mark. Connecting with the Community and the World of Work, v. 52(8), pp. 68–71.

Strauss, P., U-Mackey, A., and Crothers, C. (2014). 'They drag my marks down!' – challenges faced by lecturers in the allocation of marks for multicultural group projects. Intercultural Education, v.25(3), pp. 229–241.

Zhang, B., and Ohland, M.W. (2009). How to assign individualized scores on a group project: An empirical evaluation. Applied Measurement in Education, v. 22, pp. 290–308.

CHAPTER 23

Using GVT-Based Projects in the Pre-College Curriculum

OLEH LESKIV, X-CULTURE, INC.

Too often, we give children answers to remember
rather than problems to solve."
Roger Lewin
British science writer

Summary

1. If you are looking for a tool for enabling students` practical learning, teamwork, and individual approaches, try a GVT-based project!
2. The project demands a free educational environment; however, it can be effectively integrated even into tightly regulated curriculums.
3. It is not necessary to rely only on straight-A students, as wild cards can surprise you!
4. Do not try to incorporate all materials into the school timetable, but use an integrative approach and cooperate with colleagues.
5. Modern schooling is not about giving standard correct answers, but it is about how to think creatively and seek new solutions! Remember this during the evaluation of students` results.

1. Advantages for students, teachers, schools, and society.

"Why should we do this?" This is a reasonable question that teachers can hear from their students before the start of a GVT-based project, and they have to be ready to give a convincing and motivating answer. If this question comes into students` minds after the project, the situation can be much worse. This is a sign of ineffective work and wasted time. The following chapter was prepared in order to avoid this type of situation. We have to note that all the recommendations provided in this chapter are the result of a combination of the author`s personal experience participating in GVT-based projects and modern educational concepts which are spread in Western and some Asian countries. So, let us begin.

Four parties benefit from GVT-based project usage in the school curriculum: students who participate, teachers (instructors), school administration, and society at large. GVT-based projects rely on experiential learning and playing, which is particularly important in the case of younger pre-college students. It is a lot more comfortable for kids to explore the world in a playful way, using interactive games as a simplified model of natural and social phenomena. Thus, the main benefits of participation in a GVT-based project for pre-college students are the following.

1. Acquiring new knowledge through games.
2. Obtaining international experience of team cooperation with peers.

3. Resolving complex real-life challenges which demand a comprehensive examination of the particular cases.
4. Training new skills like cross-cultural communication, usage of online communication tools, formal writing and presentations, and the psychological skills of communication with inefficient teammates.
5. Improving students` prospects in terms of employability and university education.

Using GVT-based projects such as X-Culture in the pre-college curriculum allows for enhancing the student`s theoretical knowledge and developing practical skills in the fields of Microeconomics, Management, Marketing, Political Geography, Computer Science, English, and Psychology. The main purpose of a GVT-based project is not accumulating theory data in students` minds but teaching students to work effectively in cooperation with foreign colleagues. During the theoretical part of the project, students receive the needful knowledge and skills they need to do well in the practical phase.

A GVT-based project offers important benefits for a teacher and an entire school as well. The teacher is given the opportunity to exchange experience with foreign counterparts. This factor is extremely important for young professors. As students` supervisors, teachers have the opportunity to increase their professional level (if the project profile and teacher`s specialization are similar). The supervisor gains access to new training methodologies, pedagogical materials, etc. In addition, a GVT-based project is a great source of primary data that may be useful for scientific investigators.

Schools have three major advantages of participating in GVT-based projects:

1. Extensions of international engagement;
2. Reputation benefits;
3. An increasing level of teaching and learning can be shown up in the form of integrated lessons and more effective usage of information technologies. For example, at the author`s school, students were excited to use interactive touchscreens to communicate with their teammates and develop a graphic promotion for the project client company.

The general public is also interested in the integration of GVT-based projects into school curriculums because such convergence is a great starting point for students` professional growth. It provides useful preparation for university applicants and employees who already have theoretical knowledge and useful, practical experience in the field of their specialization. However, far more important is the fact that the increase of international communication among young members of society gives us a good reason to face the future with optimism and believe that inhuman phenomena such as military conflicts, racism and religious bias will finally be eliminated.

The use of GVT-based projects in the school curriculum fully meets the requirements of modern pedagogy, which are based on an individual approach, case study methodology, critical thinking instead of memorization, innovative technologies, creative scopes, and a practical component of teaching. The author`s observations show that students who participate in GVT-based projects demonstrate more educational progress than their colleges. The former participants are also much more motivated, disciplined, and focused on their ambitious plans.

Therefore, we can argue that GVT-based projects should be incorporated into the school curriculums as an effective method of modern teaching.

2. Before the project starts: implementation of GVT-based project into the school curriculum and selection of students.

2.1. INTEGRATION PECULIARITIES

Our experience shows that, depending on the country and type of school, teachers can use one of the following options for participation in a GVT-based project:

A. Direct integration of a GVT-based project into the curriculum and school schedule. This can be done in the following ways:

A.1. A GVT-based project as a full, separate subject;

A.2. A GVT-based project as a structural part of the existing state curriculum.

Option A.1 requires establishing a new curriculum. Therefore, this option is available mostly for Western state schools. Nevertheless, even for countries with state-regulated curriculums, option A.1 can be actual for private schools and public author's schools.

Alternative A.2 is for most Western, Latin American, and some Asian countries. In the case of X-Culture, the most suitable humanitarian subjects for integration might be Economics, Political Geography, Civic Education, Basic Business Management, Basic Marketing, and Cultural Studies.

B. Indirect integration of a GVT-based project in the state-approved curriculum. In most countries, schoolteachers may modify state programs to meet their own teaching requirements. In that case, the project may be considered as:

B.1. Mandatory workshops of the state curriculum;

B.2. Optional additional sessions for most active students.

According to the research (Nordmann, 2009, p. 34–35), options B.1 and B.2 are only available mostly in African, Southeast Asian, and Middle Eastern countries (see Table 1).

There is a growing tendency to shift from restricted state curriculums to flexible local ones. Thus, depending on the county, the integration degree of GVT-based projects can be different.

2.2. STUDENT SELECTION

The right choice of students participating in the project is crucial. GVT-based projects demand participants with a strong desire to learn new things, which are organized, motivated, and punctual. Moreover, only students who are skilled enough in foreign languages, primarily in English (at least at the B1 level) will be able to participate successfully. In any case, students with weak English will face tension with their colleges and be eliminated from the GVT, so there is no point for teachers to assign such students to the project. Awareness in other languages is an additional advantage because GVTs exist as multinational communities.

Besides, as the author`s experience shows, there is one factor that might mean even more than knowledge and skills – communicability and charm. Like in any other social system, the ability to deal with different people and friendships can be very helpful, even if your other skills are not prominent. First of all, a GVT-based project is based upon effective collaboration with people from other countries and exists only secondarily is a scientific training course.

Ideally, to participate in a GVT-based project, your students should possess several qualities. Only inquisitive, open-minded students can provide innovative approaches to resolving project tasks. Work in an international team means that students have to be social, conscientious, and disciplined. On the other hand, social students have to be independent enough to prepare their part of the project task

Schools freely adapt the official curriculum (16-20 Oidel points)	Schools implement an equivalent curriculum to the public one (11-15 Oidel points)	Schools implement an identical curriculum with other elements (6-10 Oidel points)	Schools have a few freedom (0-5 Oidel points)
Participation option A.1	*Participation option A.2*	*Participation option B.1*	*Participation option B.2*
Argentina	Germany	Albania	Afghanistan
Australia	Bulgaria	Brazil	Algeria
Austria	Estonia	China	Angola
Belgium	Hungary	Columbia	Saudi Arabia
Canada	Israel	Congo	Bangladesh
Chile	Norway	Costa Rica	Bolivia
Denmark	New-Zealand	Côte d'Ivoire	Cambodia
USA	Paraguay	Croatia	Cameroon
Finland	Philippines	El Salvador	Cuba
Netherlands	Portugal	Ecuador	Egypt
Poland	Rep. of Korea	Indonesia	Ethiopia
Czech Rep.	Ireland	Italy	France
UK	Romania	Lebanon	Ghana
Sweden	Slovakia	Madagascar	Greece
		Mexico	Guatemala
		Nicaragua	Honduras
		Nigeria	India
		Panama	Iraq
		Peru	Iran
		Russia	Iceland
		Rwanda	Jamaica
		Thailand	Jordan
		Switzerland	Kazakhstan
		Spain	Kenya
		Uruguay	Libya
		Ukraine	Malaysia
		Vietnam	Mali
			Mauritania
			Mongolia
			Nepal
			Pakistan
			Dominican Rep.
			Singapore
			Sudan
			Venezuela
			Zimbabwe

Table 1: Level of school autonomy and the most suitable participation option in a GVT-based project
Source: (OIDEL, 2018), (Nordmann, 2009).

successfully. All the aforementioned skills are largely innate, but at the same time, GVT-projects require certain acquired skills such as usage of languages and awareness in digital communications.

It goes without saying that teachers understandably assign A students to participate in such projects. Participation in a GVT-based project may be a teachers' award form for persistent study. However, our experience shows that there is a possibility that some of the A students do not recognize the opportunities which project provides. For such individuals, a GVT-based project might be only an ordinary teacher's task. In this case, high grades will become the top priority instead of self-development. Such a situation indicates a lack of appropriate motivation, which is partly the teachers` fault as well.

Besides, as we have seen, the global virtual team may become a great chance for students who have not been showing high results before. Such students may be classified into several groups depending on the factors that hinder the progress.

1. Non-motivated students. A GVT-based project is a great source of motivation thanks to:
   - shifting from school routine study;
   - interesting project tasks which, as a rule, are practically oriented;
   - new acquaintances with highly motivated teammates;
   - usage of modern communication technologies.

2. Introverted students who do not like to draw attention to themselves. A GVT-based project gives an opportunity for such students to reveal their potential in a way that was impossible before, thanks to the elimination of direct physical contact with other students (teammates) and the digitization of the communication process, making it less personal. Such elimination of the psychological barrier allows introverted students to feel more comfortable and confident.

3. "Black sheep" students. Unlike the students from the previous category who do not want to integrate into a class, black sheep frequently seek tight relations with classmates, but their reputation makes it tough. A GVT-based project gives such participants a great opportunity to show up themselves in the new collective. If the teacher sees that "black sheep" are not satisfied with their status and feel comfortable in a friendly community, they can be potential successful participants of a GVT-based project as long as they demonstrate a certain degree of analytical ability, curiosity, and focus on a task.

4. "Top dogs." Energetic, communicative, open-minded students who are used to attract the class' attention and can achieve good results in the project as well. Their leadership and organizational skills can be useful for GVTs. For such students, the main threat is the lack of discipline that may cause problems for other team participants and disrupt the project schedule. To avoid these negative consequences, the teacher has to make sure that the students are highly motivated from the beginning of the process.

So, based on our experience, there is no unique, single type of student who fits perfectly for a GVT-based project. In most cases, it is a matter of individual-friendly approach, motivation, and support. Likely project outcomes of described categories can be cited in the following structure (Fig. 1).

As can be seen from the illustration, "top dogs" and "black sheep" show statistically high potential for achieving excellent project results, but there is also the distinct possibility of failure (30–20% accordingly). The involvement of "A" students in the project almost guarantees the successful completion of the project task (95% in total). However, the share of excellent results may not be as big as with the first two options. Along with the previous category, introverted students can provide stable and positive outcomes (85% in total), but a lack of communication skills might prevent them from achieving more.

Before the start of the project, teachers have to warn their students about the main difficulties. The inevitable difficulties of participation in GVT-based projects are:

1. Differences in personal abilities and characters;
2. The coordination of time zones demands discipline and the sacrifice of individual interests;
3. Differences in motivation levels of GVT members, which can be a source of conflict and the reason for potential failure in completing the project task.

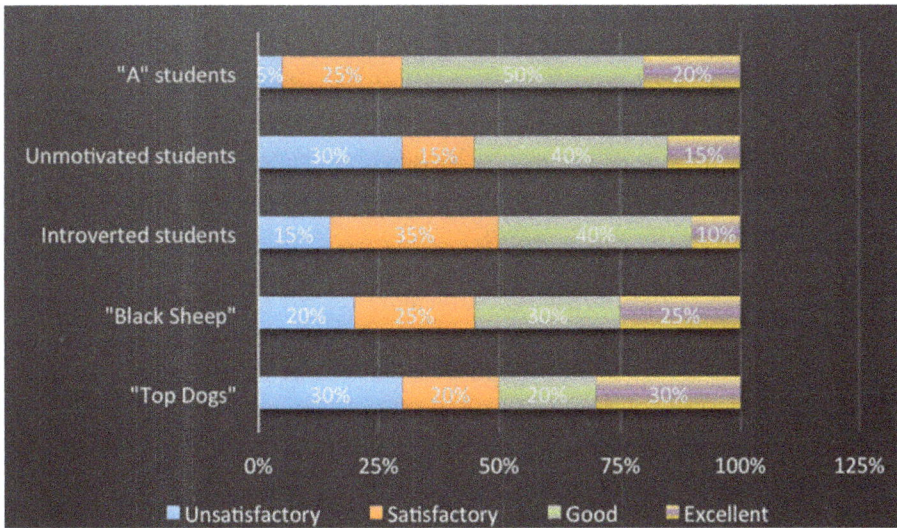

Fig.23.1 The possible results of the main student categories
Source: author data collected during participation in the X-Culture project.

Potential difficulties that are not necessarily faced by a GVT:

4. Cultural differences and stereotypes can provoke conflicts inside the GVT;
5. Different native languages cause a lack of communication among members of the GVT;
6. Lack of organization and leadership;
7. Virtual means of communication (Zwerg-Villegas, 2016, p. 139).

As supervisors, teachers have to be ready to play an active role in overcoming described difficulties. At the same time, it is vital to ensure some freedom of action for students, giving them a chance to meet the challenges alone first.

3. And here we go! The connection between lessons and GVT-based projects, teacher's ongoing support and motivation:

3.1. INTEGRATED LESSONS

Participation in GVT-based projects gives teachers a great opportunity to increase interdisciplinary connections in school. Integrated lessons allow for learning about the nature of society from different perspectives for a better understanding of the relationships. Moreover, integrated lessons correspond perfectly to the innovative (Know-Do-Be) KDB curriculum concept. In the twenty-first century, the educational philosophy is shifting from the passive cognitive realm that is based on memorizing facts and simple skills to:

- Conceptual thinking (know);
- Communication, collaboration, creativity (do);
- Lifelong learning, creating and maintaining healthy relationships, and developing social values (be) (Drake, 2018, p. 33).

Modern secondary educational systems, such as the Finnish educational system, widely use the method of integrated lessons. As mentioned above, integrated lessons help students to understand the interconnections among natural, political, economic, social, cultural spheres, and learn how to use "vacuum" disciplinary knowledge in practice, because practice always entails a complex combination of factors that have a different nature. What might such an integrated lesson that is connected with the GVT-based project look like? We can provide some examples of the integration of humanitarian subjects, developed on the basis of the X-Culture project.

Example 1: Political Geography + Macroeconomics + Law + Marketing.

One project assignment requires a new national market for a secondary school and the development of an appropriate marketing strategy for entry. Students who participate in the project decide between Austria, Slovenia, and Poland as new markets for client companies. Most likely, students or groups of students from one class would be working in different GVTs, and thus teachers have to concentrate their attention on a few countries simultaneously or distribute the material throughout a larger number of lessons. According to the client task, each GVT has to research the political, economic, and social situations of the chosen countries. This is a great opportunity for their geography professor to equip the class with relevant information. After this, the economics professor provides necessary data about vital sectors of the economy, living standards, and tax systems at the national markets. The law professor could add information regarding legislative borders in this sphere and where client companies operate. GVTs have to not only propose new products/services that might be popular in the new market, but also develop a marketing strategy for the client company. Given this, the economics professor may describe different marketing communication tools which will prove useful for promoting the company in the new market.

Based on practice, we can propose the next structure of such an integrated lesson.

1. Introduction. The students can conduct it as an announcement of the project tasks and sharing current results (3–4 min.).
2. Geographical and political features of countries (5 min.).
3. Macroeconomics (5 min.).
4. State of national educational industries. Legal enforcement of educational business (10 min.).
5. Marketing strategy of the client company. (6–7 min.).
6. Students` independent work in teams. Developing the client's strategy on the chosen market (15 min.).

The total amount of time – 45 min.

There are some other examples of the integration on the base of projects, such as X-Culture.

Example 2: Computer Science + Psychology.

While studying virtual communication platforms like social networks, Skype, Zoom, Viber, etc., students can interact with their teammates concurrently. If some personal problems of cooperation occur inside GVTs, it might be a chance for the guidance counselor to teach students how to resolve them and how to deal with unfriendly, unmotivated teammates, free-riders using GVTs` actual examples.

Example 3: History + Economics + Geography.

A combination of these closely connected subjects allows teachers to describe, in an integrated manner, political and economic unions, countries, economic areas. Such an overview would make it easier for students to choose a new profitable market for their client company.

In most teams, GVT members use English to communicate with each other. In the case that your school is not situated in an English-speaking country, but the professors of the relevant subjects are strong in English, it is possible to create lessons that are even more effective. At the same time, do not try to incorporate as many subjects as possible into one lesson, as such overload can create issues with attention span and superficial examination.

3.2. TEACHER`S ONGOING SUPPORT AND MOTIVATION.

As a rule, GVT-based projects aim to develop students` life skills. At the same time, this does not mean that teachers should not control and adjust the learning process. Teachers need to understand that participation in a GVT-based project, on average, requires 5–6 hours per week. As we mentioned earlier, before the project begins, teachers have to familiarize their students with its purpose, features, and the benefits that students receive through completing it. During the project, teachers should regularly take part in the webinars to stay informed not only about their students` activity, but also about the whole progress of the team and the newest data from organizers. The availability of this information enables teachers to provide the necessary level of support for participants.

Based on our personal experience of participation in the GVT-based project, we can propose a general structure of teachers` activities and time, as illustrated in table 2. It is noteworthy that this structure may vary depending on the specifications of a particular project, but in any case, teachers should carry out ongoing actions which allow them to monitor, evaluate, and support (adjust) participants` activity. Ongoing control enables not only the regulation of students' performance but also the detection dynamics of the psychosocial atmosphere inside the GVT.

Nature of the action		Kind of recommended activity	Time per week
Ongoing control	Ongoing monitoring	Webinars, other types of communication with project administrators and members of GVTs.	1–2 hours
	Ongoing qualitative assessment	Reviewing of interim results, preparation of recommendations for students.	3–4 hours
	Ongoing support (adjusting)	Integrated lesson: preparing and conducting.	0,5 hour
The total amount of advisable weekly activities:			4,5–6,5 hours
Ongoing support		Optional activities	
		1 hour	
		0,5 hour	
The total amount of weekly activities:			6–8 hours

It is also useful to orient students in terms of the average weekly time that is needed to participate in a GVT-based project. Research shows that most high school students around the world (about 55%) are ready to invest 3–4 hours per week in such projects. Not more than 30% of students are intended to invest more time, and 15% of students want to limit themselves to 1–2 hours per week (Zwerg-Villegas, 2016, p. 137). However, as mentioned above, this statistic is related to university students, and in the case of secondary school students, it is advisable to reduce the average weekly workload to 2–3 hours.

One of the most important aims of schooling is to teach students self-management and time management, and a GVT-based project can be very helpful in this regard. During the project, young participants have to demonstrate the ability to balance their ongoing studies and extracurricular activity in GVTs. Teachers, for their part, should take into account students' schedules and organize the teaching process appropriately. This does not mean that educators must necessarily avoid mentioning the GVT-based project during their lessons or even decrease the academic workload for GVT participants to help them to find time for resolving project tasks, as this may not necessarily improve results because there is no guarantee that students will use the additional time for this purpose. A much more effective decision is to integrate the curriculum and tasks of the project by using integrated lessons, which would save a lot of time for both teachers and students.

If the average weekly workload in a GVT-based project is 3 hours, teachers might design for the following time structure for participation in the project:

1 hour – weekly integrated lesson.

1 hour – weekly webinars with other GVT members and administration of the project.

1 hour – self-study to resolve project tasks.

Using this structure of time, teachers can control at least 2/3 of students' activity (integrated lessons and webinars), but at the same time, the last hour of independent study requires the participants of the project to develop their self-management skills. Of course, depending on project specification, this time structure may vary, but we recommend teachers to include some form of external control to monitor and adjust the progress of GVTs.

Our experience and research show that usually, participants demonstrate a high level of motivation at the start of the project. However, motivation can decrease after the beginning and closer to the end of the project. This can partly be due to underestimation of the complexities that every student faces during the project (Zwerg-Villegas, 2016). These difficulties are described in subparagraph 2. Another factor is the energy level of the participants. We have to admit that the stress level of pre-college students can grow after the project begins, not only because of their lack of experience in social communication but, as a rule, relatively weak initial abilities in planning, researching, coordinating, and independent studying. Such stress may provoke huge demotivation that is fraught with loss of willingness to participate in the project.

Based on our experience, we can propose the next main ways to motivate project participants:

1. A clear explanation of the main project benefits, for example, preferential terms of admission to universities or advantages in finding employment.
2. The positioning of the project as a reward and an opportunity for the top or the most promising students of the class.
3. Consideration of project results in the schooling process. Teachers can take into account these results, converting them into the national grade scale (see table 3).
4. Public recognition of participants who completed the project successfully through a solemn awards ceremony.
5. Events for the project participants, including conferences and seminars with guests whose specialty corresponds with the project specifications.

4. The curtains came down! Evaluation of students' results. Encouragement.

The post-project evaluation process is an important moment and requires a lot of prior preparation. The specifics of the process are largely dependent on the participation options in a GVT-based project (see subparagraph 2). If a teacher possesses a high level of curriculum freedom and involves the whole class for participation in a GVT-based project, evaluation becomes an easier task, because all the assessment criteria is the same for each student. It is much more difficult if only some students in the class take part in a GVT-based project. Below, we share our experience of harmonizing the assessment process for the project participants and the students who do not participate.

First of all, to synchronize the evaluation systems, a prior coordination of tasks is necessary. If teachers use a GVT-based project as mandatory practical training for some of their students, they need to develop a similar workshop for the rest of the class. The main characteristics of the workshop tasks have to correspond to the basic features of the GVT-based project. In this case, teachers can guarantee that conditions and evaluation criteria will be equitable for all their students. We stress the importance of equal conditions for all students to prevent potential accusations in teachers' engagement. The students who do not participate in the project should have the opportunity to show their potential capacity and talent, as well as to prove their teacher that they deserve to take part in the GVT-based project next semester. Curriculum workshops might be a good starting point for future participation in a GVT-based project.

This means that such a mandatory workshop for non-participating students should include:

1. A creative component. One of the main goals of the GVT-based project is to develop students' creativity and lateral thinking. Therefore, the workshops must include such skills.
2. Collaborative component, allocating roles, and responsibilities. The workshop should provide collective group work of 3–6 students (the average size of a GVT) to teach them to work in a team and coordinate activities effectively.
3. Providing mandatory time frames.

Based on the author's practical experience, we recommend the following example, which illustrates how harmonization between the school curriculum and the GVT-based project might be achieved.

Points of harmonization	GVT-based project	Curriculum workshop
Objects of harmonization	"X-Culture Kids"	Subject: "Economics" for eleventh-graders
Goal	Development of skills in teamwork, virtual communication, division of responsibilities, time management.	
Final result	Drafting a team report for a real enterprise in the educational sphere.	Preparing a draft business plan for a hypothetical innovative company in any segment of the market.
Task specification	Searching a new national market for a private school, designing educational toys, developing elements of the client's marketing strategy.	Description of a business idea for an innovative product/service. Description of the potential market. Developing frameworks of HR, marketing, and financial policies.

Kind of interaction between team members	Online (via e-mail, Skype, Zoom, Facebook, Viber, Trello, etc).	Online/offline
Form of final results presentation	Online, using PowerPoint or similar software.	Offline in class, using MC PowerPoint and multi-board.
Subjects of assessment	1. Client's: «Finnish School International», «Innospark». 2. Organizers: the X-Culture. 3. Instructors, teachers.	1. Teachers. 2. Invited experts: local entrepreneurs.
Team size	4–6 members	3–4 members
Evaluation scale	a 7-point scale:	a 12-point national grading scale.

1–3	looks weak	1–4
4–5	looks acceptable	5–9
6–7	looks convincing, viable	10–12

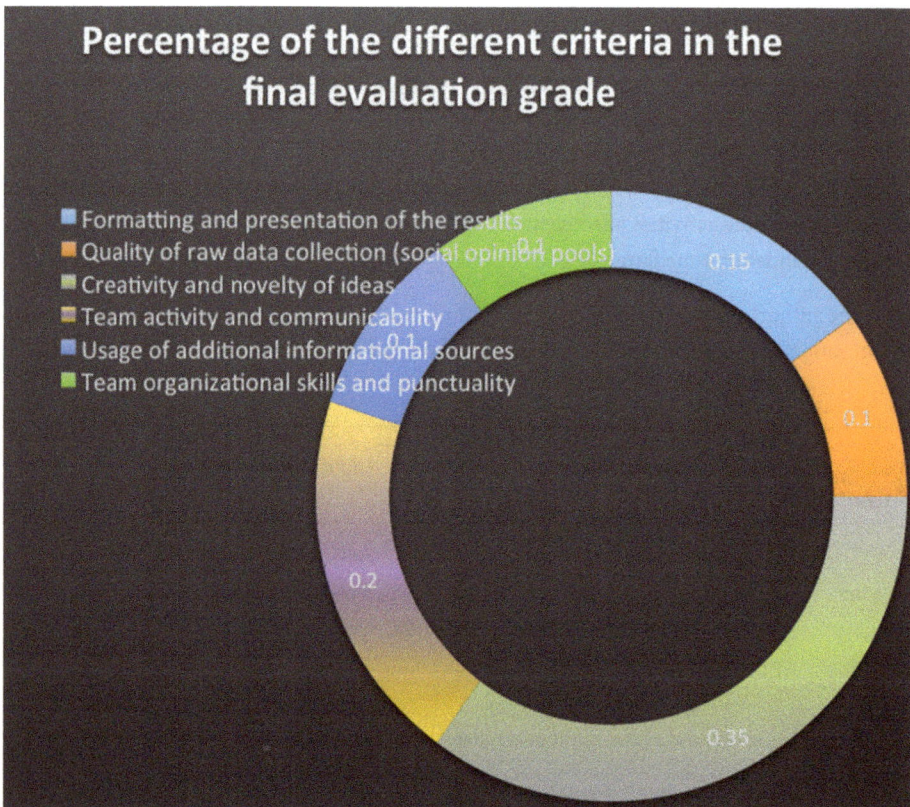

Fig. 23.2 Unified criteria for GVT-based projects/curriculum workshops assessment

Source: Prepared by the author on the basis of the X-Culture project.

After task harmonization, it is possible to highlight shared evaluation criteria. The unified assessment criteria for a GVT-based project and curriculum workshops may look like Figure 3.

Note that based on the modern schooling paradigm and specific aims of GVT projects and workshops, we propose putting students` innovativeness and lateral thinking first. The development of cooperation skills, which leads to team synergy, is one of the most important criteria as well.

Modern pedagogy insists that students must play a role in the evaluation process from the beginning (Drake, 2018). It means that the teachers and administration of the GVT-based project should be ready to correct assessment criteria before the start of the process. The implementation of students` wishes relating to the evaluation process and into post-project assessment may help to raise the motivation of the participants and increase its urgency.

Let us now turn to the assessment of the GVT`s results, specifically. The evaluation system in the GVT-based project should be flexible. This takes into account the duality of the assessment process: on the one hand, teachers have to evaluate the final work (report) of the whole international team, and on the other hand, it is preferable to take into account the individual results of each participant. As a rule, toward the end of the project, teachers have to evaluate reports from the teams in which their students participate. Besides, if teachers are able to support organizers, they can evaluate reports of other teams as well. That means that an instructor faces the challenge of being objective, otherwise, the final assessments would be completed unfairly. Teachers can also use project evaluations in the school teaching process, formatting points into the national grade system.

Outcomes

In summary, we wish to emphasize the following points:

1. A GVT-based project can provide major benefits for students, teachers, and schools. The main advantages relate to the enhancement of international cooperation and the increase of practical learning.
2. The options of project integration into schooling programs exist even in countries with a set curriculum.
3. A GVT-based project can be a great opportunity to shine, not only for A-students but for other kinds of students as well. Appropriate motivating tools must be used (special project positioning, public recognition, privileged events, and harmonization with the schooling process).
4. The integrated lessons give teachers an excellent opportunity to coordinate students` activities. At the same time, it is necessary to avoid subject overload during such classes.
5. A GVT-based project may require teachers to invest approximately 6–8 hours of mandatory and optional activities per week. Meanwhile, the recommended workload for school students should be no more than 3 hours per week.
6. It is possible to coordinate the teaching and assessment process, even if only some of the class students participate in the GVT-based project. Curriculum workshops, which give similar knowledge and train the same skills, may be a good starting point for future project participants.

Please take the recommendations given in this chapter into account, but always remain creative and be ready to act outside the box. In the end, we would like to wish our readers an enjoyable time while participating in a GVT-based project, and we recommend being open-minded and easygoing. Remember that only a joyful activity can be truly productive!

References

1. Drake, S., Reid, J. (2018). Integrated Curriculum as an Effective Way to Teach 21st Century Capabilities. Asia Pacific Journal of Educational Research, 1(1): 31–50.

2. Nordmann, J-D., Ponci, J-D., Fernandez, A. (2009). Report 2008/2009 on Freedom of Education in the World. Volume 1. Presentation of work and Synthesis of Results. Oidel. Retrieved from: http://www.oidel.org/doc/Rapport_08_09_libertes/english.pdf

3. OIDEL. (2018). Freedom of Education Index Correlations with Selected Indicators. Retrieved from: http://www.oidel.org/wp-content/uploads/2018/07/Version-anglaise_cute_3.pdf

4. Zwerg-Villegas, A., Martínez-Díaz, J. (2016). Experiential Learning with Global Virtual Teams: Developing Intercultural and Virtual Competencies. Magis, Revista Internacional de Investigación en Educación, 9(18): 129–146.

CHAPTER 24

Preparing and Guiding Students Through the Experience of Global Virtual Teams

SHERRY ANDRE, FLORIDA INTERNATIONAL UNIVERSITY

A ny instructor who has used some form of group work in a traditional or online classroom is certain to have experienced some challenges. Common issues that often emerge include limited or no contribution by some members, personality challenges, and schedule conflicts. Now, add in the use of technology and no face-to-face component. Combine this with varying time zones, a variety of cultural beliefs and behaviors, and differing technical and linguistic skills, and you are presented with a global virtual team (GVT). Is this a recipe for failure?

Fortunately, no. As more and more programs and courses expand to an online platform, GVTs are a reality that all faculty members will likely face and facilitate at some point. Even traditional face-to-face classrooms or hybrid courses may opt to participate in GVTs in an effort to broaden global awareness. More importantly, GVTs can be fun, very educational, and a great experience for students in most disciplines.

Utilizing select strategies to prepare students, support students, and guide students towards an enjoyable experience will be a critical factor for faculty who aim for successful outcomes. While each GVT will be unique, and faculty may have students participating on GVTs for various reasons, there are some tactics and techniques that may lead to more positive results for both the student and the instructor.

The remainder of this chapter will explore different methods and exercises that enhance the use of GVTs. More specifically, the content will include a review of how to prepare students for GVTs, how to support students throughout the process, and how to encourage growth and to learn through the experience.

Prepare students for the experience: Help them understand the "why."

As with most new activities, people are often naturally unsure and may have some anxiety about what to expect. Being able to openly discuss concerns and address obstacles students are likely to face will help to minimize the fears that some anticipate. For example, the instructor can benefit by introducing the project as a new opportunity that will provide additional growth beyond the educational component of the project. GVTs offer students a chance to learn about other countries, experience other cultures, and reflect on their own beliefs and biases. They are great preparation for the realities of global business and international communications. By encouraging students to view the GVT as more than just another group project, faculty have the opportunity to open the students' eyes to new learning outcomes they may not have considered previously.

It is beneficial to give students a chance to express their concerns about the upcoming experience prior to placing them on global teams. Prompting questions can be beneficial, such as: what problems do you expect to face? Or, do you expect this to be more or less challenging than a face-to-face group, and why? It is important not to minimize their concerns or pretend they won't exist. Acknowledge the realities of the challenges they will likely face, including those they may not have thought about.

Consequently, by highlighting the negatives first and minimally adding in the positives, such as the ability to connect with people from around the world or learn about new cultures, you set them up to have their expectations exceeded. Sometimes, it is better to under-promise and over-deliver than do the opposite. Let them know up front they will be challenged. They will likely experience issues and obstacles not necessarily found within traditional group work; however, if they remain open to learning from the experiences, they are more apt to grow individually and professionally. Additionally, they have the opportunity to set themselves apart with a competitive advantage over other graduates who have not participated on a GVT.

At the same time, it is important to also address traditional group dynamics, and the objections students often bring forth. Showing empathy and an understanding that not all group members will likely contribute equally and that identifying common schedules and work ethics will not always be easy demonstrates your awareness as a facilitator that such scenarios are real. If possible, share a real example from your own experience working within a professional group. Address the fact that as individuals, each person has the ability to use the experience as a learning opportunity, and the more effort they are willing to contribute, the more they are likely to take away.

Some additional pre-group exercises include:

Research countries in advance

Prior to being assigned to GVTs, create a list of potential countries that may be perceived negatively or very differently than the one where you are teaching. If known in advance, you can also use countries that will make up the GVTs your students will be on. Provide an individual assignment or in-class group work for the students to do some research about the countries.

To begin with, this provides an opportunity to introduce them to resources of value, such as cultural norms, governmental regulations, geographical locations, and other items beneficial for the team project and/or to support the global experience. Some librarians will support this with a LibGuide, or you can secure a list of valuable websites to utilize.

Next, introduce questions that will support the project and interaction with others from around the world. If time permits, you may elect to have the students first write out their perceived answers prior to having them do the research. Some questions may include:

- Identify two (2) cultural norms that are the same and two (2) that are different from your country.
- Identify three (3) cultural norms for males and females in said country.
- What are the top three (3) industries for revenue in said country?
- Can you find a business failure that occurred within that country based on a lack of understanding, translation, or perceived expectation? What happened, and how might it have been prevented?
- Compare the country's standard of living to your country.

- What are the top social media or smartphone applications used in said country?
- Geographically, where is said country located?
- What is the time difference between your country and the assigned country?
- What type of government is in place in said country?
- What type of leadership or management style is most popular in said country?
- List two (2) items you identified that surprised you the most about the said country?

After students complete prompting pre-group questions individually or as a team, it is helpful to hold a class discussion or post them to an open platform if administered in an online class. With this format, students have the opportunity to learn about multiple countries, rather than only the one they were responsible for researching.

Being able to discuss perceptions and newly acquired information is beneficial for students and helps to ease concerns. It is a great opportunity for the instructor to clarify false perceptions and acknowledge how stereotypes are formed. It often instills a sense of excitement prior to being introduced to others from different countries as well.

Bring in former students

Student peers are a great way to increase commitment and reduce anxieties about a GVT. Oftentimes, going through the experiences seems far more challenging and frustrating than it really is. At the conclusion, students will often feel a sense of accomplishment and joy at having completed the exercise. Many cherish the new connections they have made and/or feel pride in having finished the project. Allowing them to share their experiences openly and discussing the challenges, successes, and approaches taken will often be inspiring for new students. There tends to be a different level of acceptance when the students hear about the experience from others who have previously been in their position, rather than only from the instructor.

Reflect on differing personalities experienced on traditional teams

Not all students have taken the time to understand their own personality, much less that of others. Prior to being placed on a GVT, have students identify various personalities they have experienced in traditional group work. This is a good exercise to have them complete as a group in class; however, it can also be done individually. See if they can identify 5-7 different personality types. For each type, you may want to ask them the following:

- How did each personality help the team?
- How did each personality hinder the team's performance?
- Which personalities have tended to be most beneficial for a successful team experience? Why?
- What personalities have you demonstrated on a team? Did it help or hinder the team's performance?
- If you could do one (1) thing differently when participating as a team member, what would it be? Why?
- Why is it important to have a variety of personalities on a team?

Supplementing this with a lecture or discussion on team member behaviors provides more clarity and offers an opportunity to highlight personality differences. Identifying strengths and contributions varying roles provide helps students to better understand why it is beneficial for teams to consist of a variety of people.

Provide opportunities to discuss challenges

GVTs may be used for a variety of reasons, and the beneficial outcomes and purposes for administering them and/or implementing them into a course are varied. Even so, regardless of the preparation, GVTs are apt to generate challenges for students. Much of this is part of the learning process and supports many of the expected outcomes.

While faculty may be able to identify the learning taking place throughout the process, students are more apt to recognize the nuances of the experience. Providing an outlet or opportunity to share what is being experienced can be extremely beneficial. Simply learning they are not alone and have not been the only student in the class that has been placed on a difficult team can provide a sense of relief. Sharing common concerns and issues with their peers provides an outlet and opportunity to discuss solutions. A variety of options can be implemented to facilitate the process.

For an online course or a face-to-face setting, journals can be effective. Journaling allows the student to put their thoughts, feelings, and experience into words. It is important to allow this to be free-form and allow their emotions to flow naturally without restrictions. Simply writing out what is causing the frustrations or taking the time to reflect upon the experience can put the situation into a more realistic perspective. Journals help the instructor to better understand the challenges students are struggling with and offer an opportunity for discussion and support.

A slightly more formal opportunity for reflection is through discussion boards. Although often used in online or hybrid classes, discussion boards may also be used to support a face-to-face class. Here, students have an opportunity to share their concerns, successes, and questions through an open dialogue with their peers and professor. Prompting questions are suggested to initiate conversations. For example, one may offer any of the following:

- What has been the most challenging aspect of participating in a GVT? Why? Provide supporting examples.
- What has been the most surprising aspect of participating on a global virtual team? In other words, what had you expected/not expected that turned out to be very different? Provide your initial expectation versus the reality of what has taken place. Explain why you believe it was different than expected.
- What have you learned thus far as a result of participation in your GVT? This may support educational learning, personal growth, or another aspect of newly acquired knowledge. Explain and support with examples.
- To what extent have you exercised leadership skills on your GVT? Explain and provide at least one example.
- Explain how different cultures and personalities have impacted your GVT. Be sure to include supporting examples.
- If you were responsible for leading a GVT during your career, what would be the top three (3) things you would do to prepare your staff for the experience? Why?

- Have you experienced any disagreements between your team members? If so, share one (1) and explain how your team resolved/handled the situation. If not, what do you think has been the reason your team is working well together? Explain.

When leading a face-to-face course that has implemented GVTs, in-class discussions can be very effective. Place your students into groups within the classroom and provide them with some prompting questions (similar to those offered above for the discussion board posts). Allow the students ample time to discuss each among the group. It may be beneficial to share questions one at a time with everyone in the room. This will require them to focus on a specific question without attempting to jump through the list quickly.

As the students talk amongst themselves, it is likely they will find common challenges and experiences. This tends to help relieve the idea that they are the only ones on a "bad" team. It also provides an outlet to vent about some obstacles they are facing and engage with others about methods used to improve the experience. While they may be experiencing troubles among group members, it is often quite likely that technology, cultural differences, time zones, or other impeding factors may be causing alarm. Being able to discuss and share these with their peers will often lead to laughter and opportunities to identify new ways to approach issues they are facing.

After allowing groups in the class to discuss each question, instructors may opt to open up the dialogue to the entire class, depending on the number of students enrolled. Another option is to have the groups write out their answers or present the top one or two things the group would like to share with the class. Reminding students that our greatest growth opportunities often arise from our biggest challenges is another way to encourage them to continue on with a positive attitude.

Opportunities to express frustrations and share common challenges may not eliminate issues GVTs are experiencing; however, this process often provides the students in the class with a sense of comfort and provides common bonds with their peers. It also allows students and the instructor to discuss some of the cultural differences observed, challenged, or identified. There will often be enjoyable experiences shared, and excitement as students begin to offer additional information about their teammates as well.

Encourage students to reflect and grow as individuals

GVTs offers an opportunity for students to challenge their own personal biases. Using reflective exercises, ask students to write out their beliefs about different cultures and how the experience interacting with them has supported or changed their previously held perceptions.

Journaling is a good way of helping students acknowledge their preconceived views and gain an understanding of how they may have changed or been impacted by the GVT experience. Journals can be kept electronically or in a notebook. Provide a prompting question or two each week, or have the students write out their experience openly on a weekly basis. Encourage honest thoughts to be shared and acknowledge the privacy placed upon them. Instructors can elect to add their notes as feedback and/or offer one-on-one meetings to discuss further. A final reflection can be used to identify how previously perceived expectations were challenged or confirmed. Furthermore, after the GVT concludes, seek to find out if the students have gained more empathy, curiosity, understanding, or respect for those who may be different from themselves.

Reflection exercises provide students a chance to better understand what they have experienced and what they have learned. They allow for assumptions to be examined and help to solidify what took place. Many times, they will not recognize how much they have grown or learned until they have gone through the entire process and completed the project.

Enhance leadership development

Students on GVTs will often have the opportunity to take on leadership roles, whether assigned or accepted. Most students studying at the university level have some aspiration to hold management or leadership positions in the future. Remind students that GVTs provide a great avenue to begin practicing real-life skills needed to move a team forward.

Discussions regarding leadership and team dynamics can take place prior to, during, or after the GVT experience. Using in-class dialogue or online discussion board posts, instructors can develop some prompting questions to help students identify best leadership practices. Some suggested questions may include:

- How does communication impact a team's success? What are some best practices for communication?
- How can leaders on a team positively impact the outcome? What roles do they take on, and how do they help facilitate the project forward?
- If you have participated on a team previously, or based on your GVT experience, what are some things you would do differently to make the experience more successful?
- How do leaders create cohesion within a team? Is it important? Why?
- What can you take away from the experience that will make you a better leader? Explain.
- If leadership on a team is lacking, what is the impact?

During the project, encourage students to practice their leadership skills within their GVT. You may choose to have them identify how they approach non-participating team members or how they motivate others to contribute meaningful work by the deadlines set. If they have elected to do or say nothing, ask them why. Sometimes students need help connecting the opportunity to practice real-life tasks within their GVT to those they will be assigned in their careers. Faculty can help bridge this gap.

Another option is to set up a discussion board for students to share their team's successes and positive experiences. Have them identify leadership, communication, or cohesion efforts that are of value. It is often easy for students to focus on what is not working; however, when they are required to identify positive outcomes that have taken place, they can begin to appreciate the value of the experience. This offers a method of reflecting on good leadership skills and provides ideas and best practices that can be used in future roles.

While students may or may not embrace the experience of a GVT, the instructor can contribute to the approach students take. Acknowledging the challenges ahead while also preparing them for the unique experience is beneficial. Offering opportunities to reflect and discuss the experience throughout the process provides an outlet to express challenges and identify best practices. When a faculty member is able to empathize with the students and help them recognize the value being gained, the experience becomes a win-win. Not only are GVTs not going away, but they also provide a platform to expand students' knowledge and acceptance of others. When facilitated properly, most students will conclude the process feeling grateful to have had the opportunity.

CHAPTER 25

Online Collaboration and Communication Tools

RAFAEL TAMASHIRO, X-CULTURE, INC.

LYAONNE MASPEO, X-CULTURE, INC.

Tool	Best for and how to use it
Google Translate	*Best for:* Translating text *How it works:* Just paste the text, select the language you want it translated into. Done. You can also use it for conversations: https://youtu.be/K5nFWAgSlWI
Doodle	*Best for:* Finding the best time for a group meeting, but can also be used for voting on the best option. *How it works:* https://youtu.be/Mjn4LG4pmeE *Bonus:* Automatically adjusts time zones
MS Word "Track Changes"	*Best for:* If multiple people are editing the same MS Word file and you want to see who changed/added what. *How to use it:* https://youtu.be/5_knruAysnA
Skype	*Best for:* Instant messaging, audio and voice conversation, group discussions, document sharing. *How to use it:* https://youtu.be/S38e-t6rhKA *Bonus:* Always on. When a team member adds a comment, you get an instant message on your computer/smartphone.
Zoom	*Best for:* Pre-scheduled video meetings. *How to use it:* https://youtu.be/fMUxzrgZvZQ X-Culture version: https://youtu.be/ncpzQ1Y5QWk *Bonus:* Easy to schedule a meeting and add it to the calendar.
Google Docs	*Best for:* Multiple people writing the same document. *What it is:* https://youtu.be/eRqUE6IHTEA *How to use it:* https://youtu.be/OBh8bMC7XEU *X-Culture version:* https://youtu.be/YOfLwhp7FWo
Dropbox	*Best for:* Multiple people writing the same document, sharing large documents. *What is it:* https://youtu.be/ps4X1KFZ8Jo *How to use it:* https://youtu.be/zjSFC6pPkyk *Bonus:* Works with real Microsoft Office files and any other formats of files (Google Docs aren't "real" MS Office files).

Facebook Groups	*Best for:* Discussing ideas, sharing comments, keeping a record of discussions, share files
	How to use it: https://youtu.be/8KO3tK8YBJc
	Bonus: Facebook Messenger also allows you to make audio/video calls to your team members.
Viber	*Best for:* Group discussion, group calls, sharing files.
	What it is: https://youtu.be/-MQw1HtawKo
	How to use Viber Groups: https://youtu.be/pw2aPtkekGk?t=10s
WhatsApp	*Best for:* Group discussion, group calls, sharing files.
	What it is and how to use it: https://youtu.be/mhnFh1MGx4w
Google Hangout	*Best for:* Instant messaging, audio and voice conversation, group discussions, document sharing.
	How to use it: https://youtu.be/Kkgdc92KMnQ
	Bonus: Up to 10 people can participate in a video call (in Skype or Facebook usually only two, unless you have a professional account).
Slack	*Best for:* For coordination and communication in teams.
	What it is: https://youtu.be/9RJZMSsH7-g
	How to use it: https://youtu.be/s69uoRkmoWE
	Warning: A free version is available and should be enough for X-Culture teams, but a small subscription fee is required for advanced features.
Trello	*Best for:* For coordination and communication, distributing work, and tracking everyone's performance in teams.
	What it is: https://youtu.be/FMETUJ7u3U4
	How to use it: https://youtu.be/xky48zyL9iA
	Warning: A free version is available and should be enough for X-Culture teams, but a small subscription fee is required for advanced features.

Online Collaboration Tools

Email is still essential and is probably our most reliable form of online communication. However, email is often not enough. Other tools are better if the team wants to:

- Have a real-time discussion (instant text-only messaging)
- Have a voice conversation (audio)
- Have a video conversation (audio and video)
- Find a time for a meeting that fits everyone's schedule
- Co-edit a document (multiple people write the same document)
- Make a collective decision or vote on the preferred option
- Comment on each other's work and keep track of discussions.

Below is the list of tools that X-Culture teams found to be useful. The most-used tools are shown in blue:

- Schedule meetings
  - Doodle
- Real-time discussion (voice and message)
  - WhatsApp
  - Viber
  - Line
  - Facebook messenger
- Co-edit a document
  - Google Docs
  - Dropbox
  - Track Changes (feature in MS Word)
- Video conference
  - Zoom
  - Skype
  - Microsoft Teams
  - Google Meets
- Coordination and Communication
  - Trello
  - Slack

Doodle

Doodle is an online scheduling tool that can be used quickly and easily to find a date and time to meet with clients, colleagues, friends, or teams. You can download the App or use it in your browser.

When working in Global Virtual Teams, people being in different time zones is a major problem that all teams face, and saving time is key to success. So, it is recommended to learn how to use Doodle.

Video guide: https://www.youtube.com/watch?v=Af9n9cLYXcM

Step 1 - Schedule a meeting

Go to: https://doodle.com

If you are a first-time user, you can already create a Doodle without an account, as you can see in the image above. However, it is recommended that you create an account in "sign up" box, which makes it possible to manage all the Doodles that you have created, and also copy and paste old Doodles to save time.

For these guidelines, we will consider a first-time user.

Step 2 – What's the occasion?

When clicking on "create a Doodle," it will lead to the page above. Add the information about your meeting:

- Enter a title
- Add location: 9 options
- Enter a title.

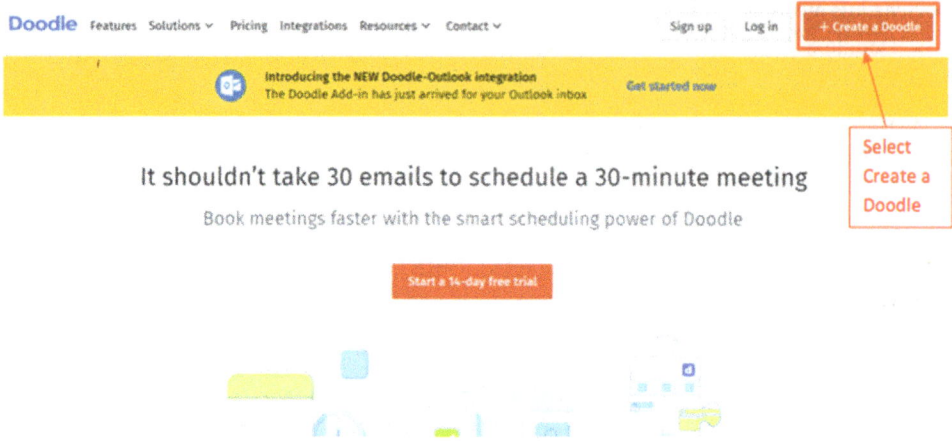

Doodle Features Solutions ˅ Pricing Integrations Resources ˅ Contact ˅   Sign up   Log in   + Create a Doodle

Introducing the NEW Doodle-Outlook integration
The Doodle Add-in has just arrived for your Outlook inbox   Get started now

It shouldn't take 30 emails to schedule a 30-minute meeting
Book meetings faster with the smart scheduling power of Doodle

Start a 14-day free trial

Select Create a Doodle

Doodle 1

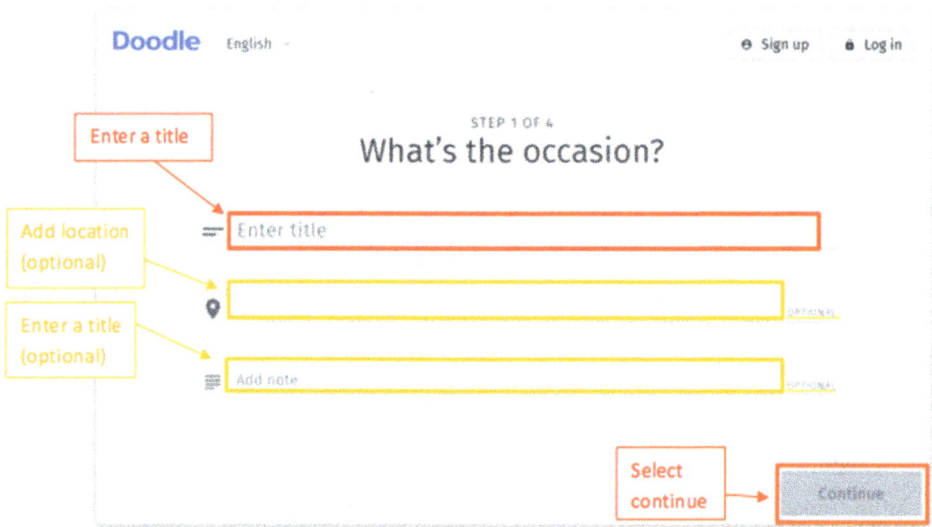

Doodle English

θ Sign up   🔒 Log in

STEP 1 OF 4
What's the occasion?

Enter a title

Enter title

Add location (optional)

OPTIONAL

Enter a title (optional)

Add note   OPTIONAL

Select continue   Continue

Doodle 2

Step 3– Options

On the next page, you will choose which dates and times are available for the meeting. You can choose the whole day or a couple of hours:

- Select your possible dates
- Select your possible times
- Select your time zone
- Click continue.

You can select as many dates and times as you like.

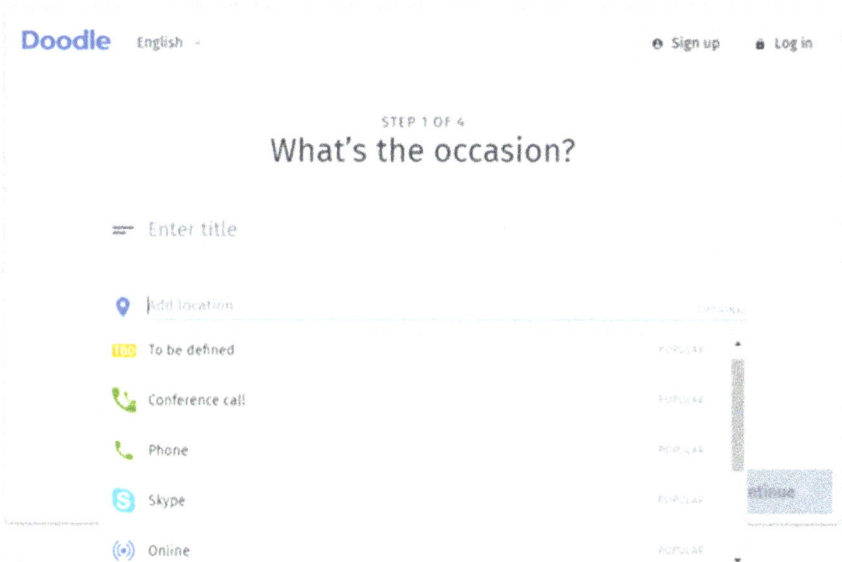

Doodle 3

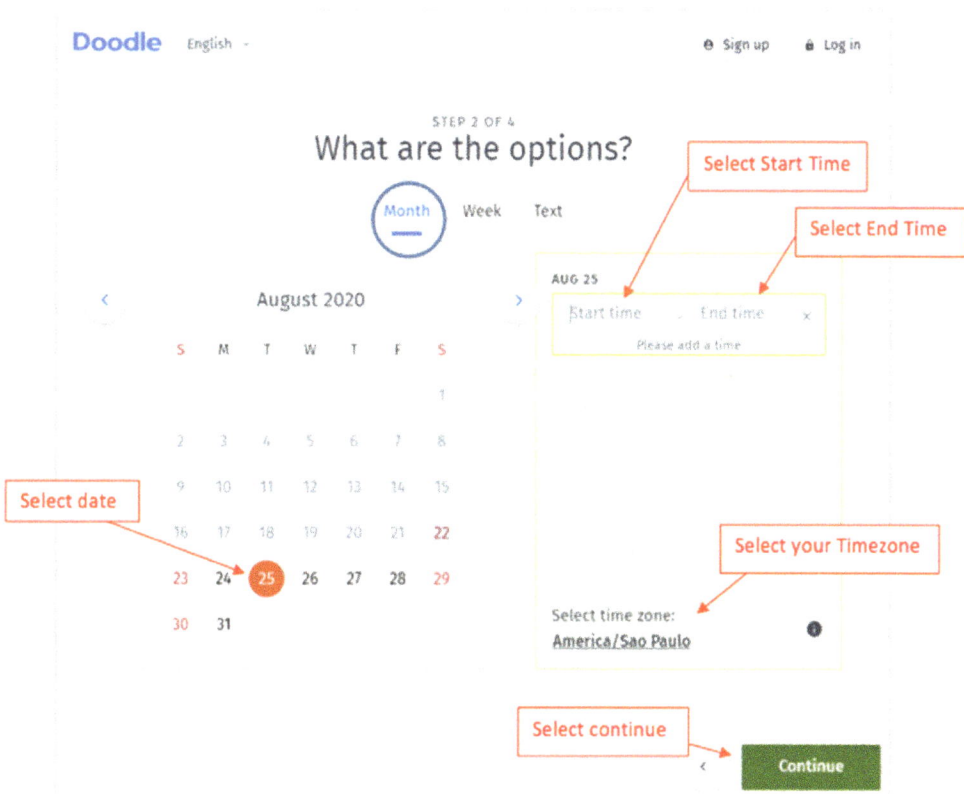

Doodle 4

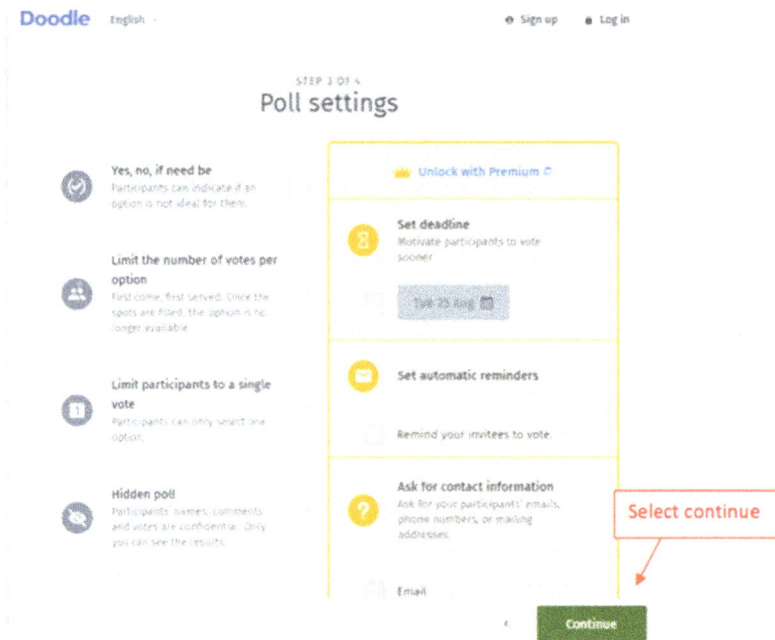

Doodle 5

Step 4 – Poll Settings

Choose your preferences for your poll.

For a typical user, you have four settings options:

- **Yes, no, if need be:**
  - Participants can indicate if an option (date/time) is not ideal for them.
- **Limit the number of votes per option:**
  - This is useful when you have a limited number of dates/times and need to have different meetings with different people. So, once the spots are filled, the option is no longer available.
- **Limit participants to a single vote:**
  - Participants can only select one option.
- **Hidden poll:**
  - Only those who created the poll can see the names, comments, and votes.

When you finish choosing the settings, click on "continue."

Step 5 – Tell the participants who you are

Add your name and your email to let the participants know who sent the poll and ask questions if needed.

Step 6– Invite the participants.

Copy the link and send it by email or WhatsApp.

After sending to all the participants, each participant will need to vote for preferred dates and times.

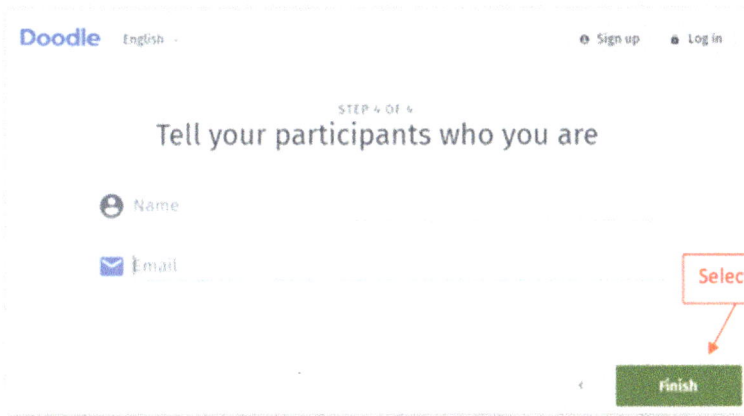

Doodle 6

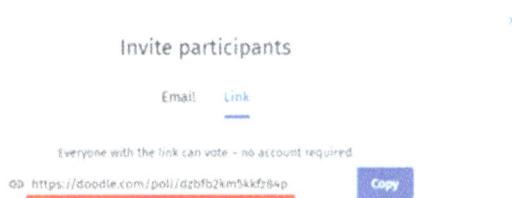

Doodle 7

Step 7–Choose the final date.

When all the participants have voted for their preferred dates and times, you will need to choose the final date:

After analyzing when is the best date and time, choose the final option.

PS: If you log in and save your templates, you can reuse them whenever you want.

Zoom

What is Zoom?

When working in GVTs, you probably won't have the opportunity to talk face to face. So, there are some useful tools such as **Zoom**. Zoom is a video communications app that allows you to set up virtual video and audio conferencing, webinars, live chats, screen-sharing, and other collaborative capabilities.

To use Zoom, please follow the guidelines below or/and watch the following video: https://www.youtube.com/watch?v=ncpzQ1Y5QWk

First, enter on https://zoom.us/

Step 1 – Sign in

If you already have an account, sign in. If you don't, create one, it's free! Using the free account, you can schedule a 40-minutes meeting maximum.

All times displayed in America/Sao Paulo

Check your timezone

Best day and time

Table   Calendar

		Aug 25 TUE 8:30 AM 9:30 AM	Aug 25 TUE 10:15 AM 11:15 AM	Aug 25 TUE 12:30 PM 1:30 PM	Aug 25 TUE 2:00 PM 3:00 PM
4 participants	+	✓2	✓4	✓2	✓2
Participant 1		✓	✓		
Participant 2			✓		
Participant 3			✓	✓	✓
Participant 4		✓	✓	✓	✓

Doodle 8

Select final option

★ Choose final option   ☺ Invite   More ⌄

Select your final option

		Aug 25 TUE 8:30 AM 9:30 AM	Aug 25 TUE 10:15 AM 11:15 AM	Aug 25 TUE 12:30 PM 1:30 PM	Aug 25 TUE 2:00 PM 3:00 PM
		✓2	✓4	✓2	✓2
final options		★	★	★	★
Participant 1		✓	✓		
Participant 2			✓		
Participant 3			✓	✓	✓
Participant 4		✓	✓	✓	✓

idar sync

Select Done

★ 1   Done

Doodle 9

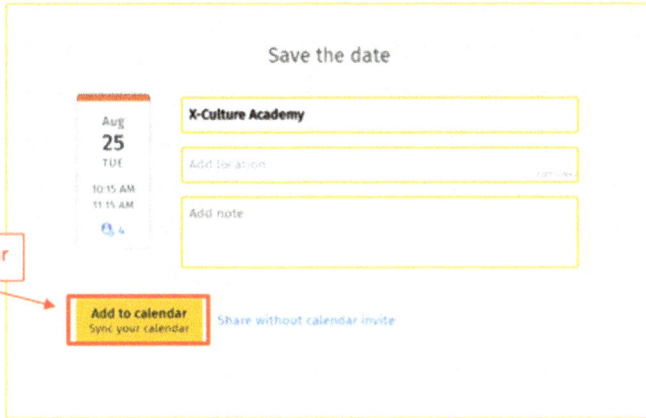

Doodle 10

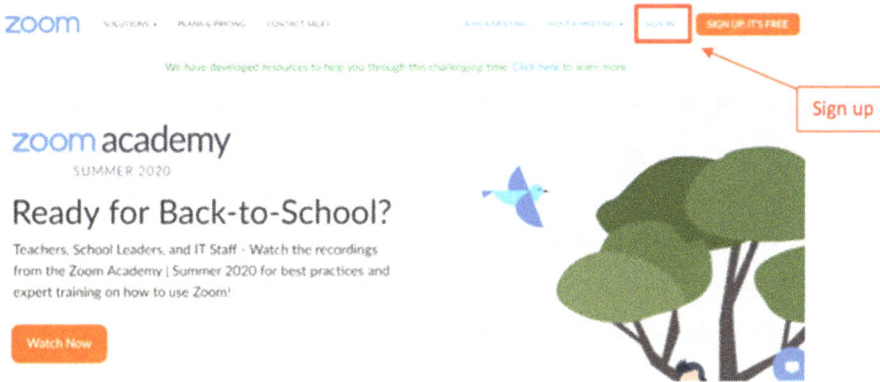

Zoom 1

Step 2 – Schedule a meeting

After signing in, schedule a meeting.

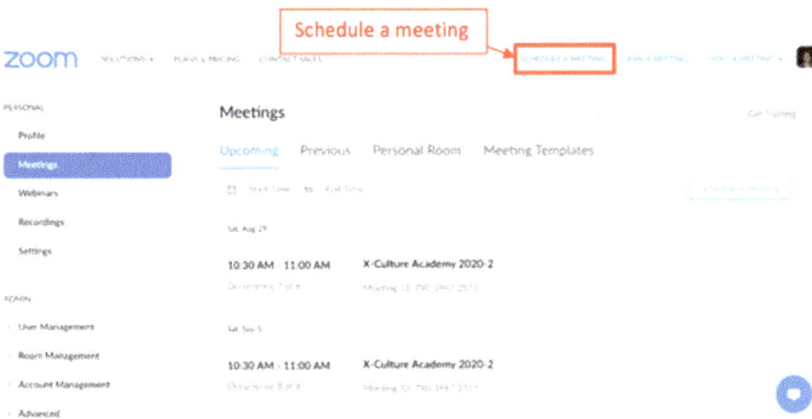

Zoom 2

Step 3 – Setting up the meeting

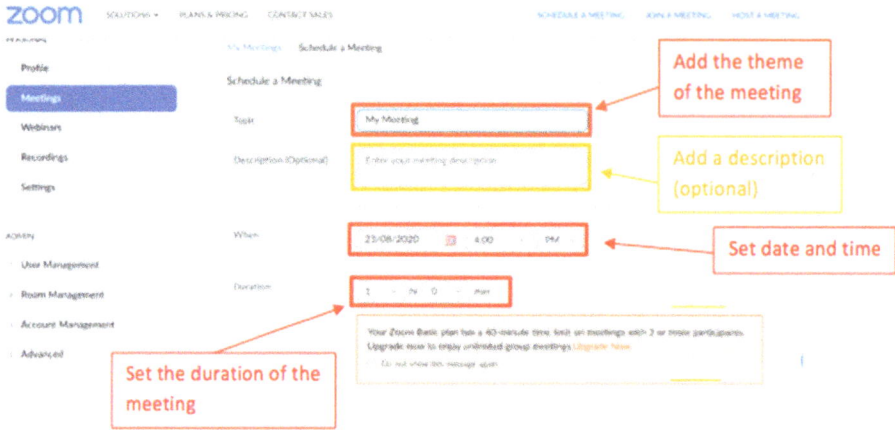

Zoom 3

1. Add a topic
2. Add a description (optional)
3. Set a date and time
4. Set the duration of the meeting
5. Select time zone
6. Save.

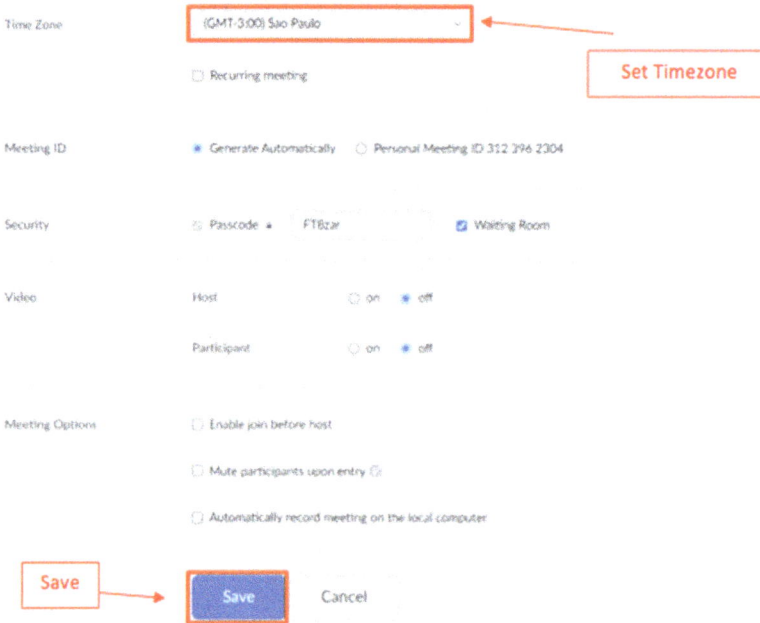

Zoom 4

Step 4 – Starting the meeting

Zoom 5

1. Copy the link
2. Send it to the participants.

Step 5 – Zoom tools

Zoom 6

Google Docs

When working in GVTs, you will need to use online tools to create and work together. So, there are some useful tools such as Google Docs. Google Docs is a very powerful real-time collaboration and document-authoring tool. It is also compatible with Microsoft Office file formats. The application allows users to create and edit files online while collaborating with other users in real-time. Also, if you want, you can share folders, spreadsheets, photos, etc. in Google Drive.

To use Google Docs, please follow the guideline below or watch the following video: https://www.youtube.com/watch?v=YOfLwhp7FWo

First, enter on https://docs.google.com/document/u/0/

Step 1 – New Document

GD 1

Step 2 – Sharing and working together

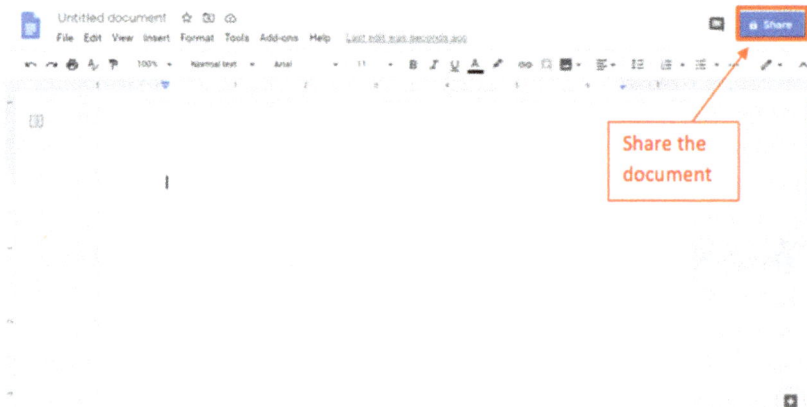

GD 2
- Name your file.

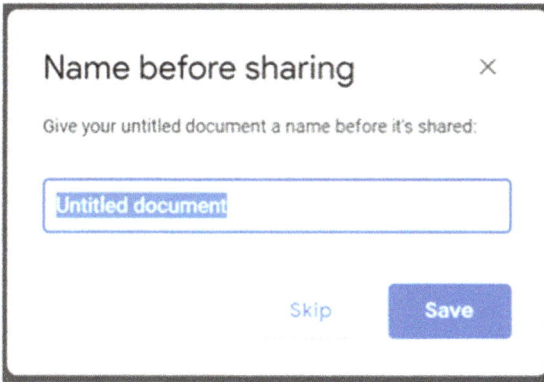

GD 3

- Share with your team workers by adding their emails or by sending the link to them.

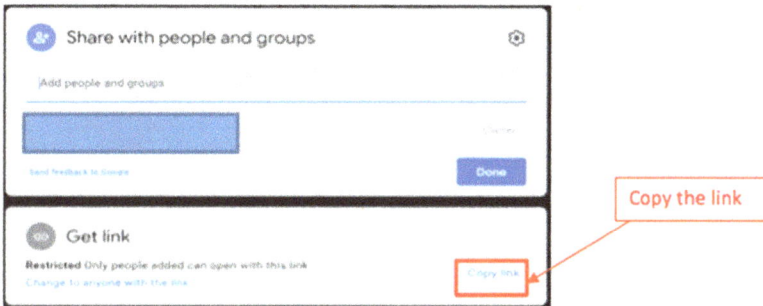

GD 4

Step 3 – Writing a document

Now, you can start writing your shared document.

- Select your font
- Font size
  - Bold
  - Italic
  - Underlined
- Text Color
- Insert link
- Insert image
  - Upload from your computer
  - Search the web
- Align
- Line spacing
- Numbered list

- Bulleted list
- Decrease indent
- Increase indent
- Editing
  - Edit
  - Suggest
  - Viewing

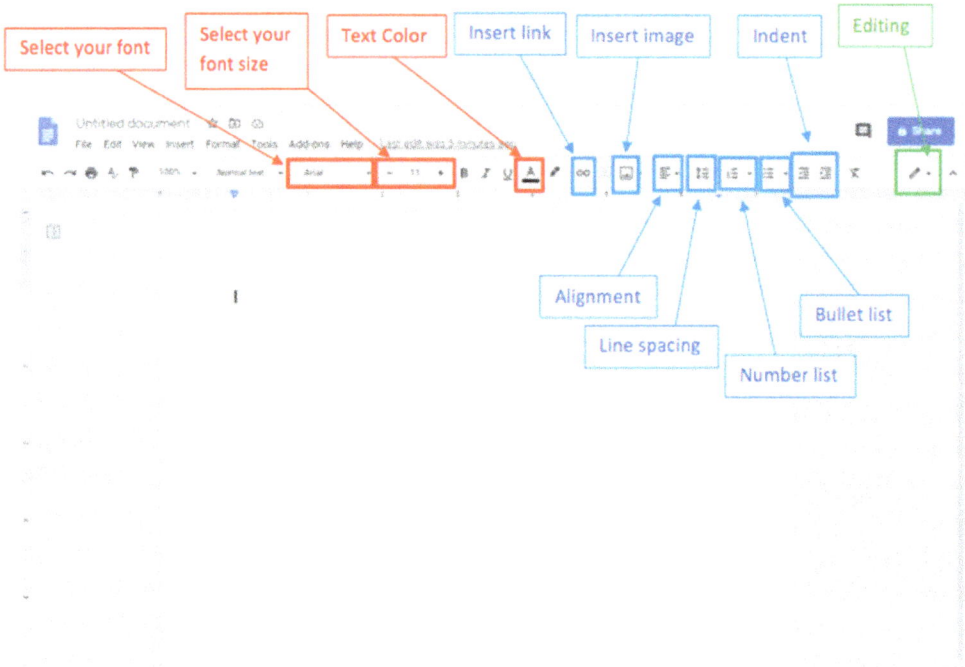

GD 5

Step 4 – Essential features

When you are comfortable with how to write in Google Docs, you can start learning its essential features such as:

- Undo
- Redo
- Spelling and Grammar – a useful tool as many of the teammates are not from English speaker countries

GD 6

File feature:

- Download the file to submit the reports
- Version history: Check who changed something and look for the previous document
- Language: choose the language for the spelling and grammar feature
- Page setup: format your report.

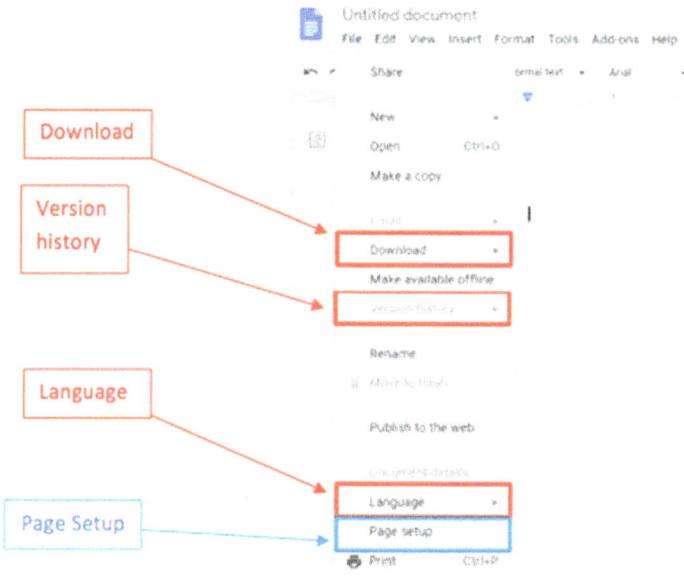

GD 7

Formatting

When clicking on Page Setup (Figure 7), the window below will appear:

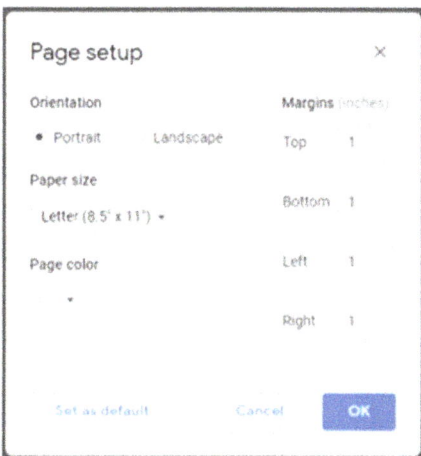

GD 8

The image shows the right Page Setup formatting for X-Culture reports.

Step 5 – Presentation features

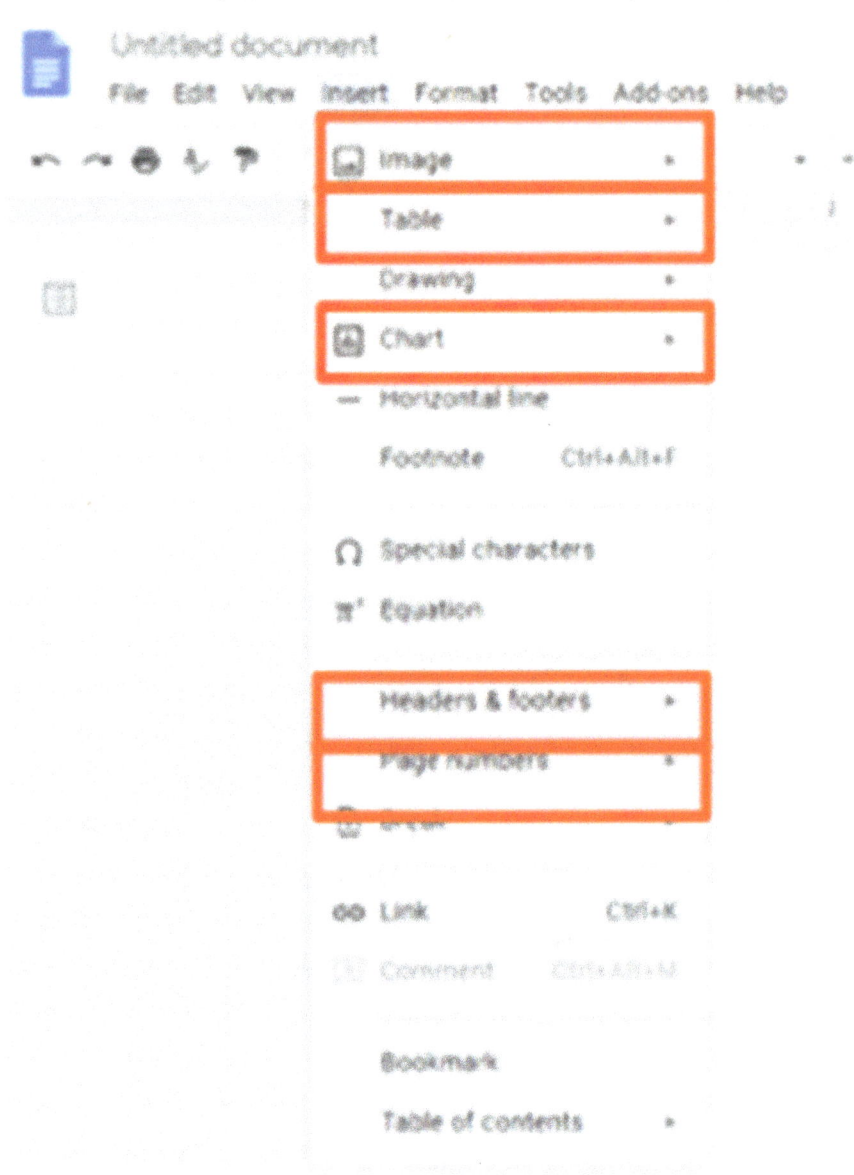

GD 9

Insert feature:

- Image: add images from your computer or the web
- Tables: add all sizes of tables
- Charts:
  - Bar
  - Column
  - Line
  - Pie
- Headers & footers
- Page numbers.

All these features are used to improve the report's presentation and allow you to visualize how it will appear.

Step 6 – Collab features

- Add comments
  - Highlight the word or phrase you want to comment about
  - Click on "Add Comment": Write your comment regarding the highlighted part.

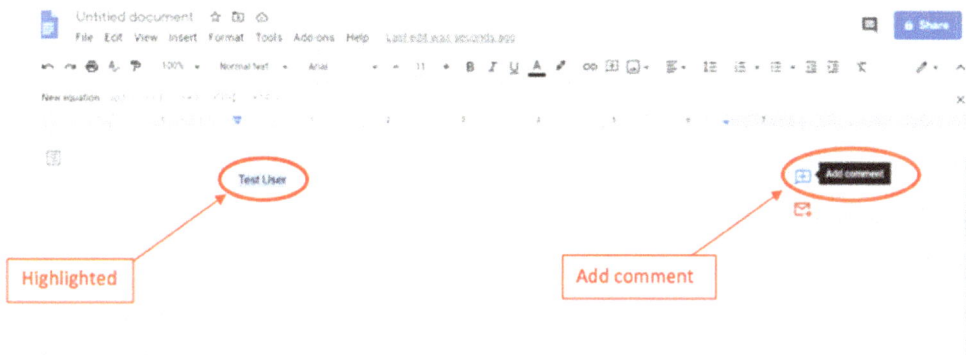

GD 10

When working as a team, it's better to comment on something you disagree with or don't understand than just change it, as people may be offended or feel unmotivated.

Dropbox

When working in GVTs, you will need to use online tools to create and work together. Dropbox is one powerful tool for this purpose. Dropbox is a file hosting service that offers cloud storage, file synchronization, personal cloud, and client software. It is also compatible with Microsoft Office and Google Docs file formats. The application allows users to create and edit files online while collaborating with other users in real-time. Also, if you want, you can share folders, spreadsheets, photos, and etc.

To use Dropbox, please follow the guideline below:

First, navigate to the following link for the basic plan: https://www.dropbox.com/basic

Step 1 – Sign in

If you already have an account, sign in. If you don't, create one, the basic plan is free! Using the free account, you get 2GB of storage.

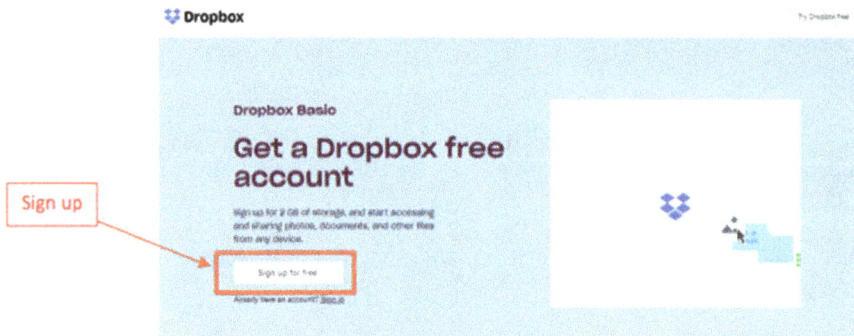

DB 1

Step 2 – Download Dropbox

If you want, you can download the program to your computer, which allows you to share and access information more quickly by synchronizing it with your computer. But if you don't want to, you can continue accessing Dropbox only through your browser.

DB 2

Step 3 – Starting a document

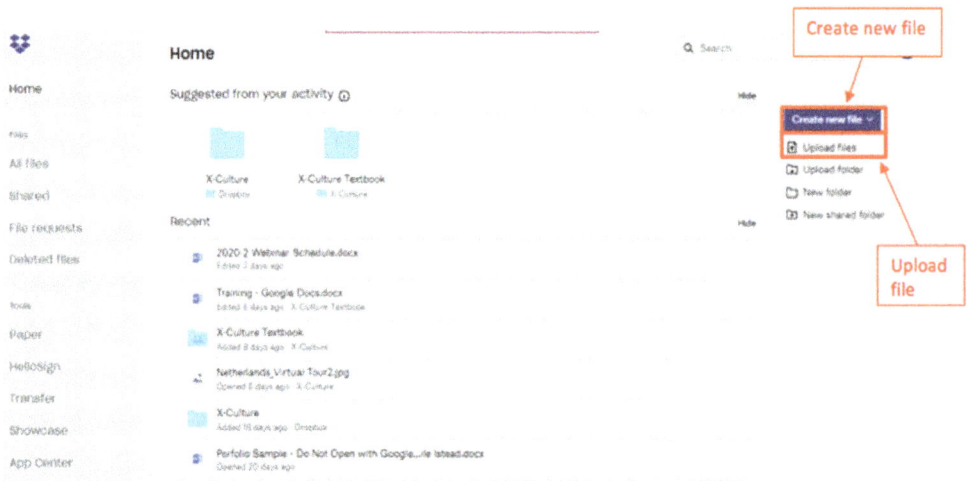

DB 3

You can create a new file or upload a file from your PC.

When clicking on "Create new file", the following options will appear:

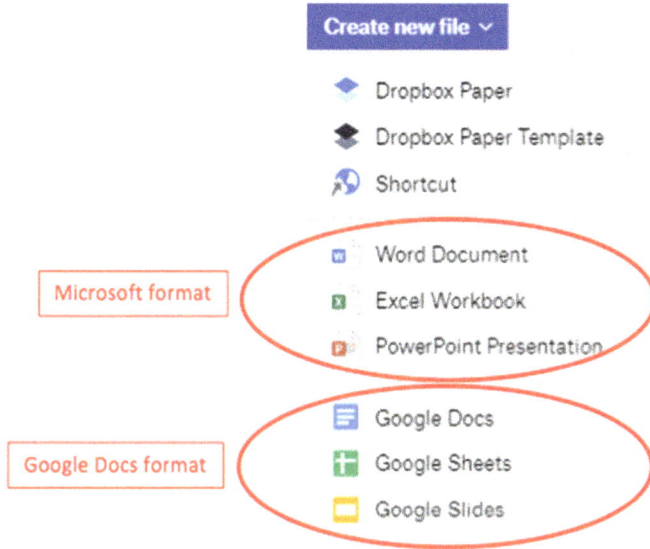

DB 4

As you can see, Dropbox is compatible with Microsoft Office and Google Docs file formats. So, you are free to choose your preferences.

Step 4 – Sharing a document

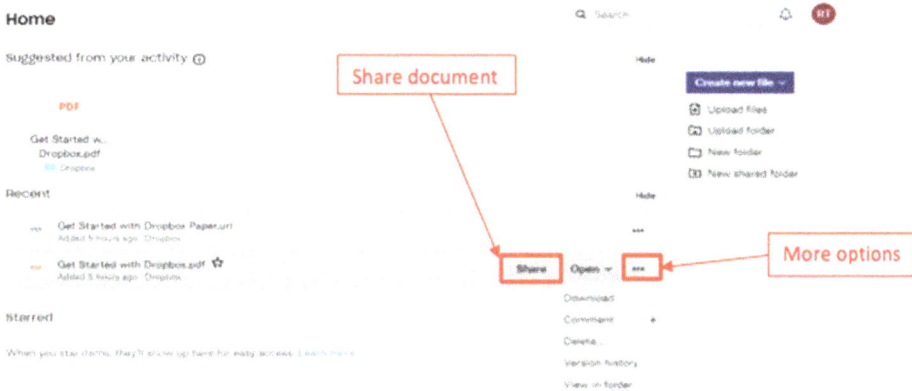

DB 5

After creating a file (figure 4), you can share, download, comment, or check it's version history. When clicking "share", it will show the image below:

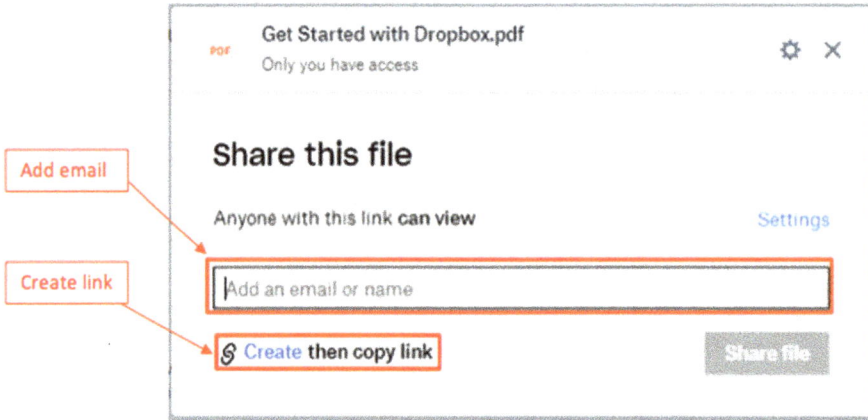

DB 6

You can share it by adding your teammates email or by creating and sharing a copied link.

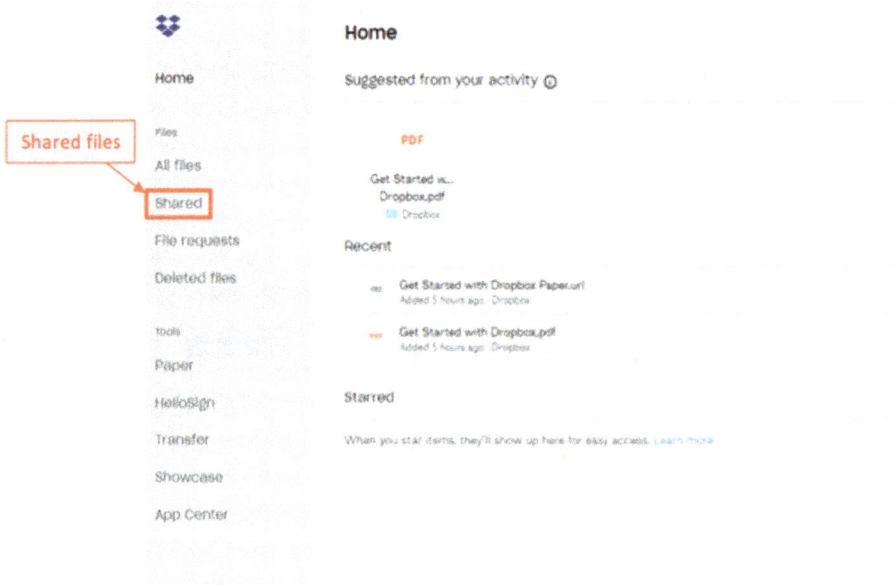

DB 7

After sharing the document, the shared document will be available files.

Track Changes in MS Word?

If you don't want to use Google Docs, there are some useful tools such as "Track Changes" in MS Word. We can use Track Changes to check all the edits that were made in the document. Therefore, it's easier to keep up with updates, assure that everyone is on the same page, and save all the report's information.

How to use Track Changes in MS Word

To use this tool, please follow the guideline below:

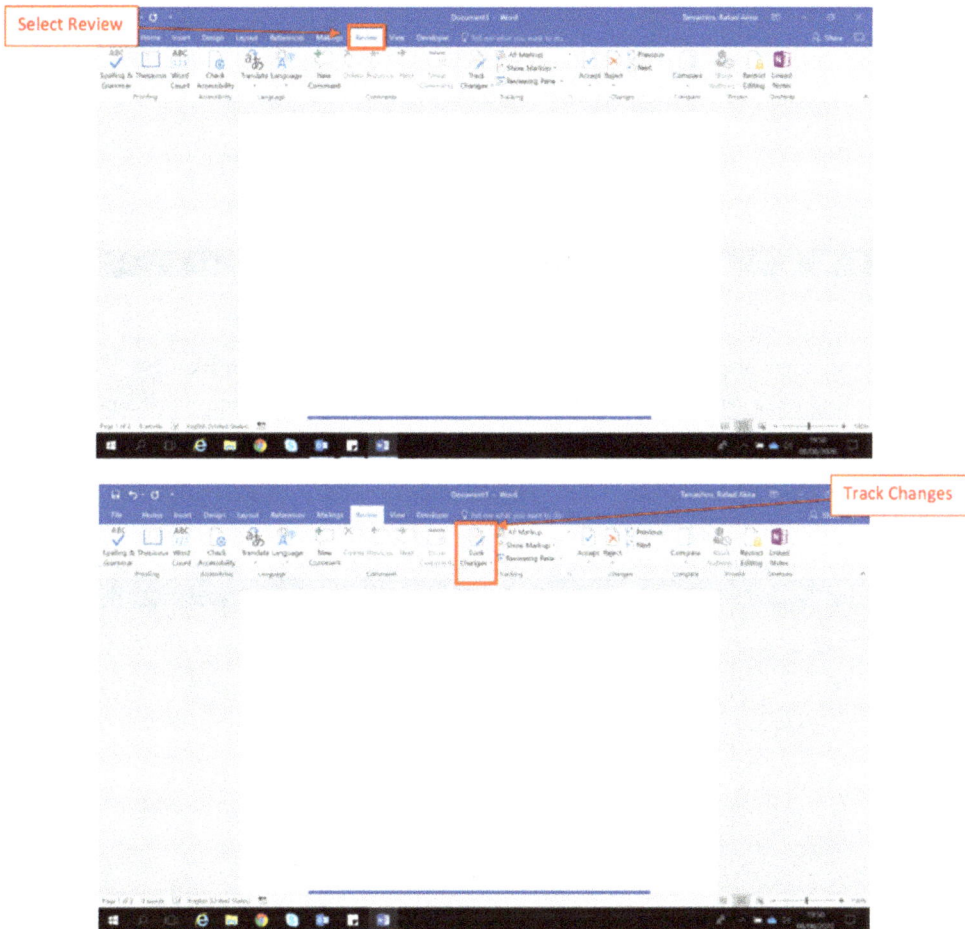

Word 1

And the Track Change tool is already ON!

Now, we are going to explain how to select the markups that MS Word has and what each one is for.

Markup Display

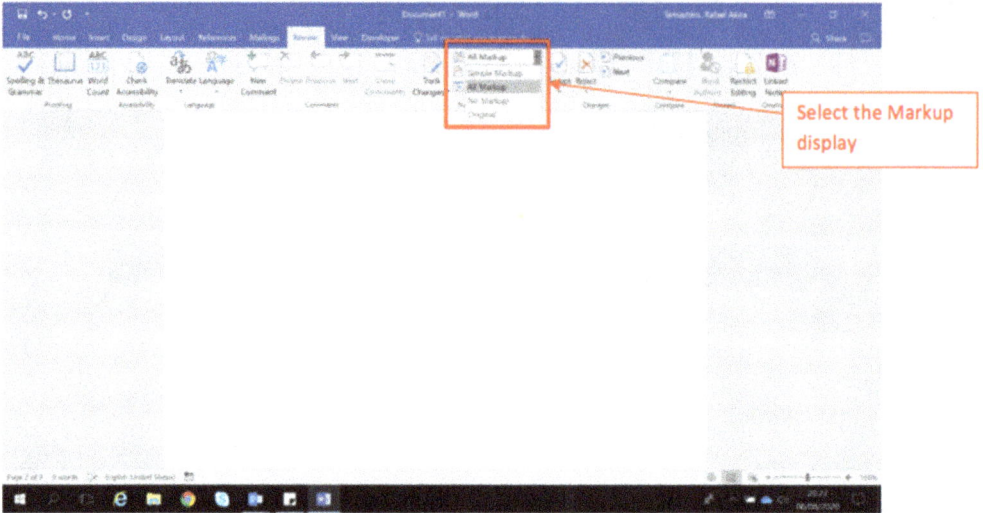

Word 2

1. Simple Markup: Displays the editor version of the content without any markup
   a. It will appear a vertical line on the left, meaning that a change was made in that location
   b. Speech bubbles on the right of the screen mean that there are comments for that location.

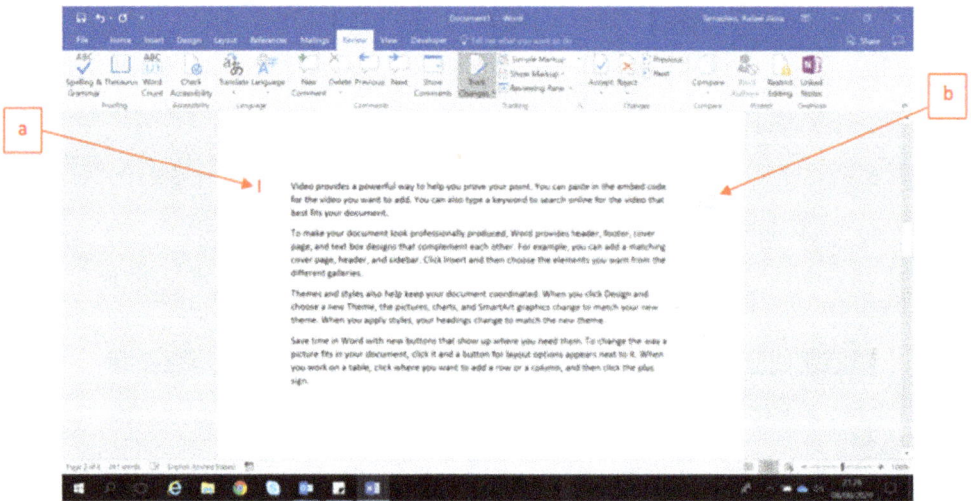

Word 3

1. All Markup: Displays all markups and comments
   a. Additional words will appear underlined
   b. Deleted words will be mentioned on the right side.

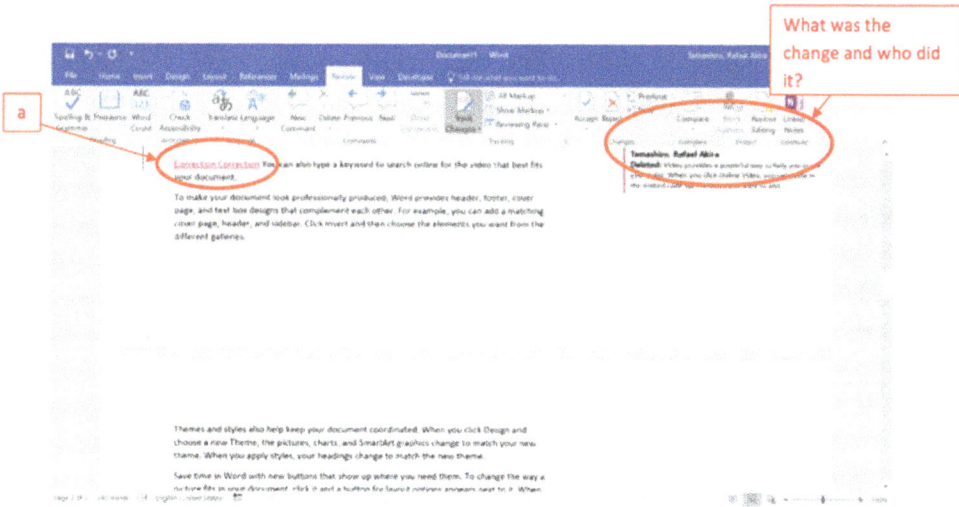

Word 4

1. No Markup: Displays the editor version with no markups and comments
2. Original: Displays the original version with no markups and comments.

Keep in mind that hiding the markups is not the same as accepting the changes; you still need to accept or reject the changes in your document before sending out the final version.

Accept or Reject Changes

Click "accept" to accept the suggested change or "reject" to reject it.

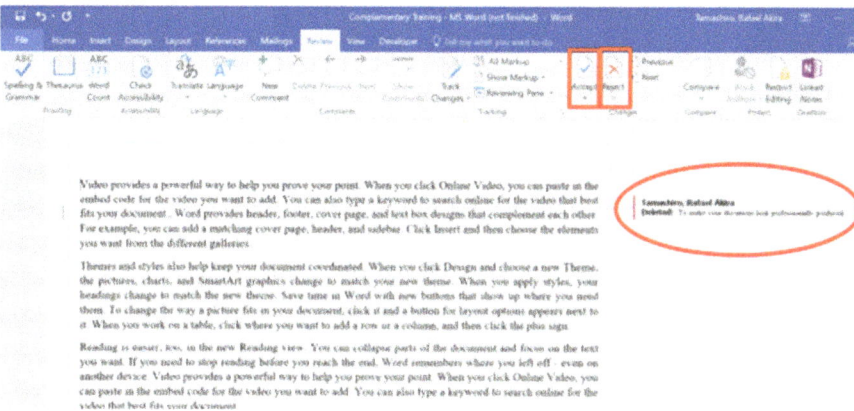

Word 5

Trello

Trello is a free online collaboration tool that helps you to manage your projects and organize its tasks.

When working in Global Virtual Teams, people are in different time zones, from different cultural backgrounds, and have different approaches on how to work, which are big problems that all teams face. Saving time is a key to success, and so, it is recommended to learn how to use Trello to increase your productivity.

To use Trello, please follow the guideline below:

First, navigate to https://trello.com/en

Step 1 – Sign in

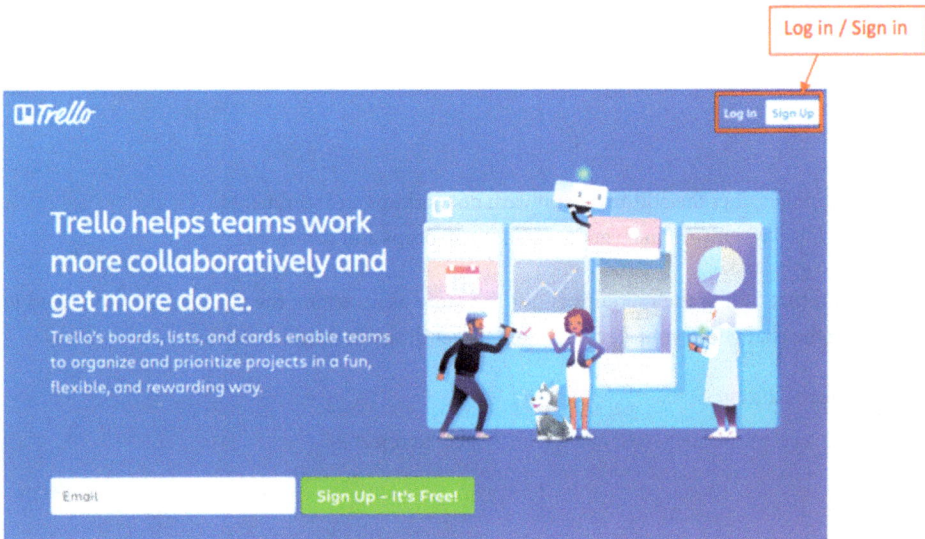

Word 6

Trello helps teams work more collaboratively and get more done. Trello's boards, lists, and cards enable teams to organize and prioritize projects in a fun, flexible, and rewarding way.

Step 2 – Creating your team

After signing in, Trello will present the image below:

- Name your team
- Choose your team type
- Add your team members (emails).

Trello 1

Step 3 – Creating a board

After creating your team, you can start to use Trello. The most important tools are highlighted below:

- Your team
- All team boards
- Members (you can add more members to the team at any time)
- Create
  - Create board
  - Create team.

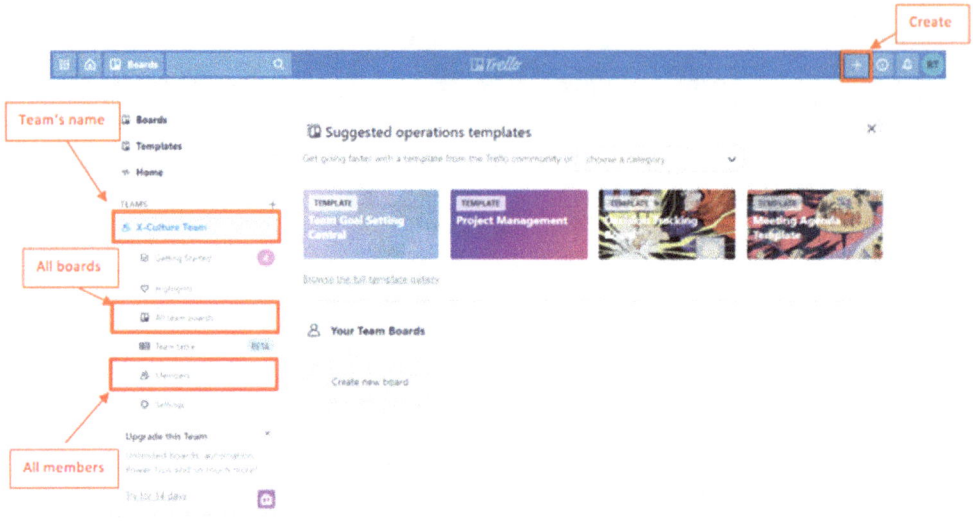

Trello 2

Add a board title

- Check the visibility of your team
  - Private (Only board members can see and edit)
  - All members of the team can see and edit
  - Public (anyone on the internet can see it, but only members of the board can edit).
- Choose background.

When clicking on "Create", the image on the right (figure 4) will appear. So, you will be able to create a new board.

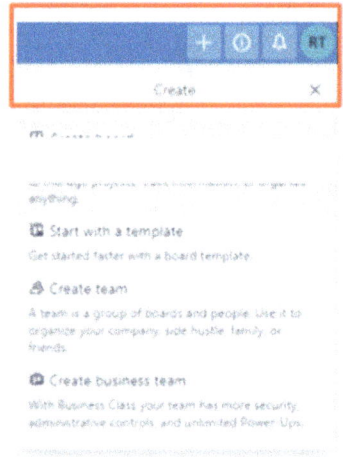

Trello 3

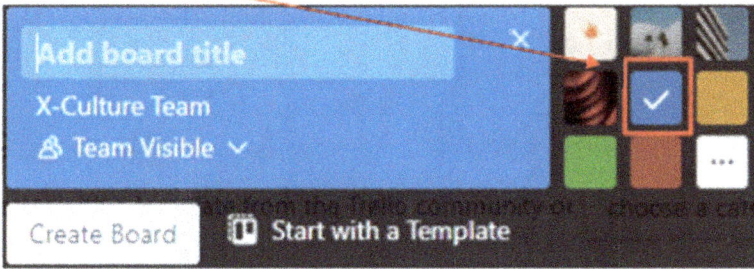

Trello 4

Step 4 – Organize your boards

On the standard template, we have "to-dos," "doing," and "done," but you are free to create more as you choose. So you need to create your tasks:

- Add all the necessary tasks.

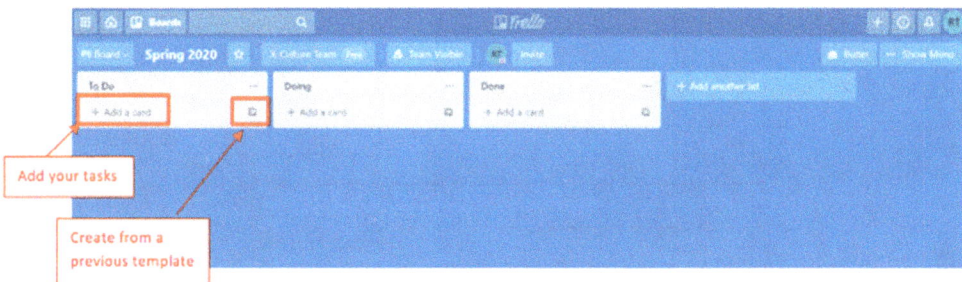

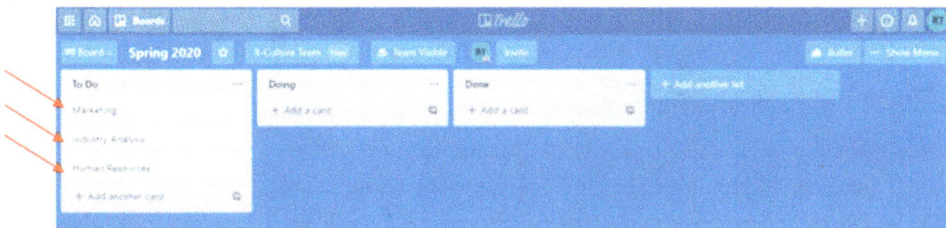

Trello 5

Now that you have created some cards, you can move the cards between the lists (click + drag to move):

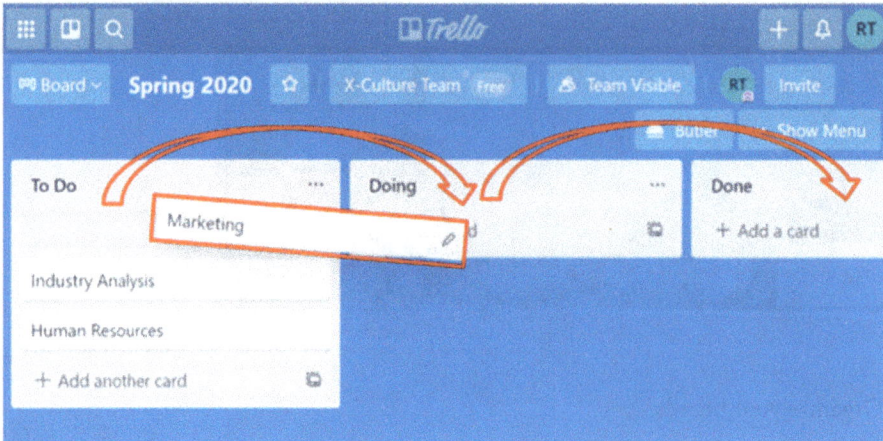

Trello 6

Step 5 – Card details

When clicking on a card, the image below will appear:

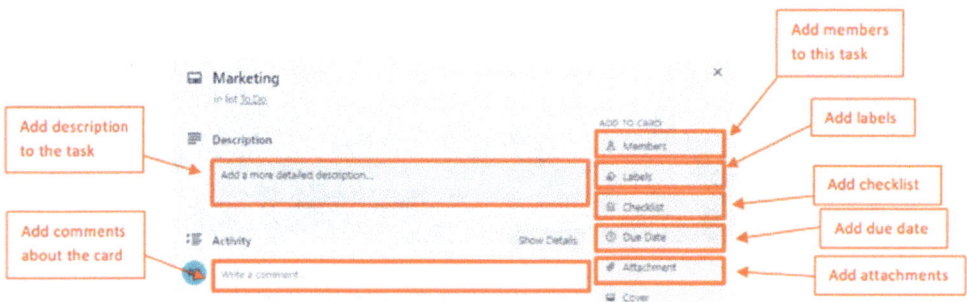

Trello 7

The card has the following features:

- Description: Add a more detailed description of the card (task)
- Comments: Add comments to communicate with your teammates
- Members: Add members to the card (will be co-working with you or you can assign someone)
- Labels: Very good for task governance
- Checklist: Create a checklist to finish the task (good for follow-up)
- Due date: define a due date for the task
  - It automatically creates a checkbox
  - When you check the box, it will show a "complete" sign
- Attachment: add all documents related to the task (photos, files, videos, websites, etc.)

As you can see, after adding all the information you want, your card will look like this:

Members in the card

Labels

Due Date

Description

Attachment (document)

Attachment (logo)

Check list

Marketing
in list To Do

MEMBERS   LABELS
[RT] +   Important Coach Admin +

DUE DATE
☑ Nov 19 at 3:44 AM COMPLETE ∨

Description
Add a more detailed description...

△ Google Drive   ▲ Enable Google Drive
Access your Drive files for a project directly from its card, or create and attach new Drive files to
a card.

X-Culture Academy Schedule
Google Drive · Nov 17

Attachments
X-Culture Academy Logo.png
Added 3 minutes ago · Comment · Delete · Edit
▢ Remove Cover

Add an attachment

☑ Checklist   Hide completed items   Delete
20%
☑ Marketing Research
Best place
Target Consumer
Channel Promotion
Review
Add an item

ADD TO CARD
⚌ Members
◉ Labels
▤ Checklist
⏱ Due Date
∅ Attachment

POWER-UPS
+ Add Power-Ups
Get Unlimited Power-Ups plus much more.
⚙ Upgrade Team

BUTLER   ⓘ
+ Add Card Button

ACTIONS
→ Move
🗐 Copy
🗗 Make Template
◉ Watch   ✅
🗃 Archive
< Share

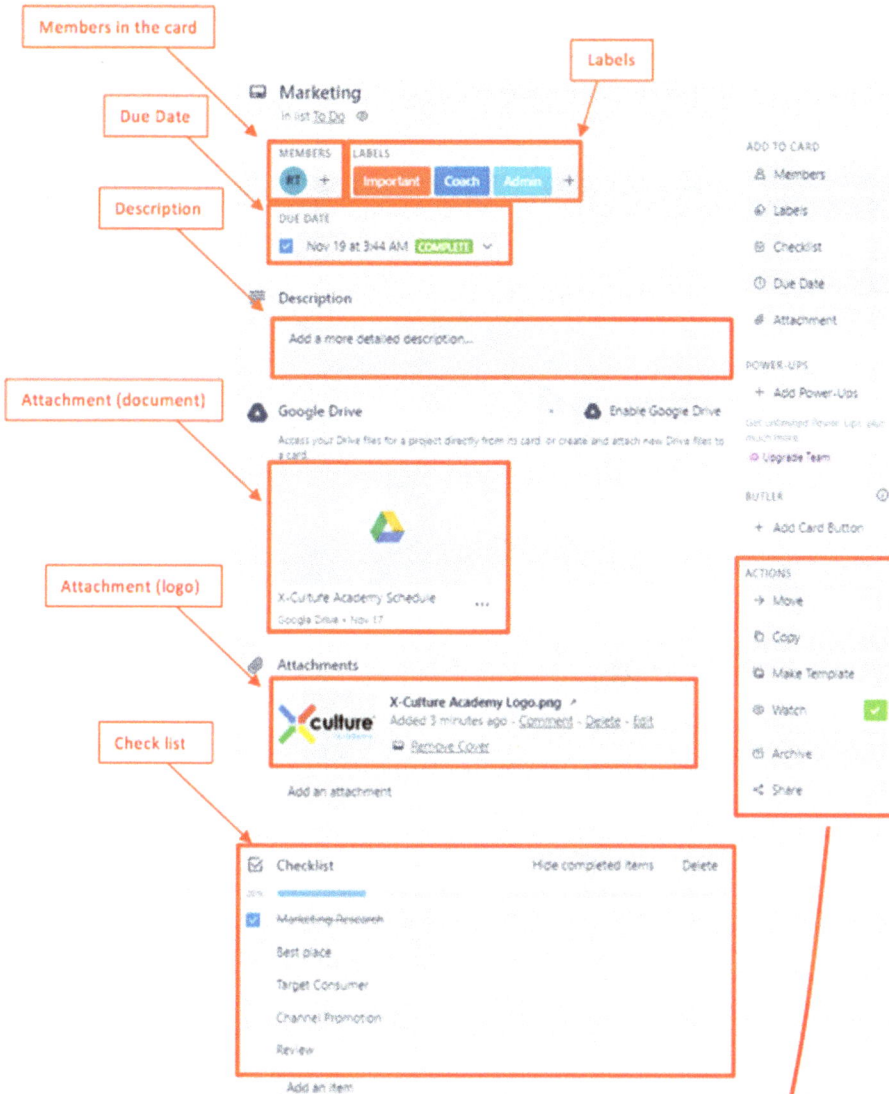

You can also take the following actions:

- Move (can move to other lists)
- Copy
- Make a template (save as template)
- Archive
- Share.

Trello 8

Step 6 – Check your calendar

All the due dates will be added to your calendar. So, if you want to check your dates, click on Board -> Calendar (Figure 11), or can click on the calendar icon on the right side (Figure 12).

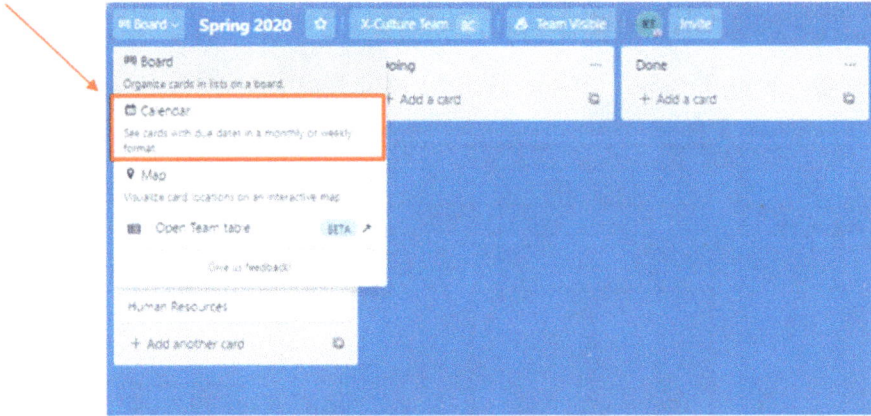

Trello 9

So, your calendar will show all the tasks with due dates and their labels.

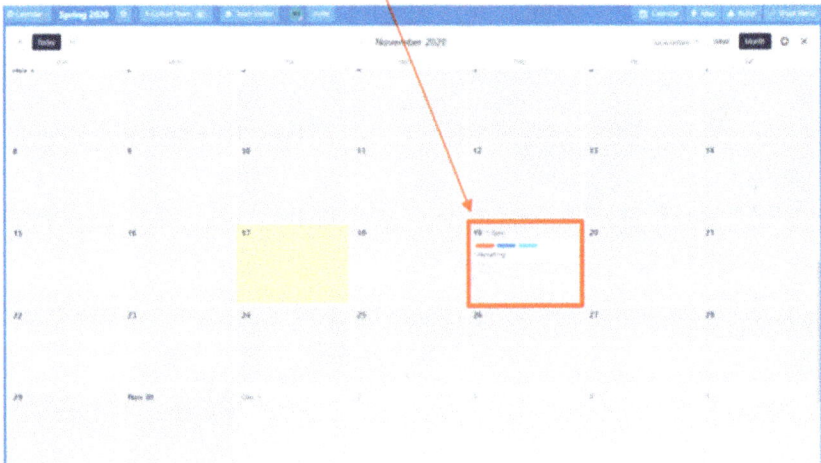

Trello 10

Virtual International Teams, Global Virtual Collaboration and Dealing with Student Aversion to Team-Based Projects

EMIL VELINOV, SKODA AUTO UNIVERSITY, CZECH REPUBLIC, EMIL.VELINOV@SAVS.CZ

TIIT ELENURM, ESTONIAN BUSINESS SCHOOL, ESTONIA, TIIT.ELENURM@EBS.EE

The book chapter proposal tackles with theories of virtual international teams and students' different perceptions on collaborating internationally in global virtual teams (GVT) based-projects. The chapter sheds light on managing virtual teams that involve students from some universities around the Baltic Sea and students studying at Tallinn and Helsinki branch of the Estonian Business School. It contributes to understanding how universities and schools deal with student unwillingness and co-operation barriers, when it comes to team-based projects on the cases of Estonia, Germany and the Czech Republic and what are lessons learnt from such projects. The book chapter tries to explain what the key pillars for successful cross-border cooperation are in regard to virtual teams among universities in different regions of Europe. At the same time, the chapter provides detailed analyses of students' aversion to different types of team work assignments, which need to be worked out and delivered by bachelor and master students in the above-mentioned countries. Furthermore, the chapter suggests strategies for dealing with cross-cultural differences, which affect the virtual collaboration among the students, who come from different cultural and geographic backgrounds and who perceive and manage differently such international virtual collaborative projects across Europe. The authors try to outline and show, how the communication and the interpersonal chemistry within the students' teams work as it is critical to the successful completion of the international virtual cooperation within the ongoing projects among the universities. Readiness to work in international virtual teams and obstacles to such work are also discussed in the broader context of globalization and innovative entrepreneurial orientations in order to explain attitudes that inhibit or support cross-cultural communication and joint project work with team members from different countries.

What is the role of GVT for the universities in selected European countries in terms of teaching International Business?

Nowadays, International Management and International Business courses are quite widely taught at business schools and universities across the Globe. Moreover, these courses are delivered not only in English but in the local language as well. The students involved in these courses often are assigned with versatile tasks such as individual assignments, group presentations and written assignments, peer reviews, critical thinking essays, etc. In this manner the students develop not only their analytical and team work skills but their entrepreneurial skills as well (Velinov et al., 2020). Parallelly with that, the universities are putting a lot of efforts in internationalizing their curricula, which is inevitable process across the business schools and universities worldwide. The students are getting connected with their counterparts from foreign universities mainly virtually through Skype, Facetime, What's App, Viber App, We Chat when it comes to Global Virtual Teams and their group assignments and tasks. It requires quite a lot of time not only for the students, but for the teachers to devote as well. International Management and International Business classes courses in general are very demanding when it comes to Global Virtual Teams (GVT) as the students need themselves to get acquainted with lots of instructions, to establish contacts with their teammates from across the globe and to maintain virtual cooperation at least for a semester. However, challenges of global virtual teams that can lead to aversion are not limited to pedagogic practices. In order to give guidance to students lecturers and tutors have to understand broader context of cooperation readiness of students and how it is influenced by online communication (Johnson, 2013) We also have to analyze implications of cultural values and practices on student aversion of cross-cultural teamwork and the role of trust building in virtual teams (Hakanen, M., Kossou, L., & Takala, T., 2016) in creating commitment to perform in virtual teams and networks.

In the book chapter are included case studies on students' aversion in GVTs from the Czech Republic and Estonia. These case studies are based on teachers' and students' impressions and experience gained from the period of 2017–2019. Thus, the book chapter tries to explain and analyze why students' aversion in GVTs exists and what are the factors, which influence students' performance.

Historically, countries as Czech Republic and Estonia are trying to shift much of their international business to export, which requires solid foreign market knowledge and proactive broadening of International Business skills. Small and open economies in Europe need access to global markets and global online networking readiness of students is essential tool for discovering and using new global business opportunities. Respectively, the business schools from these two EU countries are putting lots of time and money for internationalizing their courses, boosting international relations through different international projects, which involve students, teachers, administrators and other stakeholders. At the same time, much of the student's work is done virtually through different e-platforms and mobile apps, which enable online and offline communications among the students.

At Skoda Auto University GVTs are very recent trend in language and International Management courses, which makes the course quite exciting and attractive to the students. The university is cooperating with German, Icelandic and British universities in so called Blended Learning International Cooperation since 2017, where Czech students virtually cooperate with the counterparts in bachelor and master programs. Majority of the Czech students possess good command of English, so they relatively well understand and conduct the cooperation with their counterparts. There are around 15–20 percent foreign students from the total number of 40 students each semester, who take part in this project at Skoda Auto University. In majority of cases those are Russian speaking bachelor and master students, who speak English and Czech.

When it comes to students' aversion in the GVTs at Skoda Auto University, it is main triggered by fear of communicating out of comfort zone, low level of knowledge of foreign culture, working habits, lack of time to do GVTs work, laziness and in more rare cases discomfort in speaking English. The students from Skoda Auto University, who participate in GVTs are struggling with managing their study and work time as almost 90 percent of them are working. The students show aversion in GVTs mainly because it takes significant chunk of time according to them for tackling with their tasks in international cooperation. We need to underline that the Skoda Auto University students are burden with lots of team work load from almost each subject they are taught at the university. Therefore, the students often would ask the International Management teacher if X-Culture or BLIC are mandatory projects or optional (Bleicher et al., 2019). Also, there is relatively low-esteem especially among the Czech students when it comes to dealing with GVTs tasks and assignments accompanied with low readiness to cooperate with non-Czech students in class. Interestingly, the initial students' interest in X-Culture and BLIC is quite volatile throughout the academic year due to the fact that the students are constantly working, and they have many group assignments in each subject they study at the university. Regardless, these facts the students often are afraid of cooperating virtually with other counterparts due to the fact that they need to read information online, to contacts and maintain virtual collaboration with students from far countries, to put much efforts on motivating other teammates from the GVTs, etc. For the last two years mainly limited time available for the GVT work and fail to motivate foreign teammates in achieving the common goal are the most frequent factors towards students' aversion in GVTs at Skoda Auto University.

At the Estonian Business School students have participated in the X-Culture global projects for three years. X-Culture global projects have been applied as exam project in the international business course. X-Culture has given to many students valuable experience of online communication in multicultural teams that help growth-oriented enterprises to enter to new foreign markets. Harisalo and Miettinen (2002) already fifteen year ago explained that trust capital is the third force in entrepreneurship in addition to financial and human capital. From the trust building point of view in X-Culture an important challenge is that team members cannot choose other team members based on their earlier contacts and co-operation experience, as online teams are formed by US organizers. X-Culture organizers allocate students to virtual teams following the principle of geographical and cultural diversity of each team. Organizers try to create teams, where each team member is from a different country, although sometimes there are more than one US student in some teams. Students have to build their team consensus on the international business opportunity challenge they try to solve together by working online over a period of two and half months. Cultural collision and resulting aversion risk have been higher in teams, where students do not start form discussing their own personal career aspirations and interests that can be linked to the project. Sharing some personal information is essential for understanding situation of each student, personal values and preferences that can be taken into consideration, when tasks are set for each team member and co-operation modes agreed.

Cultural stereotypes result in aversion if students assume already before the project has started that they are more learning and result oriented that representatives of some other cultures. In addition to trust, reputation of team members is also important in group decision making frameworks (Urena et al., 2019). Estonian students generally perceive themselves as more hard working and better in time management and meeting deadlines compared to many other nationalities. Such attitude easily results in blaming team members that seem to be more relaxed to follow deadlines as bd performers. At the same time Estonian students are not used to regular feedback surveys that are used I very structured way in the X-Culture framework. They are more used to learning projects, where feedback is not given on weekly basis and teams are more independent to specify their cooperation timetable so long as the final deadline is met. One reason is that among students are many practitioners that try to align working for their employers and university studies. Sometimes they have to go on business trip and as the result they value flexibility to adjust their learning activities to job and family obligations. In university practice it means opportunity to choose between two exam time option and opportunity to negotiate with lecturers to compensate missed face-to-face class discussions by contributing to online discussions by using e-learning tools. X-Culture team could also cooperate in such ways that multitasking and flexible time use by participants is supported but inability to agree inside teams on such arrangements can lead to aversion of intensive online teamwork.

Some students that already have practical experience of working in international teams created by companies, where they are employed, are hesitant to expand their experience through university training as they feel that their international headquarters has not recognized their hard work in coordinating project team members from other countries and they are not interested to experience the same negative feelings during university studies. At the same time there are students without international business communication experience that for the first-time experience difference between cultures that focus more on structured written communication versus cultures giving higher value to rich real time communication that combines oral messages with visualization and non-verbal communication. In GVT implication of such communication preference difference is that some team members prefer synchronous Skype or messenger calls and others feel comfortable to comment texts in Google Drive or in some other cloud services. In practice synchronous communication preference means that some team members have to wake up at night to answer to Skype call from team member living in other time zones. Although majority of Estonian students have quite good knowledge of English, they often feel uncomfortable in intensive synchronous debates and prefer to make their point in writing. Mismatch of communication style and time differences can lead to dissatisfaction with the teamwork process and frustration.

Student aversion in X-Culture projects seldom, only 2–3% of students participating in X-Culture program, has led to abandoning the project. That has happened mainly if several team members from different countries have not contributed. When Estonian Business School students have been rated as low performers by other team members, their self-explanation has been of two main types: need to perform urgent job tasks or different opinions inside the team about work rules and timetables.

How we can build rigorous and manage international GVTs across the universities?

There are two teachers in International Management and one teacher in English, who are having students participating in GVTs since 2017. When it comes to BLIC teams, we try to build teams, where at least two students know each other prior to taking up on BLIC project. Thus, the synergy in the team is very likely to occur thanks to the fact that these two students possess previous experience in conducting group presentation, work or assignment. For standard occasions they know their strong and weak sides, which makes easier the work between them. Also, we try to select one ambassador from each group, who is responsible coordinating the whole group of students. At the same time, we applied different HR tests such as Belbin, MBTi, etc.to the students, so they can find better the roles and the tasks in the GVTs. Last, but not least the teachers in the International Management classes demonstrate each week new online tools to the students, so they can ease off their work when it comes to the virtual collaboration with their international counterparts. Similarly, the students are provided with study guide in International Management at the beginning of the course, which makes clear and transparent the entire assessment and curricula specifics. Then throughout the semester teams' performances are recorded in the internal study information system and Microsoft Teams group folders, which facilitates the communication between the teacher/instructor and the teams of students. In case there is a so-called free rider student from any of the groups he or she is reported by the ambassador for each of the respective group. Free rider policy enables transparent and fair assessment of each of the students and their team and it helps the teacher to better understand the interpersonal and communication chemistry of each virtual team of students.

How we can deal with students' aversion in GVTs?

At Skoda Auto University students are provided continuous support by using Microsoft Teams, Zoom, Skype, Adobe Connect, What's app, Viber app, the International Study Information System and other software platforms in order to make sure that the students are important part in the GVTs. Also, the students are provided with certificates, 20 points from the total subject grade upon completion of Blended Learning International Cooperation (BLIC) or X-Culture and even the students are invited to grade their counterparts in the GVTs.

Estonian Business School Students that participate in X-Culture projects have international business classes, where they are introduced to the main international business concepts that are relevant for X-Culture. Before students start X-Culture teamwork, they perform assignment, where they analyze GVT challenges based on relevant literature and their own experience if they have such experience. In this homework they also present their vision, how to succeed in X-Culture and propose ideas how to overcome challenges in virtual teamwork. Special attention during the international business course that is linked to X-Culture is devoted to the PESTLE analysis. Students have a special homework assignment, where they have to apply lessons learnt in the X-Culture teamwork for choosing foreign markets to some comparable Estonian product or service that can be introduced at foreign markets. This task supports transferring X-Culture experience to practical tasks of developing Estonian exports in order to avoid GVT aversion based on seeing it as an extra task isolated from their employment or entrepreneurial ambitions. In order to overcome cultural stereotypes, synergy between representatives of different cultures is stressed, when studying cultural aspects of international business. Idea that X-Culture GVT could expand global network both for travelling and further own cross-border business initiatives of students is explained. We suggest to students that base their aversion on frustration from earlier international teamwork related to their jobs to test their leadership skill in X-Culture teams if they really already have business experience. Challenge for further development of Estonian Business School is to involve EBS alumni that already have X-Culture teamwork experience to become commissioners in the X-Culture framework. When former EBS students propose meaningful tasks for global virtual teams, Estonian students understand more clearly value of such teamwork and there will be less reasons for student aversion of such online project activities.

References:

Bleicher J., Forrester P., Honal A., Velinov E. (2019) Virtual Business Projects in the Classroom: Enhancing Intercultural and Business Skills of Students. In: Gonzalez-Perez M., Lynden K., Taras V. (eds) The Palgrave Handbook of Learning and Teaching International Business and Management. Palgrave Macmillan, Cham

Brewer, P. E., & Minacori, P. (2018). A Multi-Faceted Global Virtual Team Project Linking Tech Comm Education in the US and France. In Multilingual Writing and Pedagogical Cooperation in Virtual Learning Environments (pp. 55–81). IGI Global.

Gatlin-Watts, R., Carson, M., Horton, J., Maxwell, L., & Maltby, N. (2007). A guide to global virtual teaming. Team Performance Management: An International Journal, 13(1/2), 47–52.

Hakanen, M., Kossou, L., & Takala, T. (2016). Building Interpersonal Trust in Business Networks: Enablers and Roadblocks. *The Development and Management of Interpersonal Trust in a Business Network in Health, Exercise, and Wellbeing Markets*, 4(1), 45–62.

Harisalo, R.& Miettinen E. (2002) *Trust capital. The third force of entrepreneurship*, University of Tampere. Tampere University Press.

Johnson, K. (2013). Facilitating cooperative learning in online and blended courses: An example from an integrated marketing communication course. *American Journal of Business Education*, 6(1), 33–40.

Urena, R., Kou, G., Dong, Y., Chiclana, F., & Herrera-Viedma, E. (2019). A review on trust propagation and opinion dynamics in social networks and group decision making frameworks. *Information Sciences, 478*, 461–475.

Velinov E., Ashmarina S.I., Zotova A.S. (2021) Importance of International Entrepreneurship Skills Among MBA Students: Global Comparative Study. In: Ashmarina S., Mantulenko V., Vochozka M. (eds) Engineering Economics: Decisions and Solutions from Eurasian Perspective. ENGINEERING ECONOMICS WEEK 2020. Lecture Notes in Networks and Systems, vol 139. Springer, Cham

Walker, R. C., Cardon, P. W., & Aritz, J. (2018). Enhancing Global Virtual Small Group Communication Skills. Journal of Intercultural Communication Research, 1–12.

Wihlborg, M., Friberg, E. E., Rose, K. M., & Eastham, L. (2018). Facilitating learning through an international virtual collaborative practice: A case study. Nurse education today, 61, 3–8.

Ye, X., Molitoris, I., & Anderson, D. (2018). Opening the Classroom to the World: A Grounded-Theory Study of Student Perceptions of Integrating Intercultural Competence Into Curriculum. In Curriculum Internationalization and the Future of Education (pp. 251–272). IGI Global.

Sherry Andre, Florida International University

April Beaurivage, Mount Royal University

April Beaurivage is a graduate of International Business and Marketing from Mount Royal University. She has been with X-Culture for five years where April has travelled to various symposiums, led teams through coaching and senior coaching, and now volunteers with the administration team. Currently, April is in a new graduate rotational program with the largest pest control company in the world. April is furthering her education through her studies to obtain the FITT Diploma and future completion of a Masters in International Business from the University of Victoria in Canada.

Abdulrahman Chikhouni, Mount Royal University

Abdulrahman is an associate professor of International Business at Bissett School of Business, Mount Royal University, Canada. He has been teaching undergraduate and graduate courses since 2007, and his teaching profile includes Strategy, General Management and International Business. Abdulrahman is part X-Culture since 2016 and has received many best educator awards since then. He received his Ph.D. degree in Strategy and International Business from Concordia University, Canada. His research focuses on inter-organizational networks and multinationals from emerging countries.

Swati Dhir, International Management Institute, New Delhi, India

Swati Dhir is a Fellow of Indian Institute of Management (IIM) Lucknow and completed the Fellow Program in Management (FPM). She is currently working as Associate Professor in OB/HRM area at International Institute of Management New Delhi. She has published her research work in many National and International Journals (Scopus and ABDC indexed) and attended various National and international conferences. She is a certified DiSC trainer created by John Wiley & Sons Inc., DiSC is the world's leading assessment tool used by over 45 million people to improve productivity, teamwork, and communication. Her research interests include Diversity, Work-Related Attitudes, Employee Engagement, Work Role Performance, Employee Loyalty and Strategic Thinking

Bella L. Galperin, University of Tampa

Bella L. Galperin, Ph.D. is Dana Professor of Management and Senior Associate Director of the TECO Energy Center for Leadership at the Sykes College of Business at the University of Tampa. Her interests include leadership (in Africa and the African diaspora), ethics, and workplace deviance- both destructive and constructive. She has published in the Journal of Business Ethics, International Journal of Human Resource Management, Leadership Quarterly, International Business Review, and other journals. She co-authored a book entitled, LEAD: Leadership effectiveness in Africa and the African diaspora. She is an associate editor of Journal of Managerial Psychology.

Susan Godar, William Paterson University

Ding-Yu Jiang, National Chung-Cheng University

Dr. Ding-Yu Jiang is a Professor and Chairman of Psychology and Associate Dean of College of Social Science at National Chung Cheng University, Taiwan. He received his Ph.D. in I/O Psychology from National Taiwan University (2005). In 2010, he was a Fulbright Visiting Scholar in the Department of Psychology at the University of Illinois at Urbana-Champaign. His research focuses on employee loyalty/commitment, leadership in the Chinese context, and cross-cultural psychology and management. He is an associate editor of the Chinese Journal of Psychology and Editorial Board Member of the Journal of Cross-Cultural Psychology.

William H.A. Johnson, Pennsylvania State University

Dr. William H.A. Johnson is an Associate Professor of Management at the Pennsylvania State University. He earned his Ph.D. from the Schulich School of Business, York University (Canada). He is published in peer-reviewed journals including Research Policy, Journal of Business Research, Academy of Management Education and Learning, IEEE Transactions on Engineering Management, Technovation, Journal of International Management, Journal of Intellectual Capital, and Entrepreneurship: Theory and Practice; among others. He has also written books on Innovation in China and Global Strategy. His research focuses on the knowledge-creating processes at the nexus of innovation, strategy, and international management.

Serdar Karabati, Istanbul Bilgi University

Serdar Karabati is a Professor of Management at Istanbul Bilgi University. He received his MA degree in Social Psychology and his Ph.D. degree in Management and Organization from Bogazici University. Dr. Karabati has been invited to deliver seminars and short courses at various universities across Europe on different occasions. His current research interests include work engagement, destructive leadership, and subjective well-being.

Nataliia Kochkina, Taras Shevchenko National University of Kyiv

Lei Weng Si (Clara), Macao Institute for Tourism Studies

Weng Si (Clara) is an Assistant Professor, and Acting Vice-director for the school of Hospitality Management at the Macao Institute for Tourism Studies, China. She received her Ph.D. in International Business from the University of Leeds in the United Kingdom. Her research interests rest on management education, festivals, and event management. She has published in leading management education journals and event management journals. Prior stepping into academia, Clara worked in the industries for some years and took part mostly in marketing and management.

Oleh Leskiv, X-Culture, Inc.

Oleh Leskiv is an Economics and History Teacher at Lviv Secondary School Budokan. Also, he is an Education Project Manager at Lviv IT Cluster. He received his candidate of sciences degree in Economics from the Ivan Franko National University of Lviv, Ukraine. His research and work revolve around the development of new practical-oriented curriculums for youth and issues of advertising regulation in Ukraine and the USA. Đe received the X-Culture Global Educator award for the excellent results his students showed in this international competition.

Chia-Hua (Demi) Lin, National Chung-Cheng University

Chia-Hua Lin is a Ph.D. Candidate of Industrial and Organizational Psychology at National Chung-Cheng University in Taiwan. Her research and work revolve around organizational behavior and emotions in the workplace. Her articles have appeared in book chapters and psychology and management journals.

Terri R. Lituchy, CETYS Universidad

Karen Lynden, The University of North Carolina at Greensboro

Karen Lynden is a Lecturer at the Bryan School of Business and Economics. She holds a Master of Science in Organizational Management, and currently engaged in doctoral studies. Her teaching philosophy is centered on experiential and project-based learning, teaching international business and management courses. Ms. Lynden Directs the X-Culture Coaching Program and serves as the Coordinator for the X-Culture Advisory Board. She contributes to the Academy of International Business Teaching and Education Shared Interest Group as Co-Vice Chair, Events. Her primary research interests include: global virtual teams; cross-cultural team and management topics; and organizational training and development.

Lyaonne Maspero, X-Culture Inc.

Layonne Maspero is currently completing her last year of high school. She is a senior coach within the X-Culture Project and is constantly looking for ways to be more involved in cross-cultural and global virtual teams.

Lemayon L. Melyoki, University of Dar es Salaam

Lemayon L. Melyoki is a Senior Lecturer at the University of Dar es Salaam, Tanzania. He researches and publishes in the areas of entrepreneurship, management (leadership), and governance. His publications have appeared in the Journal of Extractives and Society, Journal of Rural and Community Development, Journal of Small Business and Entrepreneurship, and Journal of International Cross Cultural Management (JICCM) and others journals. He has recently co-authored a book on â€˜Essentials of General Management in Africaâ€™ published by Taylor and Francis, Group, New York, NY 10017: USA; https://www.routledge.com/Essentials-of-General-Management-in-Africa/Melyoki-Punnett/p/book/9780367435196.

Mamata Mohapatra, International Management Institute, New Delhi

Mamta Mohapatra is Professor in the OBHR area and Dean Executive Education & International Relations at International Management Institute New Delhi. She has over two and half decades of experience in teaching, research and training activities. Author of four books and a number of published research articles in reputed journals she has acquired expertise and training skills from Harvard Business School on Participant Centered Learning.

Tim Muth, Florida Institute of Technology

Daria Panina, Texas A&M Mays Business School

Dr. Daria Panina received her Ph.D. in International HR from School of Management and Labor Relations, Rutgers University in 2002. She joined the Management Department of Mays Business School of Texas A&M University in 2003. She teaches international business and management courses at both the undergraduate and graduate levels and regularly enrolls her students in X-Culture project since 2013. Dr. Panina serves on X-Culture Advisory Board since 2020. She does research in the areas of global mindset, global competencies, and international business teaching and learning. Dr. Panina is a member of the Academy of International Business (AIB) and chairs AIB Teaching and Education shared interest group.

Floretin Popescu, HAN University of Applied Sciences

Betty Jane Punnett, University of the West Indies, Barbados

Marketa Rickley, The University of North Carolina at Greensboro

Dr. Marketa Rickley is an Assistant Professor of Management at the University of North Carolina at Greensboro. She received her Ph.D. in Management from Boston University. She conducts research at the intersection of international business and strategic management. Her work focuses on managerial selection and top management team configuration in multinational firms. Her research has been published in the Journal of Management and the Journal of World Business, among other outlets. She previously worked for two global financial firms, as an equity analyst and as the Finance Officer for asset management in Central and Eastern Europe.

Stefaan Van Ryssen

Stefaan Van Ryssen is an emeritus lecturer of international and digital marketing and sociology of music. He has extensive experience in management of MSB's and starters, mostly advising on market research, classic and digital. He started the first cross-atlantic virtual collaboration with Prof. Dr. Susan Godar of Paterson and Prof. Dr. Jean-Marc Lehu from Sobonne, Paris. He has lectured on the digital revolution in many colleges and universities all over Europe.

Thomas Anyanje Senaji, Kenya Methodist University, Kenya

Dr. Thomas Senaji is an Associate Professor of Strategic Management at The East African University in Kenya. His research and work cover leadership, knowledge management and happiness. His publications have appeared in leading management journals. He is the founding president of the International Society for Leadership and Management. He is active in the leadership effectiveness in Africa nd the African Diaspora (LEAD) and currently co-authoring with Betty Jane Punnett a text book "Essentials of Organisational Behaviour in Africa"

Ana Maria Santos Costa Soares, University of Minho

Ana Maria Soares is Associate Professor of Marketing and Strategic Management at the School of Economics and Management, University of Minho, Portugal. She teaches several undergraduate, graduate and doctoral courses in international marketing, strategy, and consumer behavior and has been participating in X-Culture since 2017. She conducts research on consumer behavior and international marketing/strategy. She has published in a variety of international peer-reviewed conferences and journals, including the International Journal of Consumer Studies, the Journal of Research in Interactive Marketing, the International Journal of Retail and Distribution Management and the Journal of Consumer Marketing.

Ali Taleb, MacEwan University

Dr. Ali Taleb is Associate Dean of Business and Associate Professor of Strategy & Global Management at Mac-Ewan University, Edmonton, Canada. His research interests belong at the intersection of strategic management, international business, and corporate citizenship. He is one of the founding editors of the 'Essentials of Business and Management in Africa' series, with Routledge, which comprises a dozen short and affordable textbooks that focus on Africa as context. Dr. Taleb â€™s scholarly work is informed by his extensive international exposure and practical business experience in both senior management capacity and management consultancy across Africa, Europe and North America.

Vas Taras, The University of North Carolina at Greensboro, X-Culture, Inc.

Dr. Vas Taras is an Associate Professor of International Business at the University of North Carolina at Greensboro, and founder and coordinator of the X-Culture Project. He received his Ph.D. in International Human Resources and Organizational Dynamics from the University of Calgary, Canada. His research and work revolve around cross-cultural and global virtual teams and experiential approaches to international business education and development. He is an Associate Editor of the Journal of International Management, the International Journal of Cross-Cultural Management and Cross-Cultural Strategic Management, and Editorial Board Member of Journal of International Business Studies and Journal of World Business.

Ernesto Tavoletti, University of Macerata

Ernesto Tavoletti is Associate Professor of Management, International Marketing and International Business Strategy at the University of Macerata. He received a degree in Economics and Commerce cum laude at the University of Bologna in 1997 and PhD in Economics and Management of Enterprises and Local Systems at the University of Firenze in 2004. He has been a board member of the PhD in Management at the University of Rome Tor Vergata from 2011 to 2013. He is a member of the Academy of International Business. He has served in the Council of Directors of the Master in Relations with Eastern Countries from 2004 to 2011, as Co-director from 2009 and as Director in 2011. From 2011 he has been coordinating the Masterâ€™s Degree in International Economic and Trade Relations. From 2014 he serves in the Council of Directors of the Master in Innovation in Public Management. His research interests focus on international business, and innovation management.

Emil Velinov, SKODA AUTO University

Emil Velinov is an Assistant Professor at Skoda Auto University in the department of Marketing and Management. He has worked for several Multinational Corporations as General Electric, Oracle and Hoerbiger in Europe, North

America and South-east Asia in Power Generation and IT sectors in Sales and Marketing in the period 2007-2015. Since he has graduated from University of Economics, Emil has published number of articles, particularly in the field of International Management and Marketing, International Business and Diversity Management. In terms of his research activities, he has been project manager in myriad of inter-institutional projects with SMEs and Municipalities from Iceland, Norway, Lichtenstein, Austria, Estonia, Bulgaria, Russia, etc. through specific financial mechanisms such as Norwegian and EEA Grants, Visegrad Funds, CEEPUS, ESKAS and DoRa Scholarships. Since 2015 he has been acting as visiting professor in Vienna University of Economics and Business, DHBW in Germany, Estonian Business School in Tallinn, Wroclaw University of Economics and SGH Warsaw in Poland, Graduate School of Management (GSOM) in St.Petersburg, Plekhnavov Russian University of Economics (PRUE), Ural Federal University in Ekaterinburg. Emil Velinov joined SKODA AUTO University at the Department of Marketing and Management in September 2017.

Robert Warmenhoven, HAN University of Applied Sciences at Arnhem, The Netherlands

Robert Warmenhoven is currently employed as a lecturer International Business at HAN University of Applied Science where he teaches to the international students. Furthermore, he is a visiting professor at Plekhanov University in Moscow, Russia. His primary teaching interests include International Business, Marketing, Consumer Behaviour and Intercultural Management. His major research interests are Cross-cultural Management, International Business and Global Virtual Teams. He obtained his master in Business Administration at the Radboud University, Nijmegen, the Netherlands. Currently, he is a member of the executive team of the X-culture project (www.X-culture.org).

www.ingramcontent.com/pod-product-compliance
Lightning Source LLC
Chambersburg PA
CBHW080513220326
41599CB00032B/6068